LIGHT IN GERMANY

LIGHT IN GERMANY

Scenes from an Unknown Enlightenment

T. J. REED

THE UNIVERSITY OF CHICAGO PRESS

CHICAGO AND LONDON

The University of Chicago Press, Chicago 60637
The University of Chicago Press, Ltd., London
© 2015 by The University of Chicago
All rights reserved. Published 2015.
Paperback edition 2016
Printed in the United States of America

24 23 22 21 20 19 18 17 16   2 3 4 5 6

ISBN-13: 978-0-226-20510-6 (cloth)
ISBN-13: 978-0-226-42183-4 (paper)
ISBN-13: 978-0-226-20524-3 (e-book)
DOI: 10.7208/chicago/9780226205243.001.0001

Library of Congress Cataloging-in-Publication Data

Reed, T. J. (Terence James), 1937– author.
    Light in Germany : scenes from an unknown Enlightenment / T. J. Reed.
        pages cm
    Includes bibliographical references and index.
    ISBN 978-0-226-20510-6 (cloth : alk. paper) — ISBN 978-0-226-20524-3 (e-book)
    1. Enlightenment—Germany. 2. Germany—Intellectual life—18th century.
    I. Title.
    DD66.R38 2015
    943'.05—dc23

                                                    2014027491

FOR ANN

CONTENTS

"Enlightenment" is a term inviting grand generalizations, friendly or in recent times often skeptical, even hostile. Either way, they blur the view of its substance, which is the thinking and actions of individual writers. I focus on central texts and episodes in which intellectual independence and ultimately personal freedom were enacted and expanded—in the social individual, in epistemology, in reflections on history, in dramatic representations, in exploration of the wider world, in science, in education, in poetic and personal fulfillment, and in a politics of peace. They are all scenes in one great drama—at any moment there is related activity by other minds and social actors going on in another part of the field. Even when not an overt theme, social and political reality is ever-present as a framework and as the force that provoked and resisted the ideas which were striving to reshape it.

There are occasional glances at parallels across Europe, but I attempt no general theory of the Enlightenment other than what its German participants themselves say and what emerges as common ground in their writing. Beyond that I offer, at least implicitly, a defense of their leading ideas, believing that these have proved their value when realized in modern secular democracies, and that their more consistent application would be a good thing—in period parlance, would be of benefit to humanity. That much needs saying given the frequent glib dismissal of Enlightenment thinking as ineffectual, irrelevant, and a thing of the past. It is none of those things.

Some of the episodes lie on what is conventionally the literary, some on the philosophical or theological side of the line, but the line is itself imprecise and permeable—Goethe's poetry contains a vital philosophy, some of Kant's essays can be read as dramatic dialogue, Lessing's greatest drama outpreaches orthodox theology. Essential light is cast equally by them all.

The perception of a fundamental unity goes back to my years as a fellow and tutor at St. John's College, Oxford, and was explored there in essays that began to develop their own coherence. Competing involvements, in particular with Thomas Mann (himself, it is true, a late adoptive child of the Enlightenment) prevented the threads from being brought together on a larger scale. Since 2004, the freedom of retirement has made that possible, resulting first in a small German volume, *Mehr Licht in Deutschland: Eine kleine Geschichte der Aufklärung* (Munich, 2009). The present study inevitably uses some of the same materials and arguments but is substantially a different book—at twice the length, covering more ground, and addressed to a not just linguistically different readership.

The work of this last decade has been generously supported by a research prize of the Alexander von Humboldt Foundation and a substantial travel grant from the Leverhulme Trust. I owe other debts of gratitude to people and institutions for their help and hospitality: to the Göttingen Georg-August-Universität and its Academy of Sciences, which made me welcome in 2004–5; to the Goethegesellschaft and the Anna-Amalia-Bibliothek in Weimar; to the Friedrich-Schiller-Universität and the Thüringer Universitäts- und Landesbibliothek in Jena; and as always to my home libraries, the Oxford Taylorian and Bodleian, and in London the British Library and the Library of the Germanic Institute.

The final station of my Oxford career, the Queen's College, has gone on providing me in retirement with cordial collegiality, a workroom, and the outstandingly friendly services of its library, college office, IT experts, common room, lodge porters, and domestic staff. For that I am deeply grateful.

Anyone working in Oxford profits from the informal discussion, often across subject borders, that is the ancient lifeblood of the place. From among numberless fruitful conversations, I remember with particular affection those with my predecessor in the Taylor Chair, Siegbert Prawer, who took a lively interest in my project right up to his death. We had hoped he would see it completed. Deeper in the past, I shake my head over the nonchalance with which, as a student of French, I chose to concentrate on the nineteenth century, well knowing that my tutor Robert Shackleton was an eminent Enlightenment scholar. This book perhaps makes some amends.

Of friends and partners in Germany, Gottfried Willems initiated my connection with Schiller's old university, and Werner Frick smoothed the way for my stay in Göttingen. The Zwiener family in Jena have over the years provided a hospitable base for a project that lay close by.

My oldest debt, for half a century of loving support and much sympathetic and alert reading, is to my wife. To her the book is dedicated.

Jim Reed
Oxford, December 2013

The editions I quote from, and the forms of reference to them, are listed at the head of the bibliography on pp. 267–68. Letters are quoted by author, recipient, and date only. I quote in English in the main text and give the original in the endnotes where the formulation is crucial, historic, or especially fine. All translations are my own unless otherwise stated. I distinguish between "Enlightenment," with an initial capital, for the historical movement, and "enlightenment," without capital or definite article, for the timeless process.

. . . or Darkness?

Light is not the thing most readily associated with Germany. Among European societies, Germany's history has taken it deepest into moral darkness. The atrocities of the twentieth century cast a long shadow over its whole political and cultural past, even if they are not seen as the inevitable product of a peculiarly German historical fate (the controversial concept of a *Sonderweg*). In moments of mistrust, the foreign observer's mind may spool back through time, as D. H. Lawrence's did in a remarkable intuitive *Letter from Germany* in 1924, all the way "to the Roman days . . . , the days of the silent forest and the dangerous lurking barbarians."[1] The tribes that ambushed Varus's Roman legions in the Teutoburg Forest in 9 CE became indeed the central myth of Germanic resistance to Romano-Western encroachment, whether cultural or military: the tribal leader Arminius (Hermann) was the hero of poetry and plays that inspired resistance to Napoleon in the so-called Wars of Liberation of 1813, the beginnings of German nationalism.

Those dark German forests are notoriously replicated on a smaller scale in German philosophical writing, which seems worlds away from the "clear and distinct ideas" of Descartes, or the lucidity and wit of Voltaire and David Hume. It can be difficult for light to break through the thickets of a German sentence. That may be a cliché, but it is not a caricature. The style of thinkers from Kant via Hegel to Heidegger gives it legitimate substance. At the other extreme, where there *are* "clear and distinct ideas" of a sort calculated to stick in the mind, they are not those of the Cartesian tradition. They are the positively lurid images of Nietzsche—his "blond beast, roving lustfully in search of booty and victory," his "barbarians of the twentieth century," his "wars like none before"[2]—and his celebration of these things stands on a perilously unclear borderline between metaphor and literal statement. Whatever the literal sense and philosophical intentions that lay behind them, Nietzsche was playing with fire when he launched them into the unpredictable realm of reception.

So it is not surprising that a German Enlightenment doesn't loom large in the common picture—even the historically literate person's picture—of European intellectual history. If people have even heard of such a thing, it has been outshone to the point of invisibility by what went on elsewhere, in the France of Voltaire and Diderot, the Scotland of Hume and Adam Smith, the America of Jefferson and Franklin, the Italy of Vico and Beccaria. So my subtitle is only a slight exaggeration.

True, there are major figures enough in the German eighteenth-century—its second half is the moment when a literary and intellectual culture suddenly bursts into flower. By the early eighteen-hundreds the French, who had long taken their own cultural hegemony for granted, were following Madame de Staël's lead[3] in seeing this German generation—Goethe, Schiller, Lessing, Kant, Herder, the Romantics—as the European leaders in poetic and intellectual innovation. The same sustained interest and excitement swept Britain. Writers from Coleridge and Carlyle to George Eliot and Matthew Arnold were shaped in their thinking by Kant, Lessing, Goethe, Heine, German historical scholarship, and the innovations of the Prussian education system. Those German names are still well enough known in the Anglophone world as names, even if the same cannot be said of their works; but they were scarcely then and are certainly not now thought of primarily as Enlightenment figures. If they are thought about at all, it is in quite other pigeonholes of historical perception, literary or philosophical.

There is thus a gap, at least as far as educated nonspecialists go, in the general awareness of eighteenth-century Germany's intellectual and literary contribution and its clear direction.

The neglect of the German Enlightenment has been made worse by Germans' deliberate shaping of their own image. From the end of the eighteenth century with the Romantic movement, and more crudely and brutally in later stages of German history, this involved rejecting the Enlightenment and all of its values in favor of a more "profound," uniquely German, intellectual (or more precisely anti-intellectual) tradition. It was difficult for defenders of reason to confront a declared irrationalism. This rival ethos was even more decisive than the predictable opposition of authoritarian social forces to any form of rational criticism.

Hence the Enlightenment has sometimes been written out of the German historical record altogether. Almost incredibly, Friedrich Meinecke's study of cosmopolitanism and the nation-state, *Weltbürgertum und Na-*

tionalstaat of 1907, contains no proper account of the title's first concept, the central Enlightenment ideal of the "citizen of the world," and has only a few oblique and derogatory references to Kant, the leading theorist of supranational intellectual and political commitment. Meinecke was, moreover, a leading German historian of ideas, by no means one of the rabid Germanicizers who rejected the Enlightenment as culturally superficial and alien to the German character. Whether through such polemicists or through thinkers with greater intellectual claims, the German cultural tradition from the Romantics onward worked predominantly to instill quite other values and declared its allegiance to very different human powers from the ones the Enlightenment set store by. Those in Germany who argued for rationality in human affairs were always struggling against a current of thought that reveled in the irrational and antirational, consciously setting itself against "Western" thinking—in a bizarre ideological geography, Germany located itself as simply not a Western land. All this is part of German history, and not just cultural history.

To cap it all, there has been some much overrated sniping from the Left. Criticism from the Right was in the nature of things, but Horkheimer and Adorno as left-wingers broke a taboo with their *Dialectic of the Enlightenment*, licensing iconoclasm from any quarter. Their title phrase has been much used as a stick with which to beat the whole Enlightenment movement. Yet their criticism is directed at modern phenomena that have questionable connection with the Enlightenment, and they hardly identify individual writers. It has had disproportionate influence because its concept is such a handy reversal for skeptics on the lookout for historic claims to debunk but not able or willing to examine the firsthand evidence. Its knotty text has perhaps been less often read than its snappy title has been exploited.[4]

Making clear the German Enlightenment's true profile involves reclaiming those major eighteenth-century names as its integral parts and agents. Kant, for instance, is not just what he is commonly seen as, a philosopher's philosopher wrestling with timeless technical problems. True, no philosopher was ever more rigorously professional. But his thinking is deeply rooted in the practical issues of his time, and he is expressly committed to opening up critical debate about society. Goethe's poetic exploration of self and world, which has been the central reference point of German literary culture ever since, is a direct enactment of the Enlightenment's aspirations for human beings generally, as free agents and observers seeking fulfillment in a world of their own. Lessing is the first shaper of modern German drama, and Schiller the classic tragedian of the high style, but in both of them the Enlightenment aim of bringing public issues into the open gives the dramatic art its sharp edge.

Conversely, their art gives the Enlightenment its passion and its poetry. The cliché that the Enlightenment was a dry business, lacking warmth and imagination, can only seem plausible (but is then a circular argument) if you fail to include the writers who realized its ideas and values in their art. Light dawns fully only in their writing. So what follows is not a description of the Enlightenment narrowly defined as a movement in abstract thought, much less a catalog of every last minor participant, but an account of the spread of light—that is, of lucid and active liberal thinking—wherever it can be found in German eighteenth-century culture. The main emphasis is indeed on the last third of the century, what is commonly called "the late Enlightenment," as if it were a separate phase. Rather, it is a maturing, the branches of a single tree, with its imaginative harvest. A tree needs time to grow and fruit.

That the writers in question operated in more various contexts than are popularly associated with the Enlightenment only goes to show how wide and deep its roots ran. With all of them you get a lot more than usual for your money. Each is several writers in one. Goethe is poet, dramatist, novelist, traveler, autobiographer, art critic, and scientist. Schiller is poet, dramatist, narrator, historian, and aesthetic philosopher. The partnership between these two men created a culture in itself. Lessing is dramatist, theologian, literary and artistic theorist, and critic—and a hair-trigger controversialist on any topic that provoked him. Georg Forster is explorer, anthropologist, and political activist. Lichtenberg is scientist and aphoristic wit. Kant illuminates all areas of philosophy and their bearing on the real world. These multifaceted writers reflect the Enlightenment's interests on all fronts in a rich and colorful display. Their names accordingly crop up repeatedly across the chapters as these touch on a wide variety of themes. And the sheer quality of the creative writing means that the German Enlightenment can lay claim to a literature at least as significant as its French counterpart, whose commonest mode is the most directly functional of literary forms, satire.

So if there is a generic character to the age's thinking, there is also immense variety. There has been too much emphasis on a pallidly unparticularized Enlightenment, especially from critics who talk as if it were one dull outdated lump and have obviously not looked at its ingredients. Enlightenment writing covers all the issues then facing—most of them still facing—mankind and sees them as necessary parts of an embracing anthropology. They range from religion (the critique of religious texts, myths, and theological doctrines, but also their subtle transmutation into secular forms and ideas) through history (the philosophical historian's search for patterns in the past that will raise people's morale for action in the present), art, and beauty (aesthetics as a formal branch of philosophy was virtually an invention of eighteenth-century Germans, but more broadly part of a European trend toward revaluing the senses against the old priority of rational abstraction) to the wider world (as in the travel experiences of Forster father and son, Captain Cook's scientists on his second circumnavigation and founders of a tradition that runs via Alexander von Humboldt down to Charles Darwin) and on down to politics (the problems of the still fragmented, prenational German lands, the complex response to the French Revolution, and issues of intercultural tolerance or its absence). All of these themes have twenty-first-century relevance, not to mention a twenty-first-century moral.

As well as the great thinkers and poets, there is a parallel cast of rulers, some of them sympathetic to the Enlightenment cause, some opposed. Some were sovereigns of the major German powers: three Austrian monarchs, Maria Theresia, Joseph II, and Leopold II; and three kings of Prussia, Frederick the Great and two Frederick Williams. Others are more minor figures, dukes good or bad: Franz of Anhalt-Dessau, the very model of an enlightened ruler; Karl Eugen of Württemberg, the classic example of absolutist tyranny and excess; and the most celebrated minor prince of all, because he had Goethe as friend and adviser, Carl August of Weimar.[5] Advisers to the other rulers likewise varied: Zedlitz, Frederick the Great's enlightened minister of education; Wöllner, co-instigator of Frederick William II's anti-Enlightenment backlash after the death of Frederick the Great; Brühl in Saxony; Erdmannsdorf, friend of Franz of Anhalt-Dessau and co-architect of his Wörlitz buildings and parks; Kaunitz, the right-hand man of Maria Theresia and Joseph II; and Montmartin, the evil genius of Karl Eugen in Württemberg. Then between the two lines stood, especially in Prussia, men who served the state as jurists, doctors, teachers, and administrators, and who met as a club to discuss, and often publish, their views on how state and society might be better ordered.

This last dual role of intelligent citizens exactly fits the historical account of how enlightenment might progress that one such servant of the Prussian state put before the thinking public. His account of enlightenment and its necessity is timeless and exemplary, but it was rooted very specifically in its time and place. It leads directly into the problems and possibilities of late eighteenth-century Germany.

CHAPTER I

Coming of Age:
The Primal Scene

It is the privilege and proper condition of a human being, arrived at the maturity of his faculties, to use and interpret experience in his own way.
—John Stuart Mill, *On Liberty*

Renaissance is an image of new birth. The Enlightenment's master image is achieved maturity, *Mündigkeit*. The two may be seen as successive phases in Europe's intellectual history. Between them as stages in a single human life lies the double-edged phenomenon of childhood. For Christianity it was a state of absolute obedience to a stern but loving father, with the development beyond dependence left wholly out of account: childhood was a permanent condition.[1] But a child grows, asks questions, and is dissatisfied with the old answers, and the young adult has the right to propose new ones. The Enlightenment takes the metaphor of childhood with full seriousness as leading to that necessary organic development. It is a philosophy of youthful innovation, not the set wisdom of old men: "Enlightenment is man's emergence from a juvenile condition which is his own fault. That *juvenile condition* is the inability to use his own understanding without someone else's guidance. It is *his own fault* if its cause is not a lack of understanding but a lack of the resolution and courage to use it without someone else's guidance. *Sapere aude!* Have the courage to use your *own* understanding is therefore the motto of enlightenment."[2]

This opening of Immanuel Kant's essay "Answer to the Question: What Is Enlightenment?" was a real answer to a real question: what exactly was this "enlightenment" about which so much was heard? The question surely needed asking before anything else in society was changed in its name. The doubter, Johann Friedrich Zöllner, himself at home in Berlin Enlightenment circles, was asking the question in the movement's own monthly publication, the *Berlinische Monatsschrift*. Kant sets the date and page number of the original question beneath the title of his reply: "(See Decemb. 1783, p. 516)."

Zöllner's puzzlement is puzzling, given how belated his question was—the German Enlightenment had been slowly establishing itself for close on a century. But as a Protestant pastor he felt disturbed by the rise of civil marriages at the expense of church ceremonies, and by the growing recognition that this should become the norm. Kant's is the most celebrated of several prompt replies,[3] not just because he was the leading German thinker of his day but because his response formulates by far the broadest vision, setting out the essential issue, which is the process of enlightenment that operates or is blocked in any society at any time. The German phrase *Ausgang des Menschen* can be read as referring both to man in general and to every single individual, "emergence" as both a timeless ideal and an eighteenth-century necessity. In its quiet way, this is a founding statement of the open secular society of modern Europe. If the propositions sound self-evident, that is because they have long been taken for granted in civilized societies, at least in principle. Most Enlightenment utterances can sound unexciting until you reflect how fundamental they are, how limited their realization has been across the world, and what constant vigilance and pressure are needed even now, even in civilized countries, to see to it that they are practiced. Any day's news is likely to show they are not, and not just in distant places.

Besides its permanent relevance, the document throws light on what was happening in Prussia in 1784, two years before Frederick the Great died. Kant's argument was meant to be radical yet reassuring: radical because change there must be—inertia is not an option for a living society—but reassuring conservatives that the mechanics of social change need not mean violent upheaval. Change must be gradual and agreed upon. That already means there must have been a meeting of divergent ideas in a forum where opinions could be expressed freely. No society can expect universal and permanent assent to the rules and conventions handed down from earlier times. These things necessarily have a limited life, if only because a new generation is born, reaches maturity, and asks why things are as they are and, more pointedly, whether they could not be better.

Kant's view is not complacent. Where once he had accepted without more ado that his were enlightened times,[4] he now expressly denies it and begins anew at ground level. At the threshold of adult life, when people come of age, they become responsible for their own actions and free to take life-changing decisions—to enter into legal contracts, to marry—which involve thinking things out for themselves. All societies recognize this transition, though historically they have located it at different points in the individual's life (thirty, twenty-one, eighteen) and at different points for different groups, rulers and subjects, men and women. The recognition is commonly low-key. The familiar phrase "coming of age" does not explicitly say what the defining quality of "age" is, nor does it positively invite independent thought. That would be asking for trouble.

Yet the link with the chronology of human life makes the transition to independence potentially universal. Far from being an abstract or elevated conception, something strictly for intellectuals or the learned, the age of reason is a necessary stage in life—or can be, if people will only take up their birthright. It *is* a right, as Kant's fellow spirit Lichtenberg emphasized: "Have the courage to think, take possession of your place."[5] This is the primal scene, true for everyone, true at all times. Elsewhere Kant defines Enlightenment simply as thinking for yourself—*Selbstdenken*.[6] The clichés about the Enlightenment—"elitist intellectualism" or "cold abstract reason"—melt away when "reason" is replaced by "thinking for yourself" and "openness to debate." There is then only good or bad thinking, and if thinkers are an elite, it is one that anybody can join. Everybody can choose to grow up.

Kant's demands are not excessive: he invokes not "reason," but the more practical everyday concept of "understanding." The young are not being required to be philosophers, only to become fully what nature has made them. There are risks and pressures, which Kant addresses frankly: courage and resolve are needed to overcome laziness and cowardice. As minors, they have necessarily been under the control of parents or guardians. But continuing to live like a minor when they have reached maturity is plainly their own fault. Coming of age has become a metaphor for intellectual and social independence.

Human growth is thus a disturbing force, the more so because it is undeniably a gift of nature, with the suprasocial authority this implies. Its challenge to an established order lies behind such confrontational terms as "young Turks" and "elder statesman."[7] "Young" implies the vigor of early life and recent maturity. The issue will be put very clearly in Goethe's drama *Torquato Tasso*, where the young poet with something original to say to society is wrong-footed and disgraced by an elder statesman who has always treated him in the way a guardian treats a juvenile.[8] How necessary, but also unwelcome, new contributions can be to a shortsighted establishment is captured in Wordsworth's image of "blind authority beating with his stick / The child that should have led him."[9]

Yet in another sense of the word, it is "natural" for people to prefer a quiet life, to accept the status quo and cause no bother, for others or themselves. Kant's arguments frequently turn on this conflict between people's better selves—what they ought to do, what was "intended" by nature (i.e., it is visibly inherent in *their* nature, or why would they have the ability to do it?)—and the way people commonly do behave. Kant neatly mimics a quiet-lifer: "It's so comfortable to be juvenile. If I have a book that exercises understanding for me, a spiritual guide who has a conscience for me, a doctor who organizes my diet for me, then I really don't need to bother myself. I don't need to think if I can simply pay; someone else will be bound to take over the tiresome business for me."[10] Kant likewise ironizes the people who take advantage of this general slackness, metaphorical "guardians"—not the Guardians Plato conceived of as running his Republic, but the people who "most kindly" (*gütigst*) set themselves up to supervise the rest of us: the pushy, the placemen, the officious, the willing agents of power, the anxious anticipators of government's intentions. Their deliberate frustrating of natural growth reaches its climax in the caricature of a full-grown human being grotesquely penned in a baby walker, a *Gängelwagen*, or controlled by leading reins—incidentally long-established, positively meant metaphors in Pietism for divine guidance and control.[11] The guardians warn grown people off learning to walk on their own by persuading them it is dangerous, whereas in reality walking can be learned at the price of the odd tumble. Walking with a firm, independent step is part of a consistent network of Kantian metaphors. He has used this one two decades earlier in the announcement of his lectures for 1765,[12] and he will use it repeatedly three years later in a new foreword to the *Critique of Pure Reason*, where he speaks of the "firm step" of the reliable new science of human knowledge that he is in the process of founding.[13]

Kant has some sympathy for the isolated individual who is subject to the pressures of society. He knows that even that odd tumble can be enough to put the timorous off trying again. It can certainly be hard to move freely, to make the leap over even the narrowest of ditches, or even just to walk with an easy stride, when one has been long constrained by shackles (*Fußschellen*). Has he mixed his metaphors here and drifted away from the image of adults being treated as mere children? Children are, after all, seldom shackled. Yet all education risks being a form of constraint,[14] and Kant's discordant metaphor unmasks the reality behind the guardians' pretended concern for the safety of their charges. Their motive is not parental benevolence but social control. These reins are made of harder stuff.

If achieving independence is difficult for the unaided individual, then what is needed to advance enlightenment is a community that will support his efforts. A social collective, what Kant calls "a public" (*Publikum*), is bound to achieve enlightenment in the end. All it needs for the purpose is freedom, and surely the most harmless kind, namely the freedom for people to use their understanding in the public forum.

The argument seems to have come round in a circle. Making use of your own understanding was the definition of enlightenment Kant began with. The freedom to use their understanding was inherent in human beings, but they still had to choose to use it; it had to be hard-won by each of them against the pressure of social discouragement and guardianly warnings—that was why a social support group was needed. Now it seems the support group itself has to be granted freedom before the process can begin.

Yet the circularity exactly reflects the historical situation in which Kant, like all Enlightenment thinkers, was living and writing, and for which he was trying to legislate with carefully unaggressive tactics. However viable the processes of debate, and however supportive the public, there was still a controlling authority without whose assent no free thought was possible. This was the absolutist ruler, the ultimate "guardian" of "God's immature children"[15]—an eighteenth-century German prince commonly claimed to be the *Landesvater*, father of his country and his subjects. Behind the euphemism, absolutist rule meant the exercise of total power without external restraint—as was still largely true of fathers in actual families. The paternal metaphor did not envisage the children's growth to independence. The "father" was not answerable to any other authority, neither to a constitution, nor to institutions, nor to critical voices in a barely nascent public realm. Why deign to listen when he or she (the gender variant here is not political correctness but historical accuracy—this is the age of Maria Theresia of Austria and Catherine the Great of Russia)—why listen when they could go on ruling as they liked? Why make concessions at all? Society runs most smoothly on conformity, not debate. In the army, it's "Don't argue, obey!" In the church, it's "Don't argue, believe!" In matters of taxation, it's "Don't argue, pay up!"[16] These examples epitomize the workings of the social mechanism. But Kant adds, in brackets as if it were an afterthought (but in fact it is the center of his strategy), "Only one single ruler in the world says: 'Argue as much as you like about whatever you like, but obey!'"[17]

Kant is again mimicking, this time putting what Frederick the Great ultimately meant into words he never spoke. The king was half Enlightenment man—to that extent a "plausible partner" in dialogue[18]—but half

Realpolitiker. He ascended the throne with a European reputation as an enlightened prince and every promise of being a ruler in that spirit, but he marked the occasion by invading Austrian Silesia in pursuit of an old territorial claim. From then on, it was the *Realpolitiker* in him who determined matters whenever the two elements conflicted. The sword was mightier than the pen.

It looks as if the peremptory words Kant imagines the king speaking were not much of a concession; the practical outcome of debate would always be a foregone conclusion. A hard-nosed ruler was allowing free discussion that could have no practical effect. Still, the concession made a valuable break in the circularity of Kant's argument, a limited license that could, with care, be exploited. All Enlightenment dealings with the powerful were attempts to insert the thin end of a wedge, to get the very possibility of argument accepted and create a bridgehead from which the forces of free thought could move out and develop a campaign, perhaps eventually with real results for society. Almost the only thing on their side was the seductive power of ideas themselves, their modish attraction for any ruler possessed of intelligence and some measure of humane goodwill. The ultimate ideal, if not a Platonic "philosopher-king" such as the young Frederick had looked like becoming, might be one who at least listened to the advice of a philosopher. Admittedly, the few attempts in history to realize that ideal had ended in disillusion.[19]

The Prussian context explains why Kant mixes reassurance with radicalism. He does it by making a subtle distinction that can work in a half-open society and perhaps ease it open a little further. Yes, obedience is indispensable, the institutions of society have to be kept running. But even for their own purposes they can do with some improvement. Dutiful officials may be able to point out how things could be improved, in a constructive rather than a subversive spirit. Citizens should accordingly lead a double life: they must do things by the book as loyal members of a stable society, but they may also question things as members of the broader community that Kant labels "a public." Indeed, not just "may," but "should": in Kant's eyes it is the intellectual's "calling." No loyalty is owed to an institution's flaws.[20]

Since Kant's time the idea of "the public" has lost much of its thrill. It may even suggest a constituency more passive than active, uniform and perhaps even conformist in its attitudes: "public opinions, private lazinesses," as Nietzsche later sneered.[21] For Kant, by contrast, public opinion was to be the product of collective private reflection—except that he does not call it private. Counterintuitively, he uses the term "private" for people's professional work, where they have to keep to the rules—what would normally be called their public function. (It is "private" only in that it concerns their personal careers.) For him, they are only truly acting publicly when they reflect outside their professional practice on how things might work better and place their suggestions before their contemporaries, perhaps even before an international audience of citizens of the world (*Weltbürger*).

Thus a clergyman is bound to preach the doctrines his church currently holds. But if he inwardly dissents, he has the right, and the higher duty, to say so before other thinking people. Religion is the most obvious case—Diderot called Christianity "the Great Prejudice"[22]—a second eighteenth-century absolutism alongside and complicit with the political form. Religious doctrines may claim immunity to change, yet they originated at a particular time under particular conditions, and no generation has the right to impose an unchangeable belief on its successors, not even by the authority of rulers, assemblies, and state treaties. Kant is no doubt thinking of the Treaty of Westphalia, which ended the Thirty Years' War with an uneasy religious settlement. To block new insight and knowledge, and thus delay the progress of enlightenment, would be—again a dramatic foundational claim—a crime against human nature.[23]

Without continual debate and gradual change, a polity must ossify and decline. To question present practices is thus a service to its long-term interests, even its survival. It is a kind of loyal rebellion. Yet it has no fixed prior aims. Its message is simply, "Think!" Kant has taken Descartes's central maxim and turned it round: *Cogito, ergo sum*, "I think, therefore I am," becomes *Estis, ergo cogitate!*: "You are [individuals with minds of your own], so think!" If you don't, you aren't![24] And in place of Descartes's comforting thesis that our awareness of thinking is the one thing not subject to doubt, and a firm basis for constructing further certainties (though this proved to be not so simple), Kant sets the unsettling proposition that the basis of adult dignity is the readiness to query everything around us.

Thinking had no fixed program because philosophy was not a conveyable content. Kant in Königsberg never claimed to teach *a* philosophy, only how to think philosophically—not the noun *Philosophie* but the verb *philosophieren*. There was no absolute authority, no ultimate book, in the way Euclid had summarized all then-known geometry.[25] From his earliest writings, Kant declares himself independent of even his greatest predecessors—Leibniz and Newton.[26] His conception of enlightenment as intellectual independence is his own practice writ large. It duly allowed him to change the face of philosophy, for his times and beyond.

If philosophical thinking was a process with no set doctrines, argument was an adventure of reason. You were only ever committed to the process, not to a prior view. You never knew where discussion would end up. If you came up against a stronger argument than yours, you made it your own: "When I meet with something that instructs me, I adopt it. The judgment of the person who refutes my judgment is my judgment, once I have weighed it against the scale of self-love."[27] As Lessing put it, the loser in a debate stood to lose only his errors.[28] That, it is true, was an ideal which necessarily conflicted with the human desire to be right, above all to *have been* right. Goethe once said that "nobody was ever convinced by their opponent's reasons."[29] But that was an exaggerated skepticism. Reason could not afford to hang on to a weak position out of bias and obstinacy, or it discredited itself and made its own operations impracticable. If you entered the debate, you were signing up to a few simple ground rules: relevant and adequate evidence, and fair and logical argument. In Lichtenberg's words, you swore an oath on the supremacy of logic.[30] Mere interests should not count, unless they could be given a rational form. All public debate must envisage an open outcome. Rationality was a risk. Debate rested on the belief that the agreed procedures would arrive at a right answer—not *your* right answer, but right in the sense that all arguments had been given due weight. It was surely "nonsensical to expect reason to produce enlightenment and yet to prescribe in advance which side it will favour."[31] Moreover, the procedures of debate were themselves open to debate.

Even this much makes it sound more technical than it really is. People engage in these processes naturally in the interactions of daily life, starting in the playground, where the violence that short-circuits argument also begins. Reason is no highfalutin, abstract affair, and certainly not the monster of abstraction that Burke attacked in his polemic against the French Revolution. Sound argument is an everyday demand and an instinctive practice of people who have no intellectual pretensions.

Kant's own argument indeed accommodates Burke's skepticism in advance. Voices for the status quo, those conservatives for whom the right moment for change, if there is one, is the last possible moment—theirs too would be a necessary input. No point of view (so Kant held, surprisingly and engagingly in this most rigorous of professional thinkers) was ever entirely wrong.[32] They all had some grain of truth, some arguable angle on the matter at hand. Their views had to be listened to—not necessarily accepted, but seriously taken issue with. That would allow for the full range of interests and opinions. So the social debate would be long, sometimes seemingly endless, and social change would be correspondingly slow. That was the price you paid for getting the ideas of debate and change accepted. Gradualism was also a recommendation in itself. The sharper, violent break of revolution—Kant was writing five years before events in France, but he foresaw the problems they were to generate—would paradoxically not produce a fundamental change in the way people thought, but merely replace one set of prejudices with another as the reins controlling the thoughtless masses.[33] Kant is for evolution. His vision of society as continual debate is a sketch of something like the democratic process, long before its institutions were remotely possible in Germany. If it seems naive, given the vast nonintellectual forces of power and interest that shape all societies, that could just as well be said of the modern faith in democracy.

Kant's caution is matched by the modesty of his claims for what has been achieved to date. Is his generation, he asks, living in an enlightened age? No, only an age of enlightenment, that is, of a movement toward enlightenment, a gradual enlightening process—the noun *Aufklärung* means the process as much as the product. Kant's distinction recognizes not just that change will always be resisted, but that a final, settled enlightenment can never be reached. That would be a contradiction in terms, since any achieved condition is the work of a given generation, so will be open to question by its successor. It was an achievement to have got the critical process started. In a fragmented eighteenth-century Germany of some three hundred absolutist governments, it could only be with the permission of individual rulers in one or two states among many small parts of an incoherent whole. In Kant's case, fortunately, it was the ruler of no ministate, someone who for his sins and qualities was foremost in the German and European public eye and hence an invaluable example. This "age of the process of enlightenment" Kant duly calls "Frederick's century."[34]

The essay seems to be ending in a blaze of flattery, and for that Kant has often been criticized. The criticism is shortsighted. For one thing, the period convention of flattery under absolutism has to be understood as the starting point for any address to the powerful. Leibniz proposed that a medal be struck in honor of Frederick I of Prussia, inscribed *gloria novi saeculi*—the glory of the new age. A rare and precious exception to the practice is Dr. Johnson's withering reply to Lord Chesterfield, the belated would-be patron of Johnson's already successful *Dictionary*. More important, Kant's flattery is not a gratuitous or self-interested currying of favor but hardheaded tactics. Frederick the Enlightener has allowed freedom of thought, has even in some matters encouraged it—he was vehemently anti-Christian and anticlerical and so was more than happy to allow criticism and satire at the expense of the church. In a private letter, Lessing was scathing about the "idiocies" (*Sottisen*) that Frederick encouraged about religion while in other respects maintaining the most slavish society in Germany.[35] This last was an exaggeration. Frederick had gone further than just religion, as Kant points out, and Prussia was certainly not the most slavish of German societies. In particular, the king had allowed discussion of new legislation that was to be embodied in a reformed Prussian code, the Allgemeines Landrecht. For example, when he noted in the margin of a draft, "Good, but a bit much. Laws must be short," Carl Gottlieb Svarez, who was one of the draftsmen under Samuel Cocceji, addressed the Society of the Friends of Enlightenment (the "Wednesday Society") on the theme "How far may and must laws be short?," warning that brief formulations put too much power in the hands of judges, which endangered civil liberty.[36]

But the free ground gained under Frederick's rule needed consolidating. Like Kant's assurances earlier in the essay that the public use of reason is the most harmless of freedoms, and that society will be kept running by "private" conformity while "public" debate proceeds, his acclaim for Frederick was designed to keep things moving in the same direction—to push the wedge further in or, in the German phrase, to cut another slice off the salami. Kant's salami tactics culminate in the wry paradox that an absolute ruler with a large army can allow his subjects more freedom than a republican government would have the confidence to do. Under the "hard husk" of a securely controlled society, the seed of independent thought might safely develop;[37] it might slowly create a people more capable of free action, and eventually the ruler might not treat the governed as mere machines in the larger machine of the state. The stability of Prussia would not suffer; indeed, it stood to gain by the free public exercise of reason in a framework of firm control. The equally paradoxical reverse proposition—that a republican state might actually close down freedoms—would shortly be borne out by the French revolutionary regimes.

Of course Kant's argument is disingenuous. His reassurances are a common Enlightenment tactic. Voltaire, in the *Lettres philosophiques*, similarly argues that "the number of those who think is extremely small, and they do not have any intention of disturbing the world."[38] But was any ruler who bothered to read these Enlightenment tracts ever taken in by such reassurances? They were a bluff that could easily be called, and anyone who emphasized the harmlessness of critical thought was only drawing attention to its real risks: *qui s'excuse, s'accuse*. Critical thinking is never harmless—not, at least, to the present interest of rulers as they perceive it. They may well not distinguish between loyal and disloyal rebellion, between constructive criticism and subversion. Any questioning of an institution and its workings, whether church, army, or tax office, will tend to destabilize it and undermine people's unthinking trust. If a vicar has been querying

orthodox doctrine, parishioners' simple faith will suffer. Officers who criticize the army are held to be "prejudicial to discipline."[39] The seeds of free
thought could—in that further organic metaphor of Kant's, they eventually
would—not just free themselves from their "hard husk," they might break
it up altogether.

Meanwhile it was a dilemma for the officials themselves, the vicar or
the officer or the tax inspector who carried out duties by the book while also
critically rethinking what it laid down. That involved an uncomfortable
doublethink and at best a halfhearted conformity.

Finally, and crucially, because all freedoms under absolutism depended
on the will or whim of a single all-powerful individual, any gains made
could not be institutionalized, and certainly not entrenched. On one of his
visits to England, Lichtenberg reflected that freedoms here were safeguarded
by a constitution, whereas any freedoms Hanover enjoyed were dependent
on the continuing goodwill of the king.[40] What the king gave, the king could
take away. In 1837 his successor Ernst August famously did, reneging on
a nonentrenched constitution.[41] Liberal measures could be reversed at the
drop of a crown. This gave urgency to Kant's argument, for in 1784 Frederick
the Great was visibly declining, and people knew what (i.e., who) was coming. Kant certainly received at least one explicit warning from the center of
things in Berlin that was probably representative of liberal fears: "Unfor-
tunately we may be heading again for sad times of zealotry and ignorance;
zealotry is already advancing with powerful strides; not everyone knows
from what quarter such dangers for the human spirit are once more to be
feared: but it is almost dangerous to entrust one's honest thoughts on the
matter to a letter."[42]

Two years later Frederick was dead. His successor, Frederick William II,
was religiose and hostile to the Enlightenment, whose definition he had no
doubts about at all: it was subversively anti-Christian, and Christianity had
the unquestionable truth. The new king was certainly not open to liberal-
izing arguments like Kant's. Indeed, the distinction of private and public
clearly provided an opening that reaction could exploit. There would be no
more enlightened royal acts, no intellectual liberty for thinkers to welcome,
no occasion for tactical flattery of the ruler. Liberal trends in church and
education were thrown sharply into reverse, and *Aufklärer* were systemati-
cally and ruthlessly attacked. Kant himself was in due course banned from
publishing on the subject of religion.[43]

So Kant's praise of Frederick the Great had not been an ignoble bowing
and scraping, any more than his program of gradual change had been feebly
conformist. Historians who make either criticism lack a feeling for Kant's

situation and his need to employ cautious tactics to ease enlightenment along. If this was an "espousal of absolutism,"[44] it was a forced marriage. How uncompromising the will behind the tactics really was is plain from what Kant had written three years earlier in—surprisingly, at first sight— the otherwise largely abstract *Critique of Pure Reason*. A footnote to the first introduction of 1781 reads: "Our age is the age of criticism, to which everything must be subjected. *Religion*, by its *sanctity*, and *legislation*, by its *majesty*, commonly try to gain exemption. But they then arouse a just suspicion against themselves, and cannot lay claim to the unfeigned respect which reason only grants to such things as have been able to sustain its free and public scrutiny."[45] Nor, he adds later, is reason any respecter of persons.[46]

This is the iron hand inside the velvet glove. That it should have shown itself at the very outset of Kant's most technical philosophical text is not after all so surprising. For as the full passage states, it was ultimately the same impulse, growing from the same social attitudes, that led both to his revision of metaphysics and to the desired scrutiny of social institutions. Kant's whole immense philosophical campaign was inseparable from his commitment to the practical cause of enlightenment.

Kant's arguments for independent thinking were not new—but then, nobody in the 1784 debate was claiming the Enlightenment itself was new. Kant was defining it in retrospect and in essence, but its first principles had been stated as early as 1691 by Christian Thomasius, sometimes credited with being the "father of the Enlightenment":

Before all else clear out the stable of your understanding, that is to say, get rid of hindrances and combat prejudices as the origin of all errors.

Begin to attack both these things, and because you have often previously had the experience of being deceived partly by other people, partly by your own overhastiness, do not any longer so easily be trusting, but start *doubting*.

Doubt the prejudice of authority . . . In exploring truth never rely on the authority of any person, whoever it may be, if you do not feel an inner certainty that the persuasion you have believed so far is necessarily connected to the already recognised fundamental truths.

Do not be put off by the cry of those who have an interest in not letting the world be wrenched out of its common errors, when they impress on you the authority of your *governors*, your *parents*, or teachers and try to frighten your conscience with the suggestion that you are grossly transgressing a natural law when you doubt the truth of what you have been taught by your superiors or preceptors and dare to deviate from their opinion.

Ethics will demonstrate to you that we are admittedly obliged to adjust our outward acting and refraining according to the will of our superiors and elders . . . but that the *understanding* is subject to no laws, because it depends on our free will.[47]

The instilling of doubt looks back to Descartes's initial principle but stops short of Kant's collective social thinking. Thomasius's reference to governors, elders, and teachers directly anticipates Kant's "guardians," but he shares Kant's caution over "outward acting" as against the inner freedom of "the understanding," very much Kant's "private/public" distinction. Still, the attack on prejudice and unquestioned authority is the critical result, the reforming arm, of the principle of independent thinking. Thomasius is a good example of the process Kant described as "disentangling oneself" (*sich herauswickeln*) from one's juvenile immaturity.[48] Thomasius recalls how he had long believed that the theologians, a social and intellectual establishment, must be right. Eventually his judgment matured, and he saw that to be thus led by the nose was itself a sin against God; innovation was not necessarily heresy.[49] Thomasius put intellectual independence into exemplary practice when he spoke out against the evil of witch trials. His refusal to believe allegations that hapless old women had made pacts with the devil is expressed in a repeated "I cannot believe it,"[50] a negative faith as resolute as Luther's "Here I stand and can do no other." There was indeed no clearer example of prejudice than the belief in witchcraft, which put the cart of condemnation before the horse of proof: "pre-judice" (*Vor-urteil*—the compound has immediate impact in German). The Enlightenment, in contrast, is epitomized by the pursuit of fair judgment, and not just in witch trials.[51]

Flesh can be put on Enlightenment principles by a real case fought out between individuals, namely another subject and ruler: the writer Friedrich Schiller and Duke Karl Eugen of Württemberg. It begins as subversive utterance by the subject, directed at but unnoticed by the ruler, then becomes a failed dialogue, the ruler refusing to hear or see the appeals of his subject— the easy option for the holder of absolute power. But the conflict left literary traces more violent than anything in Kant's circumspect tactics. Being on the receiving end of absolute power in his youth was the first lesson in history for Schiller, the future historical dramatist.

For two years in the 1740s Frederick the Great, perhaps mindful of the Hohenzollerns' Württemberg origins, stood guardian informally to the fatherless Swabian prince, keeping him out of harm's way at the Prussian court while the War of the Austrian Succession was fought in the south. In order to take up the reins of government in 1744, Karl Eugen had to be declared of age at sixteen by the Emperor Charles VII in an exceptional move (dynastic law stipulated eighteen for princes). That was not the only way coming of age among princes and nobles differed from the process for the ordinary person. The elevated were waiting to be set free not into private responsibility but, all too commonly, into public irresponsibility. Karl Eugen was an extreme example. For at least the next three decades he proved anything but mature in all but the chronological sense. He had learned nothing about frugality and service to the state from his time under Frederick's wing, or from the written advice in the personalized *Mirror for Princes* that was Frederick's parting present. Instead he continued the long-standing Württemberg tradition of ducal extravagance, confrontation with the Estates—a rudimentary form of political representation found in some German principalities—over the financing of his expenditure, and arbitrary injustice toward his subjects.[52] The visible remains of that prolonged extravagance are the several grandiose buildings that Württemberg now proudly foregrounds as tourist attractions. They typify the architecture of the period, which is an architecture not of the Enlightenment but of unenlightened absolutism. With the marked exception of Anhalt-Dessau,[53] palaces, residences, and gardens were meant to impress with pomp and oppress with power.

In the petty German states there was little to restrain rulers' human weaknesses, and too little was done to educate them for their future role. Kant complained that they were left too much freedom, because it was known they would hold power one day.[54] In the 1780s Goethe writes more picturesquely: "The tutors of young princes whom I know are like people entrusted with the course of a valley stream, their only concern is to make sure everything runs nice and calmly over the stretch they're responsible for, they build dams across and keep the water back in a nice pond, but once the boy is declared of age the dam bursts and the water goes shooting off with full force and destructiveness, carrying stones and mud with it."[55] The following year Goethe's Weimar friend Knebel writes a letter of reproach to his former pupil Prince Constantin, who after many statements of good intent was now "sensationally extending the list of tomfooleries of the German princes."[56]

Had he not been Schiller's duke, Karl Eugen would be of no more interest now than any other minor German ruler of the time. His early extravagances were no more than typical of their time and place. He spent more than the duchy could afford on buildings, ballet, opera companies, and mistresses until an allegedly "reformed" phase was forced on him in 1770 by a decision of the Imperial Council in Vienna in favor of the Estates, who had appealed against the wastrel duke. The council's judgement was called a "hereditary settlement" (Erbvergleich), a face-saving formula that could seem to apply to Karl Eugen's successors rather than just criticizing the present incumbent. For those who prefer a more romantic motivation, within a year Karl Eugen met Franziska von Hohenheim and was seemingly saved by the love of a good woman. By 1778 he was even claiming, in a "pulpit manifesto" read in churches across Württemberg, to have been "born again in true fatherly love" for his land, after excesses that were "only human," and for which he privately blamed those who had "willingly indulged" him.[57] He promised to devote "the second part of Our life" to justice and his people's welfare. But the excuse "since We are only human" is followed ominously, almost defiantly, by "and must also remain so in future"[58]—virtually a prediction of backsliding. And back he duly slid.

It was in this phase that in 1771 he founded a school. Local historians have made much of this as an enlightened act, but it had the strictly limited purpose of creating cadres of men who would owe Karl Eugen their chance in life and hence their loyalty. That was designed to mitigate the traditional Swabian contrariness. There had been earlier foundations for the training of artists and craftsmen—musicians, singers, dancers, gardeners, fine plasterers—again with the self-interested motive of saving cash on foreign talent, which would have had to be wrung from the Estates. The Karlsschule grew out of no liberal commitment to education for its own sake; it was purely instrumental. Nor was there much liberality in its regime. Its original name was "Military Preparatory School" (Militärische Pflanzschule), and the daily routine was a precise drill. Worse, pupils were required to report on each other's attitudes to religion and to the duke, cut off from contact with their families, and denied compassionate leave even when a father was dying. Karl Eugen's reply to any such request was, "I am your father."[59] Total dependence on the duke was the aim.

Karl Eugen had talent spotters who reported on likely local material; Schiller was noticed, and his father was commanded to deliver him to the Karlsschule. He held out, riskily, till the third request, in part because the boy wished to be a preacher and the school, as a foundation by a Catholic ruler in a Protestant principality that already had its own foundation for training pastors,[60] did not offer theology. Schiller was at first, abortively, put to law,[61] then to medicine. It was in both cases an education against the grain, a denial of the Enlightenment principle of self-determination, explicitly based on "the supreme guardianship of the Prince and Ruler," whose privilege and duty it was "to decide what was best for his not yet adult subjects"—this from a Tübingen professor of law in the annual ceremonial address for 1773,[62] the first one the new pupil would have heard, and no doubt with bitter feelings. Schiller's retrospects on this unenlightened regime would give free rein to old resentments: "The four hundred who surrounded me were a *single* creature, molded into a single form at odds with the plasticity of nature." Only one human impulse came irrepressibly to maturity, which he declines to name—he must mean frustrated sexuality. All individual character and natural spontaneity were lost in the "regulated tempo of a dominant order."[63] Whereas Deucalion in the Greek myth turned stones into men, this education turned men into stones.[64] This was the "hateful truth which denied every free Swabian growth and perfection."[65] Later, when Karl Eugen died, Schiller recorded "the death of old Herod"[66]— the archetypal slaughterer of young innocence.

What could not be said openly at the time could be given vent in encoded form, paradoxically in statements addressed to the duke himself. The formal requirements of the institution—a report such as all pupils had to write on everyone else's individual attitudes to God, the duke and their supervisors, and especially two speeches in praise of the duke and his mistress that had to be delivered publicly on Franziska's birthday—carry the contraband of subversive feeling, kept safe from discovery behind the flowery rhetoric these occasions demanded. The convention of flattering the great had ironic potential, since praise, however plainly exaggerated, could not be convicted of subversion: no ruler tells flatterers they cannot mean what they are saying. Schiller was plainly not seen through, or the school authorities would not have chosen him for a second command performance.

It is noticeable that, even as he ludicrously exaggerates, Schiller never actually praises the duke, but merely envisages devotion in indirect clauses that commit him to nothing: "Judge me by my own words, whether I do not love, venerate, adore you; or should I swear an oath that I revere my prince?" Which he does not do. Oaths, as a key point in the plot of Schiller's drama *Intrigue and Love* was to embody, were not taken lightly by the pious middle classes. Or again: "Let me finally sigh, that I cannot ["cannot sufficiently" is the innocent surface meaning] give thanks!"[67] The theme set for both speeches was virtue, an obvious fishing for compliments on the duke's part, which Schiller pretends cannot have been his intention, since after all "the praise of the crowd is laughed to scorn by the wise." A protégé of the duke's would blush to practice "crawling flattery (Your sons have not been taught to flatter)," which these performances in fact were plainly required to do.[68] Perhaps Schiller had in mind Cassius's comment on Julius Caesar's susceptibility to flattery: "But when I tell him he hates flatterers, / He says he does, being then most flattered."[69] One can almost hear the only with difficulty suppressed laughter of Schiller's fellow students in the audience.

Schiller's elaborate fantasies of abject praise dare to sound a darker note. All three texts conjure up Karl Eugen's death. The first recalls Schiller's father allegedly saying, "Pray for the duke's life, that he may not be torn away from you in the midst of your glorious good fortune"[70]—an unlikely scene, given the known attitudes of father and son to the enforced Karls-schule transfer. The second ends by imagining the duke's "sons" "gathered at another festive occasion! I see them wandering among the graves of the noble dead! They are weeping—weeping for Karl—Württemberg's excellent Karl! weeping for Franziska! the friend of humanity!"[71] The third fantasy is more elaborate still: "My friends! What a scene comes before my astonished mind! Do I not see a milling crowd of human generations thronging to the grave of *one* prince (alas! a prince whom I may call my father), do I not see them weeping, crying out for joy, praying over the grave of this splendid man? What! A whole world over the grave of a single man! A thousand—a million, all blessing a single man?"[72] Again, not an assertion but a rhetorical question—"Do I not see them . . ."—which amply allows the answer No! And just why is the imagined crowd crying out for joy (*jauchzen*)? As the encomium goes from excess to excess, it carries this chilling counterpoint: bringing the favorable judgment of posterity forward (even if Karl's million admirers were remotely credible) meant bringing Karl's death closer. Surely the duke cannot have been altogether comfortable as he listened. But the most Schiller could have been reproached with was tactlessness.

In the meantime Schiller's always reluctant medical career was faltering. His first passing-out dissertation was failed, partly because of its too difficult philosophical arguments (though philosophy, in particular speculation on the relation between mind and body, still made up a large part of medicine) and partly because of his disrespect for established authorities. All resistance to authority, even in the academic realm, had a whiff of rebellion. An illiberal spirit breathes in the examiners' reports, and even more so in the duke's comments confirming Schiller's failure. They recognized that the student had shown "much fire," but "precisely for that reason, and because it is really still too strong, it will be very good for him if he remains another year in the academy where his fire can be damped down a little, so that in due course, if he is diligent, he may become a really significant individual."[73] A further year, then, was to be spent under what Schiller, again with ambiguous phrasing, calls the "paternal guidance that I have already for eight years had the good fortune to enjoy in this glorious institution"—

this in the introduction to the further dissertation that his first failure had made necessary.[74] So fire was bad; it was restraint and diligence that were required for success in life. This, surely, is what Karl Moor rails against as an "ink-splattering century," not the true Enlightenment, whose ideals of individuality and independence were precisely what was here being repressed.

Karl Moor is the hero of *The Brigands* (*Die Räuber*), the play Schiller had meanwhile been hatching, which brings his rebellion into the open. Its violence of language and action made it a sensation when it was staged, safely "abroad"—across the border at Mannheim, in the Rhineland Palatinate. His success led Schiller to believe a literary career was his for the making. Certainly the only alternative was bleak. That "glorious good fortune" in the duke's service, beginning when Schiller had finally managed to graduate, turned out to be a dead-end job as medical officer to a regiment of broken-down veterans on a salary of 216 gulden a year. (For comparison, a Karlsschule professor earned a thousand, one of the duke's opera singers five thousand.) Going absent without leave to attend the first night brought Schiller a fortnight's house arrest. Complaints from a Swiss canton over a derogatory aside in the dramatic dialogue led to a ban on any further writing on other than medical subjects. Schiller was forbidden even to submit a written appeal, on pain of fortress arrest. The pen was altogether an unwelcome instrument to the duke. The poet and critical journalist C. F. D. Schubart, who had been lured back across the border into Württemberg and imprisoned without trial for a decade, was denied writing materials and could only scratch on the walls with the buckle of his belt. There is something symbolic about the aversion the powerful feel for the pen. Schubart's crime, incidentally, had been to satirize the "reformed" duke and his educational pretensions, labeling the Karlsschule a "slave plantation" and coining the epigram:

When Dionysius of Syracuse
Gave up the ways of tyranny,
What did he choose to be?
A country dominie.

Schubart's arrest and imprisonment belied the duke's moral reform. The virtuous Franziska looked on as Schubart was delivered to the Hohenasperg fortress.

Clearly, Schiller could be a writer only if he deserted his regiment and left Württemberg behind him. So on 22 September 1782 he took flight with his musician friend Andreas Streicher, later a renowned maker of pianos in

Vienna. Their escape was covered by the tumult of a ducal entertainment for the visiting Russian Grand Duke Paul and his retinue that cost 345, 000 gulden. The fugitives made for Mannheim, on whose stage Schiller was pinning his hopes. Despite, or even because of, the sensational success of *The Brigands*, he was not welcomed with open arms by the intendant of the theater, Wolfgang Heribert, Freiherr von Dalberg. Schiller's youthful wildness and subversiveness, and the fact that he had escaped from Karl Eugen's service in the neighboring duchy, were a diplomatic liability.

Dalberg had already damped down the fire of Schiller's first play by transferring its setting to the sixteenth century. That did little to reduce its obvious relevance. Historical drama in any case commonly addresses the present as much as it portrays the past, and something was plainly rotten in the state of Karl Moor's Germany. The known evils of absolutism are amply on display, and Moor attacks them with the righteous certainty of an idealist. Only radical action will serve. Trained as a doctor, Schiller takes his title-page motto from Hippocrates, father of medicine: "What medicaments will not cure, iron will cure, what iron will not cure, fire will cure." The brigands duly put people to the sword and burn towns, but the play is not a triumph. The violence is too indiscriminate, the discrepancy too great between the high-minded Karl Moor and his crude confederates. Their atrocities contaminate his aims: "How this deed weighs upon me! It has poisoned my finest works." In the end there is a larger discrepancy still, between the individual violent initiative and the task of total reform. He can no longer believe in himself as "the man to wield the avenging sword of the higher tribunals."[75] In the final words of Hippocrates' list, not quoted by Schiller, "what fire will not cure must be considered finally incurable." Is the society of the day incurable? Moor's individual rebellion, at all events, turns into a repentance that cuts at the root of Enlightenment activism: "Mercy—mercy for the boy who tried to do thy work—vengeance is thine alone."[76] A childlike helplessness has taken the place of mature independence. The rising and falling curve of the action is no doubt in part dictated by the conventional patterns of tragic drama. Even so, Karl Moor's retraction is more than just a reneging on idealistic ideas. It is also a discovery of how corruptible they are by the human factor, how dangerous the experiment with revolution is. In another saying of Hippocrates, "Judgment is uncertain, experiment is dangerous."[77] The play is a realistic small version of what the political upheavals at the end of the century—the French Revolution and the Revolutionary Wars—would show on a massive scale. Rationality, ideals, liberation, yield to internecine conflict, a Reign of Terror, and *realpolitisch* expansionism. Enlightenment is not a simple, much less a simplistic, campaign. Literature sometimes anticipates reality rather than waiting to reflect it.

What Kant thought of *The Brigands*, if he ever came across it, is not known. Like other Enlightenment men—Lichtenberg, Lessing—he was not impressed by the Sturm und Drang movement of the 1770s, in whose wake the young Schiller was writing. Certainly the violent outbursts of Schiller's dialogue, let alone Karl Moor's rebellion itself, were not what Kant's Enlightenment essay envisaged as the professional man's spare-time contribution to social debate. Yet Schiller was exercising precisely the right Kant posited for the individual who has come of age. Literature is simply a more dynamic, more expressive contribution. Technically, Schiller did not come legally of age, the boundary being then twenty-five, until 1784, aptly at almost the point in the year when Kant published his Enlightenment essay. But the substantive maturity of Schiller's protest, its stylistic wildness notwithstanding, is unquestionable.

By September of that year Schiller's hopes of a career in Mannheim were dashed. He had submitted plays that either came in too late or were too politically sensitive for Dalberg; and he had failed to get on with the actors, who satirized him as "Patchword" (*Flickwort*). His one-year contract as resident dramatist was not renewed. He still believed the stage was a prime means of communicating enlightened ideas, and indeed of restoring human community, and in June he had given an impressive address on the theme to a local society.[78] But even while working at his next grand project, the historical drama *Don Carlos*, he was harassed by debt and constantly afraid of being dragged back across the border into Württemberg, as the luckless Schubart had been. He had to find some other way to survive. He tried the already much-tried means of founding a journal (though Germany, as he knew, was awash with such initiatives by young hopefuls). A grandiloquent announcement declared that he was a citizen of the world who served no prince. On the best Enlightenment principles, his *Rhineland Thalia* was to be open for the discussion of anything that affected human happiness.[79] Schiller was living out Kant's program, offering a forum for the free interplay of opinions directed to the public good. Whether the public would also sustain his journal in the market was another question. He could only hope his notoriety as the author of *Die Räuber* and fugitive from Karl Eugen's Württemberg would attract subscribers: the public, he grandly states, is his only sovereign. This marks the modern writer's refusal of patronage, ultimately the refusal to serve power and authority. Shifted back in history but unchanged in principle, that defiant refusal goes into the central audience scene of *Don Carlos*.

Schiller did not stand editorially above the mêlée of debate—he could not, if only because the dearth of copy submitted for his untried new publication, even though its editor was a writer of some notoriety, meant he largely had to fill its pages himself. The half-finished first version of *Don Carlos* had to serve this turn. Its journal publication, incidentally, both documented and struggled with the play's unstable conception, which was shifting from a conventional tragedy of frustrated love to an Enlightenment drama of tyranny and freedom.

EASTERN EXCURSUS: *FELIX AUSTRIA?*

Another real-life drama of Enlightenment was being played out farther east. When Kant in 1784 praised the uniqueness of Frederick the Great and called the age "Frederick's century," he was forgetting an obvious competitor. Joseph II of Austria had been actively reforming since 1780. Or was Kant necessarily ignoring him? Tact and tactics may have forbidden any favorable reference to the ruler of Prussia's long-standing enemy.

The two rulers' cases are inverse rather than parallel. What in Prussia had to struggle up gradually from below in Austria was imperiously carried through from above. But then, under absolutism any effective social change could only come from above—and how else could a ruler sympathetic to enlightened values realize them but by acting on his own authority? Where the socially conservative Frederick never initiated fundamental change, Joseph was from the start committed to it. In the difficult years of joint rule with his mother,[80] he brooded on plans for more radical measures than Maria Theresia, though herself not wholly illiberal, would have countenanced. Joseph aimed at full religious tolerance, reform of the censorship, a new tax system, the abolition of serfdom, improved education, equal rights for Jews, reduction of church and papal influence, the suppression of monasteries, the redeployment of monks as parish priests and schoolteachers, the pruning of the nobility's privileges, and the replacement of their relative sinecures and nepotism by meritocratically appointed officials. The pervasive spirit was rational and economical. In his personal mode of life, Joseph, like Frederick, was frugal and averse to lavish court ceremonial. He moved the court from grandiose Schönbrunn to the more modest, and politically central, Hofburg—the exact opposite of Louis XVI's opting for the pomp of Versailles, cut off from the political realities of Paris. Again like Frederick, Joseph saw himself as the servant of the state; as rulers, they both expressly belonged to their land and their people, not vice versa,[81] and Joseph expected the same commitment from his agents. (Not surprisingly, the two rulers got on well when they met, though that did not prevent their later confrontation in the War of the Bavarian Succession.)

Joseph's reform program was sketched in advance in his *Rêveries*.[82] It included the dream that he might have a free hand for ten years. He got almost that time span, but hardly the free hand. Not even an absolutist ruler had absolute control, especially in a realm ideologically Catholic and geographically spread from Hungary to Belgium. Moreover, these and other lands making up the monarchy had their own ancient constitutional rights that could block or delay reforming impulses from the center. Precisely centralism, Joseph's rational desire for "just one body, uniformly governed" and linguistically unified, was everywhere resented. The tables could be adroitly turned on him by calling his enlightened measures despotic and tyrannical. Religious institutions could resist measures aimed at reducing their dominance in society and education by stirring up those very people who would have benefited from change. "Thus they cunningly turned the weapons of the Enlightenment against it," Georg Forster commented.[83] It was a conservative tactic Kant had foreseen, or perhaps by 1784 was already watching at work in Austria[84]—a hint that he did perhaps have Joseph in mind after all. Naturally the church opposed Joseph's toleration edict, just as the nobility resisted their loss of privileges and perquisites. But there was also the more or less covert resistance, or at least foot dragging, by Joseph's agents, his officials, and even his relatives. Unwisely, he had kept ministers in post who had served under the coregency instead of appointing new men who might at least have been more cooperative, if not enthusiastically committed.

So Joseph was engaged in a struggle on every social and geographical front. "Against the world" is scarcely an exaggeration.[85] His was enlightened despotism indeed—not merely despotism moderated by enlightenment, but despotism seeking to impose enlightenment. Joseph did, it is true, sometimes listen to advice from his ministers, who normally suggested he should proceed more gradually; but he then took his own decisions. He claimed, ironically to none other than the pope, to have an infallible inner voice. To his conservative Belgian subjects he said, "I do not need your consent to do what is right." He had extensive observation of the realities of the realm to go on—he was traveling through it for a total of two years out of the ten of his reign. That was something Enlightenment writers often called for as a safeguard against abuses a ruler would otherwise be unaware of and would surely wish (it was charitably assumed) to prevent; the practice did, however, mean Joseph was sometimes away from the center at critical moments.

As resistance to his reforms built up and his health declined, Joseph became increasingly disillusioned. Relaxing censorship in the name of "the liberty innate in Man" had unleashed not just enlightened writing but a flood of pamphlets attacking his measures,[86] and even expressions of glee as he lay dying: he might be the peasants' idol (for abolishing serfdom), but he was the bugbear of burghers and the laughingstock of the nobility.[87] Shortly before his death he was forced to revoke his Hungarian reforms, and his Belgian states unilaterally declared independence. Joseph died feeling he had failed.

Yet his achievements were numerous and many of them lasted. They were listed in an Austrian satirical novel of the day that painted, in the manner of Voltaire's *Candide*, a picture of unenlightened human behavior worldwide but then celebrated the triumph of Enlightenment under Frederick and Joseph and marked a millennium that had begun with Joseph's decisive accession in 1780—this admittedly from the still hopeful standpoint of 1783, early in Joseph's reign.[88] At this point a medallion was struck featuring Joseph's head with an inscription declaring him the love and delight of the human race—*Amor et deliciae generis humani*. Ten years later Herder recognized Joseph's despotic haste to do everything at once, but also the fundamental rightness of his policies. They embodied "only the first duty of reason, of humanity, of social rights." Joseph had seen the needs of states more deeply than any other ruler of the day.[89]

The modern historian draws much the same conclusion.[90] No other ruler brought about so much change in so short a reign—Peter the Great in Russia had three times as long to act. And beyond his national borders Joseph, like Frederick, was a highly visible example to all Europe. Even more important than his administrative measures, which included a revision of the legal code more thoroughly modern than the Prussian *Landrecht*, was the central issue of tolerance and its vital relation to the common good. In 1780 in a letter to Catherine the Great of Russia, he contrasted her (and implicitly his own) earthly priorities with papal dogmatism: "You, Madam, are happy to make all the peoples and faiths that inhabit your vast empire take the same way on earth, namely, universal collaboration to promote the well-being of the state . . . leaving them to make their own arrangements for the after-life; while those who are intolerant are struggling to prescribe a single route which all souls must take into the obscurity of eternity, and thus deprive themselves of the totality that arises from the concurrence of views, wills and actions, which a good temporal government requires."[91] The political insight, the precisely formulated distinction, and the detached, ironic tone all suggest that Joseph, though a professed devout Catholic, was indeed a philosopher-king.

Joseph's brother and successor, Leopold II, was an enlightened ruler, first as archduke of Tuscany, where he introduced penal reform in consultation with Cesare Beccaria, tried to abolish religious fraternities, and met with the same popular resistance Joseph had provoked.[92] More significant still, he negotiated an end to the Austro-Prussian hostility that had smoldered and often flared ever since 1740. But he died after two years, so the high regard in which he is sometimes held rests on barely fulfilled hopes,[93] a historical might-have-been. In any case, as long as absolutism lasted, any enlightened ruler could only be a fortunate chapter in an uncertain story. That is a measure of how inadequate enlightened absolutism was as a practice and still is as a concept.

CHAPTER 2

A World of Our Own:
An Epistemology for Action

> ... the very world, which is the world
> Of all of us, the place in which, in the end,
> We find our happiness, or not at all.
> —Wordsworth, *The Prelude* (1805)

The three great transforming "offenses to humanity's naive self-love," wrote Sigmund Freud in 1917, were the new sun-centered astronomy of Copernicus, Darwin's theory of natural selection, and his own account of the unconscious.[1] They all set limits to human self-importance, not to say hubris: Copernicus by shifting mankind from the central place in the universe that Christianity had claimed for it, Darwin by replacing the notion of a prior design of creation with the principle of spontaneous evolution; and Freud himself, as he wrote without false modesty, by displacing consciousness as the exclusive power governing human behavior.

Kant should by rights make a fourth in that list: not for nothing did he call his own fundamental argument a Copernican revolution.[2] He too marked out limits, the inherent limits of human thought, which had traditionally ranged at will, speculating without restraint on all possible and impossible objects of knowledge, to the confusion of philosophy and the advantage of its socially enthroned mistress, theology. After Kant, arbitrary speculation and the dogmas founded on it could only survive by ignoring his arguments, which in practice of course proved feasible. Positions that have had the bottom knocked out of them do live on bottomless, through social inertia, institutional self-perpetuation, and people's undue respect for authority.

Kant is not commonly credited with such a dramatic transformation. No other great thinker has ever been so undersold to the public mind, through being oversold in a misleading way. He has been left too much to philosophy specialists, cried up as their most complex and overawing private possession. The simple main thrust of his work has been obscured by technical questions that leave the wood scarcely visible for the trees. Some of this was Kant's own doing, through his style (long, intricately structured sentences) and through his "barbaric" (his word)[3] vocabulary of newly coined concepts. He thus needs rescuing from himself as well as from his interpreters.

Even would-be basic introductions plunge straight into the technicalities of the *Critique of Pure Reason*, commonly starting with "the possibility of synthetic a priori judgments." To the general reader it is not clear what this phrase means, much less why it is crucial—it is not evidently one of the problems of life that great philosophers are expected to illuminate. Back goes the volume on the shelf in favor of some work with a more obviously relevant theme—Schopenhauer on the life force, say, or Nietzsche on the Will to Power, or Hegel on the Cunning of Reason in history: all, however questionable in themselves, matters of clear urgency. It is true that Kant himself said synthetic a priori judgments were the fundamental problem of the First Critique;[4] but they are fundamental only as the means to an end, and the purport of his philosophy has properly to be understood in the light of that end, which is Kant's enlightened social commitment. Why the technical question matters will become clear later; the prior point is Kant's purpose.

He states it emphatically fifteen years before the *Critique of Pure Reason* appeared, when he is already consciously taking aim at his grand project. In a letter of 8 April 1766 to his friend the Jewish thinker Moses Mendelssohn, Kant declares his hatred of all current writing on metaphysics, of the "inflated presumptuousness of whole volumes full of insights of this kind such as are presently in vogue." He is convinced that they are following a wrong route that can only multiply illusions and errors. It is in the fullest sense a vital issue: "I am so far from regarding metaphysics itself, objectively viewed, as insignificant or dispensable, that after grasping (I believe) its nature and peculiar place in human knowledge, I have been for some time now convinced that in fact the true and lasting well-being of humanity depends on it, an estimation which will appear fantastical and excessive to anyone but you." There has to be a metaphysics, then, but one that starts all over again from scratch and feeds into practical activity. Kant regularly uses the term "metaphysics" in two opposed senses: to label the old, discredited practice, and to announce the new science that is to emerge from a rigorous critique of the old—a meta-metaphysics, as he once calls the completed *Critique of Pure Reason*.[5] It will be a philosophy for the real world

(*Weltphilosophie*) as distinct from the old, irrelevant, ingrowing scholasticism (*Schulphilosophie*). This is one consequence of a personal conversion that Kant records in an unpublished note from the 1760s: "I am myself by inclination a research scholar. I feel the whole thirst for knowledge and the avid unrest to make progress in it or also the satisfaction at every new gain. There was a time when I believed that this could all by itself constitute the honor of mankind, and I felt contempt for the mob, who know nothing of it. Rousseau set me right. This blinding privilege vanishes, I learn to honor men, and I would think myself more useless than the common workman if I did not believe that this consideration alone can bestow value: how to restore the rights of humanity."[6] So the 1760s are the crucial point at which Kant leaves the ivory tower. The third document that completes the picture is the essay on Swedenborg of 1766, itself an important station on the way to the First Critique. It ends by quoting Voltaire's parting shot in the satirical novel *Candide*, which famously ridiculed Leibniz's optimistic doctrine that "everything is for the best in the best of all possible worlds": "I end with what Voltaire makes his honest Candide finally say after so many useless scholastic conflicts: *Let us look to our happiness, go into the garden and work!*"[7] Kant has added emphasis to the quotation, not just by the italics but by the way he elaborates on Voltaire's simple phrasing. The French text says "Il faut cultiver notre jardin." Kant spells out the goal of happiness, evokes a resolute movement ("go into"), and more bluntly names the activity ("and work").[8] Two great Enlighteners join hands across the borders of nation and genre to declare the wrongheadedness of groundless speculation and the need for practical activity in the real world.

The idea will be carried further in the Latin epigraph to the First Critique, from Bacon's preface to *The Great Instauration*: "I am laboring to lay the foundations, not of a sect or doctrine, but of human utility and power." Bacon exhorts men to "deal fairly by their own interests," to "join in consultation for the common good," and to "take part in what remains to be done."

Consistently, five years after the *Critique* appeared, Kant again stresses its practical social purpose, which he hopes younger colleagues will continue to pursue. To a disciple teaching at the University of Marburg, he writes: "Continue, my dearest man, to apply your youthful powers and fine talent to the task of correcting the claims of speculative reason, which so likes to go beyond its limits, and of suppressing the constant wild enthusiasm [*Schwärmerei*] that uses those claims for its own advantage—but pursue the task without damaging the truly elevating theoretical and practical use of reason and without offering a pillow for lazy skepticism. To recognize one's powers, but also the limits of their use, makes us secure, brave, and resolute in all things good and useful."[9] The reference to his own by now accomplished work and its central point is clear: his epistemological arguments, far from being the work of an inward-looking specialist, were meant to lay the foundation for enlightened action in the social world.

Note the warning to beware of damaging reason itself with criticism of the old metaphysics. Despair at the failure of rationality as such could lead to indifference and inertia. An almost agnostic skepticism was the position Hume had ended up with. For Kant that was a dead end; in his metaphor, Hume had beached the ship of philosophy "upon the strand of skepticism, where it will duly lie and rot." Kant in contrast was concerned "to give it a pilot who, equipped with a complete chart and a compass and reliable principles of navigation drawn from a knowledge of the globe, can take the ship safely wherever he sees fit."[10] Hume's skepticism was a symptom of a more general outlook in the eighteenth-century intellectual world as Kant saw it. Skepticism was not necessarily "lazy," as the letter to Bering suggested; initially it was a sign of high standards, a wholesale rejection of traditional thinking because it was inadequate. But that could lead to resignation and indifference. Skepticism was thus only a halfway stage, a ground-clearing with no constructive replacement. It had to lead further, to critical engagement with the fundamental conditions of thought such as Kant undertakes in the First Critique. He makes the point early in that work:

> From time to time you hear people complain about the shallowness of thinking and the decline of thorough learning in our day. But I do not see that those forms of learning which have a sound basis—mathematics, natural philosophy [i.e., science], and so on—in the least deserve this charge. Rather, they maintain their old reputation for thoroughness, in the latter case even surpass it. Exactly the same spirit would prove effective in other areas of learning too, if only the correction of their basic principles had been attended to. Where such correction is lacking, indifference and doubt and finally a rigorous criticism are proofs rather of a thorough way of thinking.[11]

So Kant's own enterprise is a step beyond the stalemate of skepticism. His models are mathematics and the hard sciences, and his aim is to provide at last a sound basis for philosophy. It will be his repeated complaint that, this late in history, proper principles have never yet been laid down for his subject; and it will be his proud claim to have now done that.

Where did the problem lie, where had it always lain? Kant puts it with epigrammatic force at the opening of the First Critique: "Human reason has the particular fate in one area of knowledge that it is plagued by questions it cannot dismiss, for they are tasks set it by the nature of reason itself, but which it also cannot answer, for they go beyond all capacity of reason." We cannot, that is, avoid asking the large questions about the meaning and purpose of life, but they cannot be conclusively answered—not, at any rate, by the principles we have learned to apply to more immediate matters. Some questions, for example whether the universe is finite or infinite, whether it had a beginning or not, whether human actions are free or determined, allow of flatly contradictory answers, each with seemingly adequate logical grounds. Such cases, familiar enough to skeptics from Sextus Empiricus to Montaigne, Kant calls "antinomies," and these likewise cast doubt on reason's capacity to go beyond strict limits.[12] So where does reason end up if it tries to do this?

> Reason finds itself in this embarrassment through no fault of its own. It starts from principles whose use has been unavoidably and adequately proven in the course of experience and by experience. But when it sees that in this way its task will always remain incomplete, because the questions will never end, it has to have recourse to principles that go beyond all possible use of experience and which yet appear so innocent [*unverdächtig*] that even common sense is in agreement with them. But it thereby plunges into obscurity and contradictions, which makes it realise there must be basic errors somewhere, but it cannot discover them, because the principles it is now using, since they go beyond the limits of experience, no longer recognise any touchstone of experience. The battlefield of these endless conflicts is what we call metaphysics.[13]

Ockham's razor, familiar of course to Kant,[14] can always do with resharpening. Questions whose answers are not testable by experience are nonquestions that only waste our time. Where a Christian mystic like Pascal held all other human interests to be a diversion (*divertissement*) from salvation, the humanist Kant sees the old unreal metaphysics—ultimately, the endless religious controversies over things that cannot by their nature be known—as the true diversion from pressing earthly concerns. The moral is clear: abandon the metaphysical battlefield and mankind will be left with Candide's garden, the garden of the world, to work in. Unresolvable debates will be replaced by useful activity. That would be a liberation—liberation through limitation. It would mean an immense saving of time and intellectual effort, to say nothing of the blood that has, literally, been shed in the battlefields of theological controversy.[15] The same sense of infuriating waste is found in Kant's contemporaries, especially in relation to the endless controversies of biblical exegesis. In Goethe: "The fairy tale of Christ is the reason the world may still stand for ten million years and nobody will come to their senses, because it takes as much power of knowledge, understanding, and concepts to defend it as to combat it";[16] in Lichtenberg: "It makes your hair stand on end when you think how much time and trouble has been applied to explaining the Bible. Probably a million octavo volumes. The prize for all this effort must finally be the conclusion that the Bible is a human work like any other, a result that would have been reached long ago if our untamable credulity had not prevented it."[17] In the same spirit Gibbon touches on, but cannot possibly enter into the minutiae of, the endless ferocious disputes over Arianism and its eighteen subsects.[18] To leave all that behind would mean a new empowerment to act in and on the world. Precisely that, as Kant wrote to Bering, is what you are equipped for once you are aware of your powers and clear about their limits.

Yet Kant could not just turn his back on the conflicts still raging. One last battle had to be fought on the old field. A new, sound method must discredit the philosophical and theological metaphysics still dominant in his day. It would invalidate all speculations that were not checked by experience and that took no account of the limitations of the human mind.

Those limitations lay in the way human perception was structured by time, space, and the conceptual categories inherent in the mind—in sum, the conditions for processing the raw material conveyed by the senses. Even religious thought has had inklings of these limiting conditions.[19] Perception and knowledge of the world are necessarily and distinctively *human* perception and knowledge: we cannot escape from our own minds. This is the simple point behind the commonly misunderstood "thing in itself" (*Ding an sich*), the ultimate reality to which Kant says we do not have access. This is a statement of the obvious: *any* perceiving agents must have their own perceptual and conceptual equipment, and it is that which blocks an absolute reality from view. An unconditioned reality can be conceived but not perceived: it is inaccessible by definition. To realize and accept that is not a deprivation.

The common misunderstanding of Kant's argument and its implications is clear from the case of the tragic dramatist and suicide Heinrich von Kleist, the more poignant because Kleist only just fell short of grasping Kant's point. He began to despair of attaining reliable knowledge after reading "the Kantian philosophy." It was as if we had green glasses in place of eyes, so we could not know whether the world was really green or just looked that way to us because of some element the eye puts in.[20] But that is Kant's point: we do have specific equipment that introduces an element of its own—not greenness, but humanness. How warm Kleist was is clear from a jotting of Lichtenberg's which uses very similar terms to get at Kant's meaning: "the question whether things have an objective reality outside of ourselves is almost as foolish as the question whether the color blue really is blue."[21]

The contradiction between subjective perception and objective reality can thus be resolved: for us the world simply *is* the way we see it. Why wish to see it other than through human eyes, even supposing that were logically possible? The wish is already a betrayal of our humanity. It is not even as if there were anything special about the "thing in itself" to make it worth penetrating to. Kant calls it a "noumenon," but he makes clear that this is no more than a neutral term for what necessarily lies behind a phenomenon—"a border concept to restrict the presumption of the senses, and thus of only negative use." It has no mystical implications. Kant's noumenon is not numinous.[22]

So his whole argument boils down to a revolutionary tautology: human beings can *only* know what *human beings* can know. What other reality would be relevant for human purposes? This equating of human empirical perception with reality may at first glance seem the kind of sophistry that tries to prove black is white: "the objective is really subjective." It is not however subjective in any distorting sense, as if the mode of vision of any particular individual mind were being privileged over that of others. Rather it is a universal subjectivity, a set of prior determinations shared by the whole human race. And the only reliable source of knowledge is the raw material presented to us by our human sensory equipment and processed by our human powers of judgment. A Martian would see things differently, being differently equipped. Different kinds of creatures all inherently have a world of their own; Kant was simply inviting us to live actively in ours. It is a resolutely positive philosophy.

Kant's analysis of human knowledge, taken to its logical social conclusion, would entail Voltaire's attack on the old obscurantisms and a good deal more. That is made uncompromisingly plain in the continuation of the footnote that declares the time is ripe for critical principles in philosophy, for it also declares open season on every social institution, especially religion and politics. It is to be an age of criticism in all areas. To quote it again: "Our age is the real age of criticism, to which everything must be subject. *Religion* through its *sacredness* and *legislation* through its *majesty* commonly try to evade it. But they then arouse justified suspicion against themselves and cannot claim the unfeigned respect which reason only grants to whatever has been able to sustain its free and public examination."[23]

This is the closest Kant ever came to mounting a frontal attack in the manner of the French Enlightenment on the walls of dominant social institutions. More often he digs deep and undermines them. That is a significant long-term task: imagine a world where fundamentalists are left without any foundations. Kant's undertaking could not be more topical, then or now.

Yet his reputation with a wider public, insofar as he has one, is negative. First there is the misunderstanding, just sketched, over the "thing in itself"—the misprision that Kant wanted to show that we were deprived of something we would want to have. Then there is the associated notion that his account of reason is destructive—the very danger he warned Bering to beware of. A major factor in his reception has been the label early on attached to him as "the all-crusher," *der Alleszermalmer*. This catchword, conceivably an echo of Voltaire's antireligious motto "écrasez l'infâme," originated with Kant's friend Moses Mendelssohn, who—ironically—had not actually read the *Critique of Pure Reason*.[24] (He suffered from a nervous condition which he said made it impossible for him to read metaphysical works, and his comment was based on reports friends had given him. How much and how closely they in their turn had read Kant can only be guessed.) The coining should be read as meaning that Kant had obliterated the opposition he was targeting, which is true enough; instead, it is commonly taken to mean that Kant's teachings had destroyed the substance of rational philosophy, and nothing was left standing of all that went before him. This entirely leaves out of account what he put in its place, the firm reliance on our sense experience as the product of the conditions he analyzes. In other words, a sound grasp of the world we inhabit.

Then there are the problems raised by the way Kant presented his argument. In its very rigor and radicality his method is an indirect one. He believed he must do the most thorough job possible, must make his case against the old metaphysics stick with full technical force in the eyes of other professionals, however incompetent he thought them. Hence an epistemological argument that has the elaborateness, as Goethe said, of a labyrinth he was chary of venturing into.[25] At every twist and turn there are unfamiliar, opaque, sometimes counterintuitive labels. The main terms of the title, "critique" and "pure," are already ambiguous. Is "critique" to be read as criticism or just as survey? Is "pure" meant positively or negatively? An earlier intended title was clearer: "On the Limits of Sense Perception and Reason" (*Über die Grentzen der Sinnlichkeit und der Vernunft*).[26] Again, the contents page of the work is like the entrance hall of an immense building with pointers to mysterious departments: the transcendental aesthetic, the transcendental logic, the transcendental deduction. What these words may seem to mean to us is not what they mean to Kant. "The transcendental aesthetic" is his account of sense perception; it has nothing to do with theories of art or beauty, for which by Kant's time the word "aesthetic" had been firmly appropriated. "Aesthetic" admittedly derives from the Greek for sense perception in general, but by 1781 it was already too late to rescue the German word for that etymologically purist meaning. Then, the "transcendental logic" is not about logic in the normal sense but is Kant's account of thought processes. It is subdivided into the "transcendental analytic," which is about the understanding (*Verstand*), and the "transcendental dialectic," which is about reason (*Vernunft*). Neither of these labels has an obvious semantic connection with the respective topic.

True, a philosopher is free to define and even to invent his terms. But the lack of an intuitive link between almost every term Kant devised and its function in his argument creates an actual barrier to understanding. Examples could be multiplied. Human awareness or reflexive consciousness, what Descartes summed up simply and memorably in the *cogito*, is in Kant the "synthetic unity of apperception" (B 130ff.; III, 114), which is arrived at in the "transcendental deduction"; the world itself is at one point defined as "the mathematical entirety of all phenomena in the totality of their synthesis" (B 466; III, 301). Most important, English-speaking readers are not helped by the standard translation of the word *Anschauung* as "intuition," which makes the one central term that Kant *did* take from everyday concrete usage appear vague and mysterious, not to say mystical. The word simply means "view" or "visual impression," the physiological raw material out of which perception is made.

But the clearest case is that ubiquitous term "transcendental." It refers to Kant's fundamental thesis that there are structures inherent in the mind as conditions of the possibility of experiencing. A first objection is the word's apparent connection, not to say contamination, with the religious notion of transcendence, which made it suggest the very reverse of Kant's antimetaphysical purpose. This even misled some contemporary British commentators, who had plainly not even looked into the First Critique, into thinking Kant was a mystic. But even if one undoes that association, there is something wrong with denoting what is logically *prior* to experience by a word with the prefix "trans-," meaning "beyond," instead of a word with the prefix "pre-," meaning "before." As a Latinate academic, Kant was certainly aware of the etymology, as witness the way his original text, not followed in modern reprints, spells the word in purist fashion: "trans/scendental."

Once you get into each of Kant's arguments, of course, it becomes apparent what his meaning and his concerns are; but the technical terminology may well have turned the reader away before ever reaching that point. As Lichtenberg noted—and he was a decided admirer of Kant—the topics of the work were very interesting, but that was not something you could see at once.[27] It is a classic case of the instructions for opening the tin being inside the tin.

Helping us get into the tin is what commentaries are for, but Kant is not always well served by his commentators; as a recent down-to-earth introduction admits, commentaries on Kant often themselves need commentaries.[28] Until we know what his philosophical and above all his ultimate practical aims were, it is impossible to see what he is after with his new terminology. Where, for example, does that crucial issue of "synthetic a priori judgments" fit in? Put simply, it refers to Kant's claim to be able to explain in principle how perception and thinking work. He is presenting his account of the mind's controlling conditions and categories as not merely a definition, an unpacking of what is contained in the concept "mind" (which would be merely an "analytic" proposition); he is setting out something discursively new about them (so his propositions are "synthetic"). But these are insights of which we are to be convinced through reflection, not on the basis of empirical evidence, so they are "a priori propositions." And once we accept this account of how the mind goes about its legitimate business— of the way sensory equipment, conditions, and categories generate reliable knowledge within the bounds of possible human experience—it becomes plain how arbitrary is the procedure by which people speculate, fantasize, and then dogmatize about what plainly lies beyond those bounds. Without the touchstone of experience and an awareness of the inherent limits on what we can know, there is nothing to stop them setting up whatever notions they like—they can spin yarns about a god, his creation, his moral demands, his ultimate intentions, his rewards and punishments, and the afterlife and its various venues, blissful or hideous, all elaborated *con amore*. Churches and governments can then compel general conformity with, albeit not actual belief in, these things. Worst of all is the last station, when dogma spawns extreme action, that is, fanaticism, which Kant pithily defines in his essay of 1764, "On the Diseases of the Mind": "the fanatic is a madman who imagines he has direct inspiration and a great intimacy with the heavenly powers."[29] The point is ultimately the same one Lessing was

making when he said he would decline absolute truth even if it were offered
him by God. That is just what dogmatists and fanatics always do believe is
happening, with fatal results of which the author of *Nathan der Weise* was
aware.[30] So it is no wonder Kant said that nothing less than "the welfare of
the human race" depended on getting the metaphysical issue straight. It
still does.

Not coincidentally, Kant's position is the basis for all serious science,
where the "adventure of reason" demands that every conception be tested
against the way things can be convincingly shown to be.[31] Like Kant's patron saint, Copernicus, the scientist must not hesitate "to risk / His dream-
stuff in the fitting-rooms of fact."[32]

Yet the importance of everything Kant was arguing remains half hidden behind the veil of his terminology and style. He was aware of the accessibility problem, which he had not solved, indeed had in great measure
created. Friends and well-wishers pointed it out forcefully. Kant was not,
however, too much moved by their objections, because he mistakenly saw
it as the inevitable conflict between cogent argument and popular appeal,
and as a philosopher he was committed to achieving maximum cogency.
The conflict was in his mind as early as the lecture—alas, long lost—that
he gave at his doctoral promotion ceremony, under the title "Of the Easier
and of the Thorough Presentation of Philosophy." The title needs quoting
with precision, to make clear that the two approaches are being set against
each other.[33]

Kant later often modestly disclaims any presentational talent of his
own. He was even suspicious in an almost puritanical way of any highly
readable style, which he associated in the first place with the shallow arguments of contemporary *Popularphilosophie*, the well-meaning essays in
social ethics and general wisdom that filled middlebrow journals, appealing
to readers with some education and understanding but never delving very
deep. Kant is positively vituperative about the "semirational principles"
(*halbvernünftelnde Prinzipien*) which "shallow minds" (*schale Köpfe*) put
together for the purpose of "banal chatter" (*alltägliches Geschwätz*).[34] On a
different level, he read and reread his admired Rousseau until he was sure he
was not being seduced by the style and could be free to judge the content.[35]

Kant is sometimes represented as an anti-Enlightenment thinker precisely because his intricate thoroughness and stylistic obscurity undid the
urbane ease of the popular journals, which were a socially useful recent
acquisition of German culture under English influence. But that was a difference over standards, not over ultimate aims. (As political history shows,
people of roughly the same persuasion often lose sight of the common cause

and fall out over ways and means.) For himself, Kant felt he had to fight the rationalist schoolmen on their own ground, in the process enforcing a new set of rules. He had to defeat these people once and for all, and he believed his "barbaric" terminology was necessary for the purpose.

Yet he never makes it entirely clear why—why the plethora of new terms was needed, or why a lucid, eloquent style should be feared as a snare and a delusion. His philosophical position—reliance on the carefully checked senses, rejection of unfounded fantasy—was ultimately close to untutored common sense; but the commonsensical reader would not find it easy to see that in the form in which Kant presents it. Nietzsche hit off this paradox when he said that Kant wanted to prove ordinary people's view of the world was right, but he formulated his argument for the learned, in a way that was beyond ordinary people.[36] Kant indeed says much the same himself in a note from his posthumous papers that Nietzsche cannot have known: "A critique like this is not composed to be presented to simple people but to the subtlest reasonifiers [*Vernünftler*] who think no subject matter beyond their reach. Whereas this critique is meant to prove that these matters are indeed much too far beyond the reach of their and anyone else's speculative insight, and to thwart them in this illusion (since it is their own fault that they persist in it)."[37]

Was Kant's new terminology intended to be as precise as possible? Or did he mean to blind the opposition with science? Certainly his coinages go far beyond any need for exact denotation, nor, because of their often counterintuitive nature, do they spark a sense of sudden revelation for the reader. In what must now seem a primitive uncoupling of meaning from manner, Kant said that to have concerned himself with questions of presentation while still working out the problems of philosophical substance would have been a distraction. He just hoped his language would not leave his readers dazed for too long,[38] and that, once they got hold of his basic argument, it would be a thread to lead them out of the labyrinth.[39] If he could just get them to go along with his argument, he might undertake to popularize it somewhat, though that would be easier for others to do. He was deeply grateful to Carl Leonhard Reinhold for attempting just that in his *Letters on Kant's Philosophy* of 1788.[40] He had set out to do it himself in the *Prolegomena*, which is at least shorter, but it too makes few concessions to easy reading. He also pleads in mitigation the astounding circumstance that he wrote the whole of the First Critique, the product of twelve years' reflection, in four to five months.[41] That, he said, did not allow much time for stylistic fine-tuning.

Kant did admit that his argument might have been presented better.

Like Thomas Mann wishing he had put the visionary chapter "Snow" at the end of *The Magic Mountain* instead of in the middle, Kant said that he should perhaps have begun with the antinomies, that series of problems for which reason can construct two equally cogent but diametrically opposed answers; this might have called forth a more "blossoming style."[42] Yet he had begun with a quite sufficiently essential and indeed closely related point, since the first page of the Critique confronted the issue of reason and its limits squarely and forcefully. Far more important in practice than the sequencing of the argument was the density of style that is overwhelmingly present throughout the text of the Critique. Especially strange was Kant's failure to see that style and subject cannot properly be separated, that a way of writing is not just an exchangeable packaging but profoundly affects the substance and effect of what is said. For it was precisely his point in the First Critique that the structures of the mind determine the substance of what is experienced—that reality and form are interdependent. In the same way, style codetermines the substance of what is written.

Not quite all is lost, however, because there are moments when Kant—for all his disclaimers—emerges as a positive master of style. He can be totally lucid and immediately cogent. He can capture the essence of a complex argument in brief compass, for example the mutual dependence of mental structure and sensory input in human experience: "thoughts without content are empty, percepts without concepts are blind."[43] The chiastic epigram hits off the compromise with which Kant was balancing two things: the best of the rationalist tradition with the sensualism that the eighteenth-century was now asserting in every area of thought. Sometimes Kant even achieves beauty, as in his image for the illusion that we might achieve knowledge without the beneficial resistance of experience: "the light dove, as she cleaves the air in her free flight and feels its resistance, might imagine that in airless space her flight would be freer still."[44] And the traditional philosopher's opening of "Was ist Aufklärung?"—a proposition followed by a definition of its terms, potentially a dry enough proceeding—becomes through its simple directness as heroic a fanfare as the opening of Rousseau's *Social Contract*: "Man is born free, but is everywhere in chains." It is a serious loss that Kant did not draw on this talent more frequently and fully, failing to recognize that style, far from being an irrelevant extra, is the writer's point of contact with a waiting world.

Beyond those fine individual passages, Kant's work rests on a strong system of consistent metaphors, such that his essential message can be distilled virtually from them alone. They are all metaphors of reliability: voyaging with a compass and sound charts, guidance through the labyrinth

with Ariadne's thread, the firm gait of a confident walker. All of them counter the popular notion of a negative Kant, an epistemologist of despair and
resignation. Overarching them all is the metaphor of Copernican reversal—
thanks to Kant, the intellectual solar system can at last be seen the right
way round, with the operations of the mind at its center. Within that transformed universe there are then metaphors of successfully directed activity.
In a very early text, Kant had spoken of the "modest character of our understanding" and urged that we should therefore keep "close to the shore of the
cognitions granted to us . . . rather than putting out into the deep sea of . . .
mystical investigations."[45] The idea of human limitation is already there,
but not yet the actual querying of those mystical depths; as yet, only the
word "mystical" itself implies the actual unreality of such "investigations."
But as Kant's philosophical self-confidence grows, he turns the metaphor
into the more positive idea of a bold ocean voyage with a good compass. Our
"modest understanding" still has its limits precisely set, but now to wholly
positive effect. Beyond that contrast with the beached hulk of Hume's skepticism, Kant takes up an old baroque emblem of the island of truth toward
which we must sail and works it up into the dimensions of an epic simile.[46]
Perhaps at the back of his mind was the ship of knowledge on its way to
new continents which figures on the title page of Francis Bacon's *Novum
Organon* of 1620—Bacon after all provided the epigraph for the First Critique. But Kant is clearly also modernizing these older sources with touches
of reality taken from his reading of eighteenth-century travelers. His image
for the illusions that risk distracting us on the way to truth is the ice packs
and fog banks that misled explorers into thinking they had found land. This
exactly echoes Georg Forster's account of the bleak passage through Antarctic seas on Captain Cook's second circumnavigation.[47] Kant was an avid
reader of geographical and anthropological material, indeed of any material
concerning the real world. It was a way of making up for never in all his life
budging more than a mile or two from Königsberg (and only once making
a short and miserable voyage across a landlocked bay). To be precise, Kant
turns the baroque image round, picturing a voyage *away* from the island in
order to discover, as Cook had been sent to do, whether there is any substantial firm ground in the uncharted seas around it before we settle for the
land of truth that we already have and that we know we can rely on. The
implication is that there will turn out not to be any such, just as Cook's
voyage had proved to contemporary satisfaction that there was no southern
land mass, no Antarctic continent.

One other apt image within the architecture of Kant's system is, appropriately, that of building, especially of laying firm foundations. All too

often people had rushed to erect a structure and realized too late that the foundations were shaky. In other words, metaphysics now belatedly needed to have some proper footings put in. A medal that Kant's friends struck to commemorate his fundamental work showed the leaning tower of Pisa and bore the inscription *perscrutatis fundamentis stabilitur veritas* (when the foundations have been thoroughly examined, truth is made stable).[48] That balanced Kant's own reference to the Tower of Babel, which had been meant to reach to the heavens. Once again he develops his metaphor into an epic simile and also adapts it to his purposes by literally bringing it down to earth: the materials hubristically intended for a tower turned out to be only enough for a house. Yet this too is not negative, for the house has proved to be "just spacious enough for the conduct of our affairs on the level of experience," and, though not a tower, it is still "elevated enough to offer an overview of them."[49] A modest but sufficient dwelling, then, such as might appropriately stand in Candide's garden. The foundation metaphor is present again, almost too obvious to be noticed as such, in the title of Kant's first major essay in ethics, the "Grundlegung zur Metaphysik der Sitten." *Grundlegung*: not just foundations, but a process of *laying* foundations, work observably in progress. How Copernican Kant's revolution was in this second area of philosophy will appear later.

Kant's metaphors, then, are a vital means of communication as well as a source of literary pleasure and of much-needed refreshment for the reader of a dense exposition in which Kant seems to be, in Wordsworth's famous line on Newton, "voyaging through strange seas of thought, alone."[50] It is certainly a hard job keeping him company. Yet if we then arrange Kant's metaphors in sequence—orienting oneself, embarking on a confident voyage with chart and compass, arrival at the island, the laying of strong foundations, and the erecting of a building on a modest human scale—they make a continuous odyssey. And the building will surely turn out to be inhabited by independent-minded people whose intellectual development has matched their organic growth, who in the full sense therefore have come of age, that other metaphor which opens "What Is Enlightenment?" and is sustained for several paragraphs through images of child rearing and the child's learning to walk. The same metaphor is again prominent three years later in the second edition of the *Critique of Pure Reason*, where the new introduction speaks repeatedly of the "firm gait" or "reliable step" (*sicherer Gang*) of a reformed philosophical science.

In Kant's own critical spirit one might ask whether his account of the mind's operations and limitations is as much speculation of the kind he wanted to invalidate as anything he was attacking. Was he not now sawing

off the branch he was sitting on? One answer would be that he was not proposing a new hypothesis, alleging a new reality, or claiming a new discovery.
He was simply pointing out something that reflection—the self-reflection
of human beings—must inevitably confirm. We are indeed creatures living
in space and time, and our minds do unavoidably operate with certain preset
modes of understanding. That human beings are subject to the conditions
and categories peculiar to their species simply stands to reason. It is hardly
a speculation. But does that not then make it an analytic proposition, a definition of what human beings are? And does it not in some measure rest on
our lifelong experience of introspecting our own minds, and of observing, as
far as we can, other people's minds in operation? That, surely, would make
Kant's theses empirical propositions. It would mean in sum that Kant was
putting forward analytic a posteriori propositions, not the synthetic a priori
kind he claimed.

The answer, however, is surely: does it matter? Criticism of Kant's chosen angle and terminology takes nothing away from the force of his argument, from the truth and relevance of what he has to say about human
powers and their inherent limits and use. So the criticism is terminologi-
cally radical but not substantively damaging. Which in turn means that
what is alleged to be the "central problem" of the First Critique—"the
possibility of synthetic a priori judgments"—really should not be the thing
commentators so often give priority to, because it does not much affect the
issue at the work's center. This is simply: what can we reliably know, and
what should we stop claiming to be able to know? As Kant argued from the
outset, this has vital consequences for what, in the practical as well as the
epistemological sense, is a world of our own.

What impact did Kant's work have? "The *Critique der reinen Vernunft*
appeared—and the Universities of Germany *exploded*," wrote Coleridge in
a marginal note to his copy of Kant.[51] He was wrong about the timing. When
the work first appeared, German universities virtually ignored it. Kant's
message only slowly began to get through over the following half decade.
The growth of interest between the first (1781) and the second (1787) edition can be quantified by the reviewing space devoted to him. From four
items totaling six pages in 1781, by 1787 it had grown to seventy-five items
totaling 284 pages.[52] More to the point, there was an increasing recognition of what Kant's critical philosophy meant for orthodoxy, and not just
philosophical orthodoxy. By 1790 at the latest, the religious party was fully
aware of the threat to their fundamental beliefs: "the main cause of offense seems to the opposition to be that they cannot have any knowledge
of God, immortality, and so on."[53] Not much more was meant at the first

level by Kant's much-quoted statement that he had been obliged to undo knowledge so as to make room for faith.[54] Kant certainly retained, from his Pietist family upbringing, a belief in immortality, even while classifying it as something not knowable. (He leaves unsaid that even faith needs some sort of presumed knowledge as its starting point.) The positive phrasing in the *Critique* may also have been a defensive measure—this is the foreword to the 1787 second edition, a year into the new king's anti-Enlightenment measures, which would later specifically target Kant's account of religion. Even more significant, Kant does not specify for what faith, in what orthodoxy or unorthodoxy, he is leaving room. That leaves the door open for personal intuitions, which could—like Goethe's—have power and beauty, and above all independence.[55]

Just as powerfully as it undermined theology and the Cartesian-Leibnizian rationalism that starts in medieval fashion from assumptions about God and works deductively downward,[56] Kant's argument allied him with empirical science, notably with Newton's argument for experiment against untestable hypotheses: "for if the possibility of hypotheses is to be the test of truth and reality of things, I see not how certainty can be obtained in any science; since numerous hypotheses may be devised, which shall overcome new difficulties."[57] That was how the Aristotelian and Ptolemaic cosmogonies had been shakily rescued by epicycles arbitrarily devised to explain away irregularities in the observed orbits of the planets.

But Coleridge was right that Kant's acceptance took place largely in the universities. He became famous without his work's becoming popular—few people among the thousands who turned out to pay their respects at his funeral in Königsberg in 1803 will have known just what this local celebrity's central achievement was. Moreover, there is even now an enormous discrepancy between Kant's legendary standing and his practical effect. He has the reputation of a remote icon of philosophy, little read at first hand, scarcely recognized as the profoundly foundational thinker he is, "islanded partly by his own qualities, but partly by oceans of the wrong kind of respect."[58] We have seen why. So he is left to be pored over almost exclusively by specialists: a philosopher's philosopher. And the philosophers, engrossed as they are in the endless technicalities of Kant's hard-core theoretical works, rarely take account of his basic Enlightenment purpose, or of the letters and popular essays that make his practical aims impossible to miss. Tellingly, Theodor Adorno, in his 1959 lecture course on the First Critique, spoke of Kant's grand public declaration, "An Answer to the Question: What Is Enlightenment?" as still little known.[59] Given its centrality to students of eighteenth-century literature, Adorno can only have meant among philosophers, already a damaging division between two subcultures. That essay is the key to Kant's whole enterprise, but it is quantitatively slight beside the three monumental Critiques, works demanding the most earnest engagement of the learned. The paradox is that Kant has always been taken too seriously to be taken seriously.

CHAPTER 3

Hope in History:
Making the Past Serve the Future

Wir heißen euch hoffen.
We bid you hope.
—Goethe, "Symbolum"

Kant's "Was ist Aufklärung?" of 1784 set out a program of reflection and reform for the Prussia of his day. With cautious optimism, he showed how enlightenment might gradually take hold in this cross-section of time. In the same year a second essay, *Idea for a Universal History with a Cosmopolitan Purpose*, added the vital second coordinate, the line through time that all cross-sections would together compose. This was a still greater challenge to optimism. Did the long term have a direction? Was it one of systematic progress toward social justice and individual freedom? Did history have an arrow of direction, a human meaning?

Christians had always believed so, and written the first universal histories.[1] Secular observers have always doubted it. The idea of systematic progress is dismissed by Anglophone historians, perhaps a little too readily, as the "Whig interpretation of history." Elsewhere too skeptics have always predominated, seeing history as "little more than the register of the crimes, follies and misfortunes of mankind."[2] Yet what if a positive trend could nevertheless be made out—not as conclusive proof, but enough to strengthen people's commitment to action? Kant makes the case for hoping. His *Idea for a Universal History* imagines an account of the past such as an ideal historian might write, someone with an informed but also a philosophical mind. Nature had produced Kepler, who conceived laws for planetary motion, and then Newton, who fleshed out Kepler's principles and showed how gravity held the universe together. Could nature not oblige by producing a genius of historiography? There were observable patterns in the weather, plant growth, the statistics of human births and deaths, and the movements of the heavens. If physical reality was thus coherent, why not history? Was nature not controlling *its* rhythms and pattern too? Might she perhaps even have a plan for humankind?

Kant duly grounds his answer in observable nature, the endowments (*Anlagen*) all human beings have, which must surely be meant to achieve fulfillment. Some people are capable of thinking, acting, creating; the achievements of the few prove the potential of the many. That is surely the destiny intended for mankind, the *Bestimmung des Menschen*, a phrase originally coined by a theologian but equally inviting humanist use.[3] Why else would human beings be constituted the way they are? Their own nature, Lichtenberg wrote, was the only revelation they needed for their happiness.[4]

Kant states the conditions for human fulfillment. They are political: a free and just society within a free and just international order. Human society arose when people gave up the right to use (but by the same token were protected from) arbitrary power by joining in a community and submitting to its laws—Hobbes's argument. A similar compromise might join the peoples of the world in a peaceful association, for which Kant coins the term "league of nations" (*Völkerbund*). This external order is a precondition, and expressly *for the purpose*, of the just internal order that will foster individual fulfillment[5] The state exists to serve its citizens, not the other way round—a crucial divide among political thinkers. National expansion as an end and armed force as the means—very much Frederick the Great's prime concerns—are contrary to the people's true interests, not least because standing armies leave no money for something more vital: education. Yet even wars show a kind of crude plan working itself out, a series of experiments to shape and reshape states and their relations (Proposition 7). But there are less crude signs of progress too, in the way political systems have developed from the Greeks via the Romans and the barbarians down to modern times. Each was superseded, but "a seed of enlightenment" was always left to prepare a higher stage (Proposition 9).

All this may not seem much to go on as pointers to a plan, but perhaps not much was needed. Some few positive outcomes could generate hope, in the way the whole movement of the heavens could be extrapolated from just a few astronomical observations. Kant was concerned to inspire an attitude, not to make a rock-solid case. Optimism was more a conscious choice than a compulsion by facts. Even some appearance of a plan would foster hope in history and thus "itself further this intention of nature."

To some the whole notion might seem mere fantasy, not much better than "a novel," a standard term of dismissal in Kant's day. Yet it was a com-

forting way to present what would otherwise seem a "planless agglomera-
tion of human actions" ruled by "blind chance" (Proposition 9). As traditional Christian reassurance faded, some guarantee of meaning was a widely
felt spiritual need. The metaphor of a "plan of nature" was a "guiding thread
[*Leitfaden*] of reason" through the labyrinth of history. The thread Ariadne
gave Theseus to guide him out of the Cretan labyrinth after killing the
Minotaur became an eighteenth-century leitmotif, part of the resistance to
chaos that was a topos of the time. In Kant's essay, nature stands in for God
as an agent in what is already, if not a supporting dogma, at least an "ideology of nature."[6] Perhaps this is why near the end of the essay Kant surprisingly suggests that the idea of a plan might better be called a "justification
of providence" rather than of nature.[7] This is a relapse into the language of
Christian theodicy, whose purpose was indeed, in Milton's phrase, "to justify the ways of God to Man."

But there are crucial differences. Christian theodicy was meant to console the faithful in their tribulations. For them, too, the labyrinth stood for
the mysterious ways of providence, but at least it was the work of divine
intention, and one day they would be led out of the maze. That was eloquently stated by the principal Christian poet of the day, Klopstock.[8] For
Christians, however grim things might look, all was ultimately for the best.
It only needed passive acceptance, since the divine plan was surely real and
in uniquely powerful hands. Its concern, though, was with the other world,
and the individual's motive was hope for his own salvation. Kant's plan, in
contrast, needed active participation; its goal was this-worldly, and it was
partly altruistic, since establishing a just society was avowedly the hardest
of all tasks.[9] It would take generations to achieve, and we might not live to
see it ourselves. Kant's plan is an article of faith in a different sense from
the Christian's. It is no more than a hopeful hypothesis, which can only
become real in retrospect—a plan will only "have existed" once citizens of
the world have brought about its fulfillment by their actions. That was the
"cosmopolitan purpose" of Kant's title. History would help to make history.

Schiller was Kant's direct disciple, beginning in 1787, when he read the
essay on universal history with deep satisfaction.[10] He was just starting to
write history himself, and when he became a professor at the University
of Jena in 1789 he set out to realize Kant's program, to become the Newton Kant had looked forward to. "The universal history he will create is
designed after your plan, which he understood with a purity and fire that
made him all the more dear to me," the Jena philosopher Reinhold wrote
to Kant.[11] Schiller's project was cut short by poor health and a dispensation
from teaching. Only a few fragments exist as short essays.

That however was far from the end of Schiller's engagement with the past, nor was it the beginning. He had already been confronting history since his early dramas, not just in the obvious sense of reacting to the abuses of his own day through the rebellious gestures of *The Brigands* and unmasking the evils of an identifiable court in *Intrigue and Love*. A longer historical perspective was at work too. When the first audiences in 1784 watched a scene where the duke's subjects are sent off to fight for the English crown in America (German rulers regularly sold soldiers to the great powers to finance their luxuries), they knew that the colonists had won their independence the year before. The young lovers are sacrificed to the machinations of a corrupt court, but in the larger frame positive forces are operating. Less topical but no less real, the audience and readers of the explicitly historical drama *Don Carlos* knew that an earlier struggle, for Dutch independence, had also been finally victorious, even though its Spanish champions, Carlos and Posa, had been sacrificed. In both plays tragedy is enacted in the foreground, but history triumphs in the larger picture. Poetic justice has been done, in seventeenth- and eighteenth-century reality rather than in fiction. Hope was not misplaced.

In other words, the American War of Independence and the Rise of the Dutch Republic—allusions in *Don Carlos* suggest that in Schiller's mind the two events were related[12]—were just the kind of success story Kant wanted his ideal historian to put together. He himself could well have used recent events in America for his argument—he too was writing in 1784. Without knowing it, Schiller had been edging toward Kant's vision of history's larger movement. Having now read Kant's essay, he was consciously working in its categories as he set out on his new venture as a historian. Although writing history was at first just a way of making desperately needed money, it is clear the Dutch rebellion held his imagination beyond the completion of *Don Carlos*. He planned to write six volumes (in the end only one, though substantial, was written). Such full treatment meant shifting his focus from the center of tyranny in Madrid, which had made for claustrophobically intense drama, to the broader scene of repression in the Netherlands. The focus also shifted from royal and noble actors to a whole people. That made the lessons of Dutch liberty directly relevant in just the way Kant intended to the present and future of Schiller's own society. For it was ordinary citizens, an unheroic people of burgher merchants, who finally defeated the might of Spain. Even the great leader of the revolt, William of Orange, is described as magnanimously giving up his princely way of life and embracing poverty as just one more citizen.[13] Where once Schiller had set Karl Moor raging at the lack of great Plutarchian figures in an enfeebled present, he now saw that men on such a colossal scale were not needed.[14] The unity of the many could achieve as much as the heroic deeds of the one, helped by the waters of the Netherlands and the backs-to-the-wall desperation of the Dutch.[15] All this was meant to resonate with Schiller's middle-class readers.[16] He applies the historical lesson tendentiously to his own times: "We still have the strength they showed; we could achieve the same success if ever similar circumstances called us to similar deeds." (Sobered by events in France, he was to delete these sentences of 1788 from the 1801 reprint.)[17]

Kant's idea of a plan is also present in the way a political potential needed decisive action to make it real. The spirit of rebellion in the Dutch provinces grows, but still needs the "perfecting hand," the enlightened, enterprising mind that will seize the great moment and turn the "product of chance" into the "plan of wisdom."[18] That is the cue for William of Orange's entrance. But chance is impartial: Philip II of Spain might equally have seized the moment had he brought his personal authority to the Netherlands. But he missed his opportunity, and that gave the "work of random happening" time to ripen into "a work of the understanding."[19] There is, once again, no objective plan, just the raw material of chance that human action shapes into purpose, first tactically on the ground, then in the historian's retrospect. In an extended metaphor, "Man works, smoothes and shapes the rough stone that the times bring along; to him belongs the moment and the point, but world history is rolled by chance."[20]

There is not much consolation here for an age that needed existential reassurance. The random nature of reality is conceded; historical agents must shape it as best they can. Schiller records more such moments in his next great account, of the Thirty Years' War. Emperor Ferdinand might have brought hostilities to an end but maliciously prolonged them (he is of course the villain in the moral system of Schiller's narrative).[21] Or, again, the Protestant side missed their opportunity: "The great moment found only mediocre spirits on the stage, and the decisive point remained unexploited, because the courageous lacked power and the powerful lacked courage and resolution."[22] Human failure is the obvious pendant to decisive action.

To stress decisiveness or its lack hardly makes Schiller an original historian; but the idea that successful action creates its own teleology, which may help shape events in later periods, was a more distinctive one, and clearly an application of Kant's thesis. Schiller's reading of the past sometimes seems to relapse into a traditional, even providential view. The Dutch triumph was won against all the odds: "If it were ever allowed to weave a higher providence into human affairs, then it would be in this story, so powerfully does it seem to contradict reason and all experience."[23] It seems even "to border on the miraculous."[24] Schiller soon takes that back, saying that when all factors are considered, the miracle disappears—though a few lines on he invokes the invisible hand of fate and calls a further unexpected turn a "remarkable dispensation of heaven."[25]

Is the historian serious in straying beyond rational explanation to the intervention of higher powers? These are surely not remnants of conventional belief, any more than Kant's one reference to providence was. (Kant elsewhere firmly states that it is foolish presumption to imagine a providence working in men's interests.)[26] Schiller is certainly no Christian, and both his major histories view religion with a cold eye.[27] Is it mere rhetoric, then, perhaps to accommodate less enlightened readers? Or a way to heighten dramatic effect, turning everyday phenomena into operations of a deus ex machina? The Spanish Armada was wrecked by a great storm, a straightforward enough occurrence in nature. But at the close of Schiller's poem on Spain's "invincible fleet" ("Die unüberwindliche Flotte"), the storm is the breath of God: "God the almighty blew, / And the Armada was dispersed to the four winds."[28] God has intervened in the permanent struggle between tyranny and freedom that is history's repeated subject.[29] It certainly gives the poem a powerful close. In the end, Schiller lays aside rhetoric and metaphor and declares that the choice is ours: "it is up to us whether we stand amazed at the bold birth of chance or pay the tribute of admiration to a higher understanding."[30] At least in the happier episodes of history, the "higher understanding" is on the right side. Encouraging that belief is the pragmatic point of Enlightenment historiography.

Schiller comes fully into the open, or rather probes further into the historian's psychological depths, in the Jena Inaugural lecture he gave in 1789 between the publication of his two major historical works. It analyzes what is going on in the historian's mind when he starts to see the sequence of cause and effect as a system of means and ends, when the "blind randomness and lawless freedom" of events (das blinde Ohngefähr, die gesetzlose Freiheit) start to feel like purposeful movement. In short, when history seems to have a meaning. Yet the historian knows—or, if he doesn't, we do—that the harmonious totality (das übereinstimmende Ganze), isn't real, it is only there in his mind (freilich nur in seiner Vorstellung vorhanden). He is inserting the notion of teleological coherence into the order of things (verpflanzt sie außer sich in die Ordnung der Dinge).[31] But there is just as much out there in the "order of things" that contradicts purpose and meaning as supports them. So the historian consciously chooses the view more congenial to heart and mind. It is also a choice, on Kant's scheme, of the view that will best motivate fresh action.

Schiller doesn't make that point explicit. His emphasis is at first sight different from Kant's: when he invokes a *Naturplan* whose fine mechanisms the historian has to trace,[32] he seems to be looking wholly back to the past. The poem "Die Künstler" (The Artists), written at just this time, presents an idealized image of eighteenth-century man—mature, rational, and in control of nature—and paints a picture of continuous progress leading down from primitive times to a peaceful and civilized Europe. It expressly embraces Germany! Can this be the same writer who not so long ago was sounding the horn of revolt in *The Brigands* and flaying the absolutist courts in *Intrigue and Love*? It is not that his view has changed; he is simply showing his century from its better side,[33] in line with Kant's principle of selectivity.

The activism Kant wanted to inspire to carry things further is implicit in the pedagogic situation. Schiller is addressing an overwhelmingly youthful audience who have come en masse to experience the author of *The Brigands* live. (When a larger lecture room had to be found across town to accommodate the crowd, their wild rush through the streets made citizens fear a fire had broken out.)[34] Among these young men, Schiller says in his introduction, there must be some whose genius will help shape the coming age;[35] and he ends by urging them all not to take for granted the benefits won by the blood of past generations, but to render to future humanity the debt they cannot repay to their dead predecessors.[36] It is a call not to brigandly rebellion, but to citizenly engagement in furtherance of enlightened aims—precisely Kant's "cosmopolitan purpose."

Amazingly, for modern German historians Schiller might as well never have existed. The essay collection *Deutsche Historiker*, edited by none other than Hans-Ulrich Wehler, five volumes in the 1970s and another four a decade later, includes nothing at all on Schiller, and this despite its express warning that a discipline is lost if it forgets its founding fathers.[37] At seven names per volume, a total of sixty-three favored historians. Might Schiller have squeezed in at number sixty-four, in a collection that stretches all the way back to his predecessors and contemporaries, Pufendorf, Möser, Schlözer, and Spittler? It looks unlikely. The omission only confirms a neglect reaching back to Meinecke and Ranke, and often visibly part of the long-standing German irrationalist aversion to that Enlightenment of which Schiller's historical writings are a major part.[38]

The Enlightenment itself is commonly criticized, not to say ridiculed, for an optimistic belief in progress as sketched in Schiller's inaugural lecture. Its propositions are allegedly naive when set against hard reality. But what do the terms "optimistic," "belief," "reality," and "progress" mean? For the Enlightenment, reality was something to be not supinely accepted but deliberately shaped. Optimism was the belief that this was possible. Progress was never certain, never assumed, simply to be hoped and worked for. Like so much in the Enlightenment, it was a conception not of things as they are, but of things as they might and should be. "Reality" was not ignored: Schiller shows that the historian is fully conscious of competing facts and is choosing a positive view as a pragmatic policy.

How does the allegedly greater realism of later historians look in comparison, a comparison that their arrogant dismissal of the Enlightenment positively invites? The usual touchstone is Ranke's claim, in the four words that are all most people have read of him, to tell it allegedly "as it really was" (*wie es eigentlich gewesen*). In context, this is not the program for a new method commonly credited ever since with founding modern historiography,[39] but a passing swipe at the Enlightenment from a young scholar out to establish a profile for himself in his first published work: "People have assigned to history the office of judging the past, of informing the present for the benefit of future years. Such elevated offices the present essay does not undertake: it merely sets out to show how it really was."[40] It is hard to see how certain themes could be treated without some element of judgment: the Spanish Fury in the Netherlands, the atrocities of the Thirty Years' War, and a great deal more that has happened since. Objectivity doesn't mean abstaining from judgment, but scrupulously balancing evidence while making clear your standpoint. A standpoint is unavoidable. No historical account can claim to equate with reality; once the raw material is treated, it is not "really" (*eigentlich*) anything; it has become the historian's own reality and property (*Eigentum*), peculiar to him, even peculiar (*eigentümlich*) tout court.[41] Ranke's own peculiarity is plain, and it is far from the objectivity that his famous formula is assumed to require. His theoretical statements are few and far between,[42] but they show a consistent relapse into pre-Enlightenment thinking. At crucial moments of history, what may seem chance, he argues, is God's finger determining the outcome.[43] Nations are themselves not the cloudy formations of social-contract theory but the thoughts of God.[44] History is a sacred hieroglyph.[45] Nothing that exists, exists without God.[46] This transcendent ground of history needs no proving;[47] it is what the historian's (allegedly untheological) efforts all spring from.[48]

None of this is meant to sound provisional, hypothetical, hopeful. Ranke states it as fact, or, to be precise (given the nature of the content and the dismissal of any need for proof), as dogma. What the Enlightenment had secularized, Ranke has resacralized. His position also has a clear political angle. In his Berlin Inaugural of 1836, he contradicts his own argument of twelve years before, that history is not there to serve present and later generations (or, as the Enlightenment would have put it, humanity). He now calls historical knowledge the necessary basis for contemporary politics, because without it everything would be left to that old bogeyman "blind chance." This turns out to mean the activities of prejudiced individuals who prefer extremes to what is "just and healthy," and who, like eighteenth-century philosophers with their universal theories, are always querying the present political arrangements.[49] All these are the familiar conservative arguments against anyone who disturbs the status quo.

What kind of realism is this that set the tone for nineteenth-century German historiography? It is commonly labeled "historicism" and traced back to Herder, whom it certainly echoes—the idea that history is "the march of God through nature," or that "the finger of the Almighty is responsible for all earthly upheavals."[50] But Ranke is not just taking cognizance of the events of history or the form of a society, but demanding that they be accepted without question. He is not so much following Herder as making the same barefaced demands as Hegel. Where Ranke's authority is God, Hegel's is Reason—his peculiar conception of reason—which equally lacks intellectual underpinning and expressly rejects all counterargument. That Reason actually governs history, Hegel says, is the only thought philosophy brings to its study.[51] And quite enough, too, since precisely that, as Burckhardt crisply retorted, is what would need proving.[52] Kant's argument was for applying Reason to the historical process, not for assuming Reason was inherent in it.

Hegel's pronouncements on society just as patently beg the question. In the well-known phrase from the foreword to the *Philosophy of Right*, what is real is rational and vice versa; and Hegel bad-mouths anyone who questions the status quo.[53] Even where Ranke does not quote Hegel, the philosopher's sophistries are always there in the background.[54] Their common position, as Nietzsche was to point out, is not realism but fatalism, a kowtowing to reality, intellectual *Realpolitik*. Fatalism is fine when the fates are favorable, as they were to nineteenth-century Prussia, where Ranke was the social and intellectual authority in history and Hegel in philosophy. They and their successors—Droysen, Treitschke, Sybel—were riding the wave, as Prussia was, launched on what they saw—though they didn't call it that—as a *Sonderweg*, a unique historical path that could be seen wholly as triumph, not yet as tragedy.[55] The "Prussian school" claimed roots in Herder's "historicism," but its concentration on the rise of a single nation was a long way from Herder's vision of the uniqueness of *all* cultures, and his liberal acceptance of their diverse contributions to *Humanität*.

In his vehement attack on the endorsement of the actual, Nietzsche was fighting an Enlightenment rearguard action—not a role for which he is much known. When he rejects Hegel's "naked admiration of success," his "idolatry of the factual," a German tradition embodied in Luther's "prudent indulgence of power" and embodied now again in Ranke, the "born classic advocate of every stronger side,"[56] or when he reserves the right to say that what happened should not have happened—in all this Nietzsche is reasserting the Enlightenment's distinction between fact and value, the way the world is and the way it ought to be. Like the Enlightenment again, he insists on the need for youthful new beginnings against Hegel's notion that we live in a late time when the only thing philosophy can and should do is to take cognizance of whatever has happened[57]—a gray science that can rejuvenate nothing, for the owl of Minerva begins her flight only at dusk.[58] It is not commonly realized just how defeatist this celebrated metaphor is. Against such "congenital gray-hairedness" (*angeborene Grauhaarigkeit*), and in support of vital new impulses and a new generation in their struggle against "the blind force of facts,"[59] Nietzsche prescribes searching the past for examples that will inspire action, a practice he calls "monumental history."[60] That is not commonly heard as the echo it surely is of Kant's "history with a cosmopolitan intention."

For a true realism, sober and in thrall to no worldly power, we have to return to Schiller: "the world as the object of history is at root nothing but the struggle of natural forces with each other and with human freedom, and the outcome of this struggle is what history reports to us."[61] This is the late 1790s. It is now for Schiller a world in which "mad chance rather than a wise plan seems to rule."[62] The high expectations of the French Revolution have long gone sour. As at those missed moments in the Thirty Years' War, a generation has been tested and found wanting: "the generous moment finds an unreceptive generation" (in the first draft, "a corrupt generation").[63] That is from the fifth letter of the *Ästhetische Briefe*, which impressively faces up to the question: what do you do when your hopes fail and your whole conception of history is shaken? Most of the early enthusiasts for the French Revolution suffered a severe hangover, and many of its erstwhile friends became its critics. Not so Kant. Not only did the original pan-European enthusiasm prove a "moral predisposition" (*moralische Anlage*) in humanity. The event itself, for all its "misery and atrocities," was "too great, too closely interwoven with the interests of mankind and too widespread in its influence on every part of the world for it not to be recalled to the minds of peoples when favorable circumstances arise for new attempts to be repeated," leading in the end to the desired just constitution.[64] These had been just Schiller's sentiments when he wrote his *Revolt of the Netherlands*; he now deleted the passage from a new edition.

The practical answer to the question "What now?" is that you dust yourself off and start again from first principles. Despite (or because of) his disillusion, Schiller probes deep into the constitution of human beings—its material and spiritual components; the corresponding impulses and their excesses and imbalance—and conceives a way to understand and fundamentally reshape human raw material so as to make possible a better politics. To write *Letters on the Aesthetic Education of Man* at such a juncture (1795) might seem impossibly idealistic. Realistically, he calls what he is proposing a task for more than one century.[65]

Schiller did find a ray of light in his last dramatic subject, *William Tell* (1804). In contrast to the excesses of the French Revolution, the Swiss overthrew their Austrian overlords with an extreme of moderation: a revolution, but "if it can be, without blood." Only the visibly villainous Gessler, who sets up Tell's ordeal of shooting the apple from his son's head, is seen being killed onstage. For the rest, as Benjamin Constant noted, it was "the destruction of a Bastille carried out by one man with German calm and a little hammer." Schiller spelled out the message in a dedicatory poem that contrasted the "crude forces" and "blind rage" of French revolutionary factions with the actions of a pious people humanely defending their human rights.[66]

How else to face a present crisis undaunted, if not by commemorating in Kant's spirit the solid successes, and by looking to the longer, indeed the longest possible term? The problems change little; the analyst can only follow the same guiding light of hope and principle.

EXCURSUS: AN ERRATIC BLOCK

It is difficult to place Herder. His thinking has common threads with Kant, but also inner contradictions. He was indeed a contradictory mixture—Christian and humanist, closely involved with leading writers of the Enlightenment yet positioned athwart its main line of argument, much as Rousseau was. Like his teacher Kant, Herder had a strong sense of a movement in history, but it was the standard Christian faith in a divine plan, though the term "providence" often seems interchangeable with "chance" and "fate."[67] In *One More Philosophy of History to Educate Humanity*,[68] he caricatures the rational age, whose diet of deism, science, cosmopolitanism, and tolerance can only produce a "graybeard boy" (*Greisknaben*)[69]—the opposite of Kant's later caricature of the adult forcibly kept in a baby walker. Better to have "devotion and superstition, darkness and ignorance, disorder and primitive manners," Herder argues, than the present age's "unbelief, nerveless frigidity and refinement, philosophical weariness and human misery."[70] The errors and evils of the past—authority, prejudice, despotism, priestly power, the Dark Ages—were all, if rightly understood, necessary vehicles of the good in their day, whereas excessive light cannot nourish or bring happiness. Herder's attack on contemporary rationality for being judgmental is just as judgmental in reverse, a sweeping rejection of modern Europe by a vague Rousseauian criterion of prerational vitality.

This first sketch is a gesture toward the all-embracing history Herder conceived during his early sea voyage from Riga to Nantes.[71] His attack on an age of abstraction remains itself largely abstract, a young man's contrarian cry with no clear causal analysis. But there is at least one shrewd thrust, at "our system of commerce" and the damage done across the world by the service of mammon. Though Europe no longer has slavery, "we have allowed ourselves to use and trade three continents as slaves . . . but then they are not Europeans, not Christians."[72] Such Eurocentric scorn was rife long before the Enlightenment, documented at the latest in Montaigne's essay *Des cannibales* and duly pilloried by Enlightenment writers such as Georg Forster.[73] Here were indeed evils not to be justified as necessary to any providential plan. They remain a prime concern of Herder's, and he names the guilty nations: Spain's cruelty, England's avarice, and Holland's arrogance make up the collective shame of Europe[74]—an indictment of business rationality, indeed, though hardly of Enlightenment reason.

Herder's idea of the divine plan comes with the standard Christian reservation that we cannot hope to know it. A familiar metaphor warns the inquirer off: "And if it were all a labyrinth for you, with a hundred doors closed and a hundred open, the labyrinth is a *palace of God*, for *his* grand fulfillment, perhaps for him to take his pleasure in, not for *you*!"[75] There is no sign here of the Theseus myth's guiding thread out of the labyrinth. That is apparently withheld by a God who sounds very much like a self-indulgent German autocrat.

Herder does then find a thread of his own in an ideal of *Humanität*, a broad concept he defines variously as the gradual fulfillment of best human potential, the achievement of reason and fairness in all classes and in all affairs of men, and the joint product of the creative actions of legislators, poets, artists, philosophers, inventors, and educators through the ages.[76] But, crucially, all cultures made their historical contribution by fulfilling themselves in accordance with the values they lived by. These were as real to them as ours to us, and perhaps better rather than worse: "What is the point of measuring all peoples *against us Europeans*? Where is the means of comparison? That nation which you call wild or barbarian is in essence far more humane than you."[77] (Herder even suggests, tongue in cheek, that when cannibals eat Europeans, they are doing them a special honor.)[78]

This open acceptance of every phase of history across time and space is spelled out in Herder's central work, *Ideas for the Philosophy of the History of Humanity*. Its very openness means that it verges on tautology, seeing fulfillment in the self-evident: "The Romans were and became what they were able to become: everything in their case went under or maintained itself that was able to go under or maintain itself."[79] And as a general formula: "Whatever can happen happens, and brings forth what it was able by its nature to bring forth;"[80] "Everywhere humanity is what it was able to make of itself, what it had the inclination and power to become."[81] Clearly, on this view some phases were not in any sense progress, merely progression. Progress within a culture is difficult if it is locked into its own value system. Yet Herder will reject none. He never resolves the mismatch between indiscriminate nonrational acceptance and the necessarily rational assessment of the degree of *Humanität* the individual culture has achieved. He puts his faith in the forces of nature, which will correct follies, vices, or crimes through historical trial and error—all in good time.[82] This puts off any present generation's fulfillment every bit as much as the utopian hopes for the future which Herder objected to in Kant.

Yet Herder's approach broke open contemporary thinking and became the basis for a more all-embracing historiography. Quite apart from the breadth and exuberance of his vision, his optimism was appealing, not least to his own German culture, which was now just emerging from under the shadow of a neighbor. Till then, France had been axiomatically assumed superior. It was arguably the German struggle against French hegemony that shaped Herder's thinking in the first place. The strategy for a nation to establish itself was clear. It had to feel "its *midpoint* of happiness in itself like the center of gravity in a sphere"; it needed "the prejudice of a limited nationalism."[83] This early usage—*Nationalism*—does not imply the aggressive narrowness of nineteenth-century *Nationalismus*. As yet, the national lion could still lie down with the Enlightenment lamb. Herder later speaks of a "purified patriotism," confident in itself and needing no comparison or competition with others. Its ultimate logic is one of intercultural sympathy: what you claim for yourself, you must allow to others too. Cultures must learn from, not look down on, one another; every nation must come to feel the wrong when another is abused and insulted: "There must arise a *common feeling* so that each can put itself in the place of every other. . . . If this feeling grows, there will gradually be an *alliance of all civilized nations* against any one presumptuous power."[84] This is almost Kant's League of Nations by a cultural side door. The means and end of *Humanität* is empathy (*Einfühlung*). It is a guiding principle for understanding the past, but also for living in the present. And though Herder sometimes paradoxically locates fulfilled *Humanität* in an afterlife to which this existence is just a prelude,[85] his categories are more easily understood as of the earth. History becomes both anthropology and a politics of peace. By his own roundabout route, Herder rejoins the Enlightenment.

CHAPTER 4

Talking to Tyrants:
Pens against Power

Mir gefällt's zu konversieren
Mit Gescheiten, mit Tyrannen.
I quite enjoy a conversation
With clever tyrants of our nation.
—Goethe, "Buch des Unmuts,"
West-Östlicher Divan

For all their historical high profile, Schiller and Karl Eugen are just two representative figures in what could easily become a cast of hundreds in eighteenth-century Germany, all acting out a common conflict between individual impulse and arbitrary control. That this friction generated literary form—Schiller's in every sense dramatic career is hardly conceivable without his early experience of absolutism—is also representative. In the absence of a political forum, literature was a means to confront power, to portray it and reflect critically on it. As Schiller wrote, "One particular class of people has more reason than any other to be grateful to the theater. Only here do the great hear what they seldom or never hear—the truth."[1]

Admittedly, literature could have no immediate effect; indeed, it was still trying to secure its own freedom to address the public mind. Censorship and the caution of theater intendants like Dalberg limited freedom of speech. But the multiplicity of German states, their theaters and publishing centers, and the different degrees of liberality among rulers now showed as an advantage. Censorship could not be everywhere, and no major drama of the period was prevented from putting its message before the public somewhere in some form.

The message, understandably, was often straightforward polemic and satire—there were abuses enough in Germany to justify direct attack. In

Lessing's *Emilia Galotti*, a prince's passion for a subject leads to her fiancé's murder and her virtual suicide. The local relevance of such abuse of power is only thinly veiled by the play's Italian setting, and it recurs in the Kosinski episode of Schiller's *Brigands*. His next play, *Intrigue and Love* (*Kabale und Liebe*), pillories the court of a small German state, its political corruption and cynical machinations against its powerless subjects. Knowing which small state Schiller came from, audiences and readers could put two and two together. His facts were firm—the sexual depredations of the great; the ruthless court power struggles; the threat of arbitrary imprisonment; the "subsidy treaties" with major European powers under which subjects were sold off to fight in foreign wars, as shown in the scene Dalberg cut for performance in which a contingent of local men leaves to fight on the British side in the American War of Independence.[2]

Schiller's representation of tyranny is not exaggerated. The vehemence of his style has sometimes misled critics into thinking it was,[3] but he was meeting violence with violence, a high-handed regime with a high-flown rhetoric. What may seem unrealistic was real. True, the satire can verge on melodrama. "When I enter the scene, a principality trembles," says the first minister in best hiss-the-villain style (act 1, scene 7). In order to separate two young people whose love across class boundaries threatens the minister's schemes and political position, his underling plans to blackmail the girl and make her swear an oath of silence. What use is an oath, fool? his chief asks. Answer: for people like us, it means nothing; for this class of people, everything (act 3, scene 1). Thus the dialogue as well as the action caricatures tyranny; it is given only enough voice to condemn itself. It is seen only from outside, as—legitimately enough—an object of revulsion. The same had been true of *The Brigands*, whose title page in the first edition carried the epigraph "In tirannos!"—against the tyrants! It seems not to have been of Schiller's choosing, but it shows that others could not miss seeing what he was about.

The two sides were thus entrenched, criticism confronting absolutism, with little ground for negotiation between them, certainly not for such reconciliation as comes about in the tragicomic ending of Beaumarchais's more subtly subversive *Marriage of Figaro*, a play that premiered in Paris within two weeks of Schiller's in Mannheim. Negotiation rather than conflict may have been what the German Enlightenment was pursuing, reform rather than revolution—at least as soberly laid out by Kant in "What Is Enlightenment?" That was already dialogue with a ruler, imagined dialogue yet close to the realities of the day, tentative, gradualist. Literature was more confrontational, drama especially. The genre by its nature could hardly paint the conflicts of the day in less than stark colors, and the more clearly they stood out, the less feasible conciliation was. If the ending was to be realistic, it could not be triumphal; it had necessarily to be tragic. That showed up all the more the nature of this still feudal society.

The outspokenness of *Intrigue and Love* strained Dalberg's tolerance to the limit; its author was an in-house liability. Schiller knew he was in danger of dismissal when his contract ran out, which duly happened. His lecture to a local society on the function of theater pulled no punches: he had nothing to lose. He presented the stage as a place where the great could hear the truth. Drama was a moral authority on a par with religion: its jurisdiction went beyond that of the law, it could channel enlightened thought down to the people and spread it through the whole state, barbarism and superstition would yield to victorious light.[4] Schiller did try to resell himself to Dalberg by declaring a shift to his "true vocation" of historical high tragedy, away from the explosive "bourgeois" genre.[5] His subject, the tragedy of Don Carlos, heir to the throne of Philip II of Spain, focused on the emotional hothouse situation of a son whose fiancée has been taken over for dynastic reasons by his father. Schiller called it "a family portrait in a royal house"[6]— virtually a bourgeois theme, just in a more elevated setting. Yet politics lay close to hand and soon dominated. This was sixteenth-century Spain, the age of the Inquisition and the wholesale slaughter visited on the Netherlands by the duke of Alba[7]—the most notorious tyranny of the European past.

Distance in time was not a distraction. Historical drama as far back as Shakespeare hints at contemporary issues. It can even intensify relevance by showing how an evil has persisted through time and how long overdue is the remedy. Here a political debate arises directly from the family plot. King Philip suspects a love intrigue between Carlos and the queen, but with no one to confide in among his cynical careerist courtiers, he summons Carlos's friend Marquis Posa, a man of known integrity. Posa seizes the moment and turns an audience with the king into a debate between liberal and hard-line conceptions of government, between Enlightenment ideas and the harshness of sixteenth-century *Realpolitik*.

This twist of the plot hands Posa on a plate what philosophers since antiquity had wanted: the chance to influence rulers for the better, to convert them from ambition and oppression to benevolence and justice. There were two known ways. Either catch a future ruler young, educate him before he ascends the throne, and hope the education will stick; or try to get the ear of a ruler already ruling. A true philosopher-king could not be realistically expected. Education could take written form, as in Xenophon's *Cyropedia* or Erasmus's *Institution of a Christian Prince*, or the work Frederick the Great gave the young Karl Eugen of Württemberg. It is doubtful whether these "mirrors for princes" were closely read, and whether advice in any form was ever taken seriously. What effect instruction by Aristotle in person had on the youthful Alexander the Great, other than having him sleep with an annotated Homer under his pillow (but that was the war-obsessed *Iliad*) is at best a matter for speculation. On Seneca's failure as tutor to Nero, no speculation is needed. Influencing an established ruler, as Plato tried to do with Dionysius II of Syracuse, was no more of a success. That approach had to struggle against the already established habit of power. In a discreet and undramatic way, Montaigne as adviser to Henri IV is perhaps the most successful example.

Posa tries both routes, first working on Carlos, the heir presumptive, then seizing the chance to act directly: "Why put off the happiness of mankind to the king's successor?" as Schiller's own later commentary reads.[8] The long audience scene at the play's center (act 3, scene 10) is famous for Posa's many luminous statements: "I cannot be the servant of a prince"; "Man is far more than you have thought him"; "Can he be happy if he may not think?"; "Let citizens once more be what they were, the purpose of the crown"; "Just one stroke of your pen transforms the world"; "Grant freedom of thought"; and more. But piecemeal quotation—and Schiller's finest formulations have suffered from being quoted to within an inch of their life—can distract from the tightly coherent argument that structures the scene. Posa has done past service to the crown but sought no reward and kept aloof from the court. He now declines any special favors ("I enjoy the protection of the law") and the offer of any post in the kingdom. To serve the king in any capacity would mean selling himself for purposes not his own, for mere personal advantage: "I love humanity, and in monarchies I can love nobody but myself." Montesquieu whispers in the background: the root principle of monarchies is honor, that of republics virtue. A subject is here speaking from the higher standpoint of a *Weltbürger*. What Posa could dispense as the king's agent would not be happiness as he conceives it. Indeed, his version of human happiness would make majesty tremble. Such happiness and truth as the crown can afford—Posa's image is *Münzen*, coin of the realm, the stamp of exclusive authority—is not something he is prepared to distribute. Can citizens be happy if they are not allowed to think? The refrain returns: he cannot serve a prince.

You are a Protestant! says Philip with the paranoid promptness of a Senator McCarthy sniffing out communists. Posa reassures him that they share the same faith. He even disparages religious "innovation" because it "only increases the burden of the chains it cannot quite break." (This oracular statement sounds like an indictment of Protestantism too, which soon became as repressive as the Catholic church.)

Philip sees in Posa's forthrightness a tactical substitute for flattery. Posa replies that the king is bound to think this way, since the people around him have lost all human nobility; he cannot get the response he needs from the passive instruments he has created. The wider effects of Philip's regime are immeasurably more terrible. Posa is just back from Flanders and Brabant, flourishing provinces with a fine people. It must be divine to be the father of such a people—an echo of the divine-right notion that still in the eighteenth century placed princely authority, by analogy and delegation, in direct descent from the authority of God.[9] But then he came upon burned human bones from the latest auto-da-fé of Protestant dissenters. This hits home: the stage direction reads, "tries to meet Posa's gaze, but casts his eyes down in embarrassment and confusion." As if to console him, Posa recognizes "with shuddering admiration" that the king has acted as he believed he must. This is a surprisingly tolerant response to power's old excuse— "necessitie / The tyrant's plea."[10] Yet a new way of governing must come, the happiness of the citizen will coexist with the power of princes, and "necessity will be humane."

Philip has in the meantime regrouped: when will a humane age dawn if he hesitates to act against the "curse" (still the dogmatic presumption) of the Protestant present? Flanders must be made like Spain, which flourishes in peace. Posa: the peace of a graveyard! Meanwhile a "universal springtime" is changing the shape of the world, transforming Christianity. (Is Posa *really* not a Protestant?) The wheel of history is rolling, and no human hand can seize the spokes to stop it. There is hard economic argument too: Spain's most productive subjects are fleeing and being welcomed by Elizabeth of England "with open motherly arms"—a telling contrast with Philip's "fatherly" ruthlessness. Where the king believes he is planting for eternity, he is sowing death. Such work cannot survive its individual author (a view of tyranny that history largely confirms). Philip's is the self-fulfilling prejudice of all reactionaries against the free unfolding of human potential that is part of nature's processes: the Creator allows evils to rage in the universe rather than limit freedom; he does not intervene but stays concealed behind eternal laws. Returning from cosmogony to politics, Posa pleads for an order where citizens will once more be the crown's purpose—not a revolutionary new order, but a restored original state, a contractual monarchy. If such an exemplary balance were established in Spain, it would be her positive duty to impose it on the rest of the world.

Philip has heard enough—enough to learn how the world looks through other eyes, though not enough to be convinced, and too much for Posa's safety, were it not that he is prepared to overlook these rash utterances. He even warns Posa against the Inquisition (which it later transpires has long had him in its sights). But Philip also seeks to rebut him—not just as a king, but as the more experienced man: "You will think otherwise, when once you know / Man as I know him." It is the familiar question-begging argument of old realists against young idealists, that the way things are proves this is how they have to be.[11]

Philip's human need has made possible that second variant of Enlightened tactics, gaining access to the ear of present power. The meeting of minds is made dramatically plausible. Less plausible is Schiller's projecting of Enlightenment ideas back into sixteenth-century Spain. No Posa of that time could have formulated so clearly the principles of eighteenth-century critical thought. It is also unlikely that Philip would have heard him out. (The real Philip avowedly did not listen to what people said to him in audience.)[12] Wholly plausible, on the other hand, is the king's vision of history. Posa gets the long eloquent speeches, but Philip's replies have independent substance; they are no longer the caricatural self-condemnations of Schiller's earlier villains. He has entered into the mind of the other side as he had not done before, with artistic as well as intellectual benefit. Only such genuine dialogue could show in hard terms what the Enlightenment was up against. Philip II, the duke of Alba, even the briefly glimpsed but disproportionately chilling Grand Inquisitor, who has the play's ideological last word, condemning the king's son (Philip: What have I worked for? Inquisitor: Better decomposition than freedom)—all are credible agents of darkness, convinced and, in their own illiberal terms, convincing. The play enacts the Enlightenment principle of debate with all parties, turning both sides into credible flesh-and-blood agents.

This is not to say that things are left evenly balanced. Posa in audience with the king is of course the bearer of Schiller's own convictions, before his audience, the theater public. Anachronistic in their sixteenth-century context, Posa's arguments were for Schiller's day acutely contemporary. It was absolutist rulers who were now the anachronism, a political phenomenon left behind by Enlightenment thinking—yet left behind in the other sense too, left standing as a reality that still dominated eighteenth-century German society.

Even that is not the end of the story. Besides taking the realists seriously, Schiller sees the idealist critically, as he already had his earlier exemplars,

Karl Moor in *The Brigands* and Ferdinand Walter in *Intrigue and Love*. Posa, the friend of a prince and confidant of a king, becomes a manipulator of both, and of the queen. He uses these human beings, his switches of tactic involve betrayals of trust, his dramatically and morally devious maneuvers mean he is almost as responsible for the tragic ending as is the other side. For him, just as much as for hard-nosed realists, the end justifies the means. Posa fits Schiller's later conclusion: that the idealist who thinks highly of humanity runs the risk of scorning individual human beings.[13] Like Kant's passing remark that revolution will never bring about true reform in ways of thinking,[14] this critique of activists foresees the shape of things to come in France in the 1790s. Schiller's realism about human motivation in politics, already at work in his second play, *The Conspiracy of Fiesco at Genoa* (1783),[15] will be the backbone of his later dramas, all but one of them historical.

The issues can also show through a humorous disguise. When the young future duke of Weimar heard that Christoph Martin Wieland was to be his tutor, he wrote undertaking to serve the happiness of his land and people with the help of his "personal Danischmend."[16] The ingratiating reference is to the court philosopher at the center of Wieland's *Golden Mirror*, a novel pointedly dedicated to Joseph II of Austria. Danischmend struggles with the problems a would-be reformer faces. He regales his master, Shah Gebal of Scheschian, with the history of the country's past rulers, from ideal to positively evil, with accompanying exhortations to virtue. The trouble is, the shah keeps nodding off. Mirrors for princes, even when delivered live, are not the most entertaining of genres. Communicating reason and virtue without boring the audience was indeed a general Enlightenment problem. But is the shah's sleepiness just boredom? It looks more like an evasion, conscious or not, a psychosomatic response to things the shah is reluctant to hear—home truths he cannot refute or moral lessons he does not want to act on. His yawns are part of the dialogue between philosophy and power, inadequate answers to awkward questions. In any case, breaking up Danischmend's narrative into many evening sessions already half-undoes its effect. The shah can sleep on things, regroup his resistance, waver in his resolutions, change his mind altogether, slide out of any commitment to take measures. The philosopher has to begin all over again the next day, as in another *Arabian Nights* tale. It is a marriage of Scheherazade and Sisyphus.

The shah also dismisses uncomfortable philosophy with the familiar argument that it lacks knowledge of the real world: Danischmend likes to speak about things he does not understand. Admittedly he speaks well, and that serves to pass the time. That makes him not much better than a court jester. For the shah, ideas are just one more amusement, as they had been for Dionysius of Syracuse, whom Plato tried unsuccessfully to influence. Retelling that episode in his novel *Agathon*, Wieland defined the tyrant's "conversion" as "nothing other than that he now embraced, not a nymph breathing promises of sensual pleasure, but a lovely phantom of virtue; and he became intoxicated not on Syracusan wine but on Plato's ideas," which incidentally he regards as entirely harmless.[17]

Philosophy-as-entertainment was both its strength and its weakness. Dabbling in ideas was fashionable among the highly placed, and to that extent ideas were able to infiltrate power although with no certainty of being taken seriously. For the aristocracy, said Tocqueville, they were merely ingenious intellectual games. There was no commitment to follow them wherever they might lead. And free debate was a concession the great could always withdraw. If you disagreed with them, and certainly if you worsted them in discussion, they would fall back on social rank.[18] That was at root a snobbish variant of Frederick the Great's concession: reason as much as you like about whatever you like, but obey.

So perhaps it was all just lip service anyway? Yet even lip service might slowly create a climate of opinion, which in turn might lead to substantive commitment (just as it can be the first stage in a political withdrawal from commitment). Even entertaining the great was no bad thing—what else was Wieland doing in his novel about entertaining the great? *The Golden Mirror* is a mirror for princes at one remove, communicating ideas along with the difficulty of communicating ideas. A potentially boring preachment has become a sparkling interplay.

Underneath the playful surface the situation is serious. "Danischmend, said the shah, has one small failing—as a philosopher, he enjoys the freedom to be impudent, but sometimes he abuses it." Yes, comes the reply, "philosophy *is* impudent, because it does not hesitate to tell kings they are in the wrong when they *are* in the wrong."[19] That reinforces the parallel with the court jester. Sometimes Danischmend holds back, knowing that "the truth one tells to the great must never be offensive."[20] It is a matter of judging the mood and the moment. In the novel's enlarged second edition (the first ended tamely with the tale of an ideal ruler) Danischmend finally goes too far, falls from grace, and is arrested. Humor—his and Wieland's—was only ever a means and a mask. Power is always the underlying reality, and Enlightenment activities were always dangerous. Karl Eugen of Württemberg, we saw, arbitrarily imprisoned the writer Schubart, and he held the lawyer and court official Johann Jakob Moser for five years in Schloss Hohentwiel for speaking out against his financial extortions. What Tocqueville said of the French *philosophes*—that they might complain but never had any serious cause to fear (which is not even true of them, as Voltaire and Diderot could witness)[21]—was certainly not true of their German contemporaries.

Hopeful dialogue and tactful initiatives, careful consolidation of any progress—these were the order of the day. They are embodied in Kant's implied dialogue with Frederick the Great as clearly as in Schiller's audience scene or Wieland's novel. These dialogues are at least conducted at a civilized level; Frederick was, for his time, as far from being a tyrant as could be expected. Real ruthlessness only shows through in Schiller's Grand Inquisitor and duke of Alba. What was only glimpsed there is displayed in all its grim reality in Goethe's *Egmont*. As Alba marches his army into Brussels, the chilling atmosphere exactly matches Montesquieu's metaphor of the "silent cities" that define despotism.[22] When Alba invites Egmont to debate policies, he has already planned his arrest and death.

This as conceived now in Goethe's drama *Egmont*. By a strange coincidence he treats these same historical events independently within a year of Schiller. He comes at them at first sight from a rather different angle. Where *Don Carlos* draws on grand general concepts, *Egmont* grows out of a commitment to concrete local realities as preached by Herder, the mentor of Goethe's youth. Cultures and ages should, on the principles of Herder's historicism, be accepted in all their variety, not ranked according to a single— contemporary, Eurocentric—standard of human progress. Very much in this spirit, Goethe's early historical drama *Götz von Berlichingen* had celebrated German values against alien abstraction and centralization, setting German customary law against the imposition of Roman law, and the old imperial order against the local centers of rising princely power. The success of *Götz* created a taste and a market for more of the same, with cultural variety meaning just German realities. Goethe resisted the temptation to exploit national sentiment and instead applied the principle supranationally, to the Netherlands, where alien Spanish forces had oppressed a native culture in a structurally similar way. There is a marked contrast in execution too, between Schiller's relatively pallid Spanish court figures, a web of intriguers determining a distant action, and Goethe's colorful Dutch populace, with their flamboyant representative Egmont, seen on their home ground struggling to retain their old freedoms against foreign encroachment.

On the surface that is a more immediate realism, and it is easy to label Schiller's an Enlightenment and Goethe's a "historicist" drama. Yet ultimately their common ground, of ideas and metaphors, is more important than their differences. They both argue the case for trusting, rather than suppressing, a mature people. Every one of his compatriots, says Egmont, is "a rounded individual, a little king, firm, active, capable, faithful."[23] Posa likewise exhorts Philip to be "king over millions of kings," that is, over the mature minds across his empire.[24] The peace Philip aims to impose, Posa calls "the calm of the graveyard."[25] That is exactly what Goethe's Alba brings to the Netherlands, with his army and his reputation, all set to impose a preplanned reign of terror. The scene where Egmont is arriving to meet him and fall into his trap has the stillness of terrified expectation. Again, the dismissal of human potential by Schiller's Philip ("when you once know men as I know them") is echoed by Alba's repressive paternalistic dogma: the people must be "kept like children, guided for their own good . . . A people doesn't mature, doesn't become wise; a people remains always childish."[26] Behind the cross-echoes of Goethe's and Schiller's texts, Kant's argument for the involvement in society of citizens who have come of age can be clearly heard.

Schiller's appeal to the high principle of intellectual freedom and Goethe's defense of local liberties are wholly compatible. The two writers make common cause against political constriction and social stagnation, and against the oppression spawned by religious fanaticism. The historicist vision is not so much a rival of the Enlightenment as its convincing embodiment in time and place. Indeed, the two positively need each other if either is to be fully convincing, true to Kant's epigram: "Thoughts without content are empty, percepts without concepts are blind."[27] Bringing the two together to achieve effective communication is a central problem and task of the Enlightenment: principle remains pale, reality is potentially chaotic; abstractions somehow have to be shown informing cases. That could hardly have been done more effectively than in these two convergent tragedies, which lay bare power politics and call power itself to account.

Absolute power makes all debate unreal. Philip's tolerance in and beyond the audience scene will not save Posa from an all-seeing Inquisition, and Alba has brought Egmont's arrest warrant with him from Spain. Both dialogues are, with different degrees of political cynicism, mere shadow boxing. Yet Enlightenment debates with power can sometimes work. In Goethe's *Iphigenie auf Tauris* a ruler yields to moral suasion, and in Lessing's *Nathan der Weise* a Jew teaches Sultan Saladin tolerance in the midst of the Crusades. The question is, how convincing is such a softening of absolute power?

In both plays, sacrifice and its avoidance are central. Agamemnon's daughter Iphigenie has been rescued by Diana from a death on the altar that was to ensure the Greek army a fair wind for Troy. As the first foreigner ever to be spared slaughter on arrival in Tauris and as Diana's priestess there, she has persuaded King Thoas to suspend the practice. He now threatens to restore it unless she marries him (he acutely needs an heir). The first victims would be two captive Greeks, actually her brother Orest and his friend, whom Apollo has directed here to "bring back the sister," apparently the image of Diana from the temple at Tauris. In return he will lift the curse on Orest, who is being pursued by the Furies because he has murdered his mother, who had murdered his father, who had apparently sacrificed their daughter—the well-known unhappy-families story behind the Trojan War, and the continuation of a family curse that reaches back to Tantalus.

As in Euripides' *Iphigenia in Tauris*, the Greeks plan to escape with their booty, using trickery and the authority of the priestess. Unlike Euripides' Iphigenia, who has scruples only about killing the king, Goethe's Iphigenie is torn between obedience to her brother, the surviving head of the family, and a conscience that hesitates to steal from a hospitable people she has lived among for years. At the dramatic climax she confesses the escape plan to the king, placing their three lives in his hands.

The climax is truly dramatic because Thoas is an unknown quantity. Is he a barbarian who only "reformed" to please her and is now reverting to type when balked? Or was he more deeply affected—has he only been bluffing with his threats and is open to human appeal? This whole complex is Goethe's addition, dovetailed into the ancient story in order to try the chances of an ethical outcome. The outcome is in no way a foregone conclusion, as facile criticism has sometimes suggested (Thoas allegedly just Weimar man in antique costume). The real enormity of Iphigenie's risk comes home to her even as she performs her "unheard-of deed." Her moral new start is highlighted by that formula (*unerhörte Tat*, line 1892), which was used earlier of Atreus's atrocity, murdering his brother's sons and serving them up as a meal to their father. That was just one episode from the grisly family history with which Iphigenie has tried to warn Thoas off marrying her, a continuum of violence that the planned escape would perpetuate, and that she is consciously striving to break.

Thoas rises to the ethical challenge. The doubts about his real character, which have been left open by their early confrontation (act 1, scene 3) and by her interview with his first minister,[28] are resolved in the sharp exchanges of the climactic act 5, scene 2. The tyrant shows himself to be truly enlightened. He can even ironically point out that his behavior as a "barbarian" compares well with the string of enormities Iphigenie's forebears have committed.[29] Yet the snag remains that Orest seems required by a god to make off with Diana's image. Light now dawns on him too: Apollo meant not his sister-goddess, but Orest's own sister (lines 2113ff.)—a live woman, not an inert statue. And Iphigenie has in the meantime lifted the burden of guilt from her brother's soul by psychological means—the reward Apollo promised. Orest's reinterpretation hangs on the German use of the definite article to refer to a relative (*die Schwester*) instead of a possessive adjective (*deine* or *meine Schwester*). His insight, for which there was at most an undeveloped hint in Euripides,[30] transforms what had been a crude bargain with Apollo into a meaningful prescription. The god was testing human intelligence, not blind obedience: the question was not whether Orest would do as he was told, but whether he would think the god's instruction through. That makes an arbitrary ancient deity into a subtle, rational one.

If indeed deities are necessary at all. True, Orest would never have come to Tauris without Apollo's command—that much is a necessary part of the original story, as is Iphigenie's rescue by Diana from sacrifice at Aulis. These are the mythic preconditions of the plot. But within the action on stage, resolution is the work of human agents. Iphigenie's "unheard-of" moral deed goes against the apparent intentions of Apollo. From her unease at wronging the Taurians, she grows in confidence, overcomes some movingly portrayed moments of self-doubt in the face of male authority (Orest and his planner friend Pylades) until she achieves the maturity to act by her own lights—*Mündigkeit*. How much more difficult this is for a woman, Goethe makes empathetically clear. That it is dramatized as an aim for a woman at all is already an ethical advance even on Kant, who lumps "the whole of the fairer sex" together with that portion of humanity the guardians have intimidated into passivity, and who at best thinks women talkative rather than rational.[31]

With its triumphant outcome, *Iphigenie* is substantively a feminist play, the first since Sophocles' *Antigone*. At the climax, Iphigenie twice challenges the gods to live up to her conception of them, first when she struggles to believe they will prove benevolent, something her family's whole history makes highly unlikely ("Rescue me, and save the image of you in my soul"), and a second time at the moment of decisive action ("If you are truthful as you are reputed / Then show it through your help, and glorify / The truth through me").[32] The logical point eludes her that only benevolent gods would worry about their repute with humans anyway. That is a measure of the gap between her faith and a grimmer possible reality.

If indeed the gods are a reality. It would be going too far to read the second of those two passages ontologically, as meaning "If you truly *are*, as you are reputed." Yet the play's message comes close to that secularizing sense. In Goethe's version no deus or dea ex machina intervenes, in the way Athena helps Euripides' Greeks to escape from the barbarians. In Goethe's play Diana and Apollo are at best imagined presences, projections of the characters' experience and wishes, and the source of their divergent ethics. Thoas is conventional and conservative, Orest an embittered pessimist because much battered by fate, Pylades an incorrigible optimist who thinks the gods will help those who help themselves. Iphigenie's is ethically the most advanced position, and the most complex, in that she recognizes (in the doubts and prayer of act 4, scene 5) the evidence for a dark universe, yet hopes against hope that there is a benevolent divine order. She makes that belief come true, or at least makes it work in practice, by risking everything on it and carrying the other characters along with her. That she must first struggle to convince herself makes more impressive drama than any presentation of enlightened ideals by a preacher with no problems. Too ideal a character, as Kant saw, would risk discrediting by its implausibility the values that it was meant to represent.[33]

The drama's happy outcome sticks in the craw of critics who think only tragic endings can be serious. Goethe's thinking was not so simplistic. Obviously there are situations that would not be resolved and human types—a psychopath, a concentration camp commandant—whose ruthlessness would not be moved by moral honesty. Such situations and characters had indeed been explored by earlier German dramatists in the martyr tragedies of the Baroque, especially those of Daniel Casper von Lohenstein.[34] But they are not the only situations or people that matter.[35] As Goethe said of political conflict, the poet should immerse himself in the positions of opposed parties, and if conciliation proves impossible, resolve on a tragic ending[36]—as he emphatically does in *Egmont*. But only if. Tragedy is not necessarily necessary.

The tyrant in Lessing's *Nathan der Weise* is Sultan Saladin. When the play opens he has just massacred nineteen captive Templars, but the spotlight falls, for plot reasons, on the one he has spared because he reminded the sultan of his own long-lost brother. This is the first clue to an intricate, not to say far-fetched, history that will finally unite the Muslim and Christian characters as members of one family—an allegory of the human family divided by religious fanaticism. Forbidden by his employer, the duke of Brunswick, to continue a theological controversy with the chief pastor of Hamburg, Lessing took to his "old pulpit the theater." In the process he immensely broadened the theological theme to show "the disadvantages of revealed religion for mankind, nowhere clearer to a rational man than at the time of the crusades."[37]

The "disadvantages" are plain: Saladin's atrocity, the Crusaders' resumption of war after a truce, the Christian Patriarch's plot to assassinate Saladin, and his obsessively repeated demand that the Jew Nathan be sent to the stake for adopting a Christian orphan, however benevolent this action was: "No matter, the Jew gets burnt" (act 4, scene 2)—surely, given Lessing's familiarity with Shakespeare, a response to Shylock's insistence on the "bond" that guarantees his pound of Antonio's flesh in *The Merchant of Venice.*

How, in all this, can enlightenment insert the thin end of its wedge? The discovery of family relatedness across the frontiers of fanaticism finally resolves all, though at the risk that the allegory will be read literally and tolerance will appear to depend—as in the real world it overwhelmingly does—on concrete community and blood ties rather than a wider humanity. Nathan's rhetorical question, "Are Jew and Christian sooner Jew and Christian / Than men?" (act 2, scene 5), heartwarming though it is to all good liberals, gets a dusty answer from the hard facts of religious upbringings and ethnic traditions. And this is just the time Herder was arguing against Enlightenment universalism and for the indefeasible value of cultural difference.

A breakthrough does come, through a real enough material cause. Saladin needs money for the new campaign. Why not scare money out of the rich Jew? The plain soldier-sultan is uneasy at this plan of his sister's. Even less tyrannical is the way he then presses Nathan not for his money but for his wisdom: which of the three faiths has the best reasons in its favor? The reputedly wise Nathan will surely not have stayed where the chance of birth set him down? Yet will Saladin really, as he claims, accept Nathan's reasons, to the point of changing his own religion (act 3, scene 5)? Nathan wonders (and so do we) why the ruler is consulting the thinker at all, and whether it is some kind of trap. Read as a further allegory of Lessing's own time, the scene shows eighteenth-century Germany's productive and intelligent middle class presenting power with the fruits of its two activities, commerce and reflection. More simply, dramatic logic is taking a back seat to Enlightenment purposes, concentrated in a grand set piece at this structural midpoint of the play, as they are in Schiller's *Don Carlos.*

Nathan answers Saladin's question with a parable that relativizes the absolute claims of all three religions and offers a rational alternative to conflict. A ring that makes a ruler pleasing in the sight of God and men has been passed down to the favorite son in every generation, until one father weakly promises it to each of his three sons and has to save the situation by having copies made. The true ring cannot be distinguished, any more than can "for us now" (Nathan here decodes his own fable) the true religion.[38] Like Posa in the audience scene, Nathan is aware of a vast potential audience beyond. Posa appeals to the imagined "thousands who are taking part / In this great hour" (act 3, scene 10), and when Saladin urges, "Come, then, speak! Not a soul else can hear us," Nathan replies "Would that the whole world could" (act 3, scene 7).

So the Saladin we see is apparently no tyrant. Yet this is the man who massacred the other nineteen prisoners. It seems we are meant to forget that, were it not that in the play's very last lines Saladin reminds us of it himself, with a jest at his rediscovered nephew's expense: "Look at the villain! / He knew something of it, and could try / To make me his murderer! Just you wait!" It is hard to believe one's ears at such tastelessness, in character and author. The only explanation is that potential tragedy has now collapsed into comedy, its serious issues papered over by a conventional happy ending. As part of the same drift, the fanatical Patriarch has become a grotesque caricature whose "No matter, the Jew gets burnt" by dint of repetition ends up as a near-comic refrain.

Atrocity is not so easily dissolved in smiles. Nor is it canceled out by even the most heroic moral response, as when Nathan recalls how his wife and seven sons were massacred by Christians and he still managed to rise above hatred and despair and take in the orphaned daughter of a Christian friend (act 4, scene 7). Only an insensitive audience could accept the play's comedic turn without mental reservation, especially with hindsight on the atrocities of a twentieth-century German tyranny more total than anything the Enlightenment could have conceived. Do I only imagine a particular hush in a German theater when these passages are spoken? They bespeak the central failure of the German Enlightenment and the frustration of Goethe's wish that Lessing's parable might "remind the German public for all time that it is called upon not just to watch, but to listen and to hear. May the divine sentiment of tolerance and mercy expressed in it remain a value sacred to the nation."[39]

CHAPTER 5

Cosmopolitan Quandaries:
Among Savages, Far and Near

Only the mind that thinks for itself and has explored its relation to the
manifold things around it achieves human fulfillment.
—Georg Forster, *Ansichten vom Niederrhein*

COSMOS

Forster's words make explicit what Kant's theory of knowledge left unsaid. Kant showed that the world was in principle ours, because constituted for us by our distinctive human organs of sense and understanding.
To make it fully ours in practice meant exploring it and getting to know it
in detail. Kant did it by intensive study, never leaving Königsberg. Georg
Forster did it extensively, as few in his time could: barely twenty, he had
encompassed the globe.

In 1773 his father, Johann Reinhold Forster, was hired as replacement for
the celebrated Joseph Banks, who had been the scientist on Captain Cook's
first circumnavigation. Banks pulled out from Cook's second voyage at the
last minute when his requirements of extra space on board (he planned to
bring a team of thirteen) were not met. Forster *père* had a good enough name
among English scientists to be taken on, but not much clout with anyone
else, including the admiralty, and he was hard up. Beggars can't be choos-
ers, and the two stopgap Germans had to make do with the ship's smallest
cabins, which were regularly flooded in high seas. Georg's health was per-
manently damaged by the three-year voyage.

Taking him along was not just a family convenience. He was something
of an intellectual prodigy and would play a full part in collecting and re-
cording the flora and fauna of the South Seas. He made fine drawings, later
colored in, of plant, fish, and bird specimens.[1] He also had great linguistic

and stylistic flair. On an earlier joint journey when he was just thirteen to the Volga region on behalf of the Russian crown, he had learned the language sufficiently to translate Lomonosov's history of Russia into English. He would make some sense of the language patterns of the Pacific islands. More important, his sophisticated grasp of English gave him the opportunity that first made his name as a writer. There had been an understanding that his father would compose the official account of the voyage; but the admiralty, under its First Lord, the Earl of Sandwich, rejected Johann Reinhold's initial drafts and reneged on the agreement, which allegedly also blocked any independent account the elder Forster might write. Georg was not bound by any agreement and wrote one in his father's place. *A Voyage round the World* is a seven-hundred-page text in impeccable eighteenth-century English, something his father could never have managed, as his preserved drafts show.[2] Certainly Georg used Reinhold's diaries, but, as he insisted when charged with merely lending his name to an account written by his father, he was the work's true author—"a youth scarcely twenty years of age,"[3] perhaps, yet fully mature in both his style and his substantive reflections. Here was *Mündigkeit* indeed.

Georg's reflections included a critical review of what was needed if reports of exploration were to extend knowledge, which earlier travelers' tales and the theories built on them could not reliably do. Credulity and arbitrary selectivity had in more recent times been replaced by demands for "a simple collection of facts," but this reduction had resulted only in "a confused heap of disjointed limbs which no art could render into a whole." What was needed, Forster argues in his preface, was the "penetration" to combine facts into a general view that would serve as a "thread of Ariadne" (that familiar eighteenth-century metaphor again) to lead through the labyrinth of empirical observations. The observer must know what he set out to look for, and his audience must then be clear about his angle of vision and the associated emotions, for "it was necessary for every reader to know the color of the glass through which I looked" (that other metaphor of the epistemologically aware).[4]

The color of the glass might not matter in the collecting of natural history specimens, at least not until they had begun to generate a coherent evolutionary theory, of which in Forster's time there were as yet only inklings. But he was also observing and drawing conclusions about mankind and society, about the barely known peoples and society of the Pacific islands, about the miniature society on board the *Resolution*, and about the relationship between the two groups, natives and Europeans—both their practical interactions and their relative positions in human development.

Narratives of exploration, Reinhold wrote in the English prospectus, aim to broaden knowledge, remove prejudice, and generally refine humanity. That classic Enlightenment principle was the hope and confidence of the Forsters when they set out. Georg's preface lauds the uniquely enlightened British nation's commitment to science. The Royal Society had persuaded George III to send Captain Cook on his first expedition, to observe the transit of Venus;[5] and Cook's success in finding new territories must have aroused an "enthusiasm for extending the sciences of experience" (*Erfahrungswissenschaften*),[6] or Cook would not have taken scientists on this second voyage at all. Yet the behavior of the *Resolution*'s crew was often flatly unenlightened, indeed positively anti-Enlightenment, for despite Cook's orders they repeatedly thwarted the scientists' work, "slily and enviously" killing a collection of live specimens and deliberately misleading the Forsters about locations on the chart.[7] Georg lets off steam in a footnote: "It may seem extraordinary that men of science, sent out in a ship belonging to the most enlightened nation in the world, should be cramped and deprived of the means of pursuing knowledge, in a manner which would only become a set of barbarians."[8] The whole lengthy footnote is missing from the German translation, which Forster coauthored. Presumably he wanted to shame an English readership, but not to denigrate semi-enlightened England in the eyes of a far less enlightened Germany.

Events after periodic landfalls cast an even deeper shadow over enlightenment. If two German scientists were unacceptably foreign bodies to the British crew, native peoples were even less to be respected, and certainly not to be trusted. Accounts by earlier explorers of unprovoked cruelty and cannibalism abounded, cutting starkly across the notion of the noble savage in his paradisal surroundings. Forster wrestles with the contradiction. He is moved by the natives' friendliness and hospitality, by the welcome Cook receives among people who remember him from his first voyage, by presents the natives give in no expectation of a return, and by many other signs of "the excellence of the human heart in its simple state."[9] But the women of the islands make themselves too readily available to the sailors for Georg's somewhat preachy morality. More important, some of the natives cannot resist petty pilfering. Yet were not European objects a powerful new temptation? And was it in any case right to shoot at a native for trying to steal a jacket, or for a mere gesture of disrespect or defiance?[10] There might be rascals among the natives, but for every one among them there would be fifty in Europe.[11] On several occasions when there has been a violent overreaction by the visitors, the islanders allow themselves to be reconciled. This, together with the way they have let pass many chances to

attack the sailors on shore, persuades Georg that they harbor no inherent
ill will. Repeatedly he sees how intercultural misunderstanding or tactlessness on the part of the Europeans has led to a hasty response that incenses
the islanders, whereupon a chain reaction ensues. On one terrible occasion
things get really out of hand, again over the stealing of a jacket. The party
involved, from the *Resolution*'s sister ship *Adventure*, fire on the natives
until their ammunition is exhausted. That leaves them helpless against attack; they are killed and eaten. Forster explains the European officer's excessive response: "Mr. Rowe, the unfortunate youth who had the command of
this boat, combined with many liberal sentiments the prejudices of a naval
education, which induced him to look upon all the natives of the South Sea
with contempt, and to assume that kind of right over them, with which the
Spaniards, in more barbarous ages, disposed of the lives of the American
Indians."[12] Had there been no advance on those barbarous ages? The English crew were men desensitized by their hard way of life, some of them
violent criminals who had enlisted as an alternative to imprisonment. They
showed "a horrid eagerness" to fire, upon the slightest pretense.[13] Cook
gave orders to use tolerance and restraint toward the islanders. The gross
disobedience of some officers and men was a measure of ingrained European
prejudice. On which side were the real savages? Tellingly, at one point Forster slips from the usage "they" for natives and "we" for Europeans and uses
a distancing "their" and "them" for his fellow whites. There were of course
"a few" on board "who had too great an affection for all their brethren to
desire their destruction."[14] The split between enlightenment and barbarity runs through Forster's narrative and also through the ship, which was a
floating microcosm of eighteenth-century Europe.

A ship is indeed essentially a small despotic state,[15] but James Cook
was not the kind of despot so many captains of the day were. Some of the
officers who served under him on the *Resolution* thought his discipline too
soft.[16] Yet he brought his crew through three years of hardship and danger
in often unknown waters, twice sailing deep into the Antarctic Circle, with
minimal trouble and the loss of only four lives. As with his first circumnavigation, he chose for the voyage an unpretentious collier of the kind he had
spent his early years in, sailing around the coasts of Britain. It was "a dull
sailor,"[17] but well suited to its purpose. Cook had come up through a hard
and unglamorous school where, rather than following the accepted wisdom,
he had developed his craft through reflection and native wit, *Nachdenken
und Scharfsinn*.[18] That was the Enlightenment model of intellectual independence applied to a very practical occupation. The epigraph to Forster's
essay on Cook is the Royal Society's motto, *Nullius in verba*: trust nobody's

words, see for yourself. Cook was a good judge of men,[19] and he was loved by his crew. He took measures for their health of a kind unknown in other ships of the day. Their clothes had to be regularly washed and the between-deck spaces fumigated. Their diet included sauerkraut (*Resolution* set out with sixty barrels of it), and Cook overcame first the officers' and then the men's repugnance not by compulsion but by eating the unfamiliar stuff himself. It saved them from the seaman's scourge of scurvy. But he was also concerned for the welfare of the native peoples, preventing sailors with syphilis from going ashore.[20] He was an enlightened ruler of his precarious small state, and on the larger scale an Enlightenment man in his passion for extending knowledge. He had the deep impulse of the true explorer, at the greatest possible remove from Enlightenment armchairs. It led him to go close in to every shore in a way his predecessors had been chary of doing, inching forward with a sounding lead over uncertain depths at constant risk of irreversible disaster. Thanks to Cook's three great voyages in ten years, the geographical world became fully known in outline and much of it charted in detail, a nice parallel to the three great Critiques in ten years with which Kant explored the world of the human mind. That remains true even allowing for the more limited success and final tragedy of the third voyage, when Cook was in declining health and losing his grip. It is an intriguing thought that Cook, in his early sailing years on the Baltic run, would have come within hailing distance of Kant in Königsberg.[21] Cook's was literally an *erfahrene Welt*—a world known by the experience of travel.[22]

Cook is the central figure in Forster's idea of an enlightened Europe, far more significant than the people he more than once dismissively refers to as indoor philosophers. He contrasts Britain's high-minded exploration in the cause of knowledge with Spain's exploitation of the Americas for profit. But he knew that Cook too was opening up the world for colonization and trade. On his first voyage Cook had claimed New Zealand and Australia for the crown. Second time out he was looking for a southern continent that might one day be settled, especially since the American colonies were in the process of being lost. Forster concludes after the voyage that it is now determined for all time that no southern continent exists, just as he believes Cook's earlier northern voyage proved finally that there was no northwest passage. Cook himself kept an open mind about a southern continent, but even if it existed, the ice masses he had met with made it unapproachable. Forster looks at discovered lands with an eye to their potential as future colonies.[23] He hopes that, should it come to it, the natives will be treated humanely as brothers. It seems unlikely, given the scenes he has witnessed and what he knows of the way Europeans treat Africans, to whom they should be as fathers to the still childlike natives.[24] (He makes no reference to the Atlantic triangle of the slave trade.) Sometimes he wishes the Pacific peoples had never been disturbed, and in the process corrupted and made objects of violence. At other moments it seems an inevitable development, and even desirable that the entire world should be populated with "civilized inhabitants": this in an essay on the Botany Bay settlement, where he optimistically argues that there is no reason colonists and natives need endanger each other. In the vast Australian continent, a few aborigines can surely find alternative living space[25]—although he elsewhere anticipates the need to quell the barbarians by force. He is not above complaining at the unreliable quality of the musket flints that unscrupulous manufacturers have supplied the forces with.[26] Atrocities (*Schandtaten*) there may already have been, but the final outcome will justify the means.[27]

These oscillations in Forster's thinking show up real fault lines in the Enlightenment outlook: the liberal principles he has imbibed clash with the realities he observes and the course of events he foresees. He has no Rousseauian doubts about the value of European civilization, in which for him the wisdom of past ages has been accumulated. His observations during the great voyage have dispelled the notion of an innocent Golden Age of mankind, in harmony with nature. Rousseau is associated by implication with an "orang-outang" philosophy.[28] Nor, despite his admiration for Herder, does Forster have any sense of the independent value of all cultures, which meant that no one of them should look down on another as inferior. The problem remains that the processes of contact and transfer between a "morally superior" Europe and the undeveloped world are not governed by the superior standards that Europe claims.[29] Europeans "have humanity so often on their lips and so seldom in their hearts."[30]

That is at root a distinction between theory and practice, between enlightened idealism and every kind of all-too-human *Realpolitik*. But Forster goes further and increasingly sees rationality itself as a problem. It can amount to narrow dogmatism if not broadened by empirical observation, becoming a new despotism if not softened by feeling.[31] Forster's youthful voyage and his reverence for Cook are speaking when he says that our whole judgment of reality rests on our knowledge of the Earth, on the material accessible to our senses[32]—"For in the end you really have no more than what comes in through these two small openings of the pupils and excites the vibrations of the brain! In no other way but *this* do we take in the world and its essence. The miserable twenty-four *signs* [the letters of the German alphabet] aren't enough; the *presence* of things and their immediate *effect* is something quite different."[33] Having once cast the net of experience as wide as the globe, Forster is for all forms of variety against all kinds of constricting systems, especially that of any specialized guild.[34] He actually polemicizes against Kant over an anthropological problem—the single or plural origin of the human race—accusing him of arguing theoretically, beyond the evidence.[35] In fact, the two were largely in agreement about the relation of evidence to reflection. The young Forster's preface to *Voyage* had already argued that you must have an idea of what you are looking for before you begin looking, and the mature man repeats it as the prerequisite of a "new anthropology": "To observe purposefully you have to approach the observing process with the final purposes of the observation in mind and know the points that are really at issue."[36] That was exactly Kant's position. A grasp of what he calls "general knowledge" (which, paradoxically, had to be acquired at home in one's own particular place) had to precede the knowledge of other places (which Kant counterintuitively calls "local knowledge") if anthropology was to be a science and not just "fragmentary gropings about." That priority meant that Kant's native Königsberg was enough for him as a methodological basis![37] Yet Forster associates Kant with a "despotism in thinking," and quotes half approvingly Herder's abuse of Kant as the "arch sophist and arch scholastic" of the century.[38] Forster's fears about reason, at least as far as Kant is concerned, surely stem from a confusion between reasoning as a *method* and rational conclusions as *doctrine*—which is exactly what Kant distinguished as "doing philosophy" (*Philosophieren*) as against "holding set tenets" (*Philosophie*).[39] Forster misunderstands Kant's phrase "the general reason" (*allgemeine Vernunft*), as if it were something that oppressively replaced any single individual's reason (*subjektive Vernunft*), whereas for Kant the term meant precisely the process and product of open debate between single reasoning individuals.[40]

The empiricist's problem, even once he has a workable methodology, is the sheer vastness of physical reality. When and how can its elements be made graspably coherent? Goethe's Faust aspires to grasp what holds the world together—"dass ich erkenne, was die Welt / Im Innersten zusammenhält"—but he never can. Goethe later wrote that the world as envisaged by the great empiricist Francis Bacon is boundless, while human capacities are narrowly bounded: "Before one can arrive, through even such induction as Bacon praises, at a final simplification, life is already vanishing and one's powers are consumed."[41] (Goethe's solution was to postulate "primal phenomena"—*Urphänomene*—which were both an essence of and a limit to empirical observation.) Although, or perhaps rather because, the young Forster had seen so much of the world and gained a live sense of the immensity of all the places, races, and species on the planet, and of everything that

still remained to be explored, he can sound not just awestruck but almost
desperate in the face of nature's inexhaustible richness.[42] Nature is still, as
a residue of Forster's early intense piety, an almost religious revelation. He
sets empiricism in the context of human transience and humility at the
close of the *Voyage* in an envoi taken from Petrarch:

> Vedi insieme l'uno e l'altro polo,
> Le stelle vaghe e lor viaggio torto;
> E vedi, 'l veder nostro quanto e corto.
> (Now you see the one pole and the other,
> The stars that wander in their winding courses,
> And see that all our seeing ah! how short is.)[43]

POLIS

Forster's account of the circumnavigation, in its range and detail, was a
fundamental new start to anthropology and to much else. It inspired the
travels of the great explorer and polymath Alexander von Humboldt, whose
example in turn inspired Charles Darwin—a significant German-English
tradition. Thus in the end it contributed to the fundamental relocation of
mankind in our world. Forster's book made him an academic celebrity all
across Europe, and that was where he now had to seek his fortune, and his
father's. The admiralty's hostility had spoiled any chance of the appoint-
ments in Britain that had been part of the package agreed when father and
son signed up for the voyage. Georg was welcomed everywhere else—Göttingen, Berlin, Vienna, Prague—but nowhere did golden opportunities follow, only mediocre university positions, frustrating, underpaid, and under-
resourced, first in Cassel, then in remote Polish Vilna, which seemed at first
an exciting prospect but proved intellectually and socially arid. And Forster
was contracted to stay there for eight years. Luckily he was rescued by the
invitation to join a Russian voyage of exploration. The Russians dissolved
his Polish contract, paid his Vilna debts, and, although the planned voyage
then came to nothing, let him keep the substantial advance. It was the only
act of generous patronage he ever encountered. Meanwhile he found another post, as university librarian in the Rhineland city of Mainz, which in
financial and all other respects was as unrewarding as the others. Yet it was
unexpectedly as decisive in shaping his maturity as sailing with Cook had
been for his youth. For in 1792 a French revolutionary army under Custine
captured Mainz, and Forster found himself having to decide where and how

far his principles should lead him. The liberal Enlightenment intellectual was thrown into a test of practical politics.

Forster's writing was at least implicitly political from the start, as witness his comments on colonies. At ports of call early in the world voyage, he notes the oppressive local economic and social systems. In the Pacific communities he sees samples of social and political evolution—the way peoples organize themselves, the flaws that show in the island idylls, the workings of warlike ambition, the formation of elites, the deplorable influence of priests, a fat and idle chief who resembles the "privileged parasites" back home.[44] Forster speculates on future developments, even revolution. Natural phenomena too serve political reflection. Dolphins hunting down flying fish prompt the rhetorical question, "What empire is not like a tumultuous ocean, where the great in all the pomp and magnificence of power continually persecute and contrive the destruction of the defenceless?"[45]

Political observation becomes more specific and intense in Forster's very different second book, *Ansichten vom Niederrhein*—literally "views of," but also "considered views from" the Lower Rhine. After his three years on the world's oceans, the three months of 1790 spent following the final course of the Rhine through North Germany, Belgium, and Holland seemed tame enough. But Europe was stirring. The French Revolution was under way, as yet in an orderly and nonviolent form. Meanwhile there were upheavals and violent conflict in Belgium. Unlike those in France, they did not spring directly from Enlightenment ideas. On the contrary, the attempts at reasonable and overdue reform undertaken by Joseph II in distant Vienna were resisted by local people out of superstition and conservative habit. The clergy, intent on preserving their privileges and influence, stirred up popular resistance to changes, very much in the way Kant foresaw would happen to a more enlightened guardian—namely, that when a public is accustomed to the yoke of dependence, its conservative guardians will manage to turn it against a maverick among their number who wishes to introduce reforms.[46] Joseph had tried to break the power monopoly of the church and established custom. His high-handed, absolutist way of going about enlightened change, his desire to sweep away practically all the old ways and start afresh, was deeply disturbing to a people who were just as conservative as their guardians. Forster traces the partisan and personal infighting in the Belgian cities he passes through in all its complex and sometimes confusing detail. What is clear is that reason does not operate easily on reality. Reason means moderation, the balancing of arguments, a readiness by both sides to compromise. This is the only refuge from violence. But how can reason get a purchase on the passions?[47] And if one party's claim to reason conflicts with another's, who is to be the higher impartial judge? Will the issue not necessarily be settled by sheer force? That is how polities and politics originally began. There was and still is no rational social contract: "Everywhere the arrogance of the more powerful wrests sacrifices from the weaker such as no human being is entitled to demand of another."[48] Human society is as brutal as the world of the dolphins and their quarry. These are practical objections to Kant's model of an open society of free debate. And yet, and yet: there *is* a standard of truth and rightness by which the millennial history of humankind is implicitly judged: "Reason's claims on behalf of human rights are eternal, they are strengthened rather than weakened by the violence that shouts them down. After a thousand and ten thousand victories of predatory power, a true and lasting peace will return only when every usurpation has been checked and all human beings have entered into their rights."[49] That is Enlightenment idealism, bloody but unbowed. It is in harmony with Kant's repeated insistence that "reality" is no argument against the rightness of reason, merely an aberration from reason—and an argument for reason's necessity.

Moreover, there is light not just at the end of the tunnel, but at a few points in the here and now. After the brutal chaos of Belgian politics, Holland appears as an almost ideal state, at all events a state where human fulfillment and its practical consequence of general prosperity are plain to see. The Dutch may be stolid and unexciting, but they have strong civic virtues: moral principles, a feeling for freedom, respect for public opinion, self-confidence.[50] The causal links between rationality, freedom, industry, and well-being are a telling, down-to-earth argument for Enlightenment against the cliché that it is all just theory, out of touch with reality. Here again Forster is in harmony with Kant, author of an essay attacking "The Commonplace Saying 'That May Be Right in Theory, but It Won't Do in Practice.'" In this very concrete sense Forster can say that "the first necessity of the state is to enlighten people's ideas . . . , for only in this way can the citizens' interests be rightly judged."[51] Forster's friend Lichtenberg defined Enlightenment as consisting in "the right ideas of our essential needs."[52]

Already Forster is being drawn into that central dispute between ideas and reality, Enlightenment hope and historical gloom. Issues were being worked out in the Low Countries in a way that was not possible in a country as tightly controlled and awkwardly fragmented as absolutist Germany—worked out concretely, that is, in another land, before the eyes of a detached foreign visitor, even though he was physically in their midst and had to be careful to wear the right color cockade in the right town to keep himself and his companion safe from attack. (The companion, incidentally, was that same twenty-five-year-old Alexander von Humboldt who was to draw inspiration for his career of exploration and scientific investigation from Forster's example.) The year 1790 was a tranquil time-out in Forster's life. The Russians' money gave him a brief freedom before he took up his new post at Mainz. There was nothing to suggest that, in this not obviously significant town, he would soon be in the thick of a far greater political turmoil.

That was as much a stroke of chance as circumnavigating the world had been, and it was ultimately the German princes' doing. In 1792 they invaded France, aiming to reverse a revolution that was "unjust and illegal in its principles, horrible in its methods, and disastrous in its effects," and to restore Louis XVI to the throne. They threatened Paris with "an awesome and terrible justice." The French people, so this manifesto of the Duke of Brunswick's ran on, "are sighing for the moment when they will be delivered from the yoke under which they are bowed down."[53] Of the earlier yoke from which the French people had been freed, his lordship showed no awareness. The émigré aristocrats, who had swarmed like locusts (Forster's own image) into the Rhineland states,[54] assured their German hosts that a military campaign would be a walkover. On the contrary, the Brunswick manifesto was calculated to stiffen French resistance, of which the famous artillery battle at Valmy became emblematic. Forster called it the day the French republic was both founded and saved.[55]

When the citizen army drove the Germans back, endless rain and mud made their retreat a fiasco, graphically described in Goethe's retrospective *Campagne in France* of 1822 (he was there accompanying his employer, Duke Carl August of Weimar). But it was no good Brunswick pressing Goethe to testify that the elements, not the enemy, had caused the defeat.[56] Goethe was already clear at the time that the invasion was "one of the most unfortunate enterprises in the annals of the world."[57] He claims to have told onlookers at the Valmy engagement that "from here and today a new epoch in world history begins, and you can say you were present at it."[58]

The French under General Custine followed up the German humiliation, moving on into the Rhineland. Were they coming as conquerors or as liberators? Officially they were bringing the ideas of their Revolution. Custine promised they would never give Mainz up: with luck they would occupy the whole length of the Rhine, creating a chain of republics from Holland to Switzerland.[59] The Rhine would be France's border, no longer Germany's river. It was a chance for Germans, at least of this region, to be liberated from the old petty princedoms. If on the other hand they opposed the French, they were implicitly asking for feudal absolutism back. It was a straightforward choice between the dark past and a seemingly bright future.

Forster himself nevertheless moved slowly, and his movement can be traced in all its step-by-step conscientiousness. He was no starry-eyed radical, certainly no revolutionary fanatic. Indeed, he believed Germany was not ripe for revolution and might still be changed by reform from above. A prince who made the laws work and protected the third estate need fear no revolution.[60] If only German rulers would learn a lesson (which Brunswick's arrogant attempt at regime change in France showed they so far had not), then the sight of the French volcano could still save Germany from its own earthquake.[61] Meanwhile Forster had no illusions about the imperfections of any political grouping. Still, since he had to make a choice, by mid-1792 the Jacobins got his cautious vote.[62] Even so, when Custine established a Jacobin Club in Mainz, Forster, together with "some other moderate people." hesitated to join until they saw good reason to do so.[63] These "non-enthusiasts who are determined to work for the better" did,[64] however, get drawn into committees in the university. Neutrality became more and more difficult; the best thing seemed to be to take sides but then act with firm moderate principles on the side one chose.[65] Custine offered Mainz either assimilation into France or the status of an independent republic.[66] The general mood in the town swung, now favoring the Revolution,[67] now reluctant to lose for good the living its tradesmen had been able to make by servicing the needs of the rich in this German "Sybaris."[68] True, the elector, along with the rest of the rich and powerful, had—naturally—fled, leaving "his people" to make out as best they could. So much for their ruler as a benevolent "father"! But if the French were to be defeated or were to withdraw, the old elite might soon be back. The priesthood, true to its profession, fostered a mood of contrition and fear among the populace.[69]

Then, in mid-December, the National Assembly in Paris declares all occupied lands free,[70] free also to choose incorporation into France. Forster is sucked further into the political whirlpool, made chairman of committees, president of the Jacobin Club, editor of a new newspaper *The People's Friend*. This at least is freedom of the press at last, in the city where Gutenberg invented printing.[71] Forster strives to report facts accurately, but inevitably the tone becomes propagandistic. He is the donkey everything gets loaded on. There has to be somebody, he argues, who will act and not just write.[72] If everyone claimed they were not cut out for political intrigue and the pressures of office, there would be nobody to get anything worthwhile done.[73] In the later terminology of Max Weber, he is accepting the ethics of responsibility (*Verantwortungsethik*), which lie beyond the easier ethics of ideological attitude (*Gesinnungsethik*). Inevitably he is now vilified across Germany for acting on the principles of which people approved when he merely wrote about them.[74] But acting now includes—as the most radical step of all—approving the execution of Louis XVI as a necessary security measure for the embattled republic, even as a step in accordance with natural law. Forster declares himself convinced by Barrère's arguments; he dismisses doubts about the legality of the regicide as juridical hairsplitting and sophistry.[75]

He is drawn ever further in when at the end of March he is sent to Paris as a representative of the Republic of Mainz in the National Assembly. On 30 March Mainz is accepted into the French Republic. The Revolution has entered the phase of its most intense internecine struggles, and Forster is in the eye of the storm. Metaphors of storm, hurricane, shipwreck, volcano and avalanche dominate his letters and the essays in which he struggles to make ethical and historical sense of the events he is witnessing. Can the historical and the ethical be reconciled? It is the same old story of idealism versus reality, more specifically of the Enlightenment's hopeful half-belief in a plan of nature for human fulfillment, individual and social. That hypothesis, we saw, was a secularized remake of the notion of a divine plan. Kant's luminous 1784 sketch for a *Universal History with a Cosmopolitan Intention* oscillated between "nature" and "providence" as the plan's author and guarantor. The argument was consciously provisional and above all pragmatic: the aim was to build people's morale and lead to enlightened commitment, whose success in turn would strengthen the belief in progress, which would in turn . . . and so on. The argument was precarious: too many evils in the foreground could undermine the higher hypothesis. The foreground facing Forster is grim: the Revolution now only fits a plan where it touches. While his public writings put a brave face on things, the frank view heard in his letters is that the French are nothing less than devils, heartless, deep in the sewers of self-interest and passion.[76] If there is rationality, it is a rationality devoid of feeling; a positive tyranny of reason threatens that will be worse than any other kind.[77] There is no freedom of thought; the only thing that counts in practice is the current shibboleth, the party label.[78] Forster regrets ever coming to Paris. He hangs on to the hope that good may yet come of evil, expressly calling it the "cosmopolitan" view.[79] Like Kant's, it is a shifting conception: now fate, now providence is the object of his shaky faith.[80] In that conception individuals are lost sight of; they are merely so many midges more or less in the swarm.[81] If people were to still take that overall view and believe their present suffering was justifiable, they desperately needed not to "lose our compass on the ocean of teleology, give ourselves up to blind chance, and accept that all ideas of justice and truth, goodness and greatness are mere figments of the imagination."[82] That would be not faith in fate, but fatalism; all ideas of purpose, morality, and human fulfillment would lose their meaning.[83]

These last are the public statements, from Forster's final writings before his premature death, aged barely forty, in Paris. He is putting the best interpretation he can on things, hiding the depth of his doubts, opposing the now Europe-wide disillusion with the French experiment, appealing to the long view, admitting human fallibility. The French are certainly not angels, but neither are they devils;[84] theirs is for once a revolution of self-sacrifice serving the future,[85] standing in its proper place in the sublime scheme of providence for the education of mankind.[86] He is pressing events into an ultimately rational traditional framework. Yet he is more convincing when they burst the framework in the violent metaphors of his letters, or in the published admission that the Revolution is "a natural phenomenon of a kind too rare for us to recognize its peculiar laws, it will not allow itself to be enclosed and determined in accordance with rules of reason, but must be left to run its course."[87]

This is the ultimate cosmopolitical insight. Not in the optimistic sense of Kant's vision of history as seen from the standpoint of a hopeful and active citizen of the world, but in the pessimistic sense that the two elements of the term are ultimately one. *Polis* is inescapably part of *cosmos*, and society is as much part of nature as the hunting dolphins—nature at its most raw and violent, with no guarantee of a benevolent plan for mankind.

CHAPTER 6

The Empty Heavens:
From Dogma to Ethics

to imagine excellence, and try to make it.
What does it say over the door of Heaven
But *homo fecit*?
—Richard Wilbur, "For the New Railway Station
in Rome," in *New and Collected Poems*

German Enlightenment thinking about religion achieves a decisive shift: against the dogmatic demand for belief it sets the priority of independent ethics, that is to say, an ethics not derived from divine authority but grounded in human potential, from which a conception of God may then incidentally be derived. Several major figures move in the same direction, seemingly independent of one another and across a range of literary and philosophical genres.

They have to be seen against a background of intolerance or grudging tolerance—of one sect by another, let alone of free thinkers. The Treaty of Westphalia that ended the Thirty Years' War in 1648 confirmed the uneasy compromise of a century earlier, the Peace of Augsburg of 1555, by which the religion of a population was to be the religion of its ruler. The only major difference was that Calvinism was now officially recognized. Where the many territories had been shared out between belligerent Lutherans and Catholics, there was now a tripartite distribution, an unholy trinity of intolerance, with the mutual hatred of Lutherans and Calvinists even stronger than the hatred of either for Catholicism. Friedrich von Logau back in the seventeenth century had put the obvious point: "Luth'rans, Calvinists and Papists, here we have beliefs all three. / But it leaves us wondering, where then is Christianity?"[1]

True, at least sectarianism now no longer "dictated a responsibility to exterminate the adherents of other confessions at whatever cost."[2] "At least" could just as well read "at most," for the best one can say about the tripartite situation is that, unlike in France or Britain, there was no single dominant agent of persecution—to that extent, the fragmented nature of Germany prevented the excesses of confessional strife seen in France. Yet, if there was little murderous violence, there was much intolerant practice, with expulsions of part-populations, refusals to concede recognition in the measure agreed, and plenty of verbal and physical abuse. (Jews remained the victims of intolerance, insofar as there were dogmatic energies left over to revile them.) Rulers, if not themselves actively involved, could only contribute to tolerance by keeping the parties from each other's throats. Anyone actually seeking to bridge the gap between them, as Melanchthon and Leibniz tried to do between Protestant sects and even between Protestantism and Catholicism at a European level—an unyielding Bossuet brought Leibniz's efforts to nought—was a prophet crying in the wilderness.

In a sense, the Protestant Reformation was the ancestor of the Enlightenment, as the first critical questioning of an absolute spiritual authority; but the Reformation had itself soon become a new dogmatism and begun to spawn further splinter dogmatisms, of which Calvinism was the first. Against all this fission and faction, the rational argument conducted by serious thinkers stands out for its sober linearity. But care was needed. To question or criticize the local orthodoxy in the early Enlightenment was to risk massive attack, dismissal from one's post, and even one's life. In 1690 Leipzig Christians drove Thomasius out of the university for his proto-Enlightenment teachings, and he fled to Halle, from which university, ironically, a quarter of a century later Christian Wolff was in turn driven out for showing that the Chinese had developed an adequate secular ethics—this at the very visible public ceremony of his demission of office as pro-vice-chancellor of the university. Local Pietists led by his outraged successor pressured the Prussian king, Frederick William I, to dismiss and exile Wolff on pain of death.[3] At least in fragmented Germany there was always somewhere else to go. One of Frederick the Great's first acts on acceding to the throne was to recall Wolff. Though his philosophy was by then no longer cutting-edge, his reinstatement was a moral triumph for Enlightenment freedoms.

It follows that the appearance of orthodox conformity elsewhere in Wolff's writings, or in the scientific work of the young Kant, cannot be taken at face value. Thinkers had to watch their backs against the raging of the still powerful Christian churches, their theologians and preachers. Wolff had been careful to state—vainly, as it turned out—that his ethics concerned only the happiness attainable within natural limits, not what "our theologians" ascribed to divine grace.[4] Only in the second half of the century did the climate slowly change and a greater openness become possible, despite the efforts of the bigoted. As the thin end of the wedge of rationality was pushed deeper, writers felt a growing confidence in a common project and in the intellectual solidarity they sensed around them.

Goethe, of course, never lacked a confidence all his own. In 1784, during work on *Iphigenie auf Tauris*, he wrote a poem on the nature of the divine, "Das Göttliche," which states the general possibility of human ethical progress (and, incidentally, the ultimate ground of Iphigenie's moral success). The poem is more about the human than the divine, starting with the exhortation, "Let Man be noble, helpful and good." Not on mere do-gooder grounds, but because this alone distinguishes humankind from all other known beings, as their physical constitution does not. (Goethe had recently discovered traces of an intermaxillary bone in the human skull, the seeming absence of which had been taken as proof of a gulf between men and animals.) The ethical potential of human beings is worth living up to. The poem then also salutes "the unknown higher beings" whose existence we only intuit (*ahnen*) and exhorts man to "be like them." Their conceivability sets a standard; if man rises to it, his example (*Beispiel*) will give us stronger reasons to believe in them, which may further strengthen the moral impulse.

Nature, unusually for Goethe, is declared to be unfeeling: sun, moon, and stars look down on good and evil indifferently. But within nature's iron laws, it is uniquely man who can do the impossible—distinguish, choose, judge, reward, and punish; heal and rescue; combine the elements of experience and make use of them. We revere the intuited gods as if they were human beings on a larger scale. In fact, a noble human being is not just vaguely an example of what they might be like, but more precisely a *pre-figuration*: "Let noble man be a model [*Vorbild*] / Of those intuited beings!"

The chronology becomes more precise as the poem develops. It is mankind that sets the standard. Human virtue comes first, and only then the imagining of gods. This may explain why Goethe left out, if he did, the line "Let man be like them." Though present in early manuscripts, it is missing from the manuscript collection on which the first printing of his poems in 1789 was based, and from all subsequent editions in his lifetime. Most editors assume a random oversight and restore it. Yet keeping or deleting the line clearly affects the logic. Not because, as has sometimes been objected, there would be a problem with striving to "be like" entities that are not known precisely—working to higher unknowns and desirable possibilities is the algebra of progress. Rather, if the line is omitted, man is not exhorted to live up to unknown beings already conceived of, but only to his own potential; he is to set himself moral standards and act on them. From this may flow a belief in transcendent beings. But the substance of these beings is then not at all "unknown" and only to be intuited; it is already composed of the human competences listed. The gods will have been made in our ethical image.

Whether they are then thought of as real barely matters in practice, as long as the world's problems prove malleable to those human competences. Belief will of course be subjectively decisive for the agent in a given situation, as it plainly is for Iphigenie. Even if the gods she prays to for help are projections of her own moral impulses, it is still her belief that gives her the courage to act on them. In any imagined action beyond the end of the play, its happy outcome will have strengthened her and the other characters' moral motivation; belief and action will go on reinforcing each other in a virtuous circle, and humankind can progress. Here is a structural parallel to Enlightenment thinking about history, where provisional belief in a benevolent plan of nature was meant to strengthen active commitment and bring about results that in happy hindsight would look like a plan.[5]

Thus, behind operative belief there was a psychology of belief. That was disturbing to the orthodox. Goethe's Christian friend Johann Heinrich Jacobi demanded absolute, unpsychologized belief, "a truth that is not *my* creation, but whose creature *I* am," a real *Gott*, not an essence of *das Göttliche* to be derived, at that, from human sources.[6] Goethe himself lived easily on the twin levels of immediate motivation and philosophical insight. Alongside his sophisticated analyses in poem and drama, he blithely invokes his own personal gods,[7] undoctrinal embodiments not just of ethical principles but of his sense of an individual destiny—of happiness, gratitude, security, of being at home in a beneficent world. And why should there not be this very positive projection? Revealed religions cannot claim a monopoly on spirituality, and the "revelations" they rely on are less trustworthily tangible than the immediate perceptions of the "very earthly being" Goethe declared himself to be, living out "the truth of the five senses."[8] Later in life he will explicitly reject all revelation in favor of getting on with earthly activity.[9] Already at this point he so completely trusts his perceptions that, as against Lavater's belief in the divine truth of the gospel, even an imagined "audible voice from heaven" would not make him believe "that a woman can give birth without a man, or that a dead man can be resurrected," any more than he could conceive "that water burns and fire extinguishes." Such ideas (here he turns key religious concepts against the orthodox believer) are "blasphemies against the great god and his revelation in nature."[10] This echoes Hume's position that miracles contradict our uniform experience,[11] but Goethe's visceral disbelief is balanced by an equally strong positive belief in an earthly revelation of what is surely Spinoza's *deus sive natura.*

The dual act of rejection and acceptance had already shaped two magnificent poems, "Prometheus" and "Ganymed." They are contrasting addresses to a deity, one to a Zeus in whom, in an odd mixture of ancient myth and Christian expectations, the young Prometheus once trusted as a ready help in troubles. Now disillusioned, he rejects Zeus and all his works—a heroic coming-of-age. Ganymed invokes an unnamed "all-loving father," implicitly the Zeus of the myth, but essentially a projection of the speaker's ecstatic experience of nature around him. These two opposed ideas of the same named god are not a contradiction, nor even a balance, but a sequence. "Prometheus" clears the ground of old transcendent illusions, and "Ganymed" expresses a new reverence for the world. Rejecting orthodoxy liberates feelings of gratitude and devotion more intense and eloquent than anything merely prescribed by a church. They are a kind of faith, though not yet a religion—compelling, not compulsory.

Goethe's Christian friends found it more difficult to tolerate his relaxed earthliness than he did to live with their anxious orthodoxy. Understandably so. For in an age when dissenters can no longer be conveniently burned at the stake, the orthodox party are the more threatened. They have an immense and complex structure of myths and dogmas to guard, like a seawall that can be breached at any point by doubt and criticism. The dissenter has only the patch of solid ground he stands on to defend. He has made a fresh start in earthly metaphysics, empirically and without transcendence.

Goethe is not out to convert his friends, though he does sometimes regret that they feel less at home in their skins and in the world than he does. Lavater lacks any "drop of independent feeling"; he has no sense that "the greatest joy is to dwell in oneself."[12] To Jacobi he writes, "God has cursed you with metaphysics but blessed me with physics"—that is, the scientific study of the world—"so that I may take pleasure in the contemplation of his works," for "when you say one can only *believe* in God, I tell you I set far more store by *seeing*, and when Spinoza speaks of a *scientia intuitiva . . .* his words give me the courage to devote my whole life to the observation of the things I have access to."[13] He is speaking not just as a poet, but from this point onward as an ambitiously wide-ranging empirical scientist too. From his highly visual poetry to a "seeing science" is a continuity, not a switch. A month later, once more to Jacobi, he again quotes Spinoza—"he doesn't prove the existence of God, existence *is* God"—says he prefers not to talk about metaphysics, and declares he can only recognize a higher being *in rebus singularibus* and is duly "seeking the divine *in herbis et lapidibus,*"[14] that is, collecting plants and chipping rocks. This is no longer a search for the deep principle that "holds the innermost world together" (*was die Welt / Im Innersten zusammenhält*), which was the first aspiration of Goethe's Faust, but rather a gathering of nature's manifold riches, akin to Faust's later alternative, the pursuit of cumulative experience. Science is concerned, in both senses, with grasping the real world, concerned with plenitude as well as precision. Also, for Goethe, with beauty—a leitmotif in later scientists from Georg Büchner to Darwin.[15]

Quoting Spinoza, the bogeyman of orthodoxy, was rebellion enough. So was Goethe's devotion to the observable world and a belief in its consistent reality, a faith "as vehemently earnest" as Lavater's Christian conviction.[16] This much assertiveness in a cordial but troubled friendship is the nearest Goethe comes to being polemical. Mostly he lets the believers down lightly, sometimes with a Christian allusion: "In my father's chemist's shop there are many remedies."[17] Forty years on he uses it again to reassure a correspondent from his youth who is now concerned for the aging poet's soul: "In our father's empire there are many provinces."[18] Tolerance, and the demand for tolerance, rest on a detached view of the phenomenon of belief.

Goethe's innate independence and spiritual resilience were more than a match for Lavater and Jacobi. The two had easier prey when they gratuitously harassed Moses Mendelssohn. In 1769 the religious enthusiast Lavater, further intoxicated by what he thought decisive new proofs of Christianity, challenged Mendelssohn publicly to convert from Judaism or declare his reasons for not doing so. Mendelssohn was in a cleft stick. If he failed to answer convincingly, his repute as a thinker was damaged; if he succeeded, he might be seen as attacking the dominant religion of the land. As a Jew his position in semi-enlightened Prussia was in any case precarious. In what can only be called racial laws, there were six classes of Jew with varying degrees of permission to reside, very few with full citizenship.[19] Mendelssohn was not one of these, for all his recognized distinction—recognized by the Prussian Academy, which proposed to make him a member. Frederick exercised a veto by not even replying to the proposal. With his usual equanimity, Mendelssohn said it was better to be recognized by the Academy and rejected by the king than the other way round.

Mendelssohn answered Lavater by declining to debate religion and reasserting his unshaken Jewish faith. He was not concerned to persuade and not prepared to be converted. Lavater's public challenge rebounded on him: his outrageous behavior was widely condemned, damaging such reputation as he had. He withdrew his demand—only to join some years later in a campaign against Mendelssohn pursued by Jacobi through assertions that Mendelssohn's friend Lessing, now deceased, had admitted in conversations with Jacobi to being a Spinozan pantheist. (Lessing was now dead, nobody else had been present at the conversations, and Jacobi on other evidence was not a reliable reporter.) The two Christians, self-styled admirers and earlier guests of Mendelssohn's, were joined by the obscure and obscurantist Hamann, and even on the margins by Herder. The stress of this second affair was thought at the time to have contributed to Mendelssohn's death in mid-controversy.

With these episodes we are on the edge of the Jewish Enlightenment in Prussia, the Haskalah, which is a distinct subject in itself,[20] concerning the inner-directed efforts of reformers within a tightly knit ethnic group that interlock with the age-old problem of the group's integration in the surrounding society. Both projects were made problematic by powerful traditions, of Jewish conservatism and gentile prejudice, although there were initiatives from outside the Jewish community, in particular Christian Wilhelm Dohm's historic essay "On the Civil Improvement of the Jews."[21] But unlike the central issues of the wider German Enlightenment, the question here was how Jews might become useful participant members of society, not how the divinity should be understood.

God understood as an anthropomorphic projection was a commonplace insight of the Enlightenment, most often used destructively as in Montesquieu's *mot* that if the triangles had a god, he would be bound to have three sides. Yet as "Das Göttliche" shows and *Iphigenie* illustrates, the insight can help construct a new ethics of human self-confidence. Lessing reaches a similar position by other routes. To Nathan's parable of the three indistinguishable rings, Saladin objects that religions surely *are* distinguishable, if only by their prescribed dress and food and drink. Yes, Nathan replies, but they are identical in their founding reasons. Each religion rests on reports of a revelation, and each trusts its own. Yet all human reporting is fallible, which for Hume was enough to explain away miracles. For Lessing it was "the nasty broad ditch" of historical tradition that he could not get across.[22] It had been dug deep in Hermann Samuel Reimarus's analysis of the gospel accounts, which Lessing himself published as allegedly a set of anonymous Fragments he had found in his Wolfenbüttel library. That started the dispute his ducal employer eventually forbade him to continue, which in turn generated *Nathan der Weise*.

Since the truth claims of religions are impossible to prove or decide between, the judge in Nathan's parable looks forward to a different test, by a wiser judge thousands of years hence, who will review the actions each ring has inspired. They will not prove any ring genuine, that is, will not find any one of the religions "true." The original ring may even have been lost, or perhaps the father chose to end its "tyranny," and all three may have been copies. But truth is no longer the issue. What will be tested is what effects a religion has had on believers' practice.[23] In a Christian phrase, "By their fruits ye shall know them" (Matthew 7:16 and 20). Conceivably, more than one faith might come out of the competition well. Whether losers would accept the adjudication is dubious—on form to date, it seems unlikely. For the brothers it is once again the subjective belief in a unique force that will have been psychologically crucial—even the original ring depended for its effect on being worn "in this confidence." But to the critical outside observer faith is a means, not an end. And it must be a means to good ends, as judged by humane social, even political, criteria: toleration, an end to fanaticism and conflict. Georg Forster asked not which was the genuine ring, nor even whether there was a genuine one at all, but whether there could not be fingers on which the ring did not fit, yet which were good, useful fingers.[24] Such pointedly practical questions implicitly rebutted Luther's doctrine of salvation by faith alone and for the individual alone, not by works nor through a beneficial effect on others.

Even if religious certainty were conceivable, it would still for Lessing be undesirable. In a scene much like Goethe's with a "voice from heaven," he imagines God offering him in one hand truth and in the other the impulse to pursue it, subject always to error. He would choose the second. Absolute truth is for God alone.[25] It would be dangerous for human beings, as is the illusion (it can never be more) of possessing it: "The possession of truth makes people settled, slothful, proud—." Lessing's sentence breaks off with a dash. Surely worse is to come: "opinionated, dogmatic, fanatical"? These would follow even and especially if the absolute truth really were guaranteed by God. Since that is what believers believe, the danger is real. Elsewhere Lessing writes that "not just error, but sectarian error, indeed sectarian truth make the misery of mankind."[26] Certainty is the definition and the weakness of "revealed" religions and the foundation for the intolerance of all monotheisms, as Hume pointed out.[27] Gibbon too illustrated the consequences of dogmatic certainty: the first Christian emperor, Constantine, abandoned Rome's traditional religious tolerance: "With the knowledge of truth, the Emperor imbibed the maxims of persecution."[28]

Intolerance has a potent logic flawed only (!) by that first premise of certainty. It can override morality, as when the Christian Patriarch justifies trying to assassinate Saladin because "villainy / In men's eyes is not villainy in God's" (act 1, scene 5). Kant had diagnosed such casuistry in his essay "On Diseases of the Mind": "The fanatic is really a madman who imagines he has a direct inspiration and a great familiarity with the powers of heaven. Human nature knows no more dangerous deception."[29]

To some, then and later, Lessing's suprasectarian vision and his critique of revealed religion have made him a heretic, even a dangerous atheist.[30] His writing on theology had begun with five vindications of well-known heretics, on the Enlightenment principle that a heretic was someone who thought for himself and wanted to see with his own eyes—the word "heresy" derives from the Greek for "choosing for oneself." What mattered was how sharp those eyes were.[31] That echoes Bossuet's condemnation of a heretic as "someone who has opinions of his own,"[32] but now approvingly. There was good German tradition here, in the Pietist Gottfried Arnold's "impartial" history of the church and its heretics[33]—a history that was "partial," it turns out, to the heretics. Christ was the ultimate example, attacked by the same methods that had since been used and reused against heretics, the people who asked uncomfortable questions. But what was the value of a faith that had not been tested?[34] Lessing for his part takes such testing as far as it can go, unable to continue living under one roof with the disturbing arguments of Reimarus. Publishing the Fragments was a psychological necessity as much as an act of Enlightened openness. He was "letting air into the fire in order to then extinguish it"—surely not the best method.[35] Opening up religion to rational discussion was dangerous in one of two ways. If reasoning failed to convince, Christianity was the loser; if Christianity could show it was close to rational positions, it could appear superfluous.

Yet Lessing believed he believed; he felt he was, and wanted to remain, a Christian. A late fragment captures his discomforts. The more powerful the arguments for Christianity claimed to be, the more he doubted; the more triumphal the arguments against it were, "the more inclined I was to preserve it at least in my heart."[36] That meant rescuing its essence, but also as much as he could of its substance. He had no problem distinguishing the original "religion of Christ" from the institutionalized "Christian religion,"[37] especially after his bitter conflict with the chief pastor of Hamburg, Johann Melchior Goeze. Yet there was more to Christianity than just Christ, most prominently its Bible, whose origin in fallible human reports—of Christ's teachings too, but these could be accepted on their rational value, not just on the evangelists' authority[38]—was that "nasty broad ditch."

Lessing tries finally to bridge the ditch with the metaphor of an "education of the human race" by God.[39] It has proceeded, on sound pedagogical principles, gradually. Rational truths too subtle for "young" mankind to achieve unaided were conveyed by revelation; successive "textbooks" taught mankind only what it was capable of grasping at each stage; the Old Testament established monotheism and told of earthly rewards and punishments, the more advanced New Testament introduced the notion of immortality and located reward in the afterlife; the process is still progressing, toward a "new eternal gospel," the "highest stages of enlightenment and purity," "the time of perfection, when man . . . will do good because it is good, not because arbitrary rewards are attached to it" (§§81, 85–86). Lessing finds hints of this in the "everlasting gospel" of Revelation 14:6 and in the twelfth-century mystic Joachim di Fiore, who preached (a bit too early for the divine educational scheme) a doctrine of three ages very like Lessing's own (§88–90).[40] Lessing thus ends, aptly enough, with one more heretic.

The treatise is a complex mixture. Its elements, including the education metaphor itself, have antecedents going back a long way,[41] but they are newly combined to bear on Lessing's situation. He plainly has one foot in the Enlightenment camp. A "plan for a general education of mankind" (§88) is roughly analogous to the "plan of nature" in Kant's scheme of history, and closer still to Schiller's thesis in the poem "The Artists" of 1789, that rational truths were contained for early mankind in the "advance revelation" (voraus geoffenbart, line 45) of natural beauty and artistic forms. The idea of an agency that speeds up human progress beyond what could be achieved in prerational ages is a leitmotif of the Enlightenment, an attempt to uncover the progressive in the primitive. Classic Enlightenment too is Lessing's defense of free theological discussion against the "tyranny" of censorship, which he has recently experienced (§§76, 78, 79). He anticipates Kant's objection to the infantilizing of mature adults: it is harmful to keep a grown child back, as orthodoxy would prefer, in the elementary stage (§51). He had earlier anticipated Kant's metaphor of the baby walker.[42]

But against all that, Lessing warns the advanced student who is "stamping and glowing" to move on, not to leave the elementary books behind too soon; they may still have something new to impart (§68ff.). An old attachment makes him finally reluctant to reduce the Bible to a mere means. He goes out of his way to embrace the concepts of the Trinity, original sin, and the atonement, none of them obviously "truths of reason" (§§73–75). He also leaves crucial questions unanswered or unasked. The much-discussed contradiction between two assertions—that revelation only provided more quickly what mankind would eventually have found out by itself (§4), and that religion may lead us to ideas of God that reason would never have arrived at unaided (§77)—is the least of it. More broadly, if "rational truth" requires good argument based on reliable evidence, monotheism is hardly a "truth of reason" at all. And if mankind had the concept early on—Adam and his successors allegedly came face to face with God (§6)—how exactly did it get lost? Why was immortality, a common feature of primitive religions, too advanced for the Jews of the Old Testament (§17)? Why (§18) did the Jews become the people best suited to teach the rest of humanity? How, if reason initially needs revelation (§2off.), did other peoples develop reason too? And why did they then flag and fall behind, if indeed they did? Were these "children of nature" really (§21) overtaken, and overtaken for good, by the Jews—the Greeks especially, who, despite their prominent role in eighteenth-century German thinking, are here mysteriously left out? Their superior intellectual power and clarity should have made them the obvious control group to set beside the Judeo-Christian development. Christianity is thus given too dominant a place in the history of Western thought. Did the Bible really (§65), over a period of seventeen hundred years, bring mankind more light than any other book, albeit admittedly through taxing men's brains to puzzle it out? At best that is a charitable judgment, perhaps even humorously meant, on the centuries-old preoccupation with scriptural exegesis that Kant, Goethe, and Lichtenberg all lamented as a waste of time and ingenuity.[43] Was it even light of *any* kind that the Bible brought? And what about other cultures that claim a revelation of their own? Lessing's preface refers to "all positive religions," yet he then passes over the others in silence. At the close, moved by the traditional concern of generous-minded Christians for peoples damned because born too early to know the Christian revelation—a seeming gap in divine benevolence—Lessing falls back on the old notion of the transmigration of souls. That at least leaves time for infinite repeats of earthly life: "Is not all eternity mine?" (§100). What began as an education moving forward through time has become a circling back to give everyone a chance to catch up.

So if Lessing has one foot in the Enlightenment camp, he is dragging the other foot. There is always a danger that "the man caught in myth must make the myth, not the truth, his final value."[44] Revelation has become not so much a vehicle of progress as an impediment. The metaphor of an educational progression has proved too weak to counter the powerful pull of the Bible, which has an aura beyond that of any mere elementary textbook, irrational though this may be. As Kant wrote, "A sacred book acquires even among those who don't read it (and precisely among them most of all) the greatest authority, and no amount of rational arguing can be effective against the apodictic words: '*for it is written.*'"[45] That, in society at large, is an obstacle to flexible thinking, as it had recently been for Lessing, when he strove to set the claims of the spirit against the dogmas of the letter. (The biblical literalist Goeze did not realize Lessing was trying to rescue Christianity.) The metaphor of education and its alternative of unaided reason was also flawed at base. Pupils left to their own devices do not commonly arrive at the knowledge teachers are there to impart. Only a child prodigy like Pascal could work out Euclid's theorems for himself. All this is not to disparage Lessing. The struggle of a divided mind to find grounds for belief is more revealing, and moving, than a debate between distinct parties. No other German figure, and none in the French Enlightenment either, so embodies the demands and discomforts of the intellectual challenge to belief.

Die Erziehung des Menschengeschlechts was not chronologically Lessing's last word:[46] *Nathan der Weise* would shortly try to reconcile three religions. Nevertheless, for all its narrower focus on a single religion and for all its Christian nostalgia, the *Erziehung* has in one significant respect already gone beyond Nathan's parable. There the millennia-long process will still be a competition between religious orthodoxies, to see whose religion is, if not truer, then in practice better. The *Erziehung*, in contrast, has gone beyond revelation and institutional religion altogether. It looks forward to a "time of perfection" (§85) when ethical behavior will no longer be motivated by religious belief at all. That too is of course a pious hope, but at least a rationally directed one.

For that hoped-for final perfection there is no guiding textbook; to that extent, too, Lessing's educational metaphor has broken down. The human race has finally to move beyond the divine teaching program altogether, with no indication of how the pure ethic can be achieved. The "new eternal gospel" will have to be created by human agency, and for that the "pupil" will need to have learned along the way something more essential than any specific ideas, namely the practice of independent *thinking* that was central to Kant's idea of enlightenment and his very different view of education.

So who, if not Kant, should try to lay new ethical foundations? And could ethics really do without religious concepts, commandments, and—especially—threats of eternal punishment? Gibbon's epigram about the sects in ancient Rome had not lost its topicality. They were "all considered by the people as equally true; by the philosophers as equally false; and by the magistrate as equally useful."[47] Even in Enlightenment circles it was a common view that religion was needed to keep the people under control—although this was the cynical axiom on which the repressive alliance of church and state, the Enlightenment's bêtes noires, had always operated. Not that "the people" were the only problem. Crime reached high up the social ladder, and enlightenment itself could lead the individual astray. The cynicism of Franz Moor in Schiller's *The Brigands* was, in the author's self-critical view, "the result of enlightened thinking and liberal study."[48] Spreading light, as Lichtenberg graphically suggested, brought with it the risk of causing fire.[49] Social sophisticates could be destructively vicious, as witness the schemers Valmont and Merteuil in Laclos's *Liaisons dangereuses*, to say nothing of the Marquis de Sade. Yet whether things would have been worse without religious authority in the past, or would be worse without it in the future, was unprovable. It is uncertain whether the fear of God ever stopped anyone doing what their passions moved them to do, though they may have had worries afterward. Another non sequitur was the converse equation of atheism with immorality and crime. It was disturbing to the faithful that some human beings could live and die just as well without religion: the alleged atheist Spinoza had led a blameless life, the skeptic David Hume had died a serene death. Orthodoxy thirsted for deathbed conversions that would show unbelievers finally repenting of their sinfulness. (Gellert obligingly conjured one up in his fable "Der Freigeist"—The Freethinker). Kant's friend Moses Mendelssohn took a positively defeatist view of religion-free ethics: without God, Providence, and immortality, the love of humanity was an innate weakness and goodwill among men little more than frivolity (*Geckerei*).[50] Even the classic spokesman of toleration, John Locke, had argued in his *Letter Concerning Tolerance* of 1689 that the bonds of human society could have no hold upon atheists, which plainly begged the question whether a human society needed suprahuman sanction.

In "What Is Enlightenment?" Kant focused on religious unfreedom as the "most harmful and dishonoring" of all the forms of dependency.[51] That made it the outstanding case of an authority that enlightened thinking needed to question. The very word "church" (*kirk, Kirche*) implies authority, deriving from the Greek adjective *kuriake*, "of the master."[52] It was one of Frederick the Great's virtues that he did not reinforce religious with temporal authority, as rulers anxious for stability normally did. Kant argues specifically against the dead hand of dogma that claims to fix beliefs once and for all.[53] His later full treatment, *Religion within the Bounds of Mere Reason*, deals rather with what is *outside* the bounds of valid reason as defined in the First Critique. Official ("statutory") religion was made up of speculative, indeed antirational constructs. Predestination through grace was incompatible with the idea of a just God, a "*salto mortale* of human reason"

(6:267); the atonement was a "fund" too easily available for paying off sins, past and future (266); the authority of sacred books, even and especially when not read (252), was unacceptable, as was the "usurped dominance" of the priesthood (351); devotional practices such as churchgoing, celibacy, monasticism, mortification of the flesh, and pilgrimages were all forms of fetishism that debased religion ("Afterdienst," 329).They were offerings to a god misconceived on the model of vainglorious earthly rulers who demanded ceremonial submission. It was all "pious play-acting that entailed no action" (*frommes Spielwerk und Nichtstuerei*, 320). Above all, it actually diverted attention from the one essential of religion, which was the morally good life (*guter Lebenswandel*). As Lessing's Nathan says, "How much easier pious raptures are / Than doing what is right."[54] It was left to Lichtenberg to pillory the extreme form of debased religion: that people were prepared to fight for their faith but not to live by it.[55] For him too, the only way to revere God was by fulfilling one's moral obligations. Kant elsewhere dismisses even prayer as mere currying of favor (*Gunstbewerbung*).[56]

Kant does try to distill what is ethically usable out of "the book that happens to be there" (279), as coolly distanced a way of referring to the Bible as the phrase "the saintly person of the gospel" is for Christ.[57] Such practical use does nothing to weaken his critique of established religion, on whose "blood-spattered" history he quotes the definitive epigram of Lucretius: *tantum religio potuit suadere malorum*.[58] As with the upshot of the *Critique of Pure Reason*, with its ultimately commonsense epistemology, the conclusion is a simple one: against the "delusion" of Christians, "those would-be pious favorites of heaven," Kant's peroration sets "the natural honest man who can be trusted in our everyday business and needs."[59] That comes close to what the Lord says in the "Prologue in Heaven" of Goethe's *Faust*: "A good man in his dark instinctive drive / Is conscious of the right way in the end."

Kant allows that ceremonies like baptism and the eucharist may create solidarity and edge people toward a cosmopolitan moral community while they await true enlightenment, which consists precisely in distinguishing between the essence of religion and its trappings. More important, in jettisoning most of the Christian construct as "dead in itself,"[60] he has still not abandoned the idea of a God—Kant does after all feel able to say what, as between outward shows and the moral life, will be pleasing to Him. But Kant's God *is* an idea, with none of the mythic or dogmatic substance positive religions have accreted. That is the point. Kant derives God from ethics instead of ethics from God, a Copernican reversal every bit as complete as his earlier turn in epistemology. Ethics will be a matter of doing what is right because it is right, not because it is commanded by a deity. It is much the same reversal that Goethe was feeling his way toward poetically in "Das Göttliche," and much the same moral autonomy beyond all formal faiths in which Lessing's *Erziehung des Menschengeschlechts* culminated.[61]

Then why keep God at all? Kant's First Critique had already disposed of the three traditional "proofs" of God's existence—the ontological, the cosmological and the physicotheological.[62] What could be left? Freud later scorned philosophers who "give the name of 'God' to some vague abstraction which they have created for themselves" and "can boast that they have recognised a higher, purer concept of God, although their God is now nothing more than an insubstantial shadow and no longer the powerful personality of religious doctrine."[63] That may fit some deists but does not do justice to Kant. Certainly he has cast off myths of divine might, but what is left is not a "vague abstraction." It is in a very precise way "higher and purer" than the old conception of a jealous and vengeful God, which could only spawn practices diametrically opposed to true morality.[64] Kant's conception of God has become an inner standard of moral behavior, an embodiment of ethical reflection. He plainly does not share the conventional belief in God-and-Son, and has even virtually left behind what was known as "natural religion." There were nevertheless reasons for keeping God in play. For one thing, a more outspoken atheism would still have been scandalous and bad tactics in the climate of the time. Kant was in any case from his Pietist roots not so inclined. He had expressly left room for faith in the First Critique and had been careful from his early scientific writings to avoid being denounced by Pietist orthodoxy, in Königsberg and beyond.[65] He was already being provocative enough, as events in Prussia would soon show. Above all, God was valuable as a "regulative idea" by which people might orient their lives. The "practical power" of such an idea as an internal, not external authority is already sketched in the First Critique: "We have no other standard for our actions than the behavior of this divine person within us, with which to compare, judge and improve ourselves, although we can never attain it."[66] "Si Dieu n'existait pas, il faudrait l'inventer," said Voltaire. Kant has done that.[67] As with the three-sided god of Montesquieu's triangles, a piece of French mockery is given a serious point.

How pure is "pure" in Kant's ethics? The central plank is the simple but demanding "categorical imperative." An action must be fit to stand as the embodiment of a universal principle: "Act as if the maxim of your action should become by your will a general law." It should be pure of all self-interest, self-love, or inclination (*Neigung*). A second version of the categorical imperative specifies "a general law *of nature*" (emphasis added).

That is a bold encroachment on the realm most obviously opposed to morality, namely people's natural impulses. Kant goes beyond the individual's self-interested realism of "do as you would be done by" to the all-embracing idealism of "do as you would want everyone else to do, and not just to you." Such universal consideration of other people's purposes—people *are* embodied purpose, every one of us[68]—entails positively furthering their aims and happiness. This would bring about a "realm of ends" that harmonized all their diverse aspirations, a social concept distantly echoing Rousseau's *volonté générale*, but lacking the enforcement provisions that made it potentially tyrannical.[69] Kant's conception may sound utopian, yet it is not far from the ideal of social solidarity which democracies pay lip service to and even sporadically fulfill. Kant was in any case never one for half measures. If he asks a lot of mankind, it is because he believes human beings have an inherent moral nature—so much so that, in a step that seems to undermine both his idea of an inaccessible ultimate reality and his ban on "pure" rational speculation, he declares moral freedom to be the "thing in itself" (*Wesen an sich selbst*) of human beings: they exist under this "different order of things" even while physically determined by the laws of nature.[70] This is their "intelligible" essence, though we may not know it empirically when looking at them as figures in the phenomenal world. Paradoxically, it seems human beings can inwardly *be* what cannot outwardly be *perceived*.

Kant is not naive about the chances of practical fulfillment. The human moral potential (*Anlage*) may be frustrated by an immoral tendency (*Hang*), to the point of "radical evil." That only makes a radical moral counter-principle even more pressingly needed. For Kant, a person's very awareness of choice at decisive moments proves the reality of moral freedom. As a thought experiment, he imagines two contrasting situations where a man is threatened with hanging: in one case, it is as a punishment for indulging in his favorite ("irresistible") sensual pleasure—whereupon he does after all manage to resist temptation; in the other case he is threatened by his ruler if he refuses to bear false witness against an honorable man whom the ruler wishes to ruin—not, then, just a matter of his own welfare, but a situation readily conceivable in an absolutist age, like something from an early protest drama of Schiller's, though a later passage shows it was modeled on Henry VIII's maneuvers against Anne Boleyn,[71] which shifts it safely out of German and into English history. Whether or not the man in this instance resists the political pressure, the moral possibility is clear: "He judges that he can do something because he is aware he should, and recognises in himself the freedom which, but for the moral law, would have remained unknown to him."[72]

But moral action is not sufficiently guided by examples. These, right up to Christ himself, are only recognized as exemplary in the first place through insights already arrived at rationally. The realm of experience is in any case not the best place to look for means to resist its pressures. Nor is it enough that actions should obey external commandments or perform prescribed duties—that is a matter of mere subservience to an alien will ("heteronomy"). True morality has to spring not from conformity, but from a self-determination that is an extension of the fundamental Enlightenment principle of thinking for yourself ("autonomy"). The *Bestimmung des Menschen* has to become *Selbstbestimmung*.

This is admittedly only a rational idea within a world of natural necessity, yet it is still a footpath to freedom (*Fußsteig der Freiheit*).[73] The criterion is in any case not what does happen in the world, but what ought to happen. Not even the outcome, successful or not, is as important to Kant as the purity of motivation. The "shining jewel" of ethics is the "pure will." The outcome is merely the jewel's setting.[74]

Strikingly, the terms "pure" and "experience" now have opposite values to the ones they had in the *Critique of Pure Reason*. There, for the purposes of knowledge "experience" was positive, the touchstone of truth and of whether something was even a real question. "Pure" reason was negative, addicted to vainly speculating about unknowables. In ethics, by contrast, motivation has to be "pure," which is now positive, meaning free of entanglement in the realm of "experience," which is negative. "Experience" now means the way the world is, rather than the way it should be, a realm governed by the "realistic" and self-fulfilling assumptions of people who are proud to be "men *of* the world." The arguments of the two Critiques are not contradictory; they are simply different in kind for radically different contexts. Whereas knowledge *needs* the pressure of experience—the dove could not fly in a vacuum—moral action must *resist* the pressure of experience or it cannot take off at all.

Kant's position is refreshing in its simple radicality. For what are moral principles if not demandingly absolute? Certainly not the mere façade of an easily jettisoned liberalism. The unradical alternative is to make "realistic" concessions on an increasingly slippery slope. Kant at least offers firm ground. Not for nothing did he call his first treatment of ethics a *Grundlegung*, a laying of foundations—one of those metaphors of reliability that run through his whole oeuvre. His thinking is also simple in that he believed ethical questions—for example, where do duty and justice lie?— could be grasped by a child of eight or nine. And why not? Injustice and *Realpolitik* begin in the family and the playground, where children's sense of (un)fairness seems instinctive. Kant sketches one more situation, piling pressure on the person at its center to take the self-interested way out, and still believes a child would see the moral forest for the pragmatic trees: moral discriminations are not that subtle, they are "inscribed in the human soul in the most rough-hewn and legible letters. They are not effaced when it comes to acting"[75]—this in a popular essay attacking the old saw "That's all very well in theory, but it won't work in practice." Rejecting easy, "realistic" ways out of human obligation is common to all Kant's thinking.

As one more coincidence, or manifestation of the *Zeitgeist*, Goethe's diaries from the mid-1770s show him orienting his behavior, as he adjusts to a new life at the Weimar ducal court, by a self-devised standard of "purity" that seems to involve not so much taking right decisions against the grain of the old Adam as keeping the whole tenor of his life in a felt moral equilibrium. "For days now, so pure and true in everything"; "pure peace in my soul"; "a fairly pure view of many relationships"; and most fully: "May the idea of purity which extends to the mouthful that I eat grow more and more luminous in me."[76] This virtual program is typical of Goethe's independent intuitive character, and of a deep impulse to harmony that entailed a very different ethics from Kant's confrontation with nature. Indeed, it comes close to the language of religious mysticism, yet on a wholly human basis. Spirituality—introspection, reflection, moral resolve—has no need of orthodox transcendence. Purity, in the observer and in the world he observes, will echo still in Goethe's serene last Dornburg poems of 1828.

With his incisive account of institutional religion and his secular ethics, Kant was sailing not just close to the wind but in the teeth of a storm—one of the "storms threatening reason" that Biester had predicted in the last years of Frederick the Great's intellectually permissive reign.[77] By 1793, when *Religion within the Bounds of Mere Reason* appeared, an anti-Enlightenment reaction had set in, not just the rearguard action by orthodox theology that might have been expected, but a direct intervention by Frederick the Great's successor, his religiose nephew Frederick William II (who reported that Jesus had several times appeared to him in person).[78] His Edict on Religion of 1788 explicitly targeted the Enlightenment, giving it a line to itself in bold type, much like a "wanted criminal" notice. It had scorned the Christian religion, "whose preeminence and excellence are long since proven and placed beyond all doubt."[79] "Proven" declared a debate over, its resumption forbidden. A censorship edict followed soon after. Any publication "undermining the fundamental truths of scripture" would be confiscated. Any transgression would be punished. When Karl Friedrich Bahrdt wrote a comedy about the Edict, he was jailed for two years. The populace grumbled about the compulsion to attend church and communion—

there were surely things a ruler could not command? The liberal theologian Spalding declined to preach any longer under these conditions, and the
Berlin Upper Consistory resisted a new catechism.[80] Newly trained pastors
had to toe a more narrowly orthodox line than in the past fifty years; those
already in post had to conform or face dismissal. Kant's distinction between
"private" (sticking to the institutional rule book) and "public" (communicating one's individual view of the rules) would no longer wash as it had
under Frederick II. Indeed, it arguably made the issue all the clearer to reactionaries.[81] The king in person, or his *éminence grise* Wöllner,[82] now forbade
Kant to write further on religious matters under threat of "unpleasant measures, should he prove intransigent."[83] Free discussion of religious subjects
was forbidden. Orthodox reaction was now in control. Five years later Kant
and philosophy would take their revenge.

Kant's ethical writings had fascinated Schiller since the early 1790s, but
they had not made him a passive disciple. Respect for abstract reflection in
the Kantian mode was mixed with a long-standing admiration for the quite
different mode of another extraordinary personality. Goethe inspired paradoxical mixed feelings as Schiller struggled for success and recognition, but
from 1794, when they formed a working partnership, love-hate turned into
close friendship and furnished Schiller with a new ideal. Goethe's "naive"
creativity pointed the way to a whole system, in ethics and literature, that
set spontaneity against abstraction. In the essay *On Grace and Dignity*,
Schiller conceived a human type that would not need to fight for duty
against inclination, but would have an inclination *to* duty. That was not far
from Goethe's early impulse to "purity." The argument neatly reconciled
the opposed terms of Kant's "monastic" rigorism,[84] even while conceding
that a morally lax age could perhaps do with some rigor. Schiller took care
to be tactful in correspondence with the great thinker, and Kant's reaction
to the essay was complimentary ("the treatise of a master hand") and con-
ciliatory ("we are at one in the most important principles, I see no disagree-
ment"). Diplomacy on both sides, plus Kant's failure to fully take the point
of their difference, steered them away from confrontation.[85]

Schiller was even more outspokenly secular than Kant. He approved of
Kant's translation of sacred material into philosophical ideas in *Religion
within the Bounds of mere Reason* but feared that theologians would accept
it as positive support for the authority of their texts and ignore the secularizing arguments. Kant would then merely have "patched up the rotten construct of stupidity."[86]

Schiller had not long since had his own brush with orthodoxy. In March

1788 his poem "The Gods of Greece" described more trenchantly than ever before the two radically different, ancient and modern, ways of seeing the world. "*Seeing* the world," indeed—the German term *Weltanschauung* is closer to concrete reality than any mere "belief about," and concrete reality is Schiller's concern. The poem laments the loss to human imaginative experience when polytheism gave way to monotheism.[87] The Greek gods, major and minor, were once to be seen or sensed everywhere, from Helios/Apollo driving his chariot across the heavens each day down to the nymphs and dryads embodied in every rock, stream, and tree. The world was richly varied, colorful, and experienced as something *live*. How far that was a matter of real belief among the Greeks it is hard to be sure, and Schiller at all events does not share it. But it was a practice of the imagination that transformed the world, seeing everywhere traces of the divine and reminiscences of mythic stories. Everyday phenomena were more beautiful, more intimately known, more inspiring to poets and sculptors (lines 49ff.). The gods were more human (he admittedly leaves aside the many atrocities scattered through Greek myth), and that made human beings more divine (lines 191ff.). The imaginative richness was what made Greek culture different.

Different from what? Schiller has two targets. Most extensive, and most challenging to some of his contemporaries, is the contrast with Christianity. After stanzas that review classical color, he imagines entering a sad space, obviously a Christian church, a place as dark as is the concept of a creator who can be celebrated only by rituals of renunciation (lines 101ff.). Its emblem is death as a ghastly skeleton, and among its institutional side effects has been the passing of barbaric judgments by grim men untouched by human emotion—an allusion, surely, to Schiller's old enemy the Inquisition (lines 113ff.). The colorful world of the many Greek gods has perished to enrich "One" single god—except that the new incumbent has not been, in Schiller's term, "enriched" by what culture has lost; he and his cult remain grim and gray.[88] And Schiller leaves out of account the polytheistic tendencies at the heart of Christianity, its mysterious three-in-one, Catholic Mariolatry, and plethora of saints for all seasons, which suggest that religious belief is inherently fissiparous.

Surprisingly in an Enlightenment thinker, Schiller's other target is modern science. Before he ever gets to Christianity, he laments the replacing of Apollo and his sun chariot by a "soullessly spinning ball of fire" (lines 17ff.). The world now "servilely obeys the law of gravity" (line 167), suspended in space by its own impersonal motion (line 176). Schiller might well have shown how one of these bêtes noires was undoing the other, science undermining Christianity. Yet his equal rejection of both is not inconsistent. The mathematically precise mechanism of Newton's universe left the universe just as much, in Schiller's terms, an *entgötterte Natur* (line 168). Science might well seem as bleakly antipoetic as Christian monotheism.[89]

Not surprisingly, the poem raised a furor, though not among scientists. The attacks came from the pious, notably Count Leopold von Stolberg—once a companion of Goethe's on the Swiss journey of 1775—who accused this "Naturalist" (i.e., atheist) poet of misusing poetry to poison young minds. Several writers leapt to the poem's defense—a predictable Enlightenment response, but now visibly refining the argument for freedom of thought into a claim for the particular rights of the aesthetic realm. Schiller's friend Körner argued for "art as its own purpose" and for an "aesthetic substance independent of moral value"; another friend, Huber, for the free "play of the mind" which "cannot be offensive to uncorrupted feeling." Georg Forster argued that Schiller's poem was something to be admired even without any obligation to regret the passing of the Greek gods. Körner put it in the broadest social terms: "Happy the land where art is not occupied with commissioned work, but its free gifts are gratefully enjoyed."[90]

These are subtler claims than the Enlightenment's general defense of intellectual freedom. They rise above the direct clash with orthodoxy and convention and posit a realm where evaluative judgement no longer applies at all: art is free in an even higher sense than combative freethinking. They thus belong as much to the evolution of aesthetics—Körner's formulations in particular anticipate the arguments of Kant's *Critique of Judgment*, which was just about to appear in 1790. Forster, with tongue in cheek, suggests keeping the controversy wholly in the realm of art: might not Stolberg write a *poetic* answer to Schiller's poem? "True, you cannot beg the help of the Nine Sisters for the purpose; but who knows? perhaps there may be a single Muse unknown to us dwelling in your heaven?"—an ironic echo of the way the Greek gods had been reduced to a Christian singularity.[91]

Stolberg did not rise to that challenge, but one Franz von Kleist did, an otherwise unknown member of a famous literary family. His "Praise of the One God," a declared riposte to "The Gods of Greece," appeared in Wieland's *Teutscher Merkur* in the following year.[92] Like so much Christian apologetics in verse or prose, it expatiates on the beauties of the world as if they proved a benevolent creator, and specifically the Christian one. It also decries the Greek gods, especially Venus as goddess of love, which shows how right Schiller was about Christian antisensuousness. The "beautiful world" argument had been massively varied early in the century by Barthold Hinrich Brockes in his nine volumes of poems celebrating "Earthly Delight in God." These often charming vignettes of natural phenomena always end with a doctrinal punch line.[93] That, though, was in a setting of still largely unquestioned Protestant orthodoxy. By the end of the eighteenth century Christianity in Germany was intellectually at the end of its tether.

Religion nonetheless in its many forms remained a part of human history. That left the detached phenomenological, the anthropological view. It is implied in an early letter of Goethe's to Lavater where he says he is "admittedly no anti-Christian, no un-Christian, but a decided non-Christian."[94] Often the last element alone is quoted, but all three are necessary as coordinates of Goethe's position. To be anti-Christian would have meant being an active critic à la Voltaire; to be un-Christian would have meant not being the kind of decent person for which "Christian" was conventionally a synonym, as when the Christian brother in Lessing's play says there was never a better Christian than the Jew Nathan.[95] But "non-Christian" meant simply declining to locate himself in Christian terms—Christianity was just not interesting. With skepticism taken for granted, as by this time it could be, Goethe was able to make a new start. Old beliefs were irrelevant. This was the conclusion of Prometheus's raging against Zeus, which ends with the declaration that he will simply pay no attention to him, nor will the race of beings he now sits creating: "Und dein nicht zu achten, / Wie ich!"

Christianity remained a given of the surrounding culture. It had shaped patterns of literary expression. Its doctrines might be disregarded, but its forms—language, myths, metaphors, spiritual self-questioning—were still an expressive means. The phrases and rhythms of Luther's Bible translation had gone into the bloodstream of German literary style much as the language of the Authorized Version and its vernacular predecessors went into English. Their use need have no religious implications; it was the fruit of acculturation. The first of Goethe's *Wanderer's Evening Songs*, "Der du von dem Himmel bist," with its brooding on pain and its appeal for a soothing "peace," sounds so much like a Christian prayer that for fifty years it figured in the hymnbook of the Bremen Lutheran congregation; the second—the best-known of all German poems, "Über allen Gipfeln"—echoes seventeenth-century religious meditations like Paul Gerhardt's "Nun ruhen alle Wälder." Yet its gentle survey of nature's realms, mineral, vegetable, animal, human, is an act of secular piety. Goethe's more consciously Christian formulas in a note to Charlotte von Stein—"Farewell, you dear A and O of my joys and sufferings, if I lack you what can I possess, if you are mine what can I lack?"[96]—can be read, according to taste, as sincere feeling, humor, or blasphemy.

On a larger scale than biblical echoes and allusions, the Christian and specifically Pietist practice of self-analysis provided the soil from which the psychological novel grew, and arguably indeed the entire modern form of psychological awareness, massively initiated in Germany by Karl Philipp Moritz's ten-volume collection of empirical instances, the *Magazin zur Erfahrungsseelenkunde* (Journal for Empirical Psychology).[97] Moritz also wrote the first explicitly "psychological novel" (thus its subtitle) *Anton Reiser*, which is both the product of a Pietist upbringing and the record of an escape from it. Goethe's sensational early novel of unhappy love and suicide, *The Sufferings of Young Werther*, is more intensely self-analytical still; its title alludes to Christ's Passion (*Christi Leiden/Die Leiden des jungen Werthers*). On a far larger scale, Schiller's *Über naïve und sentimentalische Dichtung*, tracing poetic history from the "naive" ancient Greeks down to the all-too-conscious moderns, with a hoped-for millennium in which the two are magically reconciled, is a secular version of the myth of innocence, fall, and salvation. All these familiar materials were forms ready to hand to convey human inwardness and reflection—there was no need to devise new ones. These were not the phantom pains left by an amputated faith, what Nietzsche called "religious afterpains" (*religiöse Nachwehen*).[98] That such means could be used spontaneously and with complete freedom meant the process of secularization was now complete.

Old materials could still of course be out of harmony with new meanings. On the most immense scale of all, Goethe's *Faust* labors to transform the Christian myth of a pact with the devil, the pursuit of forbidden knowledge, and consequent damnation into an epic drama of all-embracing earthly experience and a final surprise redemption. It uses nonchalantly assorted Christian motifs: God the Father is in his heaven at the start, visited by Mephistopheles; Christ is only mentioned once in passing, in Easter choruses; and at the close of part 2 the Virgin Mary dominates to prevent (so Goethe said) "such supernatural, scarcely imaginable things" as Faust's salvation being "lost in vagueness."[99] *Faust* is an extreme case of the potential cross-purposes of secularization. It is a bizarre mixture, deprived of its old theological-moral point yet retaining and adding to the original's amoral episodes, and still contriving to avoid the protagonist's final damnation. The treatment is so much at odds with the material that it can be seen as the most grandiose mistake in literary history.

No secularization was needed when the sixty-year-old Goethe encountered Islam: the alien religion was from the outset one more anthropological phenomenon, another rich growth from the common human impulse to transcendent belief. It yielded him new poetic means in the *West-Östlicher Divan*, an elaborate play with Islamic and pre-Islamic materials in a cycle of twelve books, 350 poems in the Persian style, plus 150 pages of well-

researched *Notes and Essays* to help understand it, the whole written over
the years from 1814 to 1818. Goethe's interest grows out of a felt affinity
with the personality and circumstances of the recently translated medieval
poet Hafiz,[100] an unorthodox celebrator of life's pleasures (though his name
means "one who knows the Koran by heart"). Not just Hafiz's love of wine
was at odds with Muslim doctrine (and in harmony with Goethe's practice).
Poetry such as Hafiz wrote was suspect. The conquering Arabs initially "attacked all books, in their view mere superfluous or harmful scribblings,
and destroyed all monuments of literature."[101] Mohammed himself "threw
a gloomy cloak of religion" over the poetic traditions of his own tribe and
prohibited fairy tales like the *Thousand and One Nights* as frivolous imaginings that "carried people out of themselves into absolute freedom."[102] For
that was the flat opposite of the prophet's purpose. Prophet and poet radically diverge. The poet "squanders his gift in enjoyment so as to produce
enjoyment, . . . he tries to be manifold, to show himself boundless in outlook and representation." The prophet, in contrast, "looks only to a single
definite purpose," using the simplest means to "gather the peoples around a
single doctrine as around a standard." People only have to believe in the one
thing he insistently repeats: "he must become and stay monotonous" (*er
muss eintönig werden und bleiben*). Against that, the manifold world is not
something you believe but something you directly know (*denn das Man-
nigfaltige glaubt man nicht, man erkennt es*).[103] This is a virtual epigram
for the gulf between the closed mind of dogma and the openness of poetry
to the experienced world. It applies not just to Islam. It exactly echoes the
letter in which Goethe decades before had set his own physical "seeing"
against Jacobi's metaphysical "believing."

The Koran's assertion "There is no doubt in this book" together with its
"boundless tautologies and repetitions" meant that "as often as we engage
with it, it repels, then attracts, then amazes us, and finally compels our reverence."[104] That conveys the open-minded persistence and mixed reactions
of Goethe the reader. Overall the book took some stomaching for this intercultural explorer, who had long since risen above dogmatic thinking. He
nevertheless rarely touches on theological doctrine, and then mostly in humorous vein, teasing both Islam and Christianity for things they have in
common—bizarre beliefs, theological disputes that will last them till Judgment Day,[105] shared hope for the joys of an afterlife.[106] As the houri says in
one poem of the *Book of Paradise*, he is "of a free humor."[107] There is rarely
anything like an Enlightenment antireligious sharpness.[108] True to the indifference of the "decided non-Christian," and equally decided non-Muslim,
things are seen from a higher, humanistic, an anthropological standpoint.

Where there definitely is sharpness, it is directed at the religious big-otry that leads to conflict, distorting the common humanity that lies deep beneath all religious beliefs. To know oneself and others (which is a fair definition of comparative anthropology) is to see that West and East cannot essentially be divided.[109] Goethe declares it "foolish that everyone praises his own beliefs," for "if 'Islam' means acceptance of a divine will, then in Islam we all live and die."[110] Where peoples are divided in mutual contempt, neither will admit that they are really striving for the same thing.[111] Ulti-mately it is God's Orient and God's Occident; North and South rest in the peace of his hands.[112] But this is once more a God above all doctrine, the embodiment not of a peace that passeth all understanding, but of a peace that would resolve all misunderstanding.

It does not, however, reduce human beings of different religions to a pale abstraction. Both the poetry and the prose of the *Divan* engage with a very specific culture and religion, taking them—for all the humor—seriously. Goethe the poet makes virtuoso play with the materials that Goethe the anthropologist has gathered. Where he finds aspects of Islam repugnant, at least it springs not from prejudice, but from conscientious, open-minded, and largely appreciative study. Avoiding prejudice (*Vorurteil*) does not mean refraining from judgment (*Urteil*); indeed, taking things seriously involves engaging frankly with manifestations good and ill and recognizing the limi-tations of one's own culture in the process. The introduction to the *Notes and Essays* presents the author as "a traveler . . . who has adapted to the best of his powers to the foreign culture, customs of the country, language, attitudes, conventions," but who "remains recognizably a foreigner by his own accent, by the insuperable inflexibility of his own nationality."[113] That states, beyond any facile optimism, the intercultural problem. The *Divan* remains a remarkable attempt at a solution.

What is emphatically abandoned in all the above cases is any doctrin-ally specific God enthroned in a promised heaven. That leaves the concept of God as very much what Kant calls a "regulative idea" in ethics, as com-mon ground between cultures, as an imagined recipient of the poet's delight in the real world. Increasingly it was a Spinozan God, *deus sive natura*, whether the terms of the phrase were read as an apposition—"God, that is, Nature"—or as an alternative: "Either God or Nature."[114] Whichever way, the world was now increasingly conceived as *natura*, a nature seen through poetically sensitive and scientifically sober eyes. What would science con-tribute to an enlightened vision?

CHAPTER 7

Apples and After:
The Gravity of Science

> O Sacred, Wise, and Wisdom-giving tree,
> Mother of science . . . And wherein lies
> Th' offence that Man should thus attain to know?
> —Milton, *Paradise Lost*, Book 9

Thus the Serpent, tempting Eve with forbidden fruit from the tree of knowledge—the original mythic story warning against the audacity of enlightenment. "The modern movement began with Adam, no, come to think of it with Eve."[1] Newton's legendary falling apple likewise led down the path to light, but he was on the side of the angels and could justify man's pursuit of knowledge before God by working out in full the mechanics of a solar system that was by now uncontroversial, or almost.[2] To that extent Newton was not after all, *pace* Wordsworth, voyaging through entirely "strange seas of thought," nor "alone."[3] Christianity at all events had nothing to fear from him, as it had from Copernicus and Galileo. Newton's majestic mathematical universe, though in theory compatible with deism or even atheism,[4] could readily be built into physicotheological apologetics. That was in line with his own Christian beliefs. His second major work, the *Opticks*, ends with a virtual sermon on "the first Creation by the Counsel of an intelligent Agent" and the standard non sequitur that "such a wonderful Uniformity in the Planetary System must be allowed the Effect of Choice."[5] Newton actually wrote on theological topics and in his later years was obsessed with biblical chronology. He nonetheless became the emblem of secular science and the era's supreme scientific authority.

Since the Renaissance, science had been building a weight of evidence designed to keep mankind's feet on the ground of reality. Whatever the intent, its effects had worked against religion. Astronomy above all had changed the relation of the world and its inhabitants to the universe, turning the once subordinate sun into the controlling center and the earth into just one of its satellites. Such diametric reversal was a fresh way of thinking, a model that could be applied to other problems. This was explicit in the declared "Copernican turn" of Kant's epistemology and was plainly inherent in his ethics.[6] Other astronomical terms likewise came into general critical use. Epicycles, the old way to explain irregularities in the movements of the planets, became a metaphor for the attempt in any intellectual field to rescue an inadequate theory through hypotheses more far-fetched than the theory they were meant to defend. The standard label for this proceeding since the Greeks was "rescuing the phenomena,"[7] a misnomer, since what was really being rescued was never the phenomena but always the theory. The archangel Raphael's astronomy lecture to Adam in book 8 of *Paradise Lost* speaks of the way "cycle and epicycle . . . contrive to save appearances"[8]—a nice ambiguity, since the word can be taken in its modern sense of deceptive appearances but was perhaps for Milton just a synonym of "phenomena" consciously echoing the Greek tag. Likewise parallax, the difference between sight lines in the observation of a distant heavenly body, was used as a metaphor for divergent views, with compromise between them as the way to achieve conceptual precision.[9] Lichtenberg illustrated the problem with the typically humorous down-to-earth example of looking past one's nose with alternate eyes closed.[10]

More substantively for the progress of science, bizarre assertions about the structure and material of the universe—Aristotle's fifty-five crystal spheres to which the stars were fixed, the axiomatic smoothness of the moon's surface, the perfect roundness of heavenly bodies, and the perfect circularity of their motions—became untenable thanks to the telescope. By intensifying human sight, the new instrument gave empiricism an enhanced authority, quite dramatically in a Christian culture so antiempirical that until the Reformation the laity were not even allowed to read their foundational book, the Bible, in their own language. Nowhere was it clearer than in astronomy that knowledge of the world must rest on observation and that arbitrary imaginings could no longer be given out as unquestionable truths. That long predated Kant's attack on the old speculative metaphysics. Seeing was believing, and sight—including metaphorically "seeing through" all forms of obfuscation—was for the Enlightenment the dominant sense. But the senses generally were rehabilitated after their long subordination under rationalism. "The senses do not deceive," Kant wrote, in a simple late summary of his epistemology. It was the understanding that could fail to read their evidence aright.[11]

But surely the sun visibly rose and set? Was that not deception by the senses? Minds as scientifically sophisticated as Lichtenberg's and Goethe's mistakenly conceded that the Copernican view meant learning the opposite of what was perceived by the senses every day.[12] Yet the move to the heliocentric system made no difference to what you *saw*. How else could the Earth's turning on its axis have made the sun visually appear?[13] What the eye could see just needed understanding more subtly. Hence the rider to Kant's simple statement: the senses only provided the raw material.[14] Empiricism involved the mind's not passively waiting to be imprinted by sense data, but actively judging them.

Understanding Newton's universe in detail was only possible, as the title of his magnum opus warned (*Philosophiae naturalis principia mathematica*), for advanced mathematical minds. Newton told a friend that "to avoid being bated by little smatterers in mathematics he designedly made it abstruse; but yet so as to be understood by able mathematicians."[15] Even a would-be popular account, like Voltaire's in the *Lettres philosophiques*, was not exactly simple for the nonscientific reader. So for most of those who swore by Newton's science, his authority rested paradoxically on faith, not understanding. Yet for any scientist to be accorded axiomatic authority was contrary to the principles of science. That way dogma lay. The danger was clear to workers in the field. More than once Lichtenberg reassures himself, and imagines himself reassuring others, that "you are as good a human being as Newton."[16] He was pleased that "the almost superhuman Newton" could be wrong, as when he "proved" by experiment and calculation that an achromatic telescope was not possible—which it later turned out it was.[17] There was no malice in Lichtenberg's comment—a week later, he is expressing his delight at a system that embraces everything from the earth's gravitational attachment to the sun right down to the shape of a dewdrop.[18] And as a collector of Enlightenment relics, he treasured Newton's death mask,[19] just as he treasured a fragment of wood cut from Captain Cook's ship *Resolution*.[20]

The young Kant needed no reasssuring about the right to intellectual independence. His very first published work claims the freedom to "rate the repute of the NEWTONS and LEIBNIZES as nothing, if it should be opposed to the discovery of the truth." It "may sometimes be of use to place a certain noble trust in one's own powers," and he blithely takes on "Wolff, Hermanns, Bernoulli, Bülfinger" and "the whole mass of philosophers before Leibniz."[21] This—if a shade grandiloquent, which is perhaps why the young Lessing felt moved to slap the young Kant down[22]—is Enlightenment intellectual independence in action. It also accords with the London Royal

Society's motto: the full form of the quotation is "Nullius in verba *magis-tri*." One must not take on trust even what an accredited master says.

Kant was no less appreciative than Lichtenberg of Newton's achieve-ment, nor resolved on opposition for its own sake. On the contrary, the scientific essay of 1755 that was his first work of lasting value, dedicated to Frederick the Great but little noted at the time (not least because its publisher went bankrupt while bringing it out), the *General History and Theory of the Heavens, or Essay on the Constitution and Mechanical Ori-gin of the Whole Universe* treated its subject explicitly "*on Newtonian Principles*." These were "the understanding's happiest attempt yet to under-stand nature."[23] But Kant did believe he could take them beyond the me-chanics of the universe to show how it actually came into being, something on which Newton had declined to utter Yet it was an obvious question to ask. Why else had creation myths arisen? If Kant's answer was speculative, at least it was taking an accepted principle, gravitation, and extrapolating its action back to the very beginnings. Gravitation was the force that first concentrated the gases and fragments floating in space into celestial bodies, or, as Kant soberly terms them, "discrete lumps."[24]

To treat not just the mechanics but the origin of the universe was to trespass on the doctrine of the creation. Kant's was to that extent a "dan-gerous voyage," that recurrent seafaring metaphor of his. Yet it raised the "promontories of new land," which would be named after the bold discov-erer as his reward.[25] Any inherent systematic tendency of matter suggested nature's independence of divine providence.[26] Christianity was not the first religious orthodoxy to face that problem. Plato had been disturbed when philosophers in his day taught the young that the world was produced by *physis* and *tyche*—nature and chance— not by the gods.[27] Democritus's at-omism declared matter eternal and thus did away with the notion of a di-vine creator. Kant clearly sees his flank is vulnerable and tries to protect himself against the watchers waiting to pounce with charges of atheism.[28] He inserts references to a "higher being" who must be the author of those shaping forces, even if nature is thereafter left to herself to operate them.[29] A modern physicist with a simplistic view of intellectual history takes at face value what were plainly defensive measures.[30] Kant almost protests too much as the tension builds up between Christian doctrine and the thrust of his inquiry, which is contained in three progressive uses of the formula "Give me but matter, and I will build you a world from it."[31] The first use defines a problem that is surely beyond human understanding to solve; the second time it has become the scientific problem with the best prospect of solution; the third time it declares that the origin of something as immense as the universe is paradoxically easier to explain than the genesis of so small a thing as a grass or a caterpillar. (We can just make out Darwin in the far future responding to this latter problem.)

Increasingly, Kant's repeated formula has the ring of a bold assertion. His later treatment of purposes in nature will argue that the idea of a designing intelligence can only ever be provisional, a heuristic means to understand natural phenomena; a self-sufficient mechanism beyond our limited human understanding is a possible alternative.[32] This scientific conundrum, of a created as against an uncreated world, is an early seed of the antinomies in the *Critique of Pure Reason*.

With an eye no doubt to Newton's rejection of gratuitous "hypotheses," Kant claims to have avoided "arbitrary fabrications." He has only invoked the known forces of attraction and repulsion, which since Newton have the status of natural laws; the problem by its nature allows no exact mathematical solution. Kant's theory is sometimes said to be discredited by his own later arguments against speculation.[33] But this early theory was not mere metaphysical speculation about things that cannot be an object of knowledge, like God or immortality, which the First Critique was to invalidate. Kant was dealing with real objects and forces, conducting a thought experiment that would be testable in later astronomical work. Taken further in France, it became the Kant-Laplace nebular hypothesis on how stars are formed. Kant's "dangerous voyage" had indeed attached his name to "new-found land."[34] The hypothesis fell out of favor in the nineteenth century, but reinvigorated in the twentieth it has become the basis of modern cosmology.

That is only part of Kant's modernity. His whole approach is in the modern scientific spirit. He thinks in the immense distances and times of an infinite expanding universe. He sees the "fixed" stars as very much in motion, though it will still take generations to map their movements. He imagines the death as well as the birth of stars, the eventual possible collapse of the universe and its phoenixlike rebirth out of the energies so released. He conceives of earthly species arising and becoming extinct, of land masses emerging from the ocean and others being swallowed up by it. He has replaced the static idea of a single creative act with the continuous evolution of new worlds and new world orders from natural forces, which will take (here he marries mathematical measurement and metaphor) whole "mountain-ranges of millions of centuries."[35] This anticipates the revolutionary Scottish geologist James Hutton's conception of deep time—"no vestige of a beginning, no prospect of an end"—right down to the cycle of erosion and renewal that explains the presence of marine shells on moun-

taintops: they were not left behind by a biblical flood but, in yet another Copernican reversal of argument, thrust up by upheavals in the earth's crust.[36]

Kant still gives a formal nod to a "supreme being" whose creativity is
as plain in a sphere one inch in diameter as in the whole Milky Way.[37] Yet
the term "supreme being" is not specifically Christian doctrine. It can be
read as yet again Spinoza's *deus sive natura*, now increasingly an alternative ("either/or") rather than an equivalence ("i.e."). Kant's repeated defense
of his science against Christian attack looks like a case of *qui s'excuse,
s'accuse*. Science's own gravitational pull is plain as he strives to carry the
inquiry beyond the "despair" of ultimate explanations that left Newton invoking the "finger of God."[38] Such reliance on divine intervention was a
slippery slope, leading to the popular delusion (*Wahn*) that nature's laws
were designed to arrange things for mankind's benefit. For if natural forces
had produced the fruitful slopes and habitable places that benefit mankind,
they had also produced dangerous cliffs and bleak deserts.[39] Yet these were
no more aimed at man than were the benefits. For the scientist, the system
only fits human interests where it touches.

Kant the scientist was thus primed to respond later in the same year to
the catastrophe of the century, the Lisbon earthquakes (there were actually
four of them). Kant wrote three essays: a first sketch, a substantial treatment, and an afterthought. He does not dwell emotionally on the massive
destruction and human suffering; rather, he is moved by scientific curiosity and the scientist's obligation to explain things to the public. So where
others raised protesting hands to heaven, Kant looks for causes deep in the
earth.[40] The hollow subterranean spaces are the firm ground of his inquiry.
They were the places where fire and water moved, linking the Lisbon disaster with harbingers and concurrent events, tremors and tidal waves as
far away as North Germany and Iceland. These in turn repeated a pattern
seen in maritime Europe as far back as 1692, and ideally one would go back
much further in geological time, into the history of the earth in the original
chaos.[41] Kant surveys oceanic and volcanic reports from all over the world,
drawing on two dozen scientists and travelers. Volcanoes seemed to release
the pressures that caused earthquakes; the direction of tremors seemed to
follow the line of rivers and mountain ranges. The rebuilding of cities should
be planned accordingly. Where Voltaire's poem on the Lisbon disaster asks
God why an earthquake had to happen in a great city when it could have
been placed safely out in a desert,[42] Kant asks European man why he built
grand palaces that an earthquake would destroy. People built more simply
and safely in Peru, with a low stone base and the rest just reeds.[43] Man must
adjust to nature, not nature to man—again the argument has the struc-

ture of Copernican reversal. If we sometimes benefit from the operation of nature's laws, we must expect sometimes to suffer. Even when we do, it is presumption (*Vorwitz*) to interpret this as divine punishment, as Lessing's old adversary Goeze was still doing in his sermons on the earthquakes, warning Hamburg to mend its ways or it will suffer the same fate.[44] Such devout prostration is in fact, Kant sees, an arrogant self-centeredness: "Man is so taken up with himself that he thinks he is the sole aim of the divine dispositions. . . . We are a part of nature and claim to be the whole thing."[45] In reality we are short-term visitors at points in a grand process to which we are otherwise irrelevant. Paradoxically, a twentieth-century ironist suggests, we might feel more at home believing we are the intended victims of destructive forces than believing they are totally indifferent to us.[46]

The Christian conundrum in which Voltaire's poem on the Lisbon disaster is, amazingly for him, still entangled[47]—how could a loving God do this to innocent people?—becomes meaningless in the light of Kant's scientific sobriety. The opposed terms of that contradiction simply cancel each other out. There is neither the personal benevolence Christians believe in, nor the arbitrary wrath they cannot then understand. In place of both there is a system of natural forces that mankind, for better or worse, has to live with. God needs no exonerating when all is nature; theodicy becomes superfluous.

Where Kant had gone beyond Newton, Goethe met him head-on. In 1790 a last-minute glance through some borrowed prisms he was about to return unused to a physicist at the University of Jena convinced him in a flash that Newton's account of color was wrong.[48] The sudden insight was typical of the way Goethe's scientific ideas originated, but the consequence of this one was twenty years of experimental labor and a color theory of his own, expounded in the longest work he ever wrote, the *Farbenlehre*. What Goethe saw at that moment in 1790 was white light on a whitewashed wall, where he expected to see all the colors of the spectrum. Colors appeared only where a dark element—the uprights of the room's window frame, for instance—defined the field. Goethe's surprise is easily explained by physics: the prism splits light into the colors of the spectrum only when it is projected as a single ray through a narrow aperture, as Newton had done. But Goethe's observation persuaded him that color was a mixture of light and darkness, rather than of many components of white light; and this became the basis of the theory he hoped would supplant Newton's. When scientists failed to take it and him seriously, his embitterment led to an increasingly obsessive and personal campaign against Newton and his followers. Was science not an open debate? Goethe's initial objection that to separate out a single ray was a distortion of nature led him to reject wholesale scientific contrivance, the use of instruments, and the translation of observed phenomena into mathematical terms—the decisive step by which Newton had made optics an exact science. The explicitly "polemical part" of Goethe's *Theory of Color* is headed "Enthüllung," which means a discrediting revelation.[49] Newton is accused of assuming what needed proving; of experimenting repetitively on a narrow front, where Goethe claims to be wide-ranging and exhaustive; of dressing up appearances in mathematics.[50] He calls Newton's theory a ghost that has held the scientific world in thrall for a hundred years;[51] the authority of his name inspires (the terminology is telling) "sacred fear"; the Newtonian school is like an "old rigid religious sect";[52] it is all prejudice, judgment before the inquiry, sleight of hand and deceitful hocus-pocus.[53] Goethe even accuses Newton of half-conscious dishonesty.[54] Whenever he reflects on theory, method, or system, he clearly has Newton in mind, even when his target is unnamed. An essay on "experiment as a bridge between subject and object" argues that a shrewd mind uses the more art, the fewer data he has, and shows his command by choosing among these a few favorites that flatter him. He manages to arrange the others so they do not contradict him; he wraps them up and removes them from the scene so that the whole "no longer resembles a free republic but a despotic court."[55] The two metaphors, drawn from the Enlightenment's old enemies, religion and absolutism, form pincers in which Newton's theory of light is held up as contrary to Enlightenment principles. The openness proper to rational argument, and specifically to science, had allegedly been replaced by dogma.

Some contemporaries clearly did just assume that Newton was an unquestionable authority, he must be right and Goethe—surely a dilettante?—wrong. Faced with this, Goethe too became increasingly dogmatic. For forty years, Weizsäcker comments, he misunderstood Newton's plain meaning.[56] Yet it was not straightforwardly a matter of dragging his feet in opposition to modern science. Goethe was using a different method from Newton, one that was scientifically legitimate in its way. He was investigating empirically across the widest field he could, hence his hundreds of experiments. It has been termed a "pretheoretical, exploratory" method, virtually starting from scratch, as opposed to Newton's "theory-oriented" approach, which worked from and toward a theory within a long conceptual tradition, and on a narrower experimental front.[57]

So as far as pure physics went, Goethe is still commonly held to have been wrong. But physics in any case wasn't everything. Part of his objection was that it turned the perceived world into mathematical abstraction, as if there were no alternative vision. Scientific progress seemed a one-way street, away from empirical reality. Yet color was surely not just a function of numbers, and it had a "sensuous-moral effect";[58] it was concrete experience, a physiological and emotional phenomenon. This is what made the human being the "greatest, most precise" observational instrument there could be.[59] Microscopes and telescopes "actually confuse the pure human sense."[60] That is an astounding judgment, given the fundamental advances both instruments had made possible. But if Goethe's approach seems obstructive, it appealed outside science to painters, with its foregrounding of effects such as the role of complementary colors and the associations different colors had. Newton's theories in comparison had scarcely touched the practice of artists, or the tradition of their thinking about color and the relations between colors that stretched back to the Renaissance. From Philipp Otto Runge to J. M. W. Turner, contemporaries responded to Goethe's perceptions, both intellectually and on canvas.[61]

For all his partisan vehemence, Goethe was self-critically aware of the pathology of scientific research: that for scientists, an opponent can become a mortal enemy (as Newton had posthumously become for him);[62] that researchers will more readily admit moral than scientific errors;[63] that staying within the bounds of specialism makes for "stubbornness," while going outside them leads to "inadequacy."[64] Prominent scientists were already decreeing that minute monographic work was the order of the day, yet for Goethe such detailed research needed to be built into a general picture.[65] It was the start of the modern problem of scientific specialization.

Goethe's demanding and wholly spontaneous solution involved working more than "adequately" across the whole field of science. Dilettante he was not, if commitment, experiment, and intensity of thought are the criteria. There are few areas he did not touch, indeed work on extensively— the range was made possible by the freedom and duties of his position in Weimar, to say nothing of his sheer appetite for the material world. He came to botany via work on the ducal forests, to mineralogy via attempts to reopen an old silver mine at Ilmenau, to anatomy and the sciences generally through contacts with the nearby university at Jena, for which he was administratively responsible. But these were all only the first occasions for what soon became an all-embracing enthusiasm. And in any single phase Goethe is looking beyond it to a larger picture: "What most delights me now is the plant world, which is pursuing me. . . . It forces itself on me, I no longer reflect on it, it all comes to meet me, and the immense realm is simplifying itself in my mind so that soon I shall be able to read off the most difficult problem. . . . It is a perception of the essential form with which so to speak nature constantly plays, and playing brings forth the manifold forms of life. Had I time in the short space of one lifetime, I believe I could extend it to all the realms of nature—to her whole realm."[66]

A year later, through another sudden aperçu in a Palermo garden,[67] this "essential form"—the phrase is clearly a dynamic transposition of Spinoza's dry scholastic term "formal essence"—becomes the *Urpflanze* or "primal plant." This was both the originating pattern for all plants, yet also, for Goethe, a form directly visible in each and every one. He later realized it was more concept than percept; but, more important, it was a boundary concept, "explaining everything but not itself explicable."[68] It was paralleled by other "primal phenomena" (*Urphänomene*) that he discerned across the whole of nature. There were limits to scientific analysis: "The highest happiness of the thinking being is to have investigated what can be investigated and to calmly revere what cannot."[69] What may look, again, like obscurantism is a concern for the human scale, including its timescale. Goethe elaborates the wistful "had I but time" in the letter to Charlotte into reservations about the empiricism of Francis Bacon, "for whom in the breadth of the phenomenal world everything had equal status." But how could their overwhelming mass ever be embraced? "Before induction, even such induction as Bacon extols, can achieve simplification and finality, life passes and one's powers are consumed,"[70] as Bacon himself had indeed realized.

Goethe's answer is to see the single instance as concretely containing all. The "highest insight" was that fact contained theory: do not look behind the phenomena, they are themselves the theory.[71] "What is the general? The individual case. What is the particular? Millions of cases"[72]—another Copernican reversal. The value of the "primal phenomenon" was to be, precisely, symbolic—Goethe elsewhere calls his *Urpflanze* a "symbolic plant."[73] Natural laws as he conceives them are physically *present in* the forms of nature, not something to be inferred from them and drawing attention away from them into the realm of abstraction.

The human scale is also secured by turning scientific ideas into poetry—not just didactic poetry, as with Lucretius, but love poetry. The elegy "Metamorphosis of Plants" expounds Goethe's theory of plant evolution as an address to the poet's mistress. She needs a clue to the puzzling mass of plants in the garden around her. He offers it. *Werdend* (becoming)[74]—strong emphasis, metrical and intellectual, falls on the key word—then exemplifies the concept by following the divergent possible paths of development from a simple origin in the "primal plant." Once again the general grows out of the particular. He ends by celebrating the way their love developed. Its varieties of feeling are equally part of the natural nexus, as emotions have been for Goethe since his earliest poetry.

Love apart, the act of explaining his ideas to a woman was one more attempt at intellectual wholeness. Woman was a measure of the accessibility of science, not because she was a lesser intelligence, but because she represented the larger life of humanity against the isolating intensity of specialists. Goethe is following in the footsteps of Rousseau, who similarly addressed his botanical reflections to ladies.[75] Sometimes, as in that plant-life letter to Frau von Stein, Goethe despaired of giving anyone else "the eye for it and the joy of it."[76] But he introduced her to osteology and to geology, with a playfully satanic offer to show her from a height "the kingdoms of the earth and the glory of them."[77] Even with Goethe's enthusiasm, success was on a knife edge: Charlotte was a shade surprised that he managed to interest her in "the nasty bones and the dreary realm of stones."[78]

The vision of plant variation arising from simple beginnings points the way to evolution and genetics, as does the antiteleological statement in the parallel poem "Metamorphosis of Animals" that every creature is its own self-sufficient purpose.[79] In botany Goethe goes beyond Linnaeus's system of discrete static species to a dynamic of continual change—from taxonomy to morphology (the latter term is Goethe's coining). Juxtaposition becomes transition, the fixed Great Chain of Being lurches into movement: it is a major turning point in the history of science. In anatomy Goethe goes beyond the line theology had traditionally drawn between man and the rest of creation. One crux left a small gap: human beings allegedly lacked the intermaxillary bone found in animals. Goethe, however, observed it in the faint vestigial suture left where the two halves of the facial bone structure come together during gestation. He announced the discovery not apologetically as a continuity that degraded mankind, but with exhilaration, as the "keystone," the finishing touch of humanity.[80]

Nature's continuity was a mobile order,[81] not a rigid system: "Natural system, a contradiction in terms. Nature has no system, she has—she is—life and sequence from an unknown center to an unknowable boundary."[82] But within that boundary there were similarities across all of nature's realms; decipher her handwriting in one, it will be readable in any other.[83]

The scientist was formulating what the young poet had intuited when he linked the bursting forth of plant growth, birdsong, and human emotion in a single verb, *dringen*.[84] His science had grown out of that passionate embracing of the world and still retained the force of poetic vision, so much so that he could feel convinced he was concretely seeing what was for others an abstract idea.[85] That was the ticklish issue in his first real conversation with Schiller. As they were leaving a meeting of the Jena scientific society, Schiller objected to the "fragmented" (i.e., overly specialized) scientific treatment of nature, which was unappealing to the layman. That was a cue for Goethe to state his holistic doctrines, which involved precisely "taking nature not in separate pieces, but active and living, striving from the whole into the parts."[86] Harmony gave way to tension when Schiller expressed doubt about whether Goethe could see his *Urpflanze*—it was plainly no more than an "idea." Goethe huffed and puffed, but they agreed, just, to differ, and out of that agreement grew a relationship of complementarity rather than conflict. They realized they were on the same path between real and ideal, empirical and theoretical, merely traversing it from opposite ends and bound to meet midway, to the benefit of both.

Schiller had trained as a doctor, so—within medicine's then limits—as a scientist. Despite or because of that, he had no evident sympathy for science and a jaundiced view of modern cosmology, where the sun was a "soullessly spinning ball of fire."[87] He seems not to have realized the transforming effect that science was having on ways of seeing the world. In the already accomplished young scientist Alexander von Humboldt Schiller could see only "the naked, sharp-edged understanding that shamelessly claims to have completely measured nature, which is always ungraspable and in all her aspects venerable and unfathomable, and with an impudence that I do not understand makes his formulas, which are often only empty words and only ever narrow concepts, into the measure of nature. He has no imagination; and he thus lacks in my judgment the most necessary capacity for his science—for nature must be contemplated and felt, in its individual phenomena as in its highest laws." All this, prefaced by "About Alexander, I have as yet no proper judgment"![88] The destructive utterance has echoes of that Jena conversation. Indeed, Schiller seems to want to out-Goethe Goethe in his insistence on wholeness—though Goethe himself unreservedly admired the young Humboldt, whose science was in fact very much in his own holistic spirit and owed much to his inspiration. Perhaps Schiller was touchy over Humboldt's leading Goethe deeper into the natural sciences.[89] At best, Schiller's writing off of Humboldt, already a significant figure in science and destined to be the leading German scientist of midcentury, is an extreme case of Schiller's suspicion that specialization has a dehumanizing effect. This, in a less unpleasantly ad hominem form, was the insight he had already arrived at, that the specialist is sacrificing his human wholeness for the good, or at least the technical advance, of humanity: "Only by concentrating all the energy of our mind in *one* focal point and drawing our whole being together in a single force do we give this force wings and take it artificially beyond the limits nature seems to have set to it." All the strength of human sight put together could never have seen the moons of Jupiter that the telescope shows the astronomer. Just as certainly, all human thinking collectively could never have risen to infinitesimal calculus or the *Critique of Pure Reason* if the rational powers of certain individuals had not been separated from the sensuous world so as to concentrate on these high abstractions.[90] Was there no way of bringing such people back into their full humanity? "Can the individual really be meant, in the pursuit of some larger purpose, to lose out on his whole self?"[91] But in this context, the *Letters on the Aesthetic Education of Man*, Schiller was already casting a net far wider than science, drawing together art, philosophy, and politics in a prescription for the flaws in humanity that the disappointed hopes of the French Revolution had again made plain.

Schiller could not have been more wrong about Humboldt. Humboldt was the natural continuator of Goethe, whose all-embracing vision had influenced him as a young man; of Georg Forster's voyages (he had been Forster's companion on his Rhineland journey); and of Kant's experience-based theory of knowledge. He admired Kant's analysis of the Lisbon earthquakes and his work on the nebular hypothesis.[92] Humboldt was the extreme empiricist, in his early years doing painful and dangerous medical experiments on his own body. To collect materials for his science, he covered vast tracts of the globe, especially the jungles of South America, at considerable peril. With the inadequate equipment of the day, he climbed (on Chimborazo) to a greater height than anyone before him. On one of his voyages he had himself lowered over the ship's side to observe the storm waves from close up. Above all, he was the very antithesis of the specialization Schiller deplored. He did intensively pursue specific lines of inquiry, especially in geology, climatology, and global plant distributions. Yet these were only the start. As the last professional scientist to do this—the only comparable figure is Buffon—he had the "crazy idea" of writing "a physics of the whole material world," a survey that would "embrace all created things in earth and heaven . . . from the most distant mists and circling double stars of space to the geographical distribution of plants on earth," the whole enormous enterprise to be guided by the idea of "the inner concatenation of the general with the particular."[93] It incidentally included a survey of past presentations of the world, in texts both scientific and aesthetic, showing a grasp of ancient cultures that a historian or a classicist might envy.

Humboldt's choice of title is significant. At first it was going to be "The Book of Nature," but that, as he knew, was a Christian metaphor used by the likes of the medieval thinker Albertus Magnus.[94] The word *Kosmos*, in

contrast, made the direct link back to the Greeks, with whose science—
left wholly out of Schiller's wistful evocation of their gods—Humboldt was
well acquainted. It was as if Christianity had in the interval never been.
Kosmos duly contains not a single reference to God, something that raised
reviewers' eyebrows and shocked the conservative courtiers around Friedrich Wilhelm IV of Prussia, whose favor, remarkably, Humboldt in his late
years enjoyed. More pugnaciously, Kant's continuator Pierre Laplace, when
asked by Napoleon why his book *Mécanique céleste* contained no reference to God, made "the magnificent and disdainful reply, 'Citizen Consul,
I have no need of that hypothesis.'"[95] Religion was gradually becoming neither a threat nor a target, but an irrelevance. True, there were battles with
orthodoxy still to come, most dramatically over Darwin and evolution, but
scientists no longer needed to guard their backs so anxiously against real
dangers. Tellingly, the crucial debate on Darwinism took place in a newly
opened Museum of Science at a university (Oxford), not in front of a synod
or inquisition. Science had come of age. There were significant staging posts
in its growth. Goethe in 1831 notes that Galileo died just before Newton's
birth, which, rising above his old hostility to the *Opticks*, Goethe calls "the
Christmastide of our modern times."[96] (Newton was in fact born on Christ-
mas day.) By another chance link, Humboldt died in 1859, the year *The
Origin of Species* appeared. Lichtenberg thought in even longer historical
perspective and appropriated a biblical phrase for a secular purpose: "With
Copernicus there began a new heaven and a new earth."[97]

Humboldt's star as a scientist has since waned. Scientists outside Germany seem scarcely to have heard of him; at best, they know that a current
off the west coast of South America bears his name. Paradoxically, that ignorance may be due precisely to his grand grasp. Nowadays a lasting scientific
reputation is made by some single fundamental breakthrough. Humboldt's
renown as a popularizer—his Paris and Berlin lecture courses for university
and general audiences drew hundreds, and *Kosmos* sold in the thousands—
put his individual achievements in the shade and has itself not lasted. It
would take a scientist with equally broad grasp to appreciate Humboldt's
own. Specialization has long since won; so has the movement away from
Goethean concrete experience into the abstractions of Newtonian mathematics and on into quantum mechanics. Science avowedly investigates not
the immediate sensory world but its "dark background," which its experiments "bring into the light."[98] Light, then, of a kind. But a single graspable
whole seems, precisely for that reason, not to be in sight.

Lichtenberg, as a professor of physics at Göttingen, was in principle
already on the specialist side of the divide. There was no better base for

science than this fashionable new university established in 1737, linked as it was through its founder, the Elector of Hanover, now George I of England, with the home of empiricism and intellectual freedom: "Freedom to think and write with impunity is an advantage of the place over which George rules and on which the blessing of Münchhausen rests."[99] Lichtenberg had English links of his own. He mentored a succession of visiting students, sons of the nobility. "An Englishman at Göttingen without your assistance is but a helpless mortal," wrote Sir Francis Clarke. "I have wasted the best ten years of my life taming Englishmen," wrote Lichtenberg.[100] He remained nevertheless an Anglophile. On his second trip to England, which lasted nearly a year, he moved in elevated social and scientific circles, even accompanying the king, a keen dabbler in astronomy, on a visit to the national observatory. In 1792 he was made a fellow of the Royal Society, entered in its books (under the wrong names "Gottfried Charles"!) as someone likely to become "useful." Perhaps he was more important to the Society for his position in a politically allied location than for any specific scientific achievement. Achievements there certainly were: he had made discoveries in electricity—the starlike magnetic patterns made by dust scattered on resin (the ultimate basis for photocopying) were known as "Lichtenberg figures," and he was apparently close to creating an electrical signal.[101] He worked intensively on "types of air" (*Luftarten*), that is, gases. He was fascinated by lightning and championed Benjamin Franklin's lightning conductor in Germany. He was engrossed in the whole drama of scientific advance, kept up with many areas of scientific work, knew that no subject was ever exhausted, all was in flux, today's leading edge would be tomorrow's taken-for-granted middle. But he was also increasingly aware of being himself left behind, frustratingly missing the chance to pioneer balloon flight : "I had Montgolfier's invention in my grasp."[102] He also labored under a massive lecturing stint— six hours a day, six days a week, with only a four-week vacation—which hindered his research, though it made his name as the greatest experimental demonstrator of his day. He envied the relative leisure of English professors and the rich sponsors and practitioners of science in France and Italy. And there was the nagging question whether he had spread himself too wide. Looking back, he realized that from the start of his studies he had planned too grand a structure.[103] Then there was his principle of thoroughness, of always beginning at the very beginning, at the base.[104] How far could one hope to advance from there? It was the dilemma facing the Baconian empiricist that Goethe saw.

For all these reasons, Lichtenberg the specialized scientist was left in the end a scientific generalist. And not just in his professional practice: his private intellectual life was conducted in a succession of rough-books (*Su-delbücher*) where he deals with every kind of topic. Not for nothing is the epigraph for the 1773 notebook a quotation he found in an English journal: "The whole man must move together."[105] He mixes observations and reflections on society and culture, manners and politics, psychology and sensuality (his reactions to beautiful women in particular: the same mind that could follow Newton's proofs could be distracted by a beautiful arm—but then, thinking too was an irrepressible sensuous urge),[106] religion and philosophy (he was both a clear-sighted Kantian and a convinced Spinozist), plus mathematical calculations, poems, diagrams and caricatures, ideas for essays, and even motifs for a novel. From this inchoate mixture later editors have lifted gems of wit and insight that make Lichtenberg's main modern reputation as an aphorist in a tradition stretching from the French seventeenth- and eighteenth-century *moralistes* down to Nietzsche and Karl Kraus. Certainly his aperçus are as witty as any, his angle of vision delightfully idiosyncratic. Was it "weak- or sharpsightedness" that made him "see things so differently from other people," he asked himself, in his best English.[107] But a far more absorbing picture emerges when his rough-books are read in their entirety. Lichtenberg took the term from the commercial practice of jotting the day's purchases and sales higgledy-piggledy for later transfer to a double-entry ledger. His rough-books stayed rough, their "rich confusion" too diverse to be given any simple coherence, not even that of the Shandean novel in which he sometimes hoped—impossibly—to "use everything."[108] No brief commentary can begin to do them justice: every jotting contains a compressed argument, every rereading creates a different anthology. Yet it is precisely their chaotic range and richness that makes them an Enlightenment in little, the portrait of a mind tirelessly questioning in all directions. It is the mind of a scientist, not just through the many specifically scientific speculations and sketches, sometimes minipapers, but more broadly through the mode of inquiry, the original angle, the ingenious hypothesis, the "what if," the "could we perhaps." A favored verbal form is the subjunctive.[109] There were some certainties in Lichtenberg's world: that humankind was its own sufficient revelation; that orthodox religion was incredible though ineradicable; that absolutist rulers were largely incompetent (why was it you had to pass exams to become a village doctor, but not to become a ruler?); that change was necessary and any seeming stasis only a pause; that progressive enlightenment was inevitable, though not for all levels of intelligence, and not without its dangers and drawbacks, since independent thinking might produce harmful as well as beneficial ideas, bad books as the price of good.[110]

A case in point was Lavater's fashionable "physiognomic" theory, which argued that character could be read from the structure of the face. His immense collection of images, from well-known works of art (Holbein, Titian) but also pictures and silhouettes of contemporaries, often used without the subject's knowledge, purported to uncover moral character through physical features. With the best of intentions this would serve, so Lavater's subtitle declared, the knowledge and love of humanity. But was it really knowledge, and was love the only likely result? Might people not be judged, perhaps even condemned, on their facial appearance? A man might lose his job, and, at the extreme that Lichtenberg satirically imagined, children might be hanged for looking like future criminals.[111] Lichtenberg may have felt personally got at because of his own unprepossessing body: four feet eight inches short and hunchbacked to boot.[112] What false conclusions might that not have led to? Was flesh to be the judge of spirit? What about the plug-ugly Socrates?[113] Knigge made the same point in his classic work on social relations and behavior: any exterior might hide a noble heart and a thoughtful mind.[114] Lavater's theory was a classic case of bad science, empirical observation not processed by adequate reflection. The project at first intrigued Goethe, to the point where he himself contributed to the second and third volumes and made the arrangements for the initial printing,[115] only to be increasingly repelled by the project's theological underpinning, by Lavater's Christian dogmatism, and by the obvious overinterpretation his theories involved. Goethe's own morphological work takes off immediately afterward, not as a development from but as a reaction against Lavater's naive physiognomic ideas. The naïveté is plain in the accounts of the Stolberg brothers that Goethe quotes in his autobiography as samples of Lavater's work—lengthy effusions whose results could never plausibly have been drawn from mere facial appearance.[116] When Goethe himself was the subject, Lavater read into Lips's portrait everything he already knew about the poet—the "clear, swift, accurate understanding," the "sublimity" of the upper lip, the "expression of poetic feeling and poetic power" in the nose (!).[117] Lavater often notes that the image he prints is a poor or incomplete likeness, which makes the conclusions he draws from it even more arbitrary. It was in fact a new kind of prejudice that would have been comical had it not been potentially threatening. "Physiognomizing" on the pretext of "furthering a love of humanity" recalled for Lichtenberg the way people had once burned their fellows in the name of divine love.[118]

In contrast, another empirical collection rested on ground-level evidence and careful procedures: Karl Philipp Moritz's archive of case histories in the *Magazin zur Erfahrungsseelenkunde* (Journal of Empirical Psy-

chology), ten volumes published over the decade from 1783. It drew on a
variety of earlier journals, especially the Swiss Isaak Iselin's *Ephemeriden
der Menschheit* and indeed on Lavater's *Physiognomik*. But it also applied
more widely the self-analysis Moritz was simultaneously practicing in his
"psychological novel" *Anton Reiser*, the autobiographical narrative of a
childhood in which an extreme Pietist upbringing resulted in depressive
states.[119] Moritz was following the principle explicit in his journal's later
title, *Gnothi Sauton*—Know Thyself. Parts of the novel, more fact than
fiction, appeared in the journal, whose foreword insisted on the need for
"facts and no moralizing nonsense."[120] Its first three volumes concentrated
on collecting accounts; only in later sections did a systematic review begin. Inevitably, there was too blithe an assumption of the ready applicabil-
ity of this psychologizing, and no serious method developed. The project
hovered uneasily between technicality and popular accessibility. Still, it
was virtually the start of modern psychological understanding, exploiting
but secularizing the soul-searchings of Pietism. When Moritz asks why we
should not allow the workings of the human mind to be dissected much as
is done to the human body,[121] he is unknowingly answering David Hume's
call to "glean up our experiments in this science from a cautious observation of human life" as lived "in the common course of the world."[122]
Human nature, too, was an object of science, of practical experience if not
yet of contrived laboratory experiments (which may be why Moritz abandoned his original title). It was becoming ever more widely accepted that,
in Pope's phrase, "the proper study of mankind is man," not God; "Know
then thyself, presume not God to scan"—anthropology replaced theology.
That meant not just piecemeal insights but a cumulative science to which
all observations of human thought and creativity could contribute. The potential social value was clear. Not the least of Moritz's aims, besides aid-
ing pedagogy, was to help understand the pathology of social outcasts and
criminals,[123] something that Schiller would brilliantly explore a few years
later in his fictional reworking of a real-life case, the "Criminal through
Lost Honor" (*Verbrecher aus verlorener Ehre*).

   Among Lichtenberg's own psychological insights, often introspectively
frank, was the very modern thought that more could be learned about a
person's character from their dreams than from their faces.[124] His reaction
to Lavater was not kept private but emerged from the rough-books into
public polemic and parody, in particular a mock disquisition on (pig-)tails
that was the more hilarious because *Schwanz* (tail) also colloquially means
penis.[125] Of course, judging character visually was a skill mankind had practiced from time immemorial, but it had to rest on observations of the flux

of feelings and their expression in gesture and body language, of a person's whole mode of being, of what Lichtenberg called *Pathognomik*. Lavater's fixed anatomical *Physiognomik* would not do. Lichtenberg was conceiving a broader base of experience, of experiment. Life was indeed one big experiment—on the largest scale, the French Revolution was "experimental politics"[126]—and all experimental outcomes were open.

The principles and best practice of science joined with, were practically identical with, the principles and practice of enlightenment. Science contained the necessary gravity to give humanity a firm footing in the world. The tree of knowledge was now properly rededicated to human use. Adam and Eve's had been, in the traditional phrase, a fortunate fall. Perhaps, in that Edenic origin, the fruit was simply not yet ripe enough for good eating.[127]

CHAPTER 8

Good Guardianship:
Light through Education

Education holds the great secret of the perfection of human nature.
—Immanuel Kant, *Lectures on Pedagogy*

Your educators can be nothing but your liberators.
—Friedrich Nietzsche, *Schopenhauer as Educator*

To be enlightened is to know something of the world, one's place in it and in history, one's proper rights and obligations in the present, one's prospects in the future. Achieving that clarity can be hindered by the prejudices and superstitions of one's day and place. In the guise of "socialization," they may repress the spark of independent reflection that for Kant was the individual's birthright. The chances of enlightenment thus hang initially on a more open practice of education.

Kant's "What Is Enlightenment?" leaps straight to the young adult and the problem of control by "guardians," who are the villains of the piece. It leaves out childhood, which undeniably does need guidance and protection by benevolent real guardians—parents. Meanwhile, the metaphorical guardians who want to control society will have organized an educational system, aware that minds need to be caught young while they are still inexperienced, trusting, and open to imprinting with the required beliefs. Or was there a chance of guardians more liberal than the conservatives who were Kant's target? Teachers, if anyone in society, could be agents of fulfillment.

There is no question but that European education till the verge of the eighteenth century was limited in substance and rigid in method. Even when not directly in the hands of religious orders, it was everywhere under the close control of the church. Though the classical languages and literatures bulked large as instructional material, it was not for the value of their humanistic and perilously pagan content, but as the basis for dry-as-dust grammatical exercises. Pupils' mistakes were savagely punished, as if they were a form of misbehavior.

It is not as if better principles for teaching and motivating the young were not known, and sometimes practiced, but so far only ever in private, by tutors to the nobility and gentry. John Locke's influential *Thoughts Concerning Education* (1693) were set down to advise a gentleman acquaintance on basic matters of child health and good habits, on how to establish benign fatherly authority, on what was worth studying—with an eye to career usefulness—and on how to make the subject matter attractive. Even earlier, there could have been no more liberal education than the one Montaigne enjoyed by the grace of a father who had brought back liberal ideas from his Italian journey, a direct link with Renaissance humanism. Among other things, the boy was taught Latin as his first language by the direct method— a German, one Dr. Horst, was employed who was fluent in Latin and knew no more French than his pupil yet did. When Montaigne's father later yielded to convention and sent the boy to a college (which duly corrupted his Latin), he was at least lucky enough to have a tutor who sharpened his appetite for classical poetry. The mature essayist's happy early experience inspired his recommendations to a noblewoman, Diane de Foix, comtesse de Gurson, for the education of the son Montaigne gallantly (and, as it turned out, rightly) assumed she was going to give birth to. The boy should be made capable rather than erudite—Aristotle must have nurtured abilities, not abstractions, in Alexander. One must form the pupil's judgment, not pack his head with knowledge; encourage relevance and brevity; propose no guide but reason, and a preference for truth over rhetoric, for things over words; have the boy travel and make real contact with foreign people and so become a citizen of the world, as Socrates had been. He should also learn to doubt; and the tutor should sometimes listen to the boy's own thoughts. It was a thoroughly modern conception. The great Scottish humanist and poet George Buchanan, who spent some time in Bordeaux, thought of writing a book on education based on Montaigne's experience. Montaigne makes no great claims for himself as the product of this humane regime, but posterity knows better. Meanwhile, in contrast, the public schools—which were also exclusively for the socially better situated—remained places of pedantic cramming and "blood-stained rods."[1]

Things began seriously stirring with the Bohemian Johan Amos Comenius's *Orbis sensualium pictus* (1658) and *Great Didactic* (1633–). The first opened up the classroom to the real world through the innovative use of images designed to appeal to young minds; the second, subtitled "the whole art of teaching all things to all men," laid down principles for teaching "the entire youth of both sexes, quickly, pleasantly and thoroughly." Instead of the present "Sisyphus-labour" of schools, "teachers should teach less and pupils learn more"; "noise, aversion and useless labour" should be replaced by "more leisure, enjoyment and solid progress."[2] Schooling should embrace "the poorest, the most abject and the most obscure," the seemingly "dull and stupid" too, since nobody is "so weak of intellect that it cannot be improved." Girls have "equal sharpness of mind and capacity for knowledge" (Comenius admittedly wants competent mothers, not bluestockings). All this without the need for "blows, rigour or compulsion."[3] The necessary order and sequence is to be the order of nature.[4] The model for handling the occasional unruly spirit is Plutarch's account of how Alexander the Great made the wild horse Bucephalus his own.[5]

Comenius's influence spread across Europe through translations into five languages. He was consulted by the governments of Hungary and Sweden, and but for the English Civil War would have come to advise Parliament. His emphasis on practicality, on things rather than words, on a relation to the world outside school walls, on natural development rather than imposed routine, is behind Rousseau's *Émile*, and later Johann Heinrich Pestalozzi's involvement in practical training for poor Swiss children.[6] Likewise the seemingly trivial episode in Goethe's *Götz von Berlichingen* where the knight's small son can parrot the name Jaxthausen but doesn't realize it is their own castle and village he has been learning about: his father, in contrast, "knew every path, track, and ford before I knew the name of the river, village, and castle." It is the same false priority that makes the boy want a baked apple rather than a raw one.[7] The priority of the natural has echoes elsewhere in Goethe's early work, in Faust's frustration with mere words and his urge to grasp the inner workings of the real world.[8]

But the major new influence in eighteenth-century Germany was Johann Bernhard Basedow, with his widely (not always favorably) publicized experiment, the Philanthropin in Dessau-Wörlitz. It began when Franz of Anhalt-Dessau realized the schools of his small land were "an Augean stable" that "needed a Hercules." Calling in Basedow was only one outstanding act in a lifetime of liberal rule which made his otherwise insignificant duchy (700 square kilometers, 35,000 inhabitants) into an oasis of enlightenment in a backward Germany. Wieland, as tutor to the future duke of Weimar, wished the young Carl August could spend a year there and model himself on Franz, the only one of the German rulers to deserve the cliché title "father of his people."[9] Carl August paid the first of many visits in 1776 and 1778. Already ruling in his twenties; he was much influenced by the barely older Goethe—an education of sorts.[10]

Basedow had made a reputation as a teacher, and especially as a writer on education, in works addressed to both professionals and concerned parents and even written directly for children. He had worked for a few years for the Danish crown, which was more than once a source of support for German writers at critical moments in their careers.[11] Basedow wrote on religion, on toleration, on grammar, on literacy, and especially on teaching methods. His most significant book was the *Elementarwerk* (1772), a survey of modern views of the world angled toward presentation for children, with some three hundred engravings by the leading illustrator of the day, Daniel Chodowiecki. Inevitably Basedow was controversial. He was attacked by Christians for his scientific materialism, only lightly trimmed with deism, and for his commitment to tolerance. He even compiled a hymnbook intended to further toleration by excluding all reference to doctrines that caused conflict between sects. Believers in hell, in the rightness of persecution, or in the damnation of soldiers who died unshriven in battle were energetically denounced[12]—toleration had to be itself combative. His combativeness had to be discouraged as bad publicity for his Dessau project, but it was too deep-rooted in a man always likely to fly off the handle—he called himself "the crude stirrer" (*der grobe Rührlöffel*). That promised ill for the smooth running of the school and relations with the staff. Basedow was moreover a tired man when he founded the school and already looking for someone to whom to pass the baton. He left only four years later, in 1778, and died in 1790.

Still, his flood of publications, along with his and his successors' organizational efforts, drew attention to the school's innovations, all across Europe from Britain to Russia, in France influencing Condorcet's postrevolutionary reform proposals. The original Dessau Philanthropin lasted barely twenty years, but it generated a diaspora of some sixty similar schools, of which one, founded by the writer Christian Gotthilf Salzmann on his property at Schnepfental in Thuringia still operates today as a specialist language school. Modern languages were one of Basedow's new emphases, as well as Latin without tears by something like the Montaigne direct method. Teaching classical languages in the old dull and brutal way was not so much too specialized as too limiting, the subject matter irrelevant to later life and anyway soon forgotten. The Philanthropin's new broader curriculum embraced the sciences, handicraft, gardening, gymnastics (the seed of the national movement of *Turnvater* Jahn), many kinds of sport (an early impulse toward Coubertin's revival of the Olympic Games), and school outings. Some days were spent frugally, making the students taste hardship so as to train them in resilience. The aim was to create a rounded culture and, not least, happy pupils. The shift was from gloomy passivity to cheerful engagement, and from church doctrines to a more objective grasp of the world. A program that took in more and more of known reality inevitably loosened the grip of speculative unrealities. Religion was to be separated from humane and civic teaching; children of all beliefs were to be educated together and learn toleration in practice. Undoing the dominance of religion came naturally to Basedow as one who had sat at the feet of Reimarus. He replaced church services by acts of deistic reverence of his own devising. That was too freethinking for Christians and too Christianlike for freethinkers, but Duke Franz said he always felt "improved" by these ceremonies. And as a school that, at least in its early years, was open to the children of local tailors, coachmen, masons, coopers, shoemakers (in 1777 Basedow published a *Philosophy for All Classes*), the Philanthropin was Germany's first attempt at a school system both secular and democratic.

As a well-known educator, Basedow crops up in other writing for children. Christian Felix Weisse's journal *The Children's Friend*, begun in 1776, is a chronicle in weekly installments about a Leipzig family that young readers are invited to feel part of. The children it features benefit from the interests of family friends; they go on educational trips, to the popular fair, or to see an elephant on display in their hometown. General knowledge is interwoven with mild moral teachings. Among the excitements is a report by their private tutor (they are a well-to-do family, as the dress and interiors in the frontispieces to each number show) about visiting Dessau and watching Basedow examine his pupils on a Philanthropin Open Day. The children know the reformer's name—they have been using his *Elementarwerk*. But is their enthusiastic tutor perhaps partisan? Only, he says, "for what is good."[13] They can sense that education is everywhere a hot topic.

Basedow's program included teacher training, to create a cascade effect. Many prominent liberal minds became associated with the Philanthropin, including briefly Johann Heinrich Campe, once private tutor to Wilhelm and Alexander von Humboldt, a pioneer of writing for children, author of a multivolume *General Revision of the Whole School and Educational System*, and later in charge of schools in Brunswick. Karl Friedrich Bahrdt for a time ran an offshoot Philanthropin at Marschlin in Switzerland.

Finance was as always a problem. In 1775 Basedow issued an appeal to "cosmopolitans, crowned or other" to support this school "of a quite new kind, which ought to be old"—that is, which had surely long been the obvious way to go about educating.[14] The appeal ends on a despondent note:

"I will wait and see. But I cannot wait for long." In the event, the response was good, with many prominent names listed as subscribers.[15] Duke Franz was a last resort and provided a fine new building, but he was financially stretched, feeding fifteen hundred victims of the floods in his principality. At one stage the school was housed in a palace in the Dessau-Wörlitz grounds, while Franz's heir lived in a modest house nearby—a sign of education's relative status.

Kant supported the project with public statements and letters. He publicized Basedow's appeal and commended the Philanthropin to humanity's "guardians" as a school "genuinely suited to nature and to all society's needs" and hence as "an institution from which a new order in human affairs is beginning."[16] When it was attacked, as such innovation was bound to be, he defended it in unusually blunt words. Schools throughout Europe were wrong on first principles because they "worked against nature." It was no good waiting for gradual change, schools must be totally reshaped (*umgeschaffen*), not by slow reform but by a swift revolution—strong language from a normally gradualist thinker. It becomes positively fighting talk when he calls the attacks on Basedow's project typical of the way "convention defends itself on its dung-heap." Nothing if not practical, Kant took on the job of receiving the private contributions that were necessary because "governments these days seem to have no money for improving schools."[17] Basedow asked whether education was not a higher priority than a ruler's opera house or two hundred infantry. A skeptical sympathizer asked whether rulers had any interest at all in the education of the common man.[18] More subtly, Kant tried to secure wider support from influential figures by reassuring them that Basedow's alleged extremes had been toned down by his successor, Wolke (such people were of course worried that the formal academic side was being neglected in this newfangled curriculum) and by making them feel that they were now the pioneers in an important development.[19]

It did not last. After Basedow had gone, Duke Franz in his final years became less active and effective. The school reverted to educating the upper class. It was attacked by the church, and equally by the humanists, who saw no reason to make common cause with a humane regime. Yet the project left a high-water mark for all subsequent education across Europe. Goethe was being only partly ironic when he called Basedow a prophet, one of a pair he journeyed down the Rhine with in 1774; Lavater was the other. A poem describes himself perched between them, his mind confessedly more on what he was eating than what he was hearing, a self-styled "child of this world."[20] If that phrase denotes a rootedness in secular reality, Basedow was very much on Goethe's side, a worldly prophet at the opposite pole from the transcendentalist Lavater.

Kant's involvement in the Philanthropin was not a sudden interest in preuniversity issues. He had long been giving pedagogy lectures that filled in the gap left in "What Is Enlightenment?" by dealing with a child's upbringing to the onset of puberty,[21] which he sets at thirteen or fourteen. They are a mixture of traditional principles—breast-feeding is best; giving in to a crying child will turn it into a tyrant; learning is work, not play— and new liberal thinking. Kant is for the development of self-esteem in the young without the necessity of competition; he is against corporal punishment; he is for public education, despite the financial problem that rulers are utilitarian, shortsighted, tightfisted, and unlikely ever to finance experiments in education. Regularly in other works he complains about the priority the army enjoys—80 percent of the Prussian budget—over education. Above all, Kant is for an education in social and cosmopolitan ideals that will prepare children not just for the world as it is, but for the world as it might be: not just for their own or their own nation's advantage—which is how parents and rulers see things—but for the widest general good, for this can never be damaging to the long-term interests of people and peoples. There should be equal respect for all, of whatever social class; morality should be inculcated through a collection of exemplary cases; true religion means observing the "law within us," aimed at the practice of the good life; acts of worship are not wanted, they are an opiate for the conscience, mere currying favor (*Gunstbewerbung*) with a deity; theological doctrine is not for the young; the idea of God should grow out of morality and the analogy with the human father.

These are Kant's familiar ethical and religious principles, which he is here getting in on the ground floor. Underlying them is a respect for what is natural, in the spirit of Rousseau's *Émile*. Nature can be left to look after the young creature and must not be impeded. Wrapping a baby in swaddling clothes is a curtailment of natural freedom even before what Rousseau called the chains of society are forged. Better to lay the child in an ample box, as apparently the Italians do in an *arcuccio*.[22] Kant naturally rejects those other physical constraints, leading reins and baby walkers, that provide negative metaphors in "What Is Enlightenment?" Learning to walk in the literal sense is a natural process, and the child will always learn better what it learns for itself. It might even, left to its own devices, invent writing! Kant's ultimate ideal is indeed the complete autodidact. Short of this, mere instruction is not enough. The child must learn actively to think.[23]

This brings in a central Enlightenment purpose at an age well short of physical maturity, at most at a late stage of schooling or, in those days, the start of university. It raises the question of just how the educational process is to operate. What should liberal guardians be doing? If teaching was indeed to be more than the imprinting of old assumptions on passive young minds, there were paradoxes. One was that the young were meant to think thoughts the teacher had not yet thought and so could not impart, and to criticize the thoughts the teacher did have. For if pedagogues were left in complete control of passive young minds, as Lichtenberg said, there would be no more great men: "Heaven forfend that a human being, whose true teacher nature is, should become a lump of wax on which a professor impresses his sublime image."[24] Or in the yet more extreme terms Leonardo da Vinci used, it was a poor pupil who did not surpass his master. To this end, pupils must be—paradox again—compelled to be free. (A conservative thinker would no doubt have argued that they should be left "free" to accept the status quo.)

Kant resolved the first paradox by arguing that it was not his job to teach specific thoughts, but how to think—not the noun *Gedanken* but the verb *denken*. His students must not be "carried" if they were to learn to "walk" on their own—already the opening metaphor of "What Is Enlightenment?" What they had to learn was not contained in any one book, in the way all of geometry was in Euclid.[25] This was a radical statement at a time when a lecture course normally took the form of a commentary on a published work. Frederick the Great rather surprisingly decreed in 1778 that lectures must not be of the professor's own devising but must use a recognized manual.[26] True, education inevitably meant imparting *some* standard knowledge in advance of the students' maturity, but even here there was, so Kant argued, a natural sequence. First you should inculcate understanding, then reason, and only then academic learning. Commonly the reverse happened, with the result that universities sent out into the world shallow minds with learning "stuck on," not organically "grown." Whereas the right sequence meant that, even if the final stage was never reached, the student could at least take away something useful for life.[27]

The second paradox, if not finally resolvable, could at least be eased if "compulsion" was no more than a gentle pressure encouraging free movement. That is what Herder recalled as the way of his young Königsberg professor: "He encouraged us and pleasantly compelled us to *think for ourselves*; despotism was foreign to his mind."[28] The professor was Kant. In two glowing pages Herder recalls the "happiness" of knowing the philosopher in his teaching heyday, youthful, eloquent, witty, intellectually omnivorous, subject to no sectarian commitment or worldly ambition, concerned only to extend and illuminate the truth. He places Kant in the Socratic tradition, which incidentally provides a metaphor to further ease the paradox: Socrates claimed to be a midwife, drawing out rather than imposing ideas— skilled assistance for a natural process. Herder links this with Kant's aim in the First Critique, which was, in yet another metaphor, to weed out the thorns of sophistry and let the seeds of reason and moral principle take root, once more "not through compulsion but inner freedom." The passage is the more moving for its generosity. It rises above the frictions of the years between, when Kant had reviewed the first two parts of Herder's *Ideas for a Philosophy of Human History* hurtfully.[29]

Healthy doubt and independent thinking could be learned concretely from the teacher's own example. He could be observed questioning received ideas in a stringent procedure, without facile iconoclasm. Kant certainly did this, overall by his epistemological ground clearing and specifically by keeping his early promise to disagree if necessary with even the most eminent thinkers. In a review of progress in metaphysics since Leibniz and Wolff, he calls Leibniz's theory of preestablished harmony, according to which body and mind are coordinated like two parallel clocks, "the most bizarre figment that philosophy has ever thought up."[30] It certainly had competition in Leibniz's other theory—of the monads, "a kind of enchanted world that the celebrated man was led astray into imagining."[31] Whether the work of Leibniz and Wolff counted as progress might be left to "the judgment of those who are not scared off by great names."[32] At best theirs had been a preparation for real progress, in the form, of course, of Kant's own long-overdue, thorough critique of reason.

Much educational writing up to this time had concentrated on the particular case of princes and the nobility. Under absolutism it was crucial to try to shape the future wielders of absolute power. Basedow himself had written a mirror for princes, *Agathokrator* (1771). His ideas on method for the Philanthropin arose also out of his experience of private tutoring (of his own daughter). Applying those lessons to a school was thus a genuine trickle-down process. And tutoring in the end pointed, through its own inherent problems, to the need for schools. Besides being poorly paid, treated often as servants, and in competition with parents, who undermined their authority by humiliating them in front of their charges—they were, after all, for the most part just impoverished students, commonly of theology, who had been recommended by their professors[33]—tutors were increasingly required to be well versed in all branches of knowledge, to have physical skills (riding, fencing), to be conversant with the etiquette of a society in which they were not at home, sometimes even to assist in domestic admin-istration. Nothing short of universal geniuses would do. For want of such paragons, the idea arose that parents might pool their employees, each tutor covering a single academic need—which would in effect create a school.

By one route or another, schools became increasingly the social reality, though still looked at with a jaundiced eye by the more elevated as places where a sensitive child would be submerged in the mass and damaged by crude treatment. Another school-founding movement on a much larger scale than Basedow's sprang from the Halle charity of the Pietist theologian Hermann August Francke. Originally an orphanage, it soon became a school for all levels of society, combined with an astutely run business. Like Base-dow's Philanthropin, it too embraced practical subjects and trained teach-ers. Pietism had arisen as a lay movement within the Lutheran church to renew and intensify the individual spiritual life. By the early 1700s it had become a substantial sect outside the church and a growing force in Prus-sian society, where its interests and effects often coincided with royal inten-tions—so much so that for a time it became effectively the state religion of Prussia.[34] It also created a virtual "international order" of supporters and sympathizers stretching from London to Moscow with the aim of funda-mental social reform and renewal.[35]

By 1717 some two thousand schools on Francke's Halle model had been built or planned. But what schools! Kant experienced his education at the Königsberg Fridericianum as "an enslaved youth" (*Jugendsklaverei*)[36] under what a schoolfellow in retrospect called "the pedantic discipline of fanatics" (*poenitenda fanaticorum disciplina*).[37] It was a discipline in which prayer, devotional exercises, sermons, and catechizings dominated and pervaded the curriculum. Moreover, from being a fresh impulse Pietism had hard-ened into a virtual book of rules for spiritual breakthrough that involved constant probing into the state of the pupil's soul to check for the requisite attitudes. Pietist discipline did not allow for independent spiritual growth. So deeply pious a person as Susanne von Klettenberg, the young Goethe's friend and guide in his brief religious phase, was reproved for omitting the required "struggle of contrition" (*Bußkampf*).[38] Cheerfulness during the soul's struggles was a bad sign. Gloom and a hangdog look were the right way to curry favor with teachers, because allegedly these were what God wanted. They were easy to playact, and it may well have been the system-induced hypocrisy of Kant's schooling that shaped his later abhorrence of outward religious shows, while his home experience of a quiet, unpreten-tious Pietist faith was the source of the priority he gave to the practical good life. The hardline Pietists, incidentally, were still very much in control of

Kant's Königsberg in his early professional years, and it is against them that he takes the precautions in his scientific writings noted earlier.[39] Meanwhile, the young Herder was being exploited as a scribe by a Königsberg writer of Pietist tracts, who at the same time did what he could to prevent the boy, already a voracious reader, from taking up study by strengthening the prejudices of Herder's parents against the idea.[40] Herder overcame them, made an early career as a teacher as well as a preacher, and, in the exhilaration of his liberating sea voyage from Riga to Nantes, conceived a grandiose vision of an education in every aspect of modern knowledge, which he blithely hoped the Empress Catherine would favor for his home province of Livonia.[41]

Kant later expressly targeted the Pietist practice of constant introspection. To construct a narrative out of one's inner history was the royal road to mental confusion about imagined higher inspirations and mysterious forces, leading to "illuminatism or terrorism" (by which he presumably means the bipolar extremes of religious experience, the ecstatic and the abject), for it all stemmed from autosuggestion. Kant instances the devotional writings of a Pietist authority, Madame Bourignon; the "terrified and terrifying" notions of Pascal;[42] and the lifelong broodings of Albrecht von Haller, the poet and scientist at the head of the enlightened new university of Göttingen, who nevertheless had to seek consolation for his "frightened soul" from a theological colleague.[43]

That early experience of Kant's is paralleled by the schooling of Friedrich Nicolai, later the leading publisher and tireless champion of the Enlightenment. As the child of an averagely pious family, he found the "archpietism" of his Franckean school oppressive, with its authoritarian methods, its intensive preaching, its exclusion of all material unrelated to the "breakthrough of grace" and "the Lord Jesus in us," and its invitation to playact piety. He was rescued by transfer to the Realschule in the Berlin Kochstrasse. There dictate was replaced by demonstration and control by guidance.[44]

An even more drastic account of a grim childhood and education is Karl Philipp Moritz's autobiographical novel *Anton Reiser*. The young Anton/Moritz is brought up in a loveless home in strict practices à la Bourignon. They leave him mentally scarred: "He felt doubly now the sad effects of the superstition that had been inculcated in him from earliest childhood—his sufferings could be called, literally, *sufferings of the imagination*—but for him they were real sufferings, they robbed him of the joys of his youth." At the time, he is just thirteen.[45]

Nothing could more clearly illustrate the truly wise principle of Lessing's Nathan that children needed love before Christianity.[46] Anton's early religious gloom, continuing in obsessive self-observation and aggravated by poverty, oppression, and repeated failures with teachers and priests, together generate in him what can be read as melancholy;[47] but it is not the literary kind fashionable in the eighteenth century, nor is it—despite the book's subtitle, *A Psychological Novel*—an endogenous psychological condition. It is clearly brought on by a distorted and distorting education. What is worse, the boy has real potential, to learn and to write. Sometimes his talent wins him favor and admiration, only for some twist of chance or faux pas of his own to cast him back into the depths. Occasionally "enlivening light" breaks through and he experiences for the first time the *"bliss of thinking."*[48] Altogether his resilience is remarkable. It is helped by compensating literary and acting ambitions, but these engender more fantasies, with alternating highs and lows of their own. The story ends abruptly in unresolved frustration and uncertainty.

The real-life Moritz went on to become first a teacher, then headmaster of the Berlin Graues Kloster school—who better for the teaching profession than someone who had been put through the mill himself in such ghastly ways? Unsurprisingly, he shows a deep concern that pupils not suffer injustice; they must tell him if he has inadvertently inflicted it. He also produced, alongside his novels and aesthetic essays, some basic teaching tools, a "Logic for Children" that organizes common experience into binary categories, and an even more fundamental "New ABC Book," subtitled, in best Enlightenment style, "A Child's Introduction to Thinking." The thinking in its examples can be distinctly pointed. "U" is for *Ungleichheit* (inequality), and the accompanying picture is of plants very unequal in size, a cedar and a hyssop. But the caption runs counter to the picture: "Poor and lowly people are formed exactly like the rich and noble. So the rich and noble cannot be compared with the cedar, and the lowly man with the hyssop. Every human being is in need of help. When the poor and lowly are ill, they need help. And when the rich and noble are weak and ill, they too need help. . . . Nobody must despise anyone else. For to be a human being is the highest dignity."[49] The gesture of benevolence toward the upper classes does not take the edge off Moritz's egalitarianism. Elsewhere he writes that even the lowest laborer should be given the sense of his own worth, for the very last of human beings is "still a masterpiece on earth."[50]

A later novel, *Andreas Hartknopf*, contains much educational reflection and controversy, including an account of two men inspired by a stay in Basedow's Philanthropin to become itinerant teachers and reform "the old routine where stick and rod still ruled."[51] It again states a firm commitment to the lowly of society: "Let others look after the happy people and make them happier still through beautiful paintings, beautiful statues and beautiful poems—if I can only contribute something to making the *un*-happy people a little happier in their way, through health, contentment and work—Somebody has got to tackle the great structure of human happiness from the bottom, if it is not to fall into ruin."[52]

What this commitment was also tackling was a prejudice widespread even among Enlightenment writers: that the common people were too stupid and superstitious to be educable. It was of course a circular argument: they were superstitious *because* uneducated; and on closer examination, they were not necessarily stupid either. Diderot for one came to see that keeping the people in a state of ignorance was a political tool of the powerful, and as part of his fruitless advice to Catherine the Great he urged her to provide her peasants with basic instruction. Voltaire was at first vehemently opposed to educating the "canaille," but came to see that the ordinary people observable in England, the Dutch Republic, and his local Geneva had potential.[53] Artisans had to think, read, and strive to extend their knowledge. From what class had leading figures of the age sprung? Wolff was the son of a tanner, Kant of a saddler, Haydn of an impoverished cartwright. Workers had a grasp of the real world. A bookbinder doing a job in Goethe's house "told me his story and talked about his life. Every word he spoke was as weighty as gold and I refer you to a dozen of Lavater's pleonasms to convey the reverence [*Ehrfurcht*] I felt for this man."[54] Goethe's metaphor is apt, as is his term of comparison—a craftsman works to the gold standard of experience. To be in touch with things rather than words was in line with current educational thinking, and ultimately with the deeper movement away from, in Kant's terms, a "philosophy for the Schools" toward a "philosophy for the world."

Some rulers were beginning to see broader education as a national concern. When Duke Moritz of Saxony founded the celebrated college of Schulpforta, it was to ensure "that there should not come to be a shortage of learned people in our lands."[55] That sounds liberal enough; but economics, not the cultivation that enriches lives, was commonly the prime motive for government, as—lip service apart—it has largely remained. Acts of founding could be instrumental to the point of cold calculation, as with Karl Eugen's Württemberg "slave plantation."[56] Frederick the Great's "general regulation for country schools" of 1763 was practical and down to earth, stipulating six hours a day for peasant children from ages five to fourteen. Peasant schools (*Landschulen*) had been pioneered in Prussia by Friedrich Eberhard von Rochow on his own private estate.[57] But money, space, and books were in such short supply that the effect was limited. In any case,

Frederick had no faith in education, as witness his pessimistic comment to Sulzer, his chief inspector of schools.[58] There are known cases where the king declined to support the children of bourgeois seeking to better themselves through education.[59] The new regulation revived old decrees whose purpose, as in other principalities, had merely been to make religious instruction practicable.[60] (At the other social extreme, Casanova, of all people, was invited to instruct cadet classes; he declined.)[61]

But the influence of religion in Prussia was now waning as the prominent Pietists died out and the anticlerical Frederick was on the throne. Education moved in a secular and liberal direction under Frederick's minister of state, Karl Abraham von Zedlitz, who had close connections with the Berlin Enlightenment. Kant dedicated the second edition of the *Critique of Pure Reason* to him, not just as minister of education but as a "lover and enlightened connoisseur of the sciences."[62] There were more substantial connections: Zedlitz's secretary, Johann Erich Biester, was one of the two editors of the *Berlinische Monatschrift*, the principal organ of the Berlin Enlightenment. A portrait of Zedlitz was the frontispiece of its first number. The other editor, Friedrich Gedike, was headmaster of the Friedrichwerder grammar school. That completed a progressive triangle: enlightenment, education, publishing. Publication was the modern extension of that freedom of the pen that was in turn an extension of freedom of speech and, in Kant's view, "the sole protection of the people's rights."[63]

Kant's dedication of his magnum opus to Zedlitz was no empty compliment. The minister was a discriminating reader who regularly attended philosophy lectures, and he had a clear sense of the right balance between professional training and humane education. He asked Kant's advice on how to keep students from concentrating entirely on bread-and-butter lectures and make them understand "that the little bit of judges' work [*das bischen Richterey*] and even theology and medicine become infinitely easier and more secure in the application if the pupil has more philosophical knowledge; that one is only a judge, barrister, preacher, doctor for a few hours a day and is for far more of the time a human being, needing other kinds of knowledge.—In short, all this is what you must teach me how to make the students understand." Mere printed instructions and regulations would not suffice, they would be worse than the bread-and-butter lectures themselves.[64]

In just this spirit Schiller a few years later marks his arrival on the university scene with a fierce attack on narrowly instrumental study. The opening of his inaugural lecture deals with right and wrong motivation. The "bread-and-butter man" (*der Brotgelehrte*) studies only for career purposes with his eye on what a future employer will require. Time spent on broader interests would for him be a waste. Once established, he leaves study behind. New ideas alarm him because they threaten the acquired knowledge by which he makes his living, so he is against reformers and quick to cry heretic. Since what he has studied offers no intrinsic reward, it must bring him honors and income. If that fails, he has nothing to fall back on. Against that, the "philosophic mind" looks for the links between subjects, tries to extend his knowledge, is excited by new ideas and discoveries, and, if they upset his whole system, will start building over again. He recognizes others' contributions: all minds are working for him, where every mind potentially works against the bread-and-butter man. As implied by Zedlitz's request to Kant, the practical value of education is not undermined but enhanced by a broader, open-minded program. The free play of the mind over the materials of learning is as good for society as freedom of thought is.

Schiller's own education had been far from ideal, pressing him into molds for which he was ill fitted. The one compensation for the rigors of the Karlsschule was a teacher of true pedagogical flair and commitment, a young philosopher and author who would continue discussion with his pupils outside the classroom. Johann Friedrich Abel introduced Schiller to the sensualist thinking of contemporary Europe, and in a dramatic public address he evoked the nature of genius in terms calculated to inspire any young talent that was being kept close in an illiberal system.[65] Even the most instrumental program may let some true education slip in.

Advances of liberal reflection, insofar as they were already taking effect in educational practice and institutions, could not be guaranteed permanent. The setting was still absolutism, where any gain was temporary and precarious. When Kant declared that his was not an enlightened age, it was no abstraction. He must have known in 1784 that Frederick the Great was fading, to be succeeded two years later by his very differently inclined nephew. Would the age maintain even the gradual progress that Kant envisaged? Or would its beginnings prove to have been just a lucid interval between phases of arbitrary rule and recrudescent religion?

The religiose Frederick William II's edict on religion was the answer. Schools too were affected. Under minister Zedlitz, they had no longer been supervised by the church but had their own secular organization. Zedlitz was replaced by Wöllner, who among other things issued a new compendium of dogma, which pupils were required to learn by heart.[66] He was the real author of the edict; and since this was aimed not just at present incumbents but at new ordinands, it struck at the places where they studied: the universities. Were they free to think and teach as they thought right?

It turned out not. Universities had long been suspected of intellectual subversion, their teachers of philosophy in particular. They included figures who were at least semiorthodox— Descartes, Leibniz, Wolff, Pufendorf, and Thomasius.[67] There were now informers in the audience at lectures on Kant's thought.[68] And in 1794 Kant received the following from on high:

> Our august person has for a considerable time now perceived with great displeasure that you are misusing your philosophy for the distortion and disparagement of many of the main and fundamental doctrines of holy writ and Christianity; that you have in particular done this in your book: "Religion within the bounds of mere reason," and similarly in other lesser works. We had expected better of you, since you must yourself realise how irresponsibly you are thereby acting contrary to your duty as a teacher of the young and contrary to Our very well known intentions as father of this land. We require your most prompt, most conscientious compliance and expect that you will avoid our extreme disfavour by not being guilty of the like in future, but will in accordance with your duty apply your standing and your talents to implement ever more fully Our fatherly intention; failing which, in the case of continued obstinacy, you are infallibly to expect unpleasant measures.[69]

It was signed on behalf of the king by Wöllner, who, again, probably composed it.

This echoed the accusations against Socrates ("corrupter of the youth of Athens"), in recent times the threats to Thomasius and Wolff, and most immediately Bahrdt's two-year sentence for his comedy on the edict. Kant gave the required undertaking, which the Enlightenment party regretted as a triumph for its enemies and a serious loss for the good cause.[70] Conceivably, Kant's wide repute might have stood him in good stead if he had chosen to resist. He had offers of refuge at other universities, and the fugitive Wolff had, after all, won in the end. But Kant was now over seventy and perhaps "too familiar with the history of martyrs to wish to join them."[71] Publishing *Religion within the Bounds of Mere Reason* at just the time he did had been bold enough. His reply to the king absolutely denied the charges (a touch disingenuously, since the book had after all dismissed central Christian practices) but it emphasized that universities were the sole judges of intellectual matters. Kant also styled himself "Your Majesty's most devoted subject," so his undertaking only applied to the present monarch, whose death soon after in 1797 left Kant free to write as he pleased. The new regime restored a secular school authority and even set up a commission to look into Wöllner's malfeasance. With an appreciative nod to the new ruler, Kant printed his exchange with the old one, adding a sideswipe at the Pietistic obscurantists who had infringed the rights of scholarly inquiry and frightened off potential ordinands in droves. All this as foreword to an essay on the role of philosophy in universities and ultimately, as ever with Kant, in life.

The Conflict of the Faculties is not just Kant's answer to a single act of autocracy. He uses the occasion to overturn the traditional hierarchy that subordinated philosophy to the "higher," cadre-training faculties of medicine, law, and theology. Theology was the most powerful, having license to oversee and control the work of all the others, much like the political commissars of twentieth-century regimes. Philosophy was assigned a purely preparatory role. Yet this left an ambiguity that could be exploited. In 1713 Frederick William I had prescribed a year of philosophy and literature, to lay "good foundations" before the student proceeded to the "superior faculties." If learning to think, or at least to think about thinking, was a necessary foundation for career training, it was surely not just a pass-fail exam in something that could then be left behind. Nor was it clear—to Kant, at any rate—that the bread-and-butter subjects did indeed proceed by the light of philosophical reason. Rather, they operated by their respective rulebooks: the Bible, not rationality; the legal code, not natural law; the medical manuals, not empirical anatomy. If philosophy was the handmaid of theology, as the theologians liked to say, was she to come after with its train or go ahead with a torch?[72] All three "higher" faculties liked to keep philosophy at a safe distance, for fear it would damage their statutory authority. But if they went off the rational rails, said Kant, philosophy was going to strip them of the "brilliant feathers" they had borrowed from the state's authority; it would deal with them "on a footing of freedom and equality."[73] That was a plain echo of the French Republic's principles of liberty and equality. The third of the trio, fraternity, was missing through precisely the hierarchical division within the academic world. The French echo is confirmed when the cadre trainers are said to be "on the Right of the parliament of learning," "defending governmental statutes," while the philosophers are the necessary "oppositional party" on the Left[74]—the layout of the French National Convention that has been basic to the political vocabulary ever since.

Philosophy had no ambition to dominate in the way theology had always done, but only to make sure truth was indeed the basis for the professional activities which a university trained young people for. That did, however, mean the "foundation" subject was at the top of the hierarchy. Even state power had no right to dictate what was true,[75] as Frederick William had presumed to do with his edict. In the old Latin tag, Caesar is not above the grammarians. Kant applies another Latin tag to philosophers: they are like the Roman consuls whose task was to ensure no harm came to the state.[76] Truth is, after all, in the state's ultimate interests, even though in the short term the state may "only ever want to dominate," that is, to have its own way, and may decry dissenting *Aufklärer* as offensive, even dangerous.[77] All of which puts in more outspoken terms the argument of "What Is Enlightenment?" For if the state were to seek philosophers' advice, then the results of what the earlier essay called their "private" (= professional) activity would spread and influence society more directly than any "public" contributions they made to social debate. In an ironically apt biblical tag, "the last would become first."[78] Kant had turned the academic world upside down—or rather the right way up. It was one more Copernican reversal.[79]

When, soon afterward in 1802, consultations began for a Berlin university, a friend and correspondent of Kant's submitted the more extreme proposal that the theological faculty should be banned altogether and assimilated into philosophy: now that religion's documents and dogmas had been discredited, there was a need for rational and moral substitutes. This openly drew the logical conclusions from Kant's own writings.[80] Much the same was argued in less revolutionary but firm form in Schleiermacher's submission: "The real university is contained only in the philosophical faculty, the other three by contrast are specialized schools."[81] But when the University of Berlin was eventually founded in 1810 in a brief window of liberal reform following Prussia's traumatic defeat at Jena-Auerstedt in 1806, the principles of academic freedom set out by Wilhelm von Humboldt, with philosophy as the binding force of all academic study, were weakened by conservative politicians, and Humboldt was driven to resign.[82] Nevertheless, his year and a half as head of the section for public instruction shaped Prussian school and university education. The split between research and teaching, as the tasks respectively of academies and universities, was resolved in his celebrated declaration of their unity and interdependence, the *Einheit von Forschung und Lehre*, which has ever since been the guiding light of good universities everywhere; while the standards of Prussian education at all levels—"intelligently planned to meet their intelligent wants"—became for serious observers like Matthew Arnold an example to Europe, especially to benighted Victorian Britain, where there was "next to no love for the things of the mind."[83]

Still, there could be doubts about enlightenment's disturbing effects of a more subtle kind than Zöllner's original query or Frederick William's backlash. Outside events imposed a new perspective. Deep unease shows up in the way Goethe reshapes one of his major works. In the first of his two Wilhelm Meister novels, the themes of self-discovery and fulfillment, education and enlightenment, are central. *Wilhelm Meister's Apprenticeship* is the canonical novel of education (*Bildungsroman*) that established this genre as the German alternative to the social novel dominant in English, French, and Russian literature.[84] The hero's socialization, achieved or failed, became canonical too.

A first draft from the 1770s, *Wilhelm Meister's Theatrical Mission*, was one of the fragmentary works on Goethe's desk and conscience when he left for Italy in September 1786.[85] After his return in 1788, he completed the very different *Apprenticeship*, published in 1796. Between conception and completion stood the French Revolution. Goethe's much-quoted declaration that it was "a revolution for me too" can be applied precisely to the genesis of his novel.[86]

Wilhelm's "theatrical mission" begins when he abandons a family business trip and joins a troupe of traveling players. He has dabbled in writing; he also aspires to act and soon does so with some success. At the close of the fragment, he has an offer from an established director and must take a final decision whether to join the theatrical world. There is every reason to do so:

> At last he felt the full strength of his youth, shook himself, and with a free and courageous eye confronted the present, behind which joyful images of the future clustered. So here I am, he said to himself, not at a parting of the ways but at my destination and not daring to take the last step, not daring to seize it.
>
> Indeed, if ever a calling, a mission, was clear and explicit, it is this one. It all seems to be happening purely by chance and none of my doing, and yet everything is as I once thought it out, as I intended. . . .
>
> This is where I wanted to escape to, and I've been gently led here; I wanted to try and join Serlo's company, and now he's seeking me out and offering me conditions that I couldn't expect as a beginner.

He nevertheless still hesitates, so the director Serlo and two actresses press him for an answer: "'A little Yes,' said Philine coaxingly.—'Yes, then,' replied Wilhelm."[87] The narrative tone is as positive as the content; there is no suggestion that Wilhelm is making a mistake, no hint of irony, and certainly no irony in the fragment's title.

Wilhelm's "mission" is not, however, just a matter of his personal career. His passion is part of the theater mania of his generation. For young spirits cooped up in a stifling bourgeois society, out of touch with nature, lacking citizenly rights or scope for development in a fragmented, small-state Germany, the theater seemed a way of personal escape, as it did to Anton Reiser. Actors preaching the voice of nature were listened to like pastors preaching the word of God.[88] But the theater was also seen, significantly, as a means to create a coherent national life. By reversing the normal sequence in which a nation generates a culture, might not culture generate a nation? The theater was the most obvious public place to focus this interest. The young Schiller felt convinced there was enough common ground of distinctively German thought and feeling that dramas with deliberately national subjects could make manifest (as Goethe's *Götz von Berlichingen* had begun to do): "If we were to see a national stage established, we would also become a nation. What bound Greece so firmly together? What drew the people so irresistibly to their stage? Nothing but the patriotic content of the plays, the Greek spirit, the great overwhelming interest of the state, the better humanity, that breathed in them." Moreover, the stage could be the channel for light to spread down through society, educating the public; national feeling and enlightenment would go hand in hand (it would not always be so). Thus Schiller's address to a Mannheim society in 1784.[89] But the self-styled "national theaters", in Mannheim, in Hamburg, in Vienna, failed to transcend local limits—or failed altogether.[90]

The aspiration to German unity via culture was not innocuous, even leaving aside the critical content of much contemporary drama. If the movement did have a unifying effect, that could well destabilize the many small states, which were all intent on remaining separate and sovereign. Through much of the nineteenth century, the pressure for unification would seem to their governments as much a threat as French-style revolution. A single national capital, if unification ever came to that, could be a focus of upheaval, as Paris had proved to be since 1789. This is the context in which to understand aright Goethe's essay "Literary Sansculottism" of 1795—just when he was completing the *Apprenticeship*. It is a fierce riposte to a critic who had asked why there were no "classic" German writers. To which Goethe: You can only expect an outstanding national writer if you have a nation; classic writers presuppose conditions quite unlike Germany's: a significant history with coherent consequences, a society of sophisticated thinking and profound feeling, an intense national spirit in the writer, a high level of surrounding national culture. How could all this be brought about? And should it be? Surprisingly, no: "We will not wish for the radical upheavals [*Umwälzungen*] that could prepare the way for classic works in Germany."[91] That surely means the political transformation it would take to unify a fragmented Germany. In the mid-1790s it needed no saying where political upheavals could lead: to partisan conflict, chaos, a reign of terror.[92] The risks of trying to create a nation by cultural means—French philosophy was held to be a major cause of the Revolution—were clear. And since Wilhelm's theatrical mission had aspired to nothing less, the novel's old conception would no longer do. It needed not completing, but rescinding—not just retreatment, but retreat.

The new theme had to be the hero's mistakes, and only now does the work become a Bildungsroman. (Goethe later misleadingly projected the educative intention back into the novel's beginnings.)[93] Wilhelm has made "mistake after mistake, aberration upon aberration," foremost among them that he had "not the least potential" for the theater.[94] Not trial and error, then, just plain error; his "education" is the realization of how wrong he was. Where the first version took his talent seriously, now it is not allowed to have been real. His self-critical insight is aided, indeed required, by the older advisers and educators who increasingly surround him. The value of "guardians" is expressly declared.[95] They are the members of the "Society of the Tower"—the motif echoes the period fascination with Freemasonry and other secret societies—which has all along been benevolently watching over Wilhelm, indeed secretly guiding him. They have recorded his every move, and he accepts their account of his life as the truth about himself.[96] He has so lost self-confidence that he wishes he had been even less free to follow his inclinations: "Why did these people, who were so well informed about him and about what was good for him, not guide him more strictly, more seriously, why did they favor his games instead of leading him away from them?"[97] He has plainly lost what Kant called "the resolution and courage to use his understanding without someone else's guidance," lost what the close of the *Theatrical Mission* called the "free and courageous eye" with which he could "confront the present, behind which joyful images of the future clustered." There too he felt he had been guided, but that was no more than a metaphor for the chain of fortunate chance. His "mission" was of his own making; he was not "sent" by any outside agency. Now, however, individualism has yielded to a controlling authority—the active ambition of a spirited young adult has become the passive resignation of a biddable juvenile. "Education" is reduced again to socialization.

It is a strange turn for a writer who had himself always lived, and would go on living, by the principles of self-confidence and self-expression. Why this *Pseudokonfession*?[98] It seems unlikely Goethe was aware that the changed emphasis of his novel was so direct an effect of the French Revolution. More probably the disquiet, apprehension, and horror that set in across Europe when the Revolution turned violent had created a new atmosphere that weighed on his imagination so that the ideals of independence and youthful initiative gave way to an anxious search for security and control.

He was not alone in this. Schiller, since 1794 Goethe's literary partner, presents (briefly) the same symptoms. He too—surprisingly, given the political thrust of his early work—had not been among the Revolution's enthusiasts. He joined the disillusioned the more readily, especially after the regicide. His dark mood found expression in a series of letters to the Danish prince who had granted him a three-year pension. So far from achieving a "monarchy of reason" and a "regeneration of politics," events in France had "removed all such hopes for centuries." A corrupt generation (*eine verderbte Generation*) had failed to use the favorable moment of opportunity, that key concept of Schiller the historian. Mankind had plainly not yet outgrown the need for "rule by guardians" (*vormundschaftliche Gewalt*). But these letters proved to be only a first draft of a substantial philosophical work, the *Letters on the Aesthetic Education of Man* (1795).[99] Tellingly, the accent there has shifted. The desperate appeal to old-style rule has gone, and "guardianship" is, explicitly following Kant, a negative factor;[100] the present generation is no longer "corrupt," but at worst "unreceptive" (*unempfänglich*);[101] most significant, the political "hopes lost for centuries" have now become the sober but positive commitment to "a task for more than one century."[102] How far Schiller has recovered from the initial shock is clear from the program of an active education that his title declares. The Enlightenment is wounded but not dead.

Goethe too later presents a formal program for education, but on a less grand scale than Schiller's and at the lower level of school teaching. In a sequel to the *Apprenticeship*, the *Years of Travel*, Wilhelm discovers the son of his dead first love and puts him to school in a meticulously organized "Pedagogical Province." Here there are elaborate rituals meant to inculcate reverence for God, Earth, Man, and Self. Nature admittedly can contribute much to upbringing, but reverence has to be learned.[103] It is a form of enlightenment, perhaps, but a regimented one. At most, resistance stirs in the boy himself when he is initiated into ritual postures: "He obeyed, but soon called out: 'I don't like this much . . . ; how long is it going on?'" He goes through the motions "with such a saucy expression, that one could observe he hadn't seen a secret meaning in it."[104]

In historical retrospect, the would-be utopia is potentially dystopian. Youth groups in uniform with uniform gestures? German youth have been there twice in the twentieth century, in uniforms brown or blue. Even without these disquieting pre-echoes of ideological control, the Province's collective discipline is at the opposite end of the educational spectrum from individual self-development.

More might be, and has been, said against this late novel as a sign of the author's hardening arteries;[105] but Goethe can be defended against himself if we open larger vistas and distinguish the social being from the poet. His educational prescriptions surely embody the empirical man's views rather than the poet's vision. They are detached social reflections rather than his characteristic response of feeling and language to lived experience, which continued to the very end. If the Enlightenment ideal of education is personal fulfillment to the limits of an individual's potential, then Goethe's monumental contribution to *Bildung* is surely his full creative record, especially his lyrical life's work. That has still to be savored.

CHAPTER 9

Communication and Beyond:
Means or End?

Humanity is the sense of participation and the capacity to communicate intimately and generally; which qualities together make up the sociability of mankind.
—Immanuel Kant, *Critique of Judgment*

MEANS . . .

Enlightenment had to live by communication and access to the public. It needed means to spread its message. Education might work in the long term but depended on a society that had already progressed some way toward enlightenment—a circular process. To achieve an adequate school system was a prolonged, diffuse campaign. A more immediate means was publication, the more vital because Germany lacked a focus for live intellectual contact like Paris, London, or St. Petersburg. Vienna, with the heavy censorship that lasted up to the time of Joseph II, frustrated any hopes that it might become such an intellectual center, just as it disappointed Lessing's hopes of developing a national theater there. The leading German Enlightenment centers—Leipzig, Berlin—correspondingly had the leading publishers.

The most direct means of communication was journals. There were plenty of these—over the century they ran to thousands—though with very mixed motivations: scholarly, like Thomasius's *Monatsgespräche*, a monthly review of academic publications; didactic-*cum*-commercial, with the plethora of bourgeois moral weeklies; literary, with Wieland's *Teutscher Merkur*; intellectually comprehensive, with Nicolai's "Universal German Library" (*Allgemeine deutsche Bibliothek*, hereafter *AdB*); or ambitious-*cum*-idealistic, with the young Schiller's *Thalia*.

They all contributed something to the Enlightenment cause, Thomasius not least by publishing in German—a departure from his model, the *Acta Eruditorum*, which since 1682 had been reviewing in Latin, at that time the academic lingua franca. Schiller's journal was meant to keep his name before the public and help him eke out a living, but it also declared a classic Enlightenment commitment to open debate. The moral weeklies had some sense of mission, offering guidance on manners in a form that was entertaining and, at typically just eight octavo pages, less time-consuming than books. They were reading matter for habitual nonreaders, a new bourgeois (and perhaps largely feminine) public. They scarcely achieved the quality of their model, the English *Spectator*, with its cast of credible characters around Sir Roger de Coverley. But with their likewise self-defining titles— "The Patriot," "The Observer," "The Honest Man," "The Man without Prejudice," "The Bride," "Discourses of the Painters," "The Rational Lady-Critics," even "The Poor Scholar"—they often created a sense of character and hit an informally personal tone that helped move German prose toward clarity.[1] In an increasingly crowded niche, a weekly might go to the wall, but it could be reborn under another name promising a new angle on familiar material. The weeklies preached social conformity and tolerance, fulfillment of the duties of bourgeois life, and moderation in its enjoyment. They were critical of academic pedantry, overuse of foreign words, social affectation, and the empty conventions of higher-ups. In short, they shared and encouraged the best values of their middle-class readership. (They reached no lower down the social scale.) They were compatible with religious orthodoxy, except insofar as reading them may have distracted from the Bible or the devotional texts that were only just beginning to lose their longstanding domination of the book market. That reflected in a small way the trend of the time away from doctrine to ethics. They were certainly not political; ruling was left to rulers. All this was the mildest possible form of enlightenment. Independent thinking was not part of the program.

It was central to the *Berlinische Monatsschrift*, which from 1783 was the organ of the Berlin Enlightenment, specifically of the Wednesday Society, or Society of Friends of Enlightenment, founded in the same year. Its dozen (later two dozen) members were writers, clerics, an eminent doctor, and public officials, including two compilers of the Prussian Civil Code then in progress. They met monthly outside their professional work to "clarify each other's thinking" on social issues, some of them current administrative business which could thus to some extent be processed informally in advance of official decisions.[2] That embodied Kant's adroit compromise between a state employee's private and public functions. All the more so when talks given at the Society became essays in the journal, along with work by other hands—it published Kant's two interlocking essays of 1784 that set out his vision of enlightenment and history.

The journal declared itself nonpartisan and committed to independent thinking, though that already made it a partisan of enlightenment—form was substance. Critical responses were explicitly welcomed and lively controversy followed, most famously when Zöllner's skeptical query from within the Society of Friends launched the debate on the very nature and effects of enlightenment. In the editors' metaphor, the journal was a flint whose sparks would create light and warmth, though it might get chipped to pieces in the process. But there were no two ways about the commitment to debunking prejudice and popular superstition—the flint had an indestructible core of rationality.[3] Biester called it "a Protestant monthly," an apt but surprisingly rare explicit linking of the Enlightenment with its rebellious religious ancestor. Biester was the most forthright objector to the controversial practice of letting northern Catholics use Protestant churches for their services. It was of course an enlightened duty to be tolerant; towns were actually competing for the title. But was this not a perilous infiltration? After all, no reciprocity was forthcoming in the Catholic south. Indeed, Protestants in Austria were still suffering severe discrimination despite Joseph II's toleration edict. Christian Garve argued that these were old worries and exaggerated fears; he believed in the irreversible progress of enlightenment in Europe—Catholics would surely never return to the notion of papal infallibility . . . ?[4]

Holding the rational ring while being one of the contestants was clearly a problem. But at least it would all be open to public view. The Friends of the Enlightenment were a discreet but not a secret society. They were implicitly under the patronage of education minister Zedlitz, with his portrait as the frontispiece of the journal's first number. The practice of publishing their papers made clear they had no closely guarded secrets.

(Secret societies, to digress for a moment, were a widespread phenomenon of the day, and an obsession in the mind of governments, which commonly take suspicion to extremes. Yet their contribution to spreading the Enlightenment boils down to very little. They had no significant secrets, as Lessing discovered when he became a Freemason, and as Wieland confirmed. It was their almost coquettish flaunting of secrecy that made the authorities fear subversive plots. Only Adam Weisshaupt's Bavarian Illuminati ever had overtly political ambitions, though it was unclear how these could conceivably be realized. They were certainly not remotely in the same class as the later Italian *carbonari*. Secret societies contributed nothing intellectually to the Enlightenment and achieved nothing that was distinct from it. At best, they brought together men of goodwill who were in favor of social progress, but whose energies they then diverted into a new structure of hierarchical offices and bizarre rituals. These were accepted, strangely, by many good minds that had shaken themselves free of the Christian version— Abel, Knigge, Forster, Voss, Goethe, Nicolai, Gedike, Biester, Kanter, Hartknoch, and the young Frederick. The Freemasons in particular fell down glaringly on their stated aim to admit members from all classes—something that really would have been a distinctive achievement in that age. There was also much all-too-human strife within and between societies. While it may not be surprising that so many leading figures joined simply to see what was going on, a curiosity—and disillusionment—acted out in Lessing's Masonic dialogues *Ernst und Falk*, it is striking that they nearly all left, sometimes in vehemently expressed disgust, as Herder and Forster did. Wieland, as always, remained ironically detached.[5] Only Goethe stayed on, no doubt for purely social reasons. Schiller was courted but never succumbed. As a feature in the Enlightenment landscape, the secret societies merit this much attention, but as a force measurably furthering enlightenment, nothing more.)

The aspirations of the *Berlin Monthly* to wide debate were pursued on an immensely larger scale in Nicolai's *AdB*. He set out to review all new German books, good and bad. As a publisher himself, Nicolai knew that in commerce marketability always trumped quality and spawned quantity. It was a heroic undertaking of his to try and keep up with the growth of the German market at a time when it had gone from 1,650 titles a year in 1769 to 4,000 in 1800. It now risked, as he said, "suffocating in its own unhealthy fat."[6] From small beginnings with a handful of pressed friends, the *AdB* eventually had a team of five hundred reviewers, and over a span of forty years they accumulated 217 octavo volumes containing 60,000 individual reviews. Nicolai drew his contributors from as wide a geographical spread as possible in the cause of cultural unity in a still not unified country. He imposed no editorial program, with two exceptions. One was a declared opposition to Catholicism—the Enlightenment was indeed a Protestant movement. The other opposition was to the influence of Kant, both to his philosophical substance, which Nicolai fundamentally misunderstood, and to his style, which seemed to be making new writers "isolate themselves" from the public behind obscure verbiage[7]—and communication was the lifeblood of the Enlightenment. For Kant, reciprocally, Nicolai belonged to the trend of popular philosophy, "a disgusting mishmash of random observations and half-rational principles, lapped up by shallow minds that need something usable for daily chit-chat"; anybody could make writing accessible to the common understanding if it lacked serious analysis.[8] So an issue of style set two men against each other who had enough common ground to have been allies: both were empiricists, both hostile to empty speculation and religious fetishism, both ultimately pursuing the same clarity and the same practical reforms.

As the leading Enlightenment reviewing organ, the *AdB* kept up with major controversies. It dealt with twenty-nine books and pamphlets on the Wolfenbüttel fragments and gave even more critical attention to Frederick Wilhelm II's Edict on Religion (six hundred pages reviewing ninety-two books and pamphlets, with twenty-five pages directly on the Edict and eight on the follow-up censorship edict). It was duly banned for eight months. Otherwise it survived the anti-Enlightenment reign, though only by moving its operations from Berlin first to Jena and then to Dessau.

Nicolai also wrote himself. Of his novels, the highly successful *Life and Opinions of Sebaldus Nothanker* was a telling attack on intolerance, primitive in its literary methods but no more primitive than the evils it targeted. A major undertaking was his twelve-volume critical record of travels the length and breadth of Germany. Taken all together, Nicolai's was a heroic Enlightenment life.[9] He deserved better than to be scorned as a comic dinosaur by Goethe and Schiller from their newly won cultural heights in the 1790s. The scorn was personal and small-minded. Nicolai had given offense to them both with entirely reasonable criticisms, early on of Goethe's *Werther* and later of Schiller's *Aesthetic Letters*. In the jointly authored satirical *Xenia* of the 1790s, they directed more hostile epigrams at him than at any other single target. A man who had been an equal partner of Lessing and Mendelssohn and labored so long in a good cause deserved to be taken more seriously.[10] It was one more human failure to recognize common ground beneath surface conflict.

The motive for Wieland's *Teutscher Merkur*, the longest-lived literary organ of the age (1773–1810), was even more consciously national than the *AdB*, but more specifically literary (Nicolai had been less concerned with belles lettres than with ideas). Wieland aspired to a "national journal" that would foster a "national spirit."[11] To raise the quality of contemporary writing, he printed the best texts he could find or write himself and privately encouraged young authors (Schiller, later Heinrich von Kleist, and even the young Goethe who had publicly poked fun at him).[12] His method was not frontal preaching, but stylistic elegance, urbane wit, and a touch of Sternean playfulness with his medium, an embodiment of the Horatian *dulce et utile*. He sometimes added anonymous footnotes countering his own printed views—an intriguing way to be nonpartisan. His aim was to stay above the mêlée, shaping opposed contemporary views into dialogue, as in the *Göttergespräche*, where a liberal Jupiter and a conservative Juno debate religion, government, revolution, and enlightenment with historical figures ranging from antiquity to Elizabeth I of England. But this was 1791; the French Revolution had not yet taken a violent turn, hopes were still high, and progress seemed probable.

As things in Paris got worse, nonpartisan analysis meant in turn criticizing (though also to some degree empathizing with) all parties to the political conflict. Serious engagement was forced on the *Merkur* not least because what was being played out in France might well spill over the border, since German rulers and the nobility were as blind to the need for moderate reform as the French ancien régime had been. The French émigré nobility were provoking German intervention, and the Germans were radicalizing French republican sentiment with the Declaration of Pillnitz and the duke of Brunswick's manifesto, followed by the disastrous invasion itself. The French were moving beyond a constitutional monarchy to a republic, while the king and his party were intriguing and evading (and being caught at it). Then came the regicide, grim yet perhaps unavoidable given the external threat to restore the monarchy along the old corrupt lines. There was surely no turning the clock back so completely. And now the French were transforming the alleged export of revolutionary ideals into expansionist wars. Practically every move, of both sides, was wrong; but "wrong" was a judgment of moderate reason, itself only ever "right" from some distance or in retrospect—which was no ground for staying silent as events developed. There was nothing wrong with a wholehearted conclusion, provided it was not a foregone one. Otherwise, total nonpartisanship meant ineffectual fence-sitting. The greater the issue, the more vital it was to come down on one side.

Wieland's arguments, with events and with himself, show him to be one of the fairest, most lucid minds of the day. His quality as an Enlightenment thinker needs to be emphasized after a history of depreciation in his later years, when his fiction was attacked as immoral, his urbanity as Frenchified. His were among the first German books to be burned, by the so-called Göttingen Grove, a group of Klopstock enthusiasts and aggressive Germanicizers. The reputation Wieland enjoyed for much of his lifetime has never been fully restored. Yet his qualities as an elegant stylist, skilled versifier, and absorbing narrator, and as a scholar and translator even more at home in the works of antiquity than either Goethe or Schiller, made him a classic at a time when literary refinement was barely known in Germany.[13]

One last effort to unite major writers and the German cultural public around a single project was Schiller's journal *Die Horen*, launched in 1794 with the keen support of his Stuttgart publisher, Cotta. Schiller had also signed up to but quickly withdrew from a contract to edit a "General European Journal of Political Affairs." He pleaded health reasons and the likelihood such a journal would make a loss, but deep down he was simply uneasy with treating politics directly.[14] Indeed, in the announcement of the *Horen* he set his face firmly against politics, which had dominated public discussion since the French Revolution, in favor of what was *"purely human* and elevated above all influence of the times."

And yet, and yet. . . . There could never be a sharp separation between pure humanity and real events. The journal was avowedly going to serve "the formation of better concepts, purer principles and nobler manners, from which ultimately all true improvement of society depends."[15] So apparently there were indirect means to achieve what direct frontal debate could not. Schiller's own major contribution to his journal, the *Letters on the Aesthetic Education of Man*, would spell that out in great depth. He assigns to art and aesthetic experience nothing less than the reshaping of humanity for a better politics after the disillusion of revolutionary violence in France. An ambitious aesthetic theory builds a bridge between high-minded journal communication and the realm of art.

. . . OR END?

Art is the one orderly product our muddling race has produced.
—E. M. Forster, "Art for Art's Sake," in *Two Cheers for Democracy*

So could art itself be used for purposes of enlightenment? The still optimistic young Schiller had celebrated the stage as the channel through which "from the thinking better part of the people the light of truth streams down and spreads throughout the state," conquering the night of barbarity and prejudice.[16] But turning ideas directly into literature was a tricky process. Art does not thrive on explicitness, and poetry should not preach. It was also risky—a subtle point of Kant's—to embody ideals in a fictive figure, such as "a wise man in a novel." If he seemed too good to be true, it might make the ideal itself look like a mere "poetic fabrication."[17] But for the reference to "a novel," Kant might have had Lessing's Nathan in mind. The archetypal wise man is at the limits of credibility when his faith in ultimate meaning and guidance overcomes the slaughter of his wife and seven sons. As a further case in point, Schopenhauer found too much showcased virtue in the characters of Lessing's *Minna von Barnhelm*; he contrasts more "implacable" writers—Homer and Shakespeare.[18] Any facile happy ending risked becoming Enlightenment kitsch, and it is not clear that "sentimental stories" about basic human situations would readily touch hearts that were proof against rational appeal.[19] Lessing's brave attempt in *Nathan der Weise* is an obvious test case, its contemporary reception (see above, p. 76) not encouraging.

It was a more straightforward matter to convey socially critical ideas, as in the many works that pilloried absolutism. Besides dramas working with historical analogy (*Don Carlos, Egmont*), or with thinly veiled local reference (*Emilia Galotti, The Brigands, Intrigue and Love*), there were short, sharp attacks of a more open kind, none more powerful than Bürger's poem of outrage at the destruction of crops by a prince's hunting party, with its repeated question, who does this man think he is? and its final denial of rule by divine right.[20] A notable subgenre was the poetic imagining of Judgment Day, as in Schiller's "The Evil Monarchs," Schubart's "A Burial Vault for Princes," and the (literally) apocalyptic ending to Canto 18 of Klopstock's epic *The Messiah*. Princely courts became symbols of luxury and corruption, as contrasted with bourgeois uprightness and the people's poverty. The palace was an emblem of oppressive power and of something rotten in the state of Germany. In a little-noticed passage, Schiller records an imagined foreigner's impressions (the grandiose final metaphor recalls his own medical training):

I have seen perhaps the high point of splendor and riches. The triumph of human hand over the stubborn resistance of nature often astonished me—but the misery dwelling nearby soon infected my pleasurable wonderment. A hollow-eyed figure of hunger that begs from me in the flowery avenues of a princely pleasure garden, a shingle hut on the point of collapse that stands facing a pompous palace—how swiftly this brings down my soaring pride! My imagination completes the picture. I now see the curses of thousands teeming like a mass of voracious worms in this braggart world of decomposition. Everything that was elevated and charming becomes repellent to me. I realize that it is nothing more than a diseased, wasting body, whose eyes and cheeks burn with the hectic hues of fever and feign a flourishing life while gangrene and putrefaction rage in the expiring lungs.

This comes, of all places, in the preface to an art-historical essay: a Danish traveler has come to Mannheim to view the celebrated collection of classical casts.[21] Even more remarkably, the palace emblem crops up at the very beginning of Kant's treatise on aesthetics, the *Critique of Judgment*:

> If anyone asks me whether I find the palace I see before me beautiful, I may, it is true, say: I don't like things of that kind that are made merely to be gawped at, or, like that Iroquois chief, that nothing in Paris pleased him so much as the street food stalls; I may also rail in best Rousseauian fashion at the vanity of the great who expend the sweat of the people on such superfluous things; finally, I can very easily persuade myself that, if I were to find myself on a desert island without hope of ever returning among men and were able simply by wishing it to conjure up such a splendid structure, I would not even give myself that much trouble if I already had a hut that made me comfortable enough. All this can be granted and endorsed; only it is not the issue, which is, rather, whether the mere inward representation of the object is accompanied by pleasure, however indifferent I may be in respect of the existence of the object of this representation. One can easily see that to say the object is beautiful and to prove that I have taste depends on what I inwardly make of this representation, not on ways in which I may be dependent on its existence. Everyone must admit that any judgment on beauty in which there is the least mixture of interest is very partisan and no pure judgment of taste. One must not be in the least in favor of the existence of the thing, but in this respect wholly indifferent, if one is to play the judge in matters of taste.[22]

This is Kant's first example of his central principle, the pure disinterestedness required of an experience if it is to count as aesthetic. Since as a rule Kant refrains altogether from giving examples, the strange choice stands out.[23] The forms of "interest," on Kant's theory, are the possession, use of, or desire for an object: all positively concerned with its actual existence. Aesthetic contemplation begins when these positive relations to the object are switched off, allowing it to be perceived purely as form, an end in itself. (The desire for such purity has obvious analogies with Kant's ethics.) Yet a palace is here in no way an object of desire. What needs switching off in this case is a set of *negative* relations—dislike and disapproval of showiness ("to be gawped at," "vanity of the great"), of luxury ("superfluous"—a hut would be enough on a desert island), of oppression ("sweat of the people"). All its excesses are open to fundamental Rousseauian attack. So far from needing not to be "in favor of the existence of the thing" or even "wholly indifferent" to it, the viewer of the palace has to resist strong feelings in favor of its *non*existence, a positively revolutionary kind of "interest"! He must forcibly restrain any critical animus or partisanship for a more just world.

That Kant was himself committed to social criticism we know from the footnote early in the First Critique that declared an "age of criticism," in which everything, religion and legislation included, must submit to rational inquiry.[24] The formulations in the present passage—the legitimacy of Rousseauian vehemence in its proper place, the preference for simplicity over luxury, the sympathy with an exploited populace—show the critical impulse is very much alive. Evoking these attitudes so fully, if only to exclude them, suggests how powerfully Kant himself, in the thin disguise of the imagined viewer of a palace, is being borne along on the tide of contemporary feeling. The passage is an eloquent *praeteritio*.

Yet the theoretical thrust of the Third Critique seems to move literature and art as far away as possible from the reality that is their subject matter. So could *Don Carlos* and *Egmont* be read or watched as pure form, or a performance of *Iphigenie* experienced with no sense of moral urgency? Is Wilhelm Meister's education a mere pleasing mosaic? Is a love lyric just an exercise in verbal patterning? Is aesthetic experience overall really a subjective "pleasure without interest"?

By "subjective" Kant means that aesthetic experience involves an adjustment in the viewer's mode of seeing, not that individual viewers' experience differs. On the contrary, it is "universal" (*allgemein*). The logic is simplistic: if all the forms of interest about which individuals do differ are excluded, must not what remains be a blank sheet common to them all?[25] Yet if both the reality of the object and the individuality of the perceiver are discounted in this way, art is left looking pallid and unvital when measured against common experience. The power of art and literature surely lies, on the contrary, in working with the trace elements of people's accumulated experience. Recollections and anticipations are called up and repatterned by what is read or seen—a tragic event, a nude, a still life, a landscape, a portrait. Art and everyday life enhance each other, as is eloquently embodied in the fifth of Goethe's *Roman Elegies*, where making love and viewing sculpture are, in the fullest sense of the word, intimately related.[26]

Against such realities, as Schiller noted, Kant's view would rate arabesque above the highest human beauty.[27] So Schiller, as himself an artist taking issue with the world, set out in those letters to prove that aesthetic experience was objective, rooted in what is before the eye, not just in a special mental setting. Objectivity proved elusive: his first attempt had defined beauty as "freedom in the phenomenon", or—ambiguously—in the "appearance" of objects. That is to say, within the nexus of forces that shaped them and determined their function they could still *appear* free, provided those forces were not obtrusive. Yet that was not far removed from Kant's subjectivity—it too was arguably a mode of seeing. But there was more to come from Schiller's pen.

The theorizing impulse had been strong in Germany since the Wolffian philosopher Baumgarten first set up aesthetics as a distinct area of philosophy and made the definition of beauty the grail to pursue.[28] For Johann Joachim Winckelmann, the initiator of the German classicistic fashion, it seemed an impossible task. Beauty, "the ultimate purpose and center point of art," was "one of the great mysteries of nature, whose effect we observe and all feel, whose essence as a general concept is one of the undiscovered truths."[29] What had the greatest effect on Winckelmann personally was Greek statuary, primarily naked figures of men and gods. Eloquent descriptions—of Apollo, Antinous, the Laocoön group[30]—are interspersed in his history of ancient art among dry learned accounts of persons and periods and attributions of works from ancient Greece and Rome. The effect of his writings was immense, the start of a positive "tyranny of Greece over Germany."[31]

Telling Germans they should follow the Greeks rather than nature as a faster route to perfection was one more of the period's proposed "short cuts,"[32] yet it was also one more call to subservience, not so different from Frederick the Great's demand that Germans should imitate French classical writing. All such exhortations were cogently answered by the rhetorical question in Herder's essay on Shakespeare: if Greek art was shaped by local conditions, must German culture not also grow organically from its own local conditions? What was the soil like? What had been sown in it? What should it be able to bear? Only a fool comparing the two cultures would demand that the second be identical to the first.[33]

A different kind of dissent came from Lessing. In a way analogous to Kant, he shifted the focus away from content (Winckelmann's derivation of Greek beauty from a Greek ethos) to a demonstration that art was governed by internal technical principles. The restrained expression of suffering in the faces and limbs of the Laocoön group, which Winckelmann had put down to the "noble simplicity and calm greatness" of the stoical Greek soul, was determined rather by the "necessary limits and needs" of representation in the pursuit of beauty in visual art.[34] The ultimate conclusion was that visual art and poetry worked in fundamentally different dimensions. Painting and sculpture treated objects in space, literature actions in time. Lessing's theory arose from empirical observation and fed back into practical criticism: allegorical painting and descriptive poetry, both fashions of the day, were transgressing boundaries. This was a first commonsensical carving up of the whole field of the arts that stimulated Herder, not to disagree, but to differentiate more minutely. Only music was pure succession in time; poetry owed its effect to the "energy" (*Energie*), "force" (*Kraft*), and "meaning" (*Sinn*) that inhered in words.[35]

Lessing and Herder were quarrying from the rock face of actual works, in this case ancient ones. They were both energetic critics of contemporary writing. Herder had published a series of "Fragments"; Lessing had edited and coauthored with Nicolai a periodical of "Letters" on current literature and written two years' worth of theater criticism and dramatic theory in response to the project of a Hamburg National Theater.[36] But even Kant's highly abstract theory could have a bearing on live art and literature. Paradoxically, his theory of disinterested pleasure had a liberating effect for socially engaged writing. If a work's content was not the essential thing about it, then art could be uncoupled from questions of faith and morality, the substantive interests it had always been required to serve. Thus Goethe in Rome can admire Raphael's painting of five saints not as religious icons, but only as perfect representations of human physical existence.[37] If art was taken thus seriously as an end in itself, not a means, it could no longer legitimately be required to help inculcate belief and morals, nor could it be criticized and banned for failing to do so, or for suggesting alternative beliefs and behaviors, or even for treating these as an open question. An aesthetics of reception could thus without too great a stretch of the imagination become a license for freer artistic creation. In this way philosophy—especially given the growing status of Kant—provided an anchor for artistic freedom, with all its social consequences.

Yet "disinterested" art, for all its claims to pure formality, had a powerful and potentially disturbing "interest" of its own. It opened up all of experience to review, and even the most dispassionate review might lead to conclusions about the present state of the world. The fuller and more persuasive the picture art provided, the stronger the incentive to action. Art's distinctive freedom was already being invoked as a defense in controversies over matters of social import. The defenders of Schiller's "Gods of Greece" against Christian attack argued for an "aesthetic substance independent of moral value," for "art as its own purpose" and as the free "play of the mind."[38] This is 1788, on the eve of Kant's *Critique of Judgment*—not so much influence as a current trend of thinking.

Schiller is central to all the issues touched on so far, and his mature work carries them furthest. He had come to aesthetics by two routes. One was reflection on the nature of drama and his own creative processes, as both a problem of individual psychology and a product of deeper cultural forces. The other was Kant's three Critiques, to which his friend Körner introduced him and in which he was able to immerse himself during the three pressure-free years of his subsidy from the Danish court.

Schiller's personal problem was the sense that he had lost his early creative touch. His dramatic and poetic work was stagnating, he felt impeded by his critical consciousness, yet also needed more of it as a homeopathic cure:

> Criticism must now make good the damage it has done me. And it really has; for the boldness, the living fire that I had before I knew a single rule is something I've been lacking now for several years. I *see* myself creating and shaping, I observe the play of enthusiasm, and my imagination acts the less freely for knowing that it is no longer without witnesses. Once I've got to the point where *artifice* becomes *nature*, like a civilized person's education, the imagination will get its previous freedom back and set itself only such limits as it chooses.[39]

The problem was made worse by the contrast of Goethe's untroubled creativity, which Schiller both admired and envied—on his own melodramatic admission, it was a positive love-hate. He sought to explain it by a theory, part self-criticism, part self-defense, of creative types: spontaneous (Goethe) versus reflective (himself). Its first sketch was the extraordinary long birthday letter of 23 August 1794 that began their friendship.[40] Schiller gave this typology a historical dimension by positing a shift in Western sensibility: the ancient Greeks lived and wrote in an immediate relation to the world, which hyperconscious moderns had lost and could only yearn and strive to regain. That made all modern writing at root elegiac. Poets could only lament the lost world, or imagine it intact in fragile idyll, or satirize their own present condition—all three aspects epitomized in Schiller's own "Gods of Greece." Goethe, along with a few great names of the past (Molière, Cervantes, Shakespeare), was a rare exception in modernity. Whether as a survival or a recreation of "naive" spontaneity, Goethe's writing was immediate even when it delved deep into modern spiritual crises, as in *Werther* or *Torquato Tasso*. All these ideas came together in Schiller's short treatise *On Naive and Reflective Poetry* (1796). Thomas Mann called it "Germany's classic and exhaustive essay, which contains all others in itself and makes them superfluous."[41] Certainly it is a grandiose vision of the cultural past and a powerful tool of critical practice. Schiller applied it in a section surveying recent European literature which he called "Judgment Day," persuasively illustrating the gap cultural history had opened.

How could the gap be bridged, not least for himself? Only by taking in so much reality that his inhibiting consciousness was earthed in it; the resulting work could make it seem that world and mind were again in harmony. Schiller confessed in the same letter that he often started from a *"need* for substance" to contain emotion. In Goethe's writing he had before him a model of concrete representation. He emulates it in the massive *Wallenstein* trilogy, where hard men are driven by hard political forces and idealistic reflection is consigned to the margins. Returning the favor, Schiller's analytical mind helped sort out form and priority within Goethe's superabundant material. His input into Goethe's *Wilhelm Meister* and *Faust* was substantial. The divergence of types his essay diagnosed became a fruitful complementarity. Their cordial partnership in the decade from 1794 to Schiller's premature death also generated a correspondence of over a thousand letters that is itself a major critical commentary.

The French Revolution added an even greater problem. Schiller had never been among the early enthusiasts, and its growing violence led him to attempt two rescues. First a direct one, to defend Louis XVI with a plea to the National Convention. Schiller was not the only horrified outsider to feel so moved,[42] but he had a better chance of being heard than most, since the National Assembly had made him an honorary citizen, along with other enlightened notables.[43] But before he could finish a draft, the king had been executed. Disgusted, Schiller turned back to aesthetics. Not however as an escape. Confronted with the French failure to turn Enlightenment ideas into stable politics, he looked beyond straightforward rationality for a way to rescue the Enlightenment. The material of politics must be remolded by—of all things—an *Aesthetic Education of Man*. As the title makes plain, it is the education of the individual human being (*des Menschen*) in contrast to Lessing's education of the human race (*des Menschengeschlechts*).[44]

Aesthetics seems far removed from politics. Yet extremes met. From the start, the two realms drew metaphors from each other. That first theory of "freedom in appearance" was elaborated to read "every natural phenomenon is a free citizen, with the same rights as the most noble, and may not be *compelled* even for the sake of the whole, but absolutely must *consent* to everything."[45] That sounds like resistance to Rousseau's potentially oppressive *volonté générale*. When Schiller in a further essay analyzes beauty in movement—grace—he uses the metaphor of a monarchy ruled by a single will, yet where the individual citizen can still feel he is living by his own inclination.[46] Too rigorous a control by reason over the senses makes the government no longer liberal, too lax a hand and it ceases to be government at all.[47] Schiller's vision combines the politics of mind and matter and the psychophysiology of the body politic. Both involved the same elements, and so did art. Sense and reason, powerful feeling and sober calculation, were the ingredients of human beings. They could be balanced in a fine work of art, while their imbalance gave rise to the problems of politics. Too much violent feeling (the politics of the mob), but equally a too ruthless rationality (the lethal virtue of a Robespierre), must produce a grim outcome, as events were graphically illustrating.

That was not just an armchair analyst's view. Georg Forster saw much the same on the spot amid the turmoil of Paris. Typically of the enthusiasts in 1789, he had believed mature philosophy was now shaping the state.[48] But by 1793, "very few are true to principles; everything is blind, passionate rage, mad partisan spirit. . . . On the one side I see insight and talent without courage or strength, on the other a physical energy guided by ignorance."[49] He could only observe "self-interest and passion where one expects and demands greatness, words in place of feeling, boastfulness and ostentation in place of true substance and effect." A *"tyranny* of reason" threatened, "perhaps the most iron-hard of all."[50] These were indeed "corrupt times"[51]— this in the face of Robespierre's proud claim that the French people were a different species, two thousand years in advance of the rest of mankind.[52]

"Corrupt" was initially Schiller's key word too: the Revolution was "the most favorable moment, but it found a corrupt generation," thus the phrasing in one of the letters to his benefactor, the Duke of Schleswig-Holstein-Augustenburg.[53] But in the *Letters on the Aesthetic Education of Man* that reworked the correspondence, "corrupt" is toned down to "unreceptive." A humanity already ruined has become a humanity not yet influenced. It was worth another try. But how to restore the lost balance? There was no way the answer could come from society: society was itself the problem. The need was for some other, independent agency. For Schiller, that agency is art, and he offers a complex and rigorous argument to demonstrate it.

In the ultimate abstraction, human beings were made up of a core identity (*Person*) that was embodied in passing conditions (*Zustand*). They were a complex of form and matter, and each side of the opposition had its own drive—toward maximum "reality" (St*offtrieb*) or maximum "formality" (*Formtrieb*). In the simplest formula, the components were "life" (*Leben*) and "shape" (*Gestalt*); in beauty, the two coalesced as "living shape" (*lebende Gestalt*).[54] The new definition is simple: the stuff of life is given the benefit of form, and the rigor of form is given the content of life. Opposites are reconciled in a condition of free play, which entails its own play impulse (Sp*ieltrieb*). But beauty still contained two potential variants, an "energetic" and a "relaxing" (*schmelzend*) kind.[55] Activated singly, each could offset the opposed excess of a disturbed society, or indeed any unbalanced life; and in modern society everyone was suffering from the division of labor, all were specialists sacrificing their human wholeness so as to advance mankind. At their sublime best, they had devised differential calculus or written a *Critique of Pure Reason*. But was it right that individuals, even in such noble causes, should lose out on their fuller potential?[56] This was the seed of Hegel's and Marx's later concept of alienation (*Entfremdung*). Could human breadth and balance not be restored? To both the political and the even wider social problem, there is the one answer: the mixture that is art can work on the mixture that is the human being. Diagnosis and prescription; once more Schiller's medical training shapes his thinking.

His proposal may seem, again, idealistically detached from political realities. But it was not a matter of sending politicians to theaters and art galleries and their unruly followers back to school. Education was a matter of the whole human environment and the slow infiltration of taste. It began with ensuring that society did not have brutal entertainments—gladiatorial combat, public executions, bearbaiting, bullfighting.[57] Schiller was avowedly looking to the long term, avowedly to a task for future centuries.[58] He was also looking back for a continuity from prehistory, to the first development of decoration and pleasure in the forms and not just the usefulness of objects. That was the primitive origin of aesthetic experience, of a civilized condition that had developed over the ages alongside technology and practicality (and worse). Indeed, beautiful forms had from the first contained and inculcated what was destined to emerge eventually as rational truths—one more of those beneficial shortcuts the eighteenth century tried optimistically to make out. In a more advanced age, it meant progressively learning to see things as they were and purely for what they were, moving beyond purposes to essences (here Kant is clearly in the background) and treating phenomena with the full seriousness of play. For, paradoxically again, only in the activity of play were people fully human: "Der Mensch spielt nur, wo er in voller Bedeutung des Worts Mensch ist, und *er ist nur da ganz Mensch, wo er spielt.*"[59] The aesthetic condition had no preset purpose, it brought about no specific result, other than—but this was immense—restoring human wholeness, which would clear the ground for a fresh start.[60] To the Enlightenment mind, resilient after a historic setback, a fresh start was necessarily full of promise.

But the "aesthetic condition" was an abstraction and "art" a generalization. The job had to be done by actual artists. And if they were not to be themselves corrupted by a corrupt society, they had to be independent of their time: not its simple product and decidedly not its favorite, but able to give their culture what it needed rather than what it wanted. This is Schiller at his most prescriptive, authoritative, combative. His metaphor is extreme: the return of Agamemnon's son to avenge his father's death.[61] This is the moment when his ambitious journal meets resistance from the cultural scene he had hoped to unify; he sees himself and Goethe as a "church militant" and declares the only right relation to the public is "war"![62]

Schiller had first stated the responsibility of artists in a poem written just weeks before the Revolution. It too posited beauty as a means: "What we have here perceived as beauty / Will one day come to meet us as the truth." But it was not *just* a means, to be cast off once truth and reason were established, in the way Lessing's *Education of Mankind* foresaw the old scriptures being superseded by a pure ethic, or in the way art was finally to be superseded altogether by philosophy in Hegel's *Aesthetics*. For the artist Schiller, art and beauty were too intrinsically valuable; they would stay on at the imagined end of the historical process: "With you, the plant with which spring started, / Nature began to shape Man's soul. / With you, the garland of the harvest, / She rounds her labors to a whole."[63] Schiller's prerevolutionary faith is still there in the *Aesthetic Letters*, but thought through to a far greater and compelling depth in the shadow of a seemingly failed Revolution.

Faced with the choice between art as means and art as end, Schiller chooses both. That is no surprise. It reflects his dual commitment, as artist and cultural critic, to the order that art is and to the order it seeks to bring about. Perhaps in the end it is not so difficult to reconcile the two, the practical and political with the aesthetic. It is possible to enjoy the great scenes—Nathan and Saladin, Posa and Philipp, Egmont and Alba—on page or stage, aesthetically, as high points of drama, exemplary in the history of an art form, or to admire even the most vehement political poem for its command of rhetoric, and yet still to engage with the issues such texts embody, urgent when they were created and recurrently urgent again, their representation still potentially disturbing and activating. That always ready potential is subtly suggested in the aphorism of Jean Paul's that "books are the standing army of freedom."[64] The enjoyment of art will only be self-sufficient when—improbably—all urgency has ceased.

CHAPTER IO

The Full Earth:
A Lyrical Enlightenment

Iovis omnia plena
All things are full of Jove
—Vergil, *Eclogues*

O Erd o Sonne o Glück o Lust!
O Earth o Sun o Happiness o Pleasure!
—Goethe, "Maifest"

All the intellectual activity of these late decades of the eighteenth century would have been as nothing if it had not offered a credible basis for
lived practice. What view of life and what way of life did the Enlightenment
make possible? What was left standing, spiritually, as a result of the age of
criticism? At the centre was the modest but soundly constructed dwelling
for human beings that Kant had put up to replace the hubristic Tower of
Babel of theological speculation. He works out the contrast between these
metaphorical buildings elegantly in a late passage of the First Critique.[1] Religious doctrine was now destabilized, partly through its own visibly inadequate self-justification, Lessing's heroic efforts included, in a debate it could
never win or even hope to survive intact. Kant had never rejected faith but
had left it with no claim to count as knowledge. "Making room for faith"
was not a triumph but a fallback position, a last resort. He had shown that,
of the three traditional proofs of God's existence, the "ontological" and the
"cosmological" were "mere self-creations of thought."[2] Conjuring real existence out of mere conceptual possibility was a "miserable tautology."[3] To
then go on arbitrarily adding features that enhance the grandeur of the imagined deity was like trying to improve your bank balance by adding noughts.[4]

The entire method was, precisely, "null and void," Leibniz's arguments included.[5]

But the third—"physicotheological"—proof of God's existence Kant treats more gently. It at least took real experience as its starting point, inferring a creator from the creation. It deserved respect as "the oldest, clearest, and most suited to common human reason."[6] It motivated scientific study through the "guiding thread" of nature's unity (very much the "as if" assumption on which Kant himself later bases scientific inquiry in the *Critique of Judgment*). The richer the knowledge gained, the stronger the belief in a supreme author. Pious people would never have countenanced a "mere blindly acting eternal nature as the root of things."[7] That would have been unacceptably random, in substance even protoevolutionary (Kant's formulation echoes the hints in that direction in his early scientific writings).

True, the alleged empirical proof of God's existence still ultimately depended as much as the other two on speculation, was in fact reducible to the "ontological" argument. The creation, that is, might suggest but could not prove a "supreme being with understanding and freedom." That still needed a leap of the imagination. Strictly speaking, the world revealed only itself. So the "physico-" component carried the "theological" component only part of the way. In any case it could never prove the truth specifically of Christianity along with all its doctrines and dogmas, a point rarely taken by its defenders, then or now. The book of Genesis of course had its say, but that was merely the faith's own creation myth. To say that "the earth is full of the glory" of any particular deity only added another non sequitur.

Still, glory it remained, earthquakes and other disasters notwithstanding. Kant surveyed "an immeasurable scene of diversity, order, purposiveness, and beauty," of "endless space and infinite division . . . so that our judgment of the whole must dissolve into a speechless but all the more eloquent wonderment."[8] But why remain speechless? Wonderment could inspire poetic eloquence, monumentally so in Barthold Hinrich Brockes. Other writers' praise of the creation pales beside the range and poetic quality of his *Earthly Delight in God* (*Irdisches Vergnügen in Gott*), nine volumes published over twenty-seven years (1721–48). Brockes has been called "the church father of nature poetry,"[9] which neatly combines respect for his poetic originality with reservations about his insistent doctrinal message. His observations are real, not imaginative decoration as in much early eighteenth-century poetry. He even does some science, writing up in poetic detail an experiment with a magnifying glass that opened up the hidden structures of the infinitely small.[10] For the rest, lengthy, often delicate and insightful evocations of earthly phenomena range from the firmament, plants and birds, a rose, cherry blossom, a nightingale, down to a fly, a speck of dust, a drop of ink from his own pen, all ending with brief religious punch lines. The speck of dust is as edifying as a planet, a dewdrop is answered by teardrops of love and gratitude. A description of nightingale song not unworthy to stand beside those of Keats and Crashaw ("Music's Duel") ends with the pious point that anyone listening to it who fails to honor the creator for the air that carries sound and the ears that hear it is unworthy to enjoy either. The senses figure regularly; God made us "so wonderfully sensuous" with a purpose: "Busy yourselves then and, God to revere, / Attentively feel, taste, and see, and hear."[11] Colors reflecting sunlight on distinct parts of a fly's body make us aware of the divine gift of sight. Awe and loving gratitude can hardly be felt at all if we fail to contemplate the natural world. Yet however great the delight, it must still fall short of what the cherry-blossom poem imagines in another life: "The greatest beauty of this world / With that of heaven cannot be compared." Contemplation yields to speculation, the physical to the theological. The harmony of the overall title masks a tension: earthly delight in God is, more precisely, earthly delight plus God. It must never become self-sufficient.

For the increasingly secular mind, it did. Delight was all that was left. The other basic motives for devotion (conformism to a local religion apart)—to avert divine wrath and to request favorable interventions—had been written off by the Enlightenment. A vengeful deity was primitive superstition, and the granter of individual favors was not much more plausible; he could hardly satisfy all the divergent desires in the world,[12] most obviously the appeals of opposed sides in a war. Yet the celebratory impulse remained, as strong as ever. But who was there to thank? Thankfulness, a late poem of Goethe's reflects, draws us to something higher and purer, but always unknown, unnamed; to puzzle over it is our form of piety.[13] The impulse to thank still flowed into words, images, and tones. Poetry, the visual arts, and music could be the more eloquent for being free of prescribed belief. A new culture was slowly arising with its own earthly piety, epitomized in Diderot's cry, "Liberate God from temples, see him everywhere or say he doesn't exist."[14] That throws a bridge back across the Christian centuries to the Greek gods of Schiller's poem. The world comes into its own again, inherently valuable. The cult of nature then blossoms in nineteenth-century Romanticism; Spinoza's *deus sive natura* has become *deus qua natura*. The term "naturalist" with which Christians had attacked nonbelievers was apt enough.

Goethe exemplifies this process and its product, nobody better or earlier. He was not at first following a conscious program, just living out an exuberant response to the world of his personal experience. An innate self-confidence carries him effortlessly over the obstacles of orthodoxy, so that he sees the world with fresh eyes and captures his vision in fresh words. No doubt from his youth he was buoyed up by a higher social position than any other German writer of the age enjoyed, in a Free Imperial city (Frankfurt am Main) that was itself independent of absolutist power. No doubt, too, his antennae were sensitive to the increasingly enlightened intellectual climate. The result was "a mind not mortgaged to church or state."[15] After the adventure of reason (*sapere aude*), this was the adventure of being (*esse aude*). Kant's abstract ideal of human potential is made flesh; the individualism of freedom develops into an individualism of uniqueness.[16] Freedom *from* becomes freedom *to*: to realize one's particular self and express it.

From early on Goethe is clear he is a poet, and that this trumps any transcendent expectations. Back home from university at Leipzig to recover from near collapse, he is drawn into a Pietist group, but not wholeheartedly. He is aware they regard him "as someone who shows goodwill and some sensitivity, but is still too flighty through attachment to the world." They have given him a reverence for religion and the gospel such as the "unevangelical claptrap of our present-day pulpits" could never give. "Admittedly, with all that I'm no Christian." He is clear why: "My fiery mind, my wit, my endeavor and fairly well-founded hope to become in time a good writer are, to be honest, the most important hindrances to a complete change of mind and to accepting more avidly the pointers of grace." He is just nineteen, has published only one small set of poems,[17] but knows he is a poet, and this means being implicated—that telling oxymoron, "flighty through attachment"!—in the world.[18] The world is the subject of his poetry, the object of his curious eye, the larger home where he can happily "dwell in himself" and be creatively free—the phrases "free world," "open world," "full world" recur in poems and letters, transferred epithets for his own feelings of release.[19] The world, he later recalled, positively shared his pleasure: "I saw the world and love was in my sight, / And world and I, we reveled in delight."[20]

"Sight" was the least of it. He is fully in the world with all the confidence of that "truth of his five senses,"[21] not just observing the natural scene from a safe distance, as so much earlier nature poetry had, but moving vigorously through it and evoking it with intense and exact perceptions—dusk thickening to darkness at the horizon, morning sunlight sparkling like stars on a lake. Movement is in every sense vital. He is out skating on what may be thin ice, riding through the Alsace dusk to a lovers' meeting, being rowed on a bright day on Lake Zurich, trudging though storm and mud and singing to keep his spirits up, riding in a coach over bumpy eighteenth-century roads. Several poems cast him as a wanderer, which is what his friends called him for his practice of walking long distances before that activity was a sport. "Anything good in the way of reflections, thoughts, expression even, comes mostly when I'm moving," he noted in his diary in 1780; "sitting down I'm not good for much." The rhythms of his movement become the rhythms of his poems, as in that coach ride dragging slowly uphill ("Mühsam Berg hinauf") and careering downhill. Just as rhythmically expressive is the contrasting immobility of Prometheus's earthly home, challenging Zeus with stolid stressed syllables: "Músst mír méine Érde / Dóch lássen stéhn." Omitting the initial "du," compressing "stehen" to "stehn," reversing the usual order of "stehn lassen"—every detail embodies defiance, recalling Luther's "Hier steh ich und kann nicht anders" (Here I stand and can do no other), perhaps echoed again in the closing line: "Hier sitz' ich, forme Menschen" (Here I sit, shape human beings). Some poems are conceived—demonstrably, it is not the romanticizing legend as which it is commonly dismissed—in the moment they record: on that boat outing, or as he climbs out of the Ilm after a swim, or when he leaps out of bed to capture an inspiration without stopping to put the paper straight, or when, out on a mission for Duke Carl August, he writes him a goodnight greeting, includes a poem that came into his mind during the day's ride, the rhythmic mood draws him into writing another one.[22] Nor is it just a phenomenon of youth. In his sixties, traveling through the Rhineland and in thrall now to the poetry of Hafiz, he dashes off eight poems in the Persian mode in one day; as an old man returning embittered from Marienbad and a frustrated love for a woman fifty years his junior, from stage to stage of the coach journey he drafts what becomes the most massive, uniquely tragic poem of his life. An old calendar serves his turn.[23] Other inspirations are captured in a notebook or a diary, whatever is to hand, even on one famous occasion the wall of a hut—in Peter Johnson's enviable pun, the "Ausgabe letzter Wand"—for the most celebrated lyrical poem in the German language.[24] Emotion is caught in flight rather than recollected in tranquility, with no rhetorical throat clearing. His openings are simple and immediate, the language sometimes seemingly prosaic, but that means rooted in reality, drawing us at once into situation and standpoint. With exclamation: "How splendid nature / Shines all for me!"; "How in dawn's red / All round you glow at me, / springtime, beloved!" With imperatives, addressed to a mythic coachman: "Hurry up, Kronos, Off at a rattling trot!"; or rebelliously to the father of the gods himself: "Go cover up your heavens, Zeus!"; or, in delighted assent, to the vine growing at his window: "Grow richer, greener, you leaves." With excited or serene report: "An impulse, mount, and off careering / Wild like a hero to the fight"; "Over all the hilltops / Is peace"; "Now on classical soil I stand, inspired and elated"; "Dusk was drawing down from heaven"; "Lights are floating on the water." With personal address: "Again you fill this dearest valley / Quiet with gleaming mist"; "Do you know the land where lemons grow?" With anxious doubts and wishes: "My peace is gone, and heavy my heart"; "O if only springtime's blessing / Could be held for just one hour"; "Why did fate give us this deeper vision?"; "What can I hope for from another meeting?" "Would you go from me so quickly?" With defiance of convention: "Not for me love's torments, no"; "So that was criminal, was it, to once be inspired by Propertius?" Not to mention ghostly narrative and the "dark place" of ambiguous appearances, "the old willow trees and their gray long hair," which may be the daughters of the Erl King, who is pursuing a terrified boy.

Translators have problems rendering great poetry.[25] Even so, it is clear that Goethe's words and syntax could not be a more open code. The simplicity of both language and subject reaches out to the Common Reader; it is a democratic art. The poems spring from occasions (*Gelegenheiten*), but not in the sense of the grand public events for which "occasional verse" used to be commissioned by the great. These are occasions from a personal life, beginning sometimes as virtual diary entries (the first versions often carry dates) yet commonplace enough to be recognized by anyone, resolving the paradox that our common humanity is made up of unique individuals: "All of us are alike, it is one race that we belong to; / We are not all alike, whispers each one in his heart."[26] And the everyday is made revelatory by the way its elements are accorded serious attention. It is an art of the obvious, of things too near to be much remarked; it is also an art of communicative courtesy through the transparency of its meanings. Rarely is Goethe obscure, and when he fears he has been, he provides a commentary—to "Harz Journey in Winter," to "Primal Words. Orphic."[27] His range extends down to the most banal objects, for to the generous vision everything is connected. Goethe addresses some rough-and-ready unpunctuated lines to the would-be graphic artist: "God grant that you may love your shoe / Every deformed potato too / Try to see each object plain / Its peace and power joy and pain / And feel the whole world's held in place / By the high heaven's grand embrace."[28] It is the program for a loving realism.

Unlike Brockes's subjects, there is not much beauty or intricacy to admire in a shoe or a potato. Yet they are fit objects of an embracing love because they are all parts of one grand order under the arch of sky—"high heaven" is astronomy, not theology—in unbroken connection with everything else in the phenomenal world. Strikingly, the key concepts and rhyme words of those lines exactly echo Professor Faust's thirst for knowledge of the real world beyond academic wordmongering.[29] Moreover, the poet's exploration of the world does not stop short at sense impressions, but instinctively seeks order. Even the simple expression of delight in nature in the early poem "May Festival" unobtrusively links all the observed processes in a single verb, *dringen*: blossoms come thrusting out from every twig, the song of a thousand birds from the bushes, pleasure and bliss from every human breast. The underlying power that blesses all these things is once again love, a provisional label for the force that beyond all personal emotion holds nature together. This is not sentimentality, but something that will be amply present in much of the later poetry: an unsolemn, sacramental celebration of earthly things, a modern echo of the late Latin *Pervigilium Veneris*.

Not that for Goethe all is sweetness and light, nature happy and harmonious with no darker side. In his quest for deepest reality before he makes contact with Mephistopheles, Faust conjures up (and is duly put down by) the mighty Earth Spirit, an invention of Goethe's as much at odds with his own dramatic version of the tale as with the Christian original:

In living floods, in action's storms
I swirl up and down,
Waft back and forth,
Birth and grave,
An eternal ocean,
A weaving reweaving,
A glowing life.
I work at the roaring loom of time,
And shape the living apparel of God.[30]

The Earth Spirit may be subordinate to this deity, but he sounds otherwise very like that "blindly acting eternal nature as the root of things" that Kant knew pious people could not entertain. Likewise, the tragic hero of Goethe's first novel, *The Sufferings of Young Werther*, becomes obsessed with "the consuming force that lies hidden in the whole of nature, that has shaped nothing that does not destroy its neighbor, destroy itself. And so I reel in terror. Heaven and earth and their weaving forces all around me: I see nothing but an eternally devouring, eternally ruminating monster."[31] However joyfully the world is affirmed, tragedy remains the foil to happiness and harmony that makes them the more precious. Werther is only the first of Goethe's tragic figures, followed by Gretchen and Valentin in *Faust I*, Egmont, the dead boy in "The Erl King," Mignon and the harpist in *Wilhelm Meisters Lehrjahre*, Philemon and Baucis in *Faust II*, and Ottilie in the novel *Elective Affinities*. It can hardly be said that Goethe avoids tragedy.[32] What is true is that his work is far removed from the later cultural clichés that existence is essentially tragic and that only the tragic is to be taken seriously.

Tragedy may also be vigorously resisted, and Goethe has a vision of what that takes too. In an early review of an aesthetic theory that saw the function of art as further beautifying the agreeable impressions the Creation makes on the senses, he asks: what about the unpleasant ones? Are not storms and floods, subterranean fire and fatal elements, just as much "witnesses to nature's eternal life"? What if she were to engulf a whole civilized city in her maw? (Understood: as she already had Lisbon.) But he then argues as forcefully for the power of human response. Nature does not rear us to "gentleness and fine feeling." Rather, "she hardens her genuine children [*ihre echten Kinder*] to the pains and evils she constantly faces them with, so that we can call that man happiest who is the strongest to meet evil, to thrust it aside in defiance and go the way of his will."[33] Such is the resolve that, wherever possible, resists potential tragedy—a vitally necessary resolve, because the secular mind has no easy recourse to transcendent consolation, theodicy, an imagined afterlife. Werther does have desperate hopes for a posthumous reunion, but the ending of his story is bleak. The measured sentences, and the echoing vowels of the very last one, are like a bell tolling: "Manual workers carried him. No clergyman accompanied him."[34]

More than one early poem captures the point of balance between awe and pleasure in the face of nature. The speaker in "Welcome and Parting" sets off with pounding heart through a deserted landscape at dusk, half-seriously threatened by darkness peering out through the trees, by a mist-shrouded oak rising up as a towering giant, by the "thousand monsters" night has spawned. Precise sense perception is made metaphor: in the dusk, gaps between the branches are darker than the residual light on foliage; personified, they are "a hundred eyes."[35] As himself a "genuine child of nature," the rider has resources to match: "My courage was thousandfolder yet, / My spirit a consuming fire, / My heart entire melted in heat."[36] (These hyperboles will, alas! be revised out by a poet fifteen years older, who does not see how well poetic excess conveyed youthful feeling.) Calm comes at the sight of the beloved; there is the bliss of a too brief meeting, then the pain of parting. But that is outweighed by the happiness of being loved, however undeservedly, and especially of loving. Emotional occasion becomes mature reflection.[37]

Adventure becomes allegory. The skater in the epigrammatic "Ice-Life-Song" moves "carefree over the surface," making his own track where even the boldest have not ventured, needing some reassurance (not *so* carefree, then) for his once again pounding heart: the ice "may crack, but it won't break, / It may break, but not under you."[38] "Sea Voyage" ("Seefahrt") is a more leisurely spelling out of a benign destiny. It narrates the wait for a favorable wind, the bustle of departure, the send-off by friends who imagine the pleasures of "the first high starry nights" (*ersten hohen Sternennächte*). In the event it is all contrary winds, furled sails and a storm-tossed ship, the friends on shore now anxious. If only he had stayed safe on dry land! Is he fated to perish? He however—and it is now an objectively seen "he," not the "I" of the opening, and no longer a merchant passenger, but a seaman masterfully at home on the grim deep—stands steadfast at the wheel; the ship is the plaything of wind and wave, but his heart isn't. Shipwrecked or safely landed, he trusts in his gods.[39]

Who are the gods of this personal faith? "Götter" is a recurring exclamation in the young Goethe, almost always in this plural form, and when singular "hundred-headed."[40] He can say "fiat voluntas," but without saying whose will he means.[41] Another poem of storm-blown crisis features a guardian "Genius" who he hopes will not abandon him.[42] He is moving in elevated company, not least when—allegory again—a real coach journey becomes the journey of life to an early but triumphant end, with the postilion's horn and a clatter of hooves announcing his arrival in the underworld so that the shades of the mighty will know a prince is arriving and will rise to greet him: "Dass der Orkus vernehme, ein Fürst kommt, / Drunten von ihren Sitzen / Sich die Gewaltigen lüften."[43] Not a preexisting myth now, but mythopoeisis.

Goethe's gods are not to be feared. In youth he could summon up no sense of sin, had no great flaws to confess, knew there was moral strength within him, felt he even had a credit balance with God, who needed *his* forgiveness for not being more helpful.[44] All this was part of the Promethean ground-clearing, which Goethe himself labeled "divine impudence" (*göttliche Frechheit*).[45] As for his own gods, they had given him unasked the standard fate of all their favored ones. Once more it is a balance of delight and its opposite. The insight goes into four gnomic lines enclosed in a letter and then forgotten. They have the barely renderable power of German word order: "All things, the gods, the unending ones, gave / To their favorites, whole. / All joys, the unending ones, / All pains, the unending ones, whole."[46] Perilous incidents strengthen his faith: he survives a violent fall from his horse, he comes back from the edge of death after his Leipzig collapse, he just misses being crushed by a rockfall while inspecting the Ilmenau silver mine. His sense of direction and destiny has some of the old passive (but in his case highly personal) *Bestimmung des Menschen*, alongside an immensely active version of the new *Selbstbestimmung*. There is no distinction between his gods and the grateful confidence in his own earthly being. The gods are simply its projection.

Part of Goethe's gratitude was to his earthly father and mother for what they gave him, perhaps especially to her as the source of his lightheartedness and pleasure in storytelling ("Frohnatur und Lust zu fabulieren").[47] The personality preserved in her letters does indeed have a vivacious style all her own, even the occasional poem, and hers was the literal mother tongue he was raised in. Even more, to be her uncontested favorite was surely one source of his confidence in a higher favor. It was, Freud argued specifically apropos Goethe, "the origin of that triumphal feeling, that certainty of success which not infrequently brings success with it."[48]

Goethe had long known what the gods' favor felt like when, in his mid-seventies, he lost it, lost everything to erotic passion: "The world's all lost, myself as well I'm losing, / I, once the favorite of the gods on high."[49] While his belated infatuation with a seventeen-year-old woman lasted, thankfulness had never been stronger, but at the end of the episode it yielded to total bleakness, most sweepingly in the introductory poem of the *Trilogy of Passion*. Written last of the poems, and so chronologically the trilogy's final statement, "To Werther" devalues life itself, Goethe's own included. He tells the revenant suicide how little he lost by dying: "I stayed, you left, our fate and not our choosing, / You went before—how little you were losing."[50] It was not, however, to be Goethe's last word.

A writer like this who had escaped from conventional beliefs had a choice of allies across the cultures. For Goethe, instinctively but also in tune with fundamentals of Enlightenment thinking, such human communication was a supreme value. From the earliest days he felt a solidarity with all those whose voices had come down to him. He esteemed and loved "the testimonies that show me how thousands or even just one person before me felt exactly the same as what strengthens and sustains me. And so the word of man is for me the word of God, whether collected by priests or whores, rolled into a codex or scattered in fragments."[51] At the other end of his life he celebrates all the "sterling people" who have left a written record of themselves for later ages; they are a secular "communion of saints."[52] Specifically in science, his predecessors were the "genuine people of all ages" who "announce each other, point to each other, anticipate each other by their work."[53] "Sterling," "genuine"—Goethe's grateful accolades to his forerunners are practical and down-to-earth. At the point where his own scientific work took off from his poetic vision of nature, his great support was Spinoza and the paradoxical "atheist's reverence for God" that avowedly came closest to his own view of the world.[54] But Spinoza's pantheism was as much a confirmation as an influence.

So was the fulfillment that Italy brought. He had foreseen it as destined since childhood days, when his otherwise laconic father came alive recounting his own eight-month Italian journey.[55] There were prospects of Rome hanging on the walls and even a toy gondola to play with. After hesitations and missed chances, and after a growing obsession had made it painful even to look at a classical text, finally, at three in the morning on 3 September 1786, Goethe "crept out of Carlsbad," where the Weimar court was staying: "they wouldn't have let me go if I hadn't . . . but I wasn't going to be stopped, for it was time."[56] Arrived in Rome after superstitious fears he might be prevented at the last minute, he breathes a sigh of relief: "Only now do I begin to live, and give reverent thanks to my guardian spirit."[57]

What he found, already on the way into Italy and overwhelmingly once there, was an even fuller world—the relaxing climate, the clear light, the easygoing Italian way of life, the color and exuberance of the people, the beauty of the landscape, the rich remains of antiquity, the architecture of Palladio, the best art of the Renaissance. But he was also traveling to regain his own former exuberance, crushed under the weight of court life and especially of administration, which for his first ten years in Weimar had taken up so much of his time. He had not been invited there as a poet (none of the Weimar writers were), though providing the court with light literary fare was a chore expected of him. That was just one more thing that prevented work on two major projects (*Faust, Wilhelm Meister*) and the completion or polishing of three more (*Egmont, Iphigenie auf Tauris, Torquato Tasso*). Some or all of these were urgently needed for a collected edition, planned to revive his already fading early reputation. Above all, what he was after now was "the sense impressions that no book and no picture can give me, so that I start to take an interest in the world again."[58] It is a striking admission of loss. But now, crucially, he is on the move again, delighted, intrigued, puzzled by the sights and sounds and smells of a new world. He is in close contact with the people, tries to dress like them so as to be unobtrusive, travels alone and incognito (under one of the commonest German names, Möller) by whatever public transport is available, converses in Italian with anyone he meets—all quite unlike the standard grand tour, where as a per-

son of consequence you took your own coach and servants and carried letters of introduction to the best people along the route, thus suffering the
minimum necessary exposure to Otherness.

Though Goethe is thankfully leaving his practical activities behind, at
least they have strengthened his down-to-earth grasp of realities. His administrator's eye compares Bavaria's to Bohemia's roads, approves Tuscan
but not Vatican civic organization, devises a plan to clean up the streets of
Venice. His applied scientist's eye observes the physique and complexion of
different regional types and speculates on the causes in their diet, or relates
the weather patterns this side of the Alps to what is in store for the people
back home. And underlying all individual observations, he is consciously
traveling across the shape of Europe, its mountain ranges and watersheds.
He questions, wonders, checks, consults. Above all, he sees. He struggles
to master the input of his senses: "So much is thrusting in on me . . . , my
existence is growing like a snowball, and it's as if my mind can't grasp or
stand it all, and yet everything is developing from within, and I can't live
without that."[59] The simplest experience can suddenly become a revelation,
like seeing a small crab on the beach in Venice: "How precisely fitted to its
condition, how true! How *full of being!*"[60]

His old ideas are being made "so live, so coherent, that they may count
as new." They are realized with an almost erotic intensity that recalls the
Pygmalion myth. The sculptor "had shaped his statue with as much truth
and existence as an artist can, but when she came toward him saying 'Now
I really *am*!,' how different was the living woman from the shaped stone."[61]
Goethe speaks of revolution and repeatedly of rebirth, but he does not allow
enthusiasm to run wild. Overcompensation was a danger after the years of
yearning, so he practices a conscious discipline: "I am living frugally and
keeping calm so that objects do not find a heightened mind but themselves
heighten it. . . . All the heightening and embellishing power of the imagination cannot conceive that which is true."[62] Thus sobered, the mind of the
beholder can take on by osmosis the quality of the ancient stone all around:
"Anyone who looks about him seriously here and has eyes to see must become *solid*, he must get a conception of solidity such as was never so vivid
to him before. To me at least it seems I have never appraised the things of
this world aright as I now do here." It is as if the mass of the great buildings
has "stamped the mind with solidity."[63] This much is already achieved,
yet there is still so much to see, so much to learn—among other things,
how to draw properly, with the help of the leading resident German artist, Johann Heinrich Tischbein, for whom he also sat. And stood: the back
view of Goethe looking down from his window at the Corso, more informal

than Tischbein's famous portrait of the poet magisterially reclining in the Campagna landscape, is wonderfully suggestive of the fascination Italian life held for a fugitive northerner.

Learning will take time. Goethe begins to hint he will not be returning so soon as intended—a couple of months was the original plan. Weimar must not think he is just enjoying himself; it is not a holiday but a sabbatical. He will return a transformed and more useful man. True, the ultimate achievement is beyond reach—it would take "a lifetime of activity and practice to bring our knowledge to the highest point of purity."[64] Short of that impossible span, he manages to gradually extend his paid leave to almost two years. Some sabbatical!

His experience of art in Rome matches what he knows of natural phenomena, not by analogy but as part of a single monistic system. Hardly surprising: the ancients had a profound knowledge of the nature their art was representing. "Everything arbitrary, imagined, collapses, there is necessity, there is God."[65] "Necessity" becomes the criterion for great art, as also exemplified by Palladio—Goethe's greatest aesthetic experience as he approached Rome—and Raphael. "Imagined" or "arbitrary" means anything that goes beyond or distracts from reality. An ancient sarcophagus in Verona does not:

> You see a man beside his wife looking out of a niche as from a window, a father and mother stand with their son between them and look at one another with ineffable naturalness, a couple stretch out their hands to each other. A father seems to be taking a calm leave of his family on his deathbed. . . . I was so deeply moved in the presence of these stones that I could not hold back my tears. Here is no man in armor on his knees waiting for a joyous resurrection, what the artist has here set down with more or less skill is never anything more than the simple present of human beings, which thereby prolongs their existence and makes it permanent. They don't put their hands together, they don't look up to heaven; rather they are what they were, they stand together, they feel for each other, they love one another, and that is expressed in the stone most delightfully, often with a certain technical clumsiness.[66]

The same idea is taken up in the first of the later *Venetian Epigrams*, where death is "overwhelmed" by the "fullness" of funerary images and the life they represent.[67]

The ancient practice of commemorating presence is contrasted with the Christian aesthetics of nonpresence, of otherworldly notions not contained in visible forms but lying far beyond them, real only in the mind of the believing onlooker. Renaissance religious art was paradoxically, as Walter Pater pointed out, "the sensuous expression of conceptions which unreservedly discredit the world of sense."[68] Goethe's objection is not just ideological but aesthetic, in tune with and perhaps influenced by the central thesis of Lessing's *Laokoon*, that visual art has to deal with objects in space, it has its roots and its limits in physical reality. But Goethe does also feel revulsion at the sheer quantity of religious gore, the endless crucifixions and martyrdoms of doctrinal art. "Never a present interest, always some fantastical expectation"—the salvation or canonization that suffering promises the victim. Without such considerations, torture and death are not fit to be subjects, or certainly not the dominant subjects, of visual representation.

Violence had been done to the artists too. Seeing "the heavenly touch of Guido, a brush that should have painted only the most perfect things that strike our senses, you want to turn your eyes away from the hideous, stupid subjects which all the abusive words in the world would not be enough to degrade."[69] Painters had to do as they were told. "Of ten subjects, not one that should have been painted. . . . The great painting by Guido is everything a painter could do and everything senseless that could be ordered and demanded of a painter. . . . He had the knife at his throat, did everything he could to show he wasn't the barbarian, it was the people who had paid for the picture."[70] Some subjects do have an independent human interest. Goethe can respond to a Virgin and child as "a beautiful invention"; at least "something senseless" in doctrine is being "presented in sensuous form,"[71] a subject fundamental to human experience. He can be overwhelmed by the work of an Old Master, Mantegna, but precisely because the full force of reality has been captured: "Words can't express the sharp, confident presence these pictures contain. This whole true (not just illusory, not mendaciously effect-seeking, not playing on the imagination), this rough, pure, luminous, detailed, conscientious, delicate, circumscribed present."[72] Anti-Christian animus is set aside when individual existence is rendered as beautifully as in Raphael's painting of St. Cecilia: "A group of five saints, none of whom are of any concern to us, but whose existence is so perfect that one wishes the picture may last forever, though content with one's own dissolution."[73] In work of such supreme quality, art has transcended transcendence, embodying humanity so fully that it reconciles the viewer to his own mortality. "Existence" (*Dasein*) and "presence" (*Gegenwart*) are key terms, alongside "necessary" and "true," for the reality that is left when irrelevant or distorting superstructures have been removed. Applied to the art of writing, negative again becomes positive; excluding unrealities leaves the real substance standing, enhanced.

Yet for the time being, while still in Italy, Goethe hardly writes anything new—just two poems in nearly two years. That hardly suggests a fresh creative phase. He was of course preoccupied with the unfinished works he had brought with him. But the abstention from new writing had deeper causes. One is that words simply felt inadequate to cope with Rome's visual grandeur and historical depth: "The longer you look at objects, the less you trust yourself to say anything general about them. One would rather express the thing itself with all its parts, or just be silent."[74] There was classical tradition for that: "When you come here it is a good and necessary thing to maintain a Pythagorean silence. I could be here for years without speaking. Everything has been so thoroughly described and pronounced upon that you have to first open your eyes, first learn to see."[75] See for yourself, form your own judgment—again, a basic Enlightenment principle. Rome, though, is positively cooperating, as other realities had earlier: "You know my old way of treating nature, that's how I'm treating Rome, and already it's coming to meet me"— the prefix *entgegen*, meaning "movement toward the speaker," becomes a leitmotif of the Italian journey. All things become his allies in creating fresh experience. He declares himself a more fortunate Orestes, pursued not by the Furies but by the Muses and Graces.[76]

Meanwhile, the risk of premature writing is graphically put apropos a standard work on Italy: "How such rubbish [*Geschreibe*] shrinks when you're on the spot. It's as if you laid the book on hot coals and it slowly turned brown, then black, the pages curled and it went up in smoke."[77] Such de-scribing is literally a writing down, a devaluing of reality. That guidebook was a warning: "As long as I'm here I'm going to open my eyes, keep modestly looking, and wait to see what takes shape in my mind." For the present, fresh writing is confined to his diary and letters, with the occasional striking metaphor (the "solidity" stamped on his mind by great buildings, the coming alive of mere knowledge in the way Pygmalion's statue became a flesh-and-blood woman), though often things are simply labeled "beautiful," "fine." But the other cause is that he is in no hurry. He is in it for the long term: "I'm following my old plan and looking for something fundamental which as capital must bear interest, and am gaining so much that I can live off it for the rest of my life." This shrewd but cool strategy is followed by a more heartfelt metaphor: "Just as people say that someone who's seen a ghost can never be happy again, I would say that someone who has seen Italy properly, especially Rome, can never quite be unhappy."[78] Unsurprisingly, from the first report of his journey his mother intuited in similar terms what Italy must mean for him: "After a journey like this a man such as you are, with your knowledge, your pure, great eagle's eye for everything good, great, and beautiful, must be cheerful and happy for the rest of his life—and not just you but everybody who has the good fortune to live in the circle of your activity."[79]

Personal happiness and stylistic restraint: as early as the letter to Herder and his wife about his mind being "stamped with solidity," Goethe had defined his new condition as "seriousness without dryness, and a settled being, with joy." Add to this the principle of excluding what is superfluous as a later epigram formulates it—"Every other master we know by the things that he shows us, / Only the master of style rather by what he withholds"[80]—and Goethe's burgeoning classicism (for that is what is coming into focus) may sound less than exciting. That, however, is to leave out the revelation and revolution of sexual love—a revelation for him, a revolution for European love poetry.

Coming back to Weimar was not on the whole a happy return. There was too much resentment at his long absence, too little understanding of his new vision. The one consolation was domestic delight. A young woman of modest social background, Christiane Vulpius, became overnight his live-in mistress. Now he really could write: a cycle of twenty love poems in classical couplets, unrhymed hexameter plus pentameter, the *Roman Elegies*.[81] At a distance from Rome, he could write about Rome as the setting. The love story is straightforward: *veni, vidi, vici*. The newly arrived foreigner senses an erotic current pulsing through the city from which he is excluded, so at first he dutifully does the sights (I). But soon he is truly at home (*endlich geborgen*), provided with a mistress (II), whom he even has to reassure that he thinks no less well of her for yielding so promptly (III). This has ancient authority in the speed with which the Immortals—those gods of Greece again!—took the earthlings they fancied. Promptness and frankness are the Elegies' essence. They celebrate fulfilled mutual desire and stable affection. That goes flat contrary to the dominant tradition of the postclassical European love lyric, which positively wallows in all possible forms of unfulfillment: female mystery, worship from afar, unrequited love for a cold and cruel beloved, tragic loss, physical or social separation, star-crossed lovers, spiritual sublimation—all these are the normal (!) motifs of the genre. Perhaps only the love lyrics of Johannes Secundus or John Donne are as strong a contrarian statement as Goethe's.[82] (Donne's elegies are sometimes strikingly close to Goethe's in sentiment and phrasing.) At the extreme of the old convention, it was love's very definition to be, in Andrew Marvell's words, "begotten by despair upon impossibility."[83] This whole gloomy distortion is the first thing Goethe's new poetics excludes. At points explicitly: "Charming obstacles are something young blood delights in: / I'd rather savor in peace what is reliably mine" (XVIII).[84] But more often implicitly, through the way emotion is earthed in the tangible world. Rome itself is part of the action. The city's reality fills a several-hour gap that would otherwise have been open to the broodings separation might induce. While he waits for her (in the fiction they have rendezvous, not a shared roof) he distracts himself with the sights of Rome and reflections on the city's deep past. The only unreality is the humorous topos of asking the sun just this once not to linger over the splendors beneath. That still leaves an hour to go, but most of the wait has been filled and instead of ethereal yearning there is expectation: not a melancholy "if only!" but an anticipatory "how soon?" (XV).

Expectation is made concrete again in the progress of an autumn evening fire, the kindling now just catching, the promise of another night together. Fed with logs when she arrives, "it will blaze up and provide festive brilliance and warmth." Next morning when she stirs the embers, it will revive last night's other flames (IX). The oldest of images for passion becomes an unforced symbol. So, in another elegy, does the lamp his servant hesitates to light: why waste oil when it is not yet dark? But the lover insists, the lamp is consolation while he waits, a tangible measure of approaching dusk in place of empty wistfulness (XIV). As with the fire, memory is involved, deep cultural memory as well, for long ago the god Amor trimmed the lamp for a "triumvirate" of lover-poets: Propertius, Tibullus, Catullus.[85] That thought ends the great paean to the pleasures of being on "classical soil" (V). The traveler has a foot in both present and past, perusing the classical texts and viewing ancient art by day but learning through love at night: "And isn't it studying too when I feel her beautiful bosom / Under my hand, and explore onward down to the hips?" It is not just a nudge and a wink; the body in bed and the body on a pedestal truly illuminate each other: "Only then do I understand the marble, compare them, / See with an eye that can feel, feel with a hand that can see."[86] That he sometimes taps out his hexameters on her back is something Propertius's fiery Cynthia would not have tolerated; but this Faustine sleeps "a good almost German sleep."[87] That, for all Goethe's conscious discipleship, hits off the difference between him and his Roman models, worldly-wise tacticians to a man in what Ovid called the war of love with their passionate but bitchy mistresses. Yet the Elegies still take from Goethe's Roman predecessors the license for sexual freedom and frankness. If a culture has more than antiquarian value, it must feed into modern life. The ancients, Amor reminds the poet, were not "ancient" then! "When those happy men lived, antiquity was a *new* thing! / Live life happily—so history will live on in you!"[88] The "gate to the school of the Greeks" is still open. Education indeed.

Sunlight, firelight, lamplight: there are no dark corners in this love relation. There are no serious impediments either, only a guardian uncle who
must be got round, and no serious misunderstandings, though on one occasion his mistaken jealousy provokes her outspoken reproach to selfish
male orgasm: "You men spill out your love along with your strength and
desire / When you lie in our arms" (VI).[89] The affair meets no resistance, it
lacks coquetry, mystery, uncertainty. Love is freely given and reciprocated.
The path of true love may after all sometimes run straight. Goethe is too
much concerned with love to isolate sex—"Faustine" is a partner, not just
a sexual object—but too delighted with sex not to celebrate it enthusiastically and tenderly. The cycle is sexual, not phallic—reason enough to leave
out two poems on Priapus.[90] The Elegies are as far from the prurient and por-
nographic or even the knowingly titillating (always an eighteenth-century
option) as they are from that other self-tormenting tradition of loss and lament. Goethe's "loving realism" has created a realistic love.

Any real shadows are not of the couple's making. The thought of syphilis crosses the lover's mind, though only to reinforce his feeling of security
in these arms (XVIII). As with Priapus, a passing reference is enough, and
Goethe rightly omitted a whole elegy on this medical topic. More appropriately, death is three times remembered, once in an allusion to Cestius's
tomb pyramid in Rome (near which Keats is buried, VII), then in a reference
to the Fates (Parcae, XV), but most poignantly in the lines "Man, while you
live, be glad of the place that is warm from your loving, / Till at your fleeing foot Lethe chillingly laps" (X).[91] Loss indeed, but only after fulfilled love.

It was all too much for Weimar, socially and poetically. Carl August,
himself no saint, advised against publication. Wieland's mix of philosophy
and philandering was one thing, an eighteenth-century literary convention;
these *Elegies* were quite another. Whether or not there had been a love affair
in Rome, Goethe was now describing—revealing—what was going on just
up the road. As Charlotte von Stein put it, with whom Goethe for a decade
had been a "martyr to spiritual love,"[92] she had, tellingly, "no sense" (*keinen
Sinn*) for this kind of poetry: "When Wieland wrote salacious scenes, it all
had a moral message . . . and he was not writing them about himself."[93]

But Goethe too had a moral message: that this was the way to love and
live. Always sardonic about the boring pretentiousness of court life, the
stilted conversations and the tedious entertainments (II), he wrote a yet
more drastic elegy that Weimar was lucky not to see, scorning the finery
of upper-crust ladies in favor of erotic directness. Wool or brocade, a skirt's
a skirt for a' that, and it all has to come off anyway: "What we enjoy is the

pleasure of naked, genuine loving, / And the way our dear bed rocks and creaks as we move."[94] Love so lived was "first and last of all the world's good things" (XVIII).[95] Schiller welcomed the Elegies into his new journal, *Die Horen*, with open arms, praising the verses' "warmth, tenderness, and genuine grainy poetic spirit."[96] Any discreet cuts and exclusions were tactical, and ultimately Goethe's doing.

Despite the cool local reception, the upshot of Italy was a renewed self-confidence and the conviction of being settled in a right way of living. Goethe imagines being interviewed: "Tell us, how do you live? I live, and if man were granted / Hundreds of years, I would wish each day to be like today."[97] There is a paradoxical eloquence in not glossing "I live" any further; it is left as a richly suggestive absolute. Domestic contentment was part of it—"If I am still dear to you, a few good people remain my friends, if my girl is faithful, my child lives, my great stove burns, then I have nothing more to wish for."[98] Beyond that, Goethe knows what he owes to the generosity of his gods and of his duke. He writes a wish-list poem and ends by saying that Carl August has granted them all.[99] But these things are only the ground floor of his contentment. Goethe is no complacent bourgeois, but a man fulfilled by activity. Besides once again writing poetry, he is working as a scientist, and soon combining the two in the poems on the metamorphosis of plants and animals, and of humans too, down to the minute process of cell regeneration in the poem "Dauer im Wechsel" (Permanence in Change).

He has also undergone, as far as he ever would, the discipline of critical philosophy. Back from Italy in the autumn of 1788, he reads Kant, whose growing reputation by 1787, when the second edition of the *Critique of Pure Reason* appeared, especially in Goethe's local university of Jena, made him impossible to ignore.[100] A detail in an essay of early 1789 shows the effect precisely. Where once Goethe had contrasted his friend Jacobi's shaky realm of religious faith with his own "deep foundations of truth,"[101] he now writes of the "deepest foundations of *knowledge*, the essential nature of things *insofar as it is allowed to us* to know them in visible and graspable forms" (emphasis added).[102] He has moved back a stage, from a straightforward assertion of truth to an awareness of the process of knowing it—plainly a Kantian reservation. The result is still a Kantian confidence in the interplay of the senses with sound judgment. That matters, because at issue are the foundations of style. And the date matters, because it means Kant was there from the start in the making of the post-Italian Goethe. It is not a tenable thesis that the philosopher later rescued Goethe for some kind of spirituality from an allegedly too crude earthliness and outrageous paganism.[103]

The grandest statement of Goethe's position comes in an essay of 1805 on the art historian Winckelmann. It states as an ideal what the Greeks attained, and what moderns may yet hope to achieve:

> When the healthy nature of man operates as a single whole, when he feels the world around him as a grand, beautiful, worthy, and precious whole, when harmonious contentment grants him a pure, free pleasure—then the universe, if it could perceive itself, would cry out as having arrived at its goal and would admire the pinnacle of its own growth and essence. For what is the point of all the expenditure of suns and planets and moons, of stars and Milky Ways, of comets and galactic nebulae, of worlds born and yet to be born, if at the end a happy human being cannot rejoice in his being?[104]

This secular teleology, amply outdoing the Christian one, is a high point of Enlightenment aspiration. What Goethe called his Italian investment had indeed begun to pay dividends. The youthful ecstatic response to nature had become the well-founded vision of a mature poet. It never thereafter fundamentally changes, yet it never becomes a dull routine. Over the decade from 1794 it is refreshed and intellectually clarified through the friendship and literary partnership with Schiller. After the desolation of his friend's premature death, new discoveries strengthen it further and new cultures give it variety, enlarging that "communion of saints" who speak through time and across borders. The most substantial of these is the history and poetry of Persia.

Goethe starts from a felt affinity with the wine and song of the medieval poet Hafiz. Then, going deeper into the cultural past, he comes upon the sect of the Parsi, who "turned, in adoration of the creator, toward the sun, as the most strikingly magnificent of phenomena," a glory that "even the most lowly could daily experience." To step out into the sunlight was already an act of worship; the newborn child was baptized in these rays. The moon and stars were distant, but the sun's effects were always present: "Nothing is purer than a serene sunrise." The Parsi extended their reverence to all the elements of nature around them—air, earth, water—and strove to keep them pure; "such a gentle religion, based on the omnipresence of god in his works of the sensuous world," generated a similarly pure ethics. There are less persuasive religions than sun worship. ("The sun is God" were the last words of the great painter of light, Turner.) The sun god threatens no punishments, demands no prayers, and promises no special favors, but as the creator of the conditions that make life possible his revelation is unquestionable. Only when ritualized by Zoroaster and his priests did the original exciting vision of the Parsi become a "pious boredom."[105]

The affinities with Goethe's empirically reverent thinking are obvious. Beyond that, for modern European minds the sun had become the pivoting point for a diametrical change of worldview, and Copernican reversal an intellectual strategy. Aptly, Copernicus and Kant are jointly present in a late poem, "Vermächtnis" (Testament), that contains Goethe's mature outlook—on the consistency of matter, on the reliability of the senses when interpreted by the understanding,[106] on the rightness of enjoying earthly blessings in all their fullness,[107] on joining past and present in a symbolically eternal moment,[108] and on the poet's role in leading the way for "noble souls." Copernicus is here the wise man to whom the by now "old truth" of the heliocentric system is owed, and this in turn yields the metaphor underpinning a Kantian ethics: the "self-reliant conscience" at the individual's "inner center" is "the sun of your moral day."[109]

This poetic and philosophical summa is part of a late harvest of extraordinary poems, literally so because they are outside any known order of lyrical poetry. They distill an essence from Goethe's scientific thinking, for he is no longer investigating discrete phenomena, as he was in the two metamorphosis poems, but looking on—almost looking down, as from a God's-eye view—at the dynamic workings of the universe. He uses a language of paradoxically concrete abstraction. How else but abstractly could one try to capture such grand generalities? Yet his language, predominantly verbs of movement, powerfully visualizes process: flowing, streaming, thrusting, teeming, struggling, transforming, shaping and reshaping, yet all composing the ultimate stability of the real world: "eternal rest in God the Lord."[110] No other poetic vision is so richly compatible with the dynamic conceptions of modern science, from star formation through plate tectonics to evolution. It feels for the "inmost forces that hold the world together," what Faust in his opening monologue longed to penetrate. Goethe's alternative to Faust's devil-conjuring has been six decades of verbal magic and four of scientific hard graft. Yet the end was there in embryo from the beginning, in the way an early poem such as "Maifest" experienced single phenomena but also intuited a controlling order. And at the end as in the beginning, the emotion is still wonderment—*Erstaunen*, Kant's word too for our necessary response to the world. "Wonderment is why I'm here" (*Zum Erstaunen bin ich da*) is the last line of "Parabase," a concise lyrical retrospect on years of happy scientific work. The quoted line interrupts a sequence of ingenious formulations that have been trying to capture nature's pervasive movement. The poet finally, as it were, throws up his hands in despair—the world can

only ever be endlessly wondered at. His resignation is itself, in Kant's other
word, eloquent.

Contentment with the world has to withstand testing. The Marienbad
episode of love and loss did that at the level of emotion, demanding every
resource of personal culture and artistic ordering to cope with crisis, which
even then barely succeeds.[111] At the philosophical level, the test comes
when Goethe contemplates the remains of his long-dead friend and partner
in poetry. In 1805 Schiller's coffin had been placed in a communal vault in
Weimar; the space became overfull, and the coffins rotted. In 1826 it was
cleared and what were thought to be Schiller's bones were rescued for re-
burial. For a time the skull was in Goethe's house. With his amanuensis
Riemer and a visiting Wilhelm von Humboldt, he sat long before it. The
resulting poem, "Im ernsten Beinhaus war's" (In the grim charnel house it
was),[112] uses dense syntax and compressed word forms to enact the crush
of bones in that imagined situation; the long dead have now not even been
allowed to rest in peace. Not a place for cheerful emotion, then; and surely
"nobody can love the arid shell, / Whatever noble content once it held." Yet
the poet declares himself to be that "nobody," a rhetorical trick going back
to the *Odyssey*. In a reversal at the poem's midpoint, the eye of the initiate,
informed by osteological knowledge and friendship, makes out the one "invaluable splendid form" in the chaos, and "Feels, in this space of moldering
cold constriction, / Free and refreshed, suffused with glowing warmth, / As
if a source of life from death came springing."[113] This once again goes flatly
against a tradition, of the skull as the classic memento mori, and very specifically—this must surely have been in Goethe's mind—against its most
famous poetic expression, Hamlet brooding over the skull of Yorick. Hamlet
feels pity—"Alas! poor Yorick"—but no warmth. Memories of being carried on the jester's back a thousand times are not nostalgic but "abhorred
in the imagination", his "gorge rises" at the thought.[114] It is a second death
for Yorick; he is not celebrated but rejected in memory. Goethe resists any
such annihilation of Schiller. In the face of the common fate, he sees individuality persisting in the very bone, opening up a vision of the flood of
forms that nature endlessly creates—a vibrant counterimage to the inert
bones with which the poem began. This is the skull's "sacred meaning" and
"revelation" (line 16)—advisedly religious language, for the poem is more
than just a defiance of death's dominion. It is the liturgy of a personal faith,
a *memento vivere*. For the humanist and pantheist (the closing lines speak
of a "revelation of God-Nature") Schiller's skull is a significant relic, as
Goethe indeed called it.[115]

There is perhaps one more gesture of defiance, in the poem's chosen

form. Uniquely in Goethe's lyrical corpus, it is terza rima,[116] most famously
the verse pattern of Dante's *Divine Comedy*, newly translated in 1827 by
Karl Streckfuss. Goethe is confronting with earthly affirmation not just
Shakespeare's bleak graveyard mood, but also the great Catholic poem of
heaven and hell. There could not be a better example of "world literature"
as Goethe meant the term: not the body of works everyone wants to have
read, but the live interaction—conflict, even—between poetic visions.

After these emotional upheavals and philosophical confrontations, a late
calm sets in, first with the *Chinesisch-deutsche Jahres- und Tageszeiten*
(Chinese-German Days and Seasons) written in the role of a mandarin in
contemplative retirement. Another foreign culture, then; but he is now an
aged mandarin himself. Aptly, the fourteen delicate vignettes—of plants
and birds and colors and light and darkness—were written in his Ilm Park
retreat, the *Gartenhaus* in which he had spent his first Weimar time. Then,
after the shock of the death of Carl August, his friend and employer of fifty
years, he spends some weeks at the Renaissance castle at Dornburg above
the Saale valley near Jena, observing plants and weather, and writes his
last significant poems. The very last, titled simply "Dornburg, September
1828," is indeed a final statement, but of a quite unemphatic kind:

Früh, wenn Tal, Gebirg und Garten	When, in garden, valley, mountains,
Nebelschleiern sich enthüllen	Dawn through misty veils is spilling,
Und dem sehnlichsten Erwarten	Colors fill the flowers as fountains,
Blumenkelche bunt sich füllen,	Every utmost longing stilling,
Wenn der Äther, Wolken tragend	When the ether clouding over
Mit dem klaren Tage streitet,	Clarity of day oppresses
Und ein Ostwind, sie verjagend,	And the East Wind, airy drover,
Blaue Sonnenbahn bereitet,	Clears the blue as sun progresses,
Dankst du dann, am Blick dich weidend,	If you feast your eyes then, purely,
Reiner Brust der Großen, Holden,	Thank the gracious great one truly,
Wird die Sonne, rötlich scheidend,	Parting sun shall redden surely,
Rings den Horizont vergolden.	Gild the whole horizon newly.[117]

The single sentence the poem consists of seems at first to be just the description of a typical autumn day. It has three phases: first, the garden colors

emerge from early mists; then the wind clears the blue sky of cloud; then there is a glorious sunset. Or rather, there will be; this last phase is in the future. The other two phases are in "when" clauses, in the present tense of now, or any such time. But the last phase is in an "if" clause, and has a future verb. It states a condition on which the day's final glory depends. The golden sunset will come about, he tells himself, "if you thank" with (as the original puts it) "a pure breast." Strange! Occurrences in nature are not usually thought to be brought about by human responses. This is turning into no ordinary day. What began as present observations, or as a generalization about all such autumn days, has become symbolic. Still real, that is, because rooted in an intense early-morning experience, but also standing for a lifetime's activity and attitudes.[118] The "if" condition is one more gentle test. If he shows himself to be still what he has always been, a thankful devotee of nature as poet and as scientist, he will deserve nature's final affirmation—for that is surely who the "great and gracious" recipient of his thanks will be.

No more than a sign is promised. There is no question of immortality, something Goethe thought of as an object of idle speculation that distracted from the serious business of living. Part of that business, it is true, was to counteract transience by making ordinary things as permanent as could be through poetic remembrance. But that was a humanistic, not a religious conception.

The visionary poet is not alone in feeling at home in the universe. There is a similar ring to the sublime conclusion of Kant's *Critique of Practical Reason*: "Two things fill the mind with ever new and increasing admiration the more often and persistently they are reflected upon: *the starry firmament above me and the moral law within me.*" His conception of himself is correspondingly dual. His physical being feels a continuity with the immensity of worlds upon worlds and the limitless time of their periodic motion, albeit as a mere temporary particle in immensity. Still, there is no call to be terrified of the vast cold spaces of the universe, as Pascal or his imagined interlocutor in the *Pensées* was—on either view, terror was meant to lead the individual to God. Kant may well have had in mind the famous sentence, "Le silence éternel de ces espaces infinis m'effraie," which contains what he elsewhere calls Pascal's "excess of terrifying emotions."[119] Where the Christian apologist Pascal had exchanged science for mysticism, as Enlightenment thinkers noted with dismay,[120] Kant is speaking as a scientist. A pioneering cosmologist in his early work, he has long been at ease with the true dimensions of the universe and the processes of star birth and star death that compose the seemingly changeless firmament.[121] (Notably, there is now no longer any conventional nod to a "highest being.") But then alongside, or rather deep within, that acceptance of his physical location, there is Kant's certainty of a moral self connected to a different infinity. The two are in balance: if the first perception destroys his significance as an animal being that will soon have to hand back its briefly and inexplicably living substance to the speck in the universe that it inhabits, the second restores his value as an intelligence independent of the empirical world and its limits.[122] There is no other kind of transcendence. The combination is as firm a basis for living—not in mere resignation—as the poet in his very different mode achieved. They have both measured out the human span and accepted the limitations of living within it.

Kant was a professional teacher, but the poet may have a similar enlightening role: "For to prefigure noble spirits / Is a vocation unsurpassed."[123] A few months before he died, Goethe wrote a brief piece telling young poets what his example showed. He disclaims any direct authority, saying he has been, in the sense of a guild training system, "nobody's master." But he does claim to have been a liberator for his countrymen by showing "how the individual must live, and the artist must create, by acting on the outside world from his own inner resources," for "poetic substance is the substance of one's own life."[124]

That effect was not limited to Germany. Matthew Arnold declares Goethe to be *the* model for modern intellectual independence. There is no better succinct account than Arnold's of Goethe as a continuator and embodiment of the Enlightenment:

> Goethe's profound, imperturbable naturalism is absolutely fatal to all routine thinking; he puts the standard, once for all, inside every man instead of outside him; when he is told, such a thing must be so, there is immense authority and custom in favour of its being so, it has been held to be so for a thousand years, he answers with Olympian politeness, "But *is* it so? Is it so to *me*?" Nothing could be more really subversive of the foundations on which the old European order rested; and it may be remarked that no persons are so radically detached from this order, no persons so thoroughly modern, as those who have felt Goethe's influence most deeply.[125]

Literary individualism here becomes a model for a more general freedom. The subversion is not meant politically, although any free unfolding of personality must have social and perhaps ultimately political consequences. To have lived out this ideal before a German and eventually a European public on such a scale and with such majestic results was not just a personal triumph, but an exemplary fulfillment of the Enlightenment's hopes for humankind. In that sense Goethe was the representative figure—not typical, but exemplary and normative—of an age casually referred to ever since as the *Goethezeit*.

CHAPTER 11

Peace in Whose Time?:
The Ultimate Prize

... naked, poor, and mangled Peace,
Dear nurse of arts, plenties, and joyful births
—Shakespeare, *Henry V*, act 5, scene 2

Human potential as so conceived could only be realized in times of peace. The background to eighteenth-century culture—to everything discussed in this book so far—was the possibility or actuality of war. Though a less violent century than others, it was still as much as any other "a tract of time wherein the will to contend by battle" was ever present, true to Thomas Hobbes's definition that war is not just "actual fighting" but "the known disposition thereto"—cold war in all but name. "All other time," he says, "is peace."[1] At most a sad remnant.

The decision to wage war lay in every major ruler's hands, an option and privilege of arbitrary power, the so-called *ultima ratio regum*. Kant's critical mind could hardly overlook this fundamental issue. As early as one of his 1756 essays on the Lisbon earthquakes, he ends with the reflection that a noble-hearted prince, faced with the natural disasters that batter human beings, might spare them the further misery of war—at first sight, a surprising shift of the essay's focus. Yet its fundamental theme is human happiness and the things in nature that endanger it. War is not a natural catastrophe, but the aggressive impulse may lie so deep in human nature as to make it almost one. Still, at least it lies always in our—in somebody's—power to engage in it or avoid it.

Kant was writing in the spring of 1756, on the eve of the Seven Years' War.[2] Its imminence was clear from rumors and day-to-day troop movements; both are recorded in, among other sources, the memoirs of a Swiss national who had been pressed into the Prussian infantry.[3] As again later in

1784, Kant was implicitly addressing the king. What other ruler could be thought rational enough to prefer peace? Frederick II had come to the throne in 1740 with a reputation for enlightened ideas, Enlightenment connections (Voltaire), personal sensitivity, and cultural interests that set him against his brutal father. Early acts—abolishing judicial torture and recalling the exiled philosopher Christian Wolff—promised well. So, above all, did Frederick's explicit declaration that he proposed "to make no distinction between Our own and Our country's interests [*Vorteil*]—indeed, the interests of the country must have priority when the two are incompatible."[4] Then there was the celebrated claim to be no more than the state's first servant. Frederick was "concerned only for the well-being of his people and his state."[5]

This modest self-rededication of arbitrary power is backed up by the standard image of a frugal Frederick very different from the run of eighteenth-century princes—the snuff-stained old uniform, the dislike of court pomp and ceremony, his Potsdam retreat just an "elegant little building," "the royal bungalow."[6]

It is true Sanssouci has only a single story, but "little" it is not: its colonnade and vine terraces are grandiose, and its interiors of unsurpassable magnificence, as are the interiors of the other Prussian palaces built, extended, or refurbished in Frederick's time and under his intensive personal supervision.[7] His reign over this economically poor country, four-fifths of whose budget already went on the army, began with a burst of celebratory extravagance. The elaborate and tasteless Neues Palais was constructed after the Seven Years' War to show he still had resilience and means. As for the snuff stains, behind them lies an immensely extravagant collection of snuffboxes, where a single one could cost the equivalent of a castle or a country estate.

The propaganda image of service and modesty has been largely taken at face value, not just by pro-Prussian historians. It is true Frederick labored long hours at affairs of state and had an extraordinary if sometimes self-willed involvement in administrative matters large and small, a devotion to duty widely recognized by the population. Yet equating the interests of the people with the interests of the state was a sleight of hand that cannot survive sober definition of either. Frederick and his decisions still embody the absolutist principle "l'état, c'est moi." However enlightened his private intellectual world and his conscious intentions, his deeper drives—what Kugler indeed calls his "demonic" element[8]—determined otherwise. He was not in the least concerned with what Lichtenberg understood as "the honor of the crown," namely that it ensure "its subjects are happy to get by in a modest way with their limbs intact," rather than "slaughtering or crippling hundreds of thousands" for material advantage.[9] To say nothing of the brutality of army discipline, though that was period practice, found even in civilized Weimar and equaled or outdone by punishments in the British army and navy.

Frederick was humane enough, piecemeal, to be shocked by the numbers slaughtered in his battles, yet in the heat of the fight at Kolin in 1757, he could famously call out to the Guard as they hesitated to attack, "Fellows, do you want to live forever?"

His concern was with the very different interests of the state as he understood them. Avowedly, too, from the beginning, with the pursuit of military glory, when as the first major act of his reign in 1740 he invaded the Austrian province of Silesia, making good ancient territorial claims by a fait accompli. The move became known as the *journée des dupes*; that is, it made fools of those expecting enlightened rule by showing where the new king's real commitment lay: to aggression and aggrandizement, in short to old-style *raison d'état*. It also initiated a Hobbesian "tract of time," of war alternating with the prospect of further war.

This is not even just a case of what has been well termed a "kingship of contradictions,"[10] the obvious conflict of Enlightenment ideals with political realism. For it is an entirely realistic question whether the young king's sowing of his military wild oats actually was in the long-term interests of his state. True, Silesia was a rich province, a more worthwhile prize than the two minor Rhineland duchies Prussia also had claims to. It was large and close by, it would round out Prussian territory, it was in every sense *l'agrandissement le plus solide*. But acquiring it brought Frederick Austria's lasting hostility. Maria Theresia's intense desire for restitution of her lost province and for revenge on that "wicked man in Berlin," pursued by the single-minded diplomacy and war-planning of her Chancellor Kaunitz, overshadowed the whole of the rest of Frederick's reign. No "other time" was left for peace. There was a massive disproportion of gain and loss.

Crisis came in 1756 when, with a coalition of enemies gathering on all sides, Frederick felt compelled to move first, invading neutral Saxony and unleashing the Seven Years' War. This time, the label "preventive war" was not the usual sophistry,[11] although a considerable peace party, including the king's brother Prince Henry, argued that the potentially hostile coalition was not yet activated. Still, insofar as the compulsion was real, it was ultimately of Frederick's own making.

The final price would be 180,000 dead on the Prussian side (Frederick's own figure) and a total of 1.5 million casualties overall.[12] In those seven years, Frederick fought eight major battles, losing four and winning four, these too at enormous cost in lives. Prussia held out, just, against over-whelming odds until the lucky chance that the new Tsar Peter II, an ad-mirer of Frederick, took Russia out of the war and broke up the hostile coalition. What had got Prussia through to that point, besides the coalition partners' lack of coordination and their hesitation to act at potentially de-cisive moments, was above all Frederick's own charisma, willpower, and resilience under extreme stress, for which the only obvious parallel is Win-ston Churchill in the Second World War. The king's morale, unbroken apart from one mood of near-suicidal despair at imminent national disaster after the defeat at Kolin in 1757, is almost as strong a claim to greatness as his strategic and tactical successes. But his land was left ravaged by the march and countermarch of opposed armies—Austrians, Saxons, Russians, espe-cially Cossacks. For example, the Prussian town of Neu Ruppin, before the war 3500 people in 623 houses, was left at its end with 600 people in 150 houses.[13] In an honest retrospect, Frederick admitted that in 1740 he had acted from "ambition, self-interest, and the yearning to get himself talked about,"[14] while the Seven Years' War was the result of his and Maria There-sia's pigheadedness.[15] Most honestly of all, he could sometimes glimpse how radically opposed the interests of king and people were: "A man must be very barbarous to trouble without reason poor devils who have nothing to do with our illustrious quarrels."[16] If rulers, in period parlance, were the fathers of their peoples, Frederick in one contemporary view was a father who without much scruple sacrificed his children to the god of war.[17] For Winckelmann, who had a friend in Frederick's military entourage, he was "the devastater."[18] His own general staff came to call him the "gravedigger." The word "hero" should never be uttered without adding "God preserve humanity!"[19]

If Silesia in 1740 was the young Frederick's hubris, the Seven Years' War was his nemesis and in some measure his catharsis. When the opening cam-paign failed to be decisive and he was forced on to an ever more desperate defensive, the aim of territorial aggrandizement—for Frederick the whole point of going to war—had to yield to a stoical conception of duty and a final acceptance of the status quo ante. This time he gained nothing. (Nor, for that matter, did the coalition.) It was his last aggression, though the war of the Bavarian Succession was still to come in 1778, a half-cock campaign without a single pitched battle. In later years Frederick even on occasion made efforts to broker peace, although his known tendency to take "preven-tive" action remained a destabilizing factor in European politics—insofar as there was ever any stability in the swirl of shifting alliances and coalitions. After the war he did what he could to patch up and rebuild his country—the so-called *rétablissement*. He made some provision for soldiers' orphans and crippled veterans, though numerically it was a drop in the ocean. He raised his popularity by visiting scenes of devastation in his lands, offsetting by a public display of sympathy the fact that he was their deepest cause.

On the positive side, Prussia had henceforth to be reckoned with as an equal player, at least in European politics. (The Seven Years' War was only a sideshow to the worldwide conflict between France and Britain that extended to America, Canada, and India.) Prussia's new standing was thanks largely to the army that Frederick's grandfather and father had built up essentially for defense, a vital necessity after the bitter experience of the Thirty Years' War, but which had now proved its attacking capacity against great nations with a tradition of military prowess, Austria and France. Frederick himself could rank as a general alongside the likes of Condé, Turenne, and his youthful idol, Prince Eugen. What might have continued to be a cautious hedgehog kingdom had become a proactive major power. That, on a *realpolitisch* view, was clearly in the interests of the state. Whether it was in the interests of the Prussian people, then and thereafter, is another question.

It is the Enlightenment's question. War is the extreme case of the conflict between hard reality and humane ideal that was the Enlightenment's root perception and critical motivation. The more unquestioned the assumption that war is a normal fact of life, the more it becomes a self-fulfilling prophecy.[20] In particular, Clausewitz's dictum that war is a continuation of policy by other means smoothes away any natural threshold of inhibition, as if bringing about the mass killing of human beings were a decision no weightier than any other. An equally insidious attempt to make it seem normal is Clausewitz's metaphor that war is "merely a different kind of language and writing from politics. It has admittedly its own grammar, but not its own logic."[21] They do indeed share a common logic, which shows war to be the ultimate unenlightened act, the *ultima irratio regum*, redirecting the minds of civilized people through intensive training and an indoctrination that dehumanizes the declared enemy. The instigator, "the enlightened man who neither loves nor cares for human beings, who spills their blood like water when his pride or his acquisitiveness commands it, will work in vain at enlightenment."[22] That puts Frederick's claims and his record in confrontation at two ends of a single sentence. He was aware of the discrepancy and hoped that posterity would judge separately the ruler and the philosopher, the decent man and the politician.[23] Yet to separate them can only show how far principle yielded to practice whenever it mattered. For all his writerly activity, Frederick only rarely faced this contradiction: in the passing remarks quoted above, or in a letter of 19 November 1759 to Voltaire which speaks of the "feelings of humanity that make us to wish to make the streams of blood dry up which flood almost our whole area." Such moments of moral lucidity about the way his actions bore on his subjects still built no practical bridge between enlightened benevolence and *Realpolitik*. His claim that only great states such as he aspired to turn Prussia into were able to implement humane ideas was a feeble self-justification.[24] What about tiny Anhalt-Dessau under Duke Franz? An awareness of what this minor ruler was doing who had turned his back on a military career may have been one more reason Frederick disliked him.

The realities of conflict between enlightened intent and a militarized state can be illustrated by a superficially undramatic instance, but one that affected a large mass of the population. In 1763 Frederick set out to abolish serfdom as an offense against humanity and a heavy burden on many of his (taxpaying) peasants. Serfdom was necessary, however, to make the estates of (nontaxpaying) noble landowners economically viable. Or so they said: for were not they and their sons fully occupied with their careers as officers in his army, Frederick's overriding need? It was plain blackmail. The reform had to be dropped; only the term "serfdom" was henceforth, hypocritically, prohibited. Frederick could have called the nobles' bluff by commissioning bourgeois officers, as the massive losses in the Seven Years' War had forced him to do.[25] But that dilution did not outlast the emergency. A permanent reform was incompatible with Frederick's fixed prejudices about social class—officers must come from the nobility—which would be reaffirmed in the revised civil code.[26] So the army was the tail wagging the dog, indeed a lot more than a tail: in Mirabeau's famous *mot*, Prussia was not a land with an army, but an army with a land. A largely noble officer class remained a dominant feature of nineteenth-century Prussian society.[27]

Frederick's enlightenment, on which so many hopes had been fixed, was, like his music—he played the flute and was a more than competent composer[28]—essentially a leisure pursuit: a play with modern ideas through which sometimes, as in the *Antimachiavell*, his traditional commitments could be made out. So was the writing of French poetry, though sometimes strikingly practiced at moments of crisis and to that extent a genuine expressive outlet. As for the quality of the poetic results, a real writer but temporary courtier like Voltaire was tactful to the point of obsequiousness, which was not obviously his true opinion.[29]

That the king's literary interests did not extend to encouraging German writing—he was (Mirabeau again) "a Caesar but not an Augustus"—is a minor point. German literature flourished without him, and in spite of his culturally prejudiced attack on its promising new shoots.[30] It is doubtful how much German Frederick had actually read. There is little sign of direct knowledge in the record of his meeting with the prominent writer Gellert in 1760,[31] and the German writers Gellert named are, significantly, among the few who then occur in Frederick's essay. It is doubtful even whether the king's notoriously primitive knowledge of the language would have been up to appreciating texts of any quality. The argument that his neglect of the native culture was a stimulus and an advantage does not add up.[32] Goethe in his autobiography claims that "the king's aversion to things German was good for the shaping of literature" and that writers "did everything to get themselves noticed by the king." He quotes no instances. Patronage would, to say the least, have done no harm. After all, the French classicism Frederick idolized had thrived at the court of the Sun King.

Goethe also claims that Frederick's actions in the Seven Years' War brought "the first true and higher real-life content into German poetry" but can instance only Gleim's military poems from the Seven Years' War and Ramler's praise of the king.[33] There were disproportionately more important negative instances. Lessing's comedy *Minna von Barnhelm*, whose male lead is an unjustly disgraced officer, gives Frederick an offstage role as a rescuing deus ex machina, but there is also a good deal of criticism between the lines.[34] Most significant, when in 1789 Schiller briefly considered writing an epic on Frederick, he found the king an "uninspiring" character who would need "a gigantic amount of idealizing."[35] A later poem of Schiller's defiantly celebrates a self-made German literary culture that Frederick had left without protection and honor[36]—which is not at all the same as saying that the neglect was an advantage.

The king's cultural prejudice likewise governed the Prussian academy, which was French-led, French-manned, and French-speaking. Berlin would have been a mere outpost of Paris but for the debating circles and publishing activities that ran parallel. The ruler who had held out against Europe on the battlefield capitulated from the first to an alien culture. What remains impressive, and rare among eighteenth-century (or any other) rulers, is that Frederick had time for literature and thought at all. But the steel of his purposes remained unpenetrated by the critical thinking that was the essence of Enlightenment writing.

Kant's critical thinking returned inevitably to the problem of war as the extreme case of a reality that demanded to be questioned and as a crux for his ethics, which declared humans were ends in themselves. "Being hired to kill or be killed [is] a use of human beings as mere machines and implements in the hands of someone else (the state)"[37]—this from the start of his essay *On eternal Peace* (1795), which sets out a rational program for something that ten years earlier he could only hope would come about "God knows when."[38] In form it is a half-parodic, half-serious draft for an international treaty, with "Preliminary," "Definitive," and "Secret" articles. In substance it is a Critique of Political Unreason, that is, of the practices that conduce to armed conflict. Once again, it can be read as a dialogue with the values of the now dead king, and through him with all "the heads of state who never tire of war."[39] War is unreason not just because of the suffering it causes, but formally, in that it short-circuits all rational options—reflection, negotiation, and the search for acceptable compromise. Fanatics on both sides would rather risk defeat in a win-all/lose-all wager than settle for an unacceptable peace.[40] No adjudicating authority exists, such as the social contract has established within individual societies, so matters can only, as Hume ironically wrote, "be decided by an appeal to heaven, that is by war and violence,"[41] and their outcome is what Kant calls the *deus bonus eventus*. (Only Hegel could call this "the cunning of reason.") Given the terrible results of armed conflict, Kant says, even victorious nations should perform acts of penitence, not sing Te Deums. So here too a higher adjudicator was needed to bring about the peace between nations which is a precondition of full human development, as Kant had argued a decade ago in his *Idea for a Universal History*, and he repeats his proposal for a "league of nations." Herder too had meantime picked up the idea, cursing all wars of conquest, hoping that Frederick's would be the last, and calling for a "league of princes" to ban them at least from "civilized Europe."[42]

Eternal peace was an old dream. From Al-Farabi in the ninth century, through Marsilius of Padua in the fourteenth, Erasmus and Sebastian Franck in the sixteenth, Comenius and William Penn in the seventeenth, down to Kant's immediate predecessors the Abbé de Saint Pierre and Rousseau, it had been a necessary humane response to the horrors of human history. Kant's own plea is not all abstract idealism and emotive rhetoric. Each article in the draft treaty targets one of the practices of eighteenth-century politics that make war always likely.[43] The cap everywhere fits Frederick or his foes:

No peace shall be made with a secret mental reservation of grounds for resuming war at a later date (like Austria's ambition to regain Silesia, even after more than one treaty had definitively assigned it to Prussia); nor shall territorial claims be dug *out of the archives* (as Frederick had done, to justify taking Silesia in the first place). This view may seem pedantic, Kant ironically admits, to those who see the "honor of the state" as lying in the "constant expansion of power by whatever means"—exactly Frederick's aim.

No state shall be taken over by inheritance, marriage, exchange, or purchase (Kant omits to say: by conquest), as was common in treaties that "redrew the map." For a state is not a piece of land, but a society of people, something organic, "a tree with its own roots." Such a collective moral person cannot be reduced to an object. The right to rule over a state may be bestowed, as when Augustus the Strong of Saxony was elected king of Poland; but then the country acquires a ruler, not vice versa. Nor may *citizens be sold off* to fight for some other country than their own, a practice too widespread to need linking to any single ruler.

There shall gradually be no *standing armies* (this from the pen of a Prussian subject!) because they necessarily lead to what was not yet called an "arms race." They cost money better spent on education. The cost of maintaining them is a temptation to prefer a quick war to an expensive peace. (Frederick did indeed want his wars to be brief and brisk—*kurz und vif*—albeit by no means as an alternative to maintaining a large permanent force.)

There shall be *no national debt* as an always available war chest, the recent "invention of a trading nation," by which Kant can only mean Britain.

No state shall intervene in the constitution and government of another (not yet called "regime change"). The campaign to restore the Bourbons was one recent example. Intervention also initiated the partitions of Poland, the third of which had just been carried through at the time Kant was writing.

Kant recognizes, with Hobbes, that war is the natural condition, and that peace has to be positively instituted (*gestiftet*). This can only happen when the matter is determined by the participant members of a republic, who know what war will cost them in suffering and loss—the ship of state needs their stabilizing ballast. In contrast, an autocrat and presumed "owner" of the state can go to war on a whim; for him it is just one more leisure outing (*Lustpartie*). His other enjoyments—hunting, carousing, and living in luxury—can continue undisturbed while thousands sacrifice themselves for a cause that does not concern them; he stays out of danger. (That at least does not apply to Frederick, who was normally at the forefront of the battle.) So the requirement of *a republican constitution in all states* is the first of the "definitive articles." This sounds democratic, but Kant expressly rejects democracy as a form of popular despotism, a distinction that remains puzzling. His aversion may stem from events in postrevolutionary France, particularly from reports of the crude populism and procedural disorder that stifled debate in the National Assembly.[44]

The second definitive article states that international law shall be based on a *federation of free states*. The problem is that no state wants to give up its freedom of independent action, an attitude that for Kant is the equiva-

lent of the "wild freedom" that savages first preferred to the "rational freedom" of the social contract. The distinction between them and European
rulers is that where savages literally ate their defeated foes, rulers metaphorically gobble up the inhabitants of conquered territories to enlarge their
own armies for further war, as Frederick had done in Saxony.

If rulers go on waging wars with no interest in peace, it serves them
right if they end up in the "eternal peace" of the grave, as symbolized by the
Dutch inn sign of a graveyard to which Kant's sardonic preface refers. That
echoes Posa's riposte to Philipp II when the king claims to be restoring calm
by force throughout his realms: yes, the calm of a churchyard.[45] For by one
route or the other, peace must surely come: if not by rational agreements,
then by attrition and the final exhaustion of means and men (not yet called
MAD, the "mutually assured destruction" of twentieth-century nuclear de-
terrence). This is the hard gaze that accompanies Kant's idealism, the certain knowledge of the one inevitable end that must eventually come about
through good or evil means. In the words of Wallenstein, imperial general
in the Thirty Years' War (the real warlord, not the protagonist of Schiller's
drama): "At the last, when every land lies in ashes, they will have to make
peace."[46]

There is then a Secret Article. It is admittedly a contradiction to mix
secrecy with public law, but rulers must be allowed to save face, for it stipu-
lates that before waging war *the state shall consult the arguments of philosophers* on the possibility of peace.[47] That is something rulers would hardly
wish to admit to, even if they were prepared to contemplate it at all. It is
the familiar attempt to make power stop and take thought, the extreme instance of the Enlightenment aim to influence human affairs.

Why, Kant wonders, do hard-nosed realists even bother to dress up their
aggressions in reasons, invoking authorities on international law—Grotius,
Pufendorf, Vattel—only ever, it is true, the passages on just wars, not those
that dissuade from war altogether? But on reflection this too can be turned
to Kant's purpose, since just that much lip service to philosophy shows that
even the political class has a "moral potential" (*Anlage*).[48]

This leads in to a coda contrasting that rare bird the truly "moral politician" with the "political moralist," who at most feels the need to deny his
actions or excuse them from the solid ground of a fait accompli, as Frederick had over Silesia. But if the true moral course is followed, such is Kant's
faith, peace will be given as a consequence. In political terms, he is setting
statesmanship (*Staatsweisheit*) against mere statecraft (*Staatsklugheit*), the
pursuit of the truly desirable against the mere "art of the possible." One
notable touchstone for moral politics is that actions and the maxims that

guide them should be able to stand unashamedly before the public (what was not yet called "transparency"). Publicity was sufficient of an ideal to have an eloquent ode addressed to it in 1790.[49] It would be the most important effect of an open society and an active public. Its logical conclusion, a Freedom of Information Act, was far off in the future.

To realists, much of this would have sounded, and will always sound, utopian.[50] Unsurprisingly, Helmut von Moltke, chief of the general staff in late nineteenth-century Germany, not only dismissed the idea of eternal peace as a dream but added, "and not even a beautiful one."[51] That goes beyond mere realism to a denial of humane hope.

Such dismissals beg the question. What they claim as "reality" is for Kant not a different world with a nature of its own—harder, truer, without illusions—but the congealed remains of a deficient rationality that has always dominated. The problem is not an absolute "way things are" and an unchangeable human nature, together labeled "experience." This "experience" is merely what resulted when things were imperfectly thought through in the first place: "There can be nothing more damaging and more unworthy of a philosopher than the vulgar appeal to alleged contrary experience, which would not exist if measures true to ideas had been taken at the right time and if all good intentions had not been rendered vain by crude notions drawn, precisely, from experience."[52] It is now "not at all a question of whether this or that *does* happen, but of reason requiring what *shall* happen."[53] This would call in question many of the practices of established cultures. It need not, however, bring the world crashing down. *Fiat justitia, pereat mundus* does not mean for Kant "let justice reign, even if the world perish," but, more combatively, "let justice reign and all the villains in the world perish."[54]

As so often, Kant's almost naive radicality demands more than collective humanity seems capable of, even though achieving peace is surely humanity's deepest need. But his naïveté is something positive, a refreshing readiness to contest the most hardened prejudgments. At the very least, it makes graphically clear the dire conditions and assumptions under which people and peoples have for so long lived and continue still to live.

It also makes clear the direction change would have to take, and actually has taken in recent times, limited though the successes of supranational organizations have so far been.[55] Kant, however, was exemplary in hoping. He refused to accept his friend Moses Mendelssohn's view that there was no systematic human progress, only a succession of advances followed by relapses, a Sisyphean sequence. Mendelssohn had labored to improve the lot of Jews, necessarily with the expectation he could not do it all himself but must be followed by others. That already implied a belief in cumulative progress. Even failure was no reason—not even pragmatically, let alone morally—for abandoning belief. Admittedly, hope required the long view, but to a humanitarian that was no objection either: "Faced with the sad sight, not so much of the evils that oppress the human race through natural causes as of those which human beings do to each other, one's mind is cheered by the prospect that things may improve; and indeed by the unselfish benevolence that we, long in our graves, shall not harvest the fruits that we have helped to sow."[56] Perhaps only Kant could have written "and indeed," and not "even though we."

On Eternal Peace has remained a beacon. In the shattered and still warring Europe of March 1918, the Austrian social critic and satirist Karl Kraus wrote a poem celebrating the timeless message of Kant's *Eternal Peace* and took the passage just quoted as his epigraph. He sets the philosopher in his rightful place above the nonentities who, using war as a "continuation of policy" and setting their faces against any other option, had blundered into the most destructive conflict (so far) of all time.[57] Well might they and their perceptions be contrasted with those of the philosopher who stood above the mêlée, historically informed and alert to the wearisome repetition of old errors and catastrophes, all spawned by the unchanging crude motives. In Kraus's poem, the small figure of Kant, his physical realm just Königsberg, towers ethically above the palaces and presumptions of the powerful as the faithful subject of a far greater world.[58] In contrast, a poem of 1920 on the Emperor Franz Joseph ponders the puzzle of a personal mediocrity that can possess such disastrous power.[59] Was it "realism" to accept that?

In 1795 Kant had, relatively speaking, seen nothing yet. After fending off the Austro-Prussian invasion in 1792, the French had returned the compliment, carrying the revolutionary idea beyond their borders, a not wholly convincing mask for old-fashioned conquest, and taking the Austrian Netherlands, Speyer, Worms, and Mainz. The separate Peace of Basel at least took Prussia out of the war in the year Kant's essay was published. Perhaps that marginally strengthened his hopes. But by the time of his death in 1804, the Revolutionary Wars had given way to the Napoleonic Wars, whose scale and geographical sweep dwarfed previous horrors, with the worst still to come. In Napoleon's disastrous Russian campaign a third of the Grande Armée was provided willy-nilly by German states. Germany turned against the emperor in 1813 in the rather grandiloquently labeled Wars of Liberation (*Befreiungskriege*). Many young volunteers of the "free corps" were sacrificed, their deaths commemorated in the first performance of Beethoven's Seventh Symphony. They were idealists inspired by a new national spirit, intensified by a poetry that called up the shades of legendary ancient Germanic heroes like Arminius/Hermann,[60] annihilator of the Roman armies of Varus in the Teutoburg Forest in 9 CE. The climax came at Waterloo, when a Prussian force arrived just in time to help settle that "close-run thing", a decisive contribution in the German view, as hinted in Adolph Menzel's painting of Blücher meeting Wellington after the battle, cleverly angled to make the Prussian general the dominant figure.[61]

The sacrificial enthusiasm of the young is captured in another painting, Ferdinand Hodler's panoramic *Jena Students Going Off to Fight*, commissioned in 1908 for the university's new aula. Across a top band, in the background, a detachment of anonymous infantry is marching off; in the foreground are four individualized cavalrymen. One, in profile, is gesturing ecstatically upward; two with their backs to the viewer are preparing to mount. The last of the four is the most significant.[62] Turned toward us, arms stretched wide to get into his jacket and leaving his chest exposed, he evokes verses of Wilhelm Hauff: "Proud on horseback yesterday, / Now his chest is shot away."[63] This campaign, part of "the national rising" (*die deutsche Erhebung*), with its intellectual center in Fichte's *Addresses to the German Nation* (1808), and combined with the Romantic generation's new interest in the Germanic past, marks the start of German nationalism—a national spirit like the one that inspired French resistance to the 1792 invasion, but with a more problematic legacy.

Nothing in his lifetime, it seems, could shake Kant's belief in the progress of mankind. He looked beyond the widespread disillusionment with the French Revolution to the future prospect that seemed to be promised by Europe's first disinterested enthusiasm for such fundamental change.[64] He remained convinced republics would never wage war on each other, even though the French republic, discouragingly, had pursued expansionist wars. As far back as the *Idea for a Universal History* of 1784 and right down to the *Conflict of Faculties* of 1798,[65] he held undaunted to the view that the march of history was akin to the grand motion of the planets. Despite their occasional seemingly backward movements as seen from earth, their true course could be worked out from the observations of temporally limited human beings. But to actually see it whole and true would be the view from the sun, a reason's-eye view, rarely taken.[66]

The Enlightenment owes us no apologies if it failed. Did it fail? It certainly did not triumph. To speak, as Dilthey did, of the 1790s as a time of its dominance and the Prussian state as shaped by its spirit is to ignore the realities the Enlightenment confronted and could not topple.[67] But that is simply part of the larger movement, or immobility, of European politics. Against that background, German history has been too readily seen as leading ineluctably from the relative light of the late eighteenth century to the distant darkness of 1933. Of course continuities can be found—Bismarck's limiting social prejudices were much the same as Frederick the Great's, his readiness to use war followed in Frederick's footsteps, annexing Alsace-Lorraine with the revanchist consequences was his Silesia. The resistance to democracy throughout the period is consistent, though not peculiar to Germany. The most distinctive German thread is the irrationalism that began with the Romantics and reached its nadir in Nazism. But this was no more a peculiarly fated *Sonderweg* than any other historical development that is trivially proved necessary by the fact that it did happen. There were countervailing forces and possible branch lines.

In this complex process, the Enlightenment did not have a continuous representation and was certainly never dominant. But lucid intervals are scattered through the years, from the Prussian reform period that followed the defeat at Jena—a proof of Kant's thesis that hard outcomes may compel a recourse to reason—through the liberals of the Vormärz and Bismarckian Germany, down to the Weimar Republic. And there were always writers and thinkers who carried the torch—from Büchner, Heine, and Jung Deutschland down to the Mann brothers and Kurt Tucholsky. There is certainly no way the Enlightenment ever became responsible for its own diametrical opposite, as is sometimes bizarrely asserted. To argue against that charge, epitomized in the tag "the dialectic of Enlightenment," is as pointless as arguing with flat-earthers and Holocaust deniers. The ideas traced in the preceding chapters—an open nontheocratic society, individual liberty, freedom of speech and publication, rational debate, toleration, internal justice, external peace—speak for themselves. What society has done with (or without) those ideas is its responsibility. The Enlightenment moreover had from the start a dialectical awareness of its own, exemplified in Schiller's dual view of violent reform (Karl Moor in *The Brigands*) and rebellious subterfuge (Marquis Posa in *Don Carlos*), or in Forster's ambivalence over Pacific exploration and struggle with disillusionment in Paris, or in that first querying of enlightenment within the ranks of the Berlin Enlightenment itself, from which this book started. The dialectic is continued by responsible later scholarship, as in the scrupulous examination of anti-Semitic motifs in Kant and other writers. In that respect, a charge against Kant of occasional thoughtless prejudice sticks. But a major imputation that a "Kantian ethic" of duty could legitimately become a motive and self-justification for the perpetrators of the Shoah is decisively countered by the true Kantian argument that all compliance with outside demands for conformity—like the duties of a Nazi administrator in the Holocaust hierarchy—must be critically questioned by the ethical individual.[68]

Some writers had to carry the torch through the twentieth-century darkness itself, against all the odds, and some gave up in despair. Hope in history may fail when events are so terrible and seem so irreversible that they block the longer perspectives of Enlightenment thinking. Kraus saw the coming to power of Nazism as the end of a rational world: "Word slept the sleep of death when that world woke."[69] Faced with the Nazis' sweeping territorial and military triumphs of the 1930s and '40s, even a great activist like Ernst Toller and a historically sophisticated mind like Stefan Zweig chose suicide—serious blows to the morale of the exile community.

Thomas Mann did not despair. He held fast to the avowedly irrational conviction that Hitler would not win[70]—irrational if ever anything was by April 1941, yet rooted precisely in a positive long-term view of history: "Democracy, as the secularized form of Christianity, is not ripe for overthrow by this false missionary" (17 March 1940).[71] From the start of his exile in 1933, though already exhausted by its stresses, Mann saw Nazism in past perspective as the familiar German barbarism, and in future perspective as a movement doomed to fail because it was massively against the will of the times[72]—a classic Enlightenment mode of vision, setting a rational faith and hope against the facts. In the earlier upheavals of the 1930s Mann had coined the motto "optimism come what may" (*Optimismus quand même*).[73] Like Antonio Gramsci's formula, "pessimism of the intellect, optimism of the will,"[74] this suggests a concept "pessimoptimism." By clinging to that principle and that perspective, Mann became in the wartime United States as considerable a force in the resistance to Hitler as is conceivable for a mere man of letters.

All of which shows that what the Enlightenment preached and practiced was not so much a theory of history as a way of living in history. What other way is there? Only despair and inertia. Progressive history is made by people who go on hoping.[75] The stone that chance, in Schiller's metaphor, rolls along for humanity to work on may indeed, *pace* Kant, be the stone of Sisyphus, always needing to be pushed up the hill one more time. Perhaps Sisyphus is after all the Enlightenment's patron saint. There will at least always be a high-stone mark to encourage the next attempt.

To change metaphors, light has proved real at the end of some tunnels. For all its atrocities, the twentieth century saw the defeat of Fascism, the fall of dictatorships in Greece, Portugal, and Spain, and the overthrow of communism by revolutions that changed the very concept of revolution.[76]

To say nothing of a less dramatic but vital development in postwar Germany itself, the robust survival of the country's first ever stable democracy, and the awarding of the Nobel Peace Prize to a German, Chancellor Willy Brandt, in 1971. Like all genuine democracies, the Federal Republic is an attempt to practice Enlightenment principles. And at last a whole continent has trodden Kant's rational path to peace after wasting centuries on the destructive alternative he saw so clearly. The European Union, despite its institutional shortcomings and the frequent failure of member states to see beyond their immediate national interests, is still (be it said with fingers crossed) "the first real terrestrial space of universal peace."[77]

Toward Enlightenment

> Nobody has come up with a better project than the Enlightenment.
> —Richard Rorty, "Human Rights, Rationality and Sentimentality"

Capitalized as a period concept or presumed movement, "the Enlightenment" is too large a term to be attacked, or indeed defended, with precision. Its modern assailants commonly fail to quote or refer to individual writers or works, let alone engage with their arguments. A dismissive gesture suffices. Specific indictments of the Enlightenment for the sins of modernity, from colonialism to the Holocaust to atomic weapons, similarly lack a cogent link back to particular writers and their ideas. As contrary examples, Kant, Forster, and Herder are already critical of the beginnings of colonial exploitation; Kant's concept of duty cannot entail a willing participation in atrocity; Newton does not imply nuclear. It is impossible to recognize the real Enlightenment in such distended pseudo-causalities. Nor can the "project of the Enlightenment" even be reduced, a shade less drastically, to "the effort to subdue and dominate nature to human ends."[1]

That passing remark from a twentieth-century context shows a common confusion of Enlightenment principles with mere instrumentality. Some practical advances do of course have roots in enlightened thinking. One considerable economic activity of the day is reflected in the "philanthropic efforts" of a character in *Wilhelm Meister's Apprenticeship* to improve agricultural practice, which is said to further "the truest enlightenment."[2] To some (Gibbon, Hume, Montesquieu) the practice of trade between nations seemed likely to create peaceful interdependence. Nothing could have been more practically oriented than Diderot and D'Alembert's *Encyclopédie*. But not every application of human intelligence or ingenuity can be classed as

enlightened and its potential damaging results used to discredit the thinkers of the age.

A positive account of Enlightenment thinking likewise has to steer
clear of glib generalization. That is why the preceding chapters have dealt
with defined situations, specific works, detailed arguments. The coherence
that emerges is one that German writers may not even have been aware of.
They certainly did not think of themselves, to anything like the degree their
French contemporaries did, as a movement. They were simply reaching out
for light, as naturally as a growing plant. At most they might see themselves
as active *Aufklärer*, an unpretentiously everyday word for someone who
clears up and throws light on difficulties or obscurities, to the discomfiture
of those who want to perpetuate them.

To attempt such clearing up,, with its social and ultimately political
consequences,[3] depended on fresh critical thinking. Kant's definition of enlightenment as the emergence from juvenility into independence is not a
vague generalization but the vital seed out of which all the activities we
have looked at were generated. "Reason" was not an abstract goal, much
less an idol, and certainly not the source of deductive arguments that it
had been for Descartes and Leibniz. Reason (*Vernunft*) was now commonly
shorthand for clear, sober thinking. Indeed, what Kant first stresses in "Was
ist Aufklärung?" is the need to use one's understanding (*Verstand*), a down-
to-earth working tool. However labeled, this was a tool that everybody had
the potential and the right to use.

Enlightenment writers were thus not an elite in the word's exclusive
sense. This further cliché accusation fails to realize that innovation in ideas
can only be carried forward by an educated class, whose responsibility it
then is to communicate their findings as broadly as possible—a task we saw
Schiller unashamedly assign to the "thinking better part" of the people who
could spread light downward. The great majority needed all their time and
energies for the pressing problems of survival and the immediate pursuit of
happiness. That was bound to limit their mental horizons. Kant's charge of
laziness or cowardice as reasons for failing to "come of age" could not apply
to them. They might be suffering under tyranny, yet still not question absolutism in the abstract; they might be uneasy under religious control, yet
still not question dogma's claims to truth and authority. There were many
things they might feel, think, resent, even instinctively see through—the
ordinary person's experience of the world can generate its own commonsense insights—yet still not articulate. That had to be done on their behalf.
Thus Bürger's attack on hunting princes gave public voice to what a real

peasant must have felt but was not free to say; Lessing's *Nathan* publicly relativized revealed religion, about which there was no doubt much latent skepticism. If Schiller's words "thinking better part" of the people literally means an aristocracy, it was one with a democratic function. Writers were the representatives of the silent mass.[4]

And the Enlightenment was not just out to negate. The criticism of present ills implied positive values: justice, which is a practical subset of scrupulous argument and use of evidence; ascertainable truth, which is the fruit of unprejudiced thinking and exact science; the freedoms of thought and speech, which are the legitimate claims of adult citizens; liberal education, which is the birthright of each new generation; individual fulfillment, which is a demand inherent in the human makeup. By thorough and subtle explorations rather than dramatic confrontation in the French style, the German Enlightenment played its part in rooting these values in the European consciousness.

They have long been taken for granted in a civilized society, though constant watchfulness is needed lest commitment decline into mere lip service. Still, this is the true line of causal descent from the Enlightenment to the modern Western world.[5] One need only call to mind what social reality has looked like when the freedoms and rights the Enlightenment argued for have been denied and their proponents persecuted by authoritarian regimes[6]—communism, fascism, or Christianity in its rigidly dogmatic forms. It is a groundless cliché that we in the West live in a Christian society: those freedoms and rights were never values conceded, much less inculcated, by Christian authority. They had to be wrested from it, principally by the Enlightenment itself.

In contrast, the Enlightenment's own tradition has never been dogmatic or oppressive. As Jacob Burckhardt pointed out, it transformed the intellectual world without compelling anyone to sign up to anything.[7] To hear the complaints of its critics, one might think it had once held absolute power and abused it. Its values are not even fixed doctrines, but flexible principles with which to work. Its vision is an open offer, an invitation to help bring about a humane world, if necessary bit by bit.

If this is a conclusion, there is nothing final about it. Kant's distinction remains true: we live not in an enlightened age, only ever in an age in pursuit of enlightenment. Kant was defining and defending a process beyond the Enlightenment of his day. Enlightenment is immensely larger and richer without the capital letter, never outdated because never completed. How could it be, when there will always be new problems to face, the old unenlightened forces of interest and power to oppose, and a new generation that has to tackle them, for whom we ourselves as we grow older may be part of the problem? Each day's news brings instances of injustice, intolerance, and concealment. *Sapere aude* remains a necessary motto, made more pressing by the word that follows in the original Latin text: *Incipe*—get started.

NOTES

INTRODUCTION: . . . OR DARKNESS?

1. Lawrence, *Phoenix*, 110.

2. N 1:786; N 2:1114; N 3:690.

3. De Staël, *De l'Allemagne*.

4. Less noted is Horkheimer, "Kants Philosophie und die Aufklärung," in *Gesammelte Schriften*, vol. 7, 160ff., which declares the truth and modern necessity of Kant's Enlightenment position.

5. A concise and pungent survey of the German petty princes, good and bad, is provided in part 2 of the opening chapter of Gooch, *Germany and the French Revolution*.

CHAPTER 1. COMING OF AGE

1. Cruden's concordance to the Bible summarizes its use of "child" to mean "one weak in knowledge" and "such as are humble and docile." No development beyond that is implied. The only apparent exception is 1 Corinthians 13:11: "When I was a child, I spoke as a child, I understood as a child, I thought as a child: but when I became a man, I put away childish things"—but only, as what follows suggests, to look forward to some undefined vision. In Galatians 4:1, the subjection of children to "guardians" is brought to an end by the "father," whose inheritors they then become, still seemingly docile.

2. "Aufklärung ist der Ausgang des Menschen aus seiner selbstverschuldeten Unmündigkeit. *Unmündigkeit* ist das Unvermögen, sich seines Verstandes ohne Leitung eines anderen zu bedienen. *Selbstverschuldet* ist diese Unmündigkeit, wenn die Ursache derselben nicht am Mangel des Verstandes, sondern der Entschließung und des Mutes liegt, sich seiner ohne Leitung eines anderen zu bedienen. *Sapere aude!* Habe Mut, dich deines *eigenen* Verstandes zu bedienen! ist also der Wahlspruch der Aufklärung." K 4:169. The Latin phrase is from Horace, *Epistles* book 1, epistle 2, line 40.

3. The other German texts—by Erhard, Hamann, Herder, Lessing, Mendelssohn, Riem, Schiller, and Wieland—are printed alongside Kant's in Bahr, *Was ist Aufklärung?*

4. "Der vernünftige Geschmack unserer aufgeklärten Zeiten." In the announcement of a course of lectures on geography in 1757. K 2:3.

5. "Habe Mut zu denken, nehme [sic] Besitz von deiner Stelle" (Have the courage to think, take possession of your place). Lbg 1:130.

6. "Selbstdenken heißt: den obersten Probierstein der Wahrheit in sich selbst (d.i. in seiner eigenen Vernunft) suchen, und die Maxime, jederzeit selbst zu denken, ist die *Aufklärung*" (Thinking for yourself means: seeking the highest touchstone of truth in yourself (that is, in your own reason); and the maxim always to think for yourself is *enlightenment*). "Was heißt: sich im Denken orientieren?" (What does it mean, to take your intellectual bearings?). K 4:365.

7. The young Turks were of course an actual historical group in the Turkey of Kemal Atatürk. There are analogies elsewhere—groupings in nineteenth-century Germany (Jung Deutschland) and Italy (Giovane Italia).

8. In the quarrel scene (act 2, scene 3), both invoke the contrast of young and old, and Tasso's later reflections use the terms "guardian" and "child" against Antonio (act 4, scene 5, lines 2754ff.).

9. Wordsworth, *The Prelude* (1805 text), 3:640ff.

10. "Es ist so bequem, unmündig zu sein. Habe ich ein Buch, das für mich Verstand hat, einen Seelsorger, der für mich Gewissen hat, einen Arzt, der für mich die Diät beurteilt, so brauche ich mich ja nicht selbst zu bemühen. Ich habe nicht nötig zu denken, wenn ich nur bezahlen kann; andere werden das verdrießliche Geschäft schon für mich übernehmen." K 4:169. The subtlety lies here in the "playacting" switch to the first person, and the use of the colloquial particles *ja* and *schon*.

11. See Langen, *Der Wortschatz des deutschen Pietismus*, 313ff.

12. "Man soll [den Schüler] nicht tragen sondern leiten, wenn man will, dass er in Zukunft von sich selbst zu gehen geschickt sein soll." K 2:320.

13. "Sicherer Gang" or "sicherer Weg einer Wissenschaft." *Vorrede* to the second edition of the *Critique of Pure Reason* (1787), K 3:12, 13, 15, 17, 19, 22.

14. A strikingly similar image occurs in Montaigne's reflections on the constraints of authority in his essay on how to educate children: "Assubjettis aux cordes, nous n'avons pas de franches allures" (Accustomed to our reins, we cannot move freely). "De l'institution des enfants," in *Essais*, 183.

15. Princes as the "Vormünder seiner [Gottes] unmündigen Kinder" is a formulation from Klein's *Berlinische Monatsschrift* article, "Über Denk- und Druckfreiheit," reprinted in Hinske and Albrecht, *Was ist Aufklärung?*, 400.

16. Cf. the modern version in Alfred Döblin's novel *Berlin Alexanderplatz*: "Da ist der gute Vater Staat, / Er gängelt dich von früh bis spat. / Sein erst Gebot heißt: Mensch, berappe! / Das zweite: Halte deine Klappe!" (89) (That's your good old father state, / He keeps a tight rein early and late. / His first command is: Just fork out! / The second: Kindly shut your mouth!).

17. Did Kant not know, or was there no strict implementation, of Frederick's rescript of this same year decreeing that private individuals were not entitled to pass public critical judgments on the actions, laws, and measures of sovereigns and courts? Nor to report them in print, on the grounds that private individuals were ignorant of their circumstances and motives? Quoted in Habermas, *Strukturwandel der Öffentlichkeit*, 40.

18. Clark, *Iron Kingdom*, 255.

19. For more on this see chapter 4.

20. "Als Gelehrter hat er volle Freiheit, ja sogar den Beruf dazu." K 4:172. Cf. Jeremy Bentham's "motto of a good citizen" "under a government of Laws: to obey punctually; to censure freely." *A Fragment on Government*, quoted in Gay, *The Enlightenment*, 1:142.

21. "Öffentliche Meinungen—private Faulheiten." *Menschliches, Allzumenschliches*, N 1, 691.

22. Quoted in Gay, *The Enlightenment*, 1:340.

23. "Ein Verbrechen wider die menschliche Natur." K 4:173.

24. Thus Lichtenberg, consciously adapting Descartes: "Non cogitant, ergo non sunt." Lbg 1:708.

25. Again, the announcement of his lecture courses for the winter semester of 1765–66. K 2:320ff.

26. *Gedanken von der wahren Schätzung der lebendigen Kräfte*, K 1:5.

27. Kant, *Träume eines Geistersehers*, 1. Teil, 4. Hauptstück, K 2:364ff. Kant precisely echoes Montaigne, down to the psychology of overcoming pride: "Je me sens plus fier de la victoire que je gaigne sur moy quand, en l'ardeur mesme du combat, je me plie sous la force de mon adversaire que je me sens gré de la victoire que je gaigne sur luy par sa faiblesse." "De l'art de conférer," in *Essais* 3, viii, 1035.

28. *Rettung des Cardanus*, Lg 7:21. Montaigne again: "La cause de la vérité devroit estre la cause commune à l'un et l'autre." "De l'art de conférer," in ibid., 1034.

29. Goethe to Carl Friedrich Bachmann, 2 February 1822, WA 4:35, 256.

30. Lbg 1:570.

31. *Critique of Pure Reason*, K 3:505, B 775.

32. Cf. Hinske, "Kants Theorie von der Unmöglichkeit des totalen Irrtums."

33. K 4:170.

34. K 4:174.

35. Lessing to Friedrich Nicolai, 25 August 1769.

36. See Conrad, "Das Allgemeine Landrecht von 1794," in Büsch and Neugebauer, *Moderne preußische Geschichte*, 2:602. It is true one should not, in modern terms, make too much of this legal reform. Tocqueville argued that Prussia under its "modern head" still had a "gothic body." *L'ancien régime et la révolution*, 345ff.

37. K 4:176.

38. *Lettres philosophiques*, no. 13, in Voltaire, *Mélanges*, 42.

39. Officers in the nineteenth-century Austrian army were expressly forbidden to publish lest they damage "discipline and esprit de corps." Sheehan, *German History, 1770–1866*, 905. There have been more modern examples in Britain and the United States.

40. Lbg 2:651.

41. This was met by the resolute opposition of a group of professors, a celebrated but rare thing in German university history. The Göttingen Seven, who included the brothers Jakob and Wilhelm Grimm, all lost their posts.

42. Friedrich Viktor Plessing to Kant, 15 October 1783, K 9:244.

43. For more on this more see chapter 8.

44. Krieger, *The German Idea of Freedom*, 91.

45. K 3:7.

46. K 3:500, B 675.

47. Christian Thomasius, *Außübung der Vernunfft-Lehre*, erstes Hauptstück, §§28, 29, 87, 89, 90. Excerpted in Killy, 1:9ff. *Eltern* (parents) still also carries its more general etymological sense of "elders."

48. In "Was ist Aufklärung?," K 4:170.

49. Quoted in Hettner, *Geschichte der deutschen Literatur im achtzehnten Jahrhundert*, 86ff. Schiller to Goethe, 29 May 1799, praises Thomasius, using almost exactly Kant's metaphor, as an instance of "Loswinden . . . aus der Pedanterie des Zeitalters."

50. Thomasius, *Vom Laster der Zauberei*, 221ff.

51. All this makes the case for Thomasius as a "father of the Enlightenment," though in later years he took up a more authoritarian position. See Engfer, "Die Philosophie der Aufklärung und Friedrich II," in Ziechmann, *Panorama der Friderizianischen Zeit*, 23ff.

52. Tocqueville uses Württemberg as an example of the loss of German freedoms in the postmedieval period. *L'ancien régime et la révolution*, 341ff.

53. On Anhalt-Dessau and its ruler see below, p. 247n9.

54. In the lectures on pedagogy, K 8:458.

55. Goethe to Charlotte von Stein, 2 April 1782. Goethe's skepticism still echoes in *Faust*, part 2, lines 7336–44, where the Argonauts' legendary tutor, "the noble pedagogue" Chiron, comments: "Am Ende treiben sie's nach ihrer Weise fort, / Als wenn sie nicht erzogen wären" (When all is done, they still go on the same old way / As if they'd never had a teacher). Cf. Samuel Johnson's "Short Song of Congratulation to Sir John Lade," who had come of age and thereby into an inheritance he was clearly going to squander.

56. Karl Ludwig Knebel to Prince Constantin, 19 March 1783.

57. Burschell, *Schiller*, 43. They included his prime minister, Count Montmartin, "a smooth flatterer of those above him, a cold extorter from the duke's subjects, bankrupt when he entered his service, wealthy when he left." Ibid., 39.

58. Storz, *Karl* Eugen, 177ff.

59. Minor, *Schiller*, 1:90.

60. I.e., the Tübinger Stift, where Hölderlin, Hegel, and Schelling were classmates. Theology was commonly the start—often the only possible one—for careers that later diverged from the church.

61. Not, however, without long-term effects on many aspects of his work. See Nilges, *Schiller und das Recht*.

62. Buchwald, *Schiller*, 1:145.

63. "Ankündigung der Rheinischen Thalia," Sch 4:855f.

64. "Was kann eine gute stehende Schaubühne eigentlich wirken?" Sch 5:829.

65. Schiller to Dalberg, 6–7 October 1782.

66. Schiller to Körner, 10 December 1793.

67. "Über die Mitschüler und sich selbst." Sch 5:239, 241.

68. "Gehört allzuviel Güte, Leutseligkeit und große Freigebigkeit im engsten Verstand zur Tugend?" Sch 5:247, 249.

69. *Julius Caesar*, act 2, scene 1, lines 207ff.

70. "Über die Mitschüler." Sch 5:239.

71. "Gehört allzuviel." Sch 5:249.

72. "Die Tugend in ihren Folgen betrachtet." Sch 5:284.

73. Schiller, *Schillers Sämtliche Werke*, Goedeke ed., 1:73.

74. "Versuch über den Zusammenhang der tierischen Natur des Menschen mit seiner geistigen." Sch 5:287.

75. Sch 1: 548.

76. Sch 1:617.

77. "Iudicium anceps, experimentum periculosum"; quoted in Kant, "Theory and Practice," K 6:390.

78. "Vom Wirken der Schaubühne auf das Volk," published in 1784 as "Was kann eine gute stehende Schaubühne eigentlich wirken?"and later again retitled as "Die Schaubühne als eine moralische Anstalt betrachtet." Sch 5:818ff.

79. "Ankündigung der Rheinischen Thalia." Sch 5: 857, 855.

80. Joseph was elected Holy Roman Emperor in 1765, a position a woman could not hold. But Maria Theresia could in her own right be queen of Austria—which was part of Joseph's empire. They were thus bizarrely yoked together, with her the more conservative partner. Only after her death in 1780 was Joseph free to take his own initiatives.

81. Joseph as quoted in Herder, *Briefe zu Beförderung der Humanität* (1793), letter 10. H 7:64. The principle of the ruler serving the people is already stated in Pufendorf's constitutional writings, though it is unclear whether either king read him, especially not Frederick, whose reading was wholly French. At all events, for the agitator Breme in Goethe's fragmentary political play *Die Aufgeregten* of 1793, Frederick and Joseph are "the two monarchs whom all true democrats should worship as their saints." HA 5:202.

82. Reprinted in Beales, *Enlightenment and Reform*.

83. Forster, *Ansichten vom Niederrhein*. F 196.

84. "The thing to note here is that when the public has been brought under the yoke of immaturity by the guardians, it will compel any among them who have themselves become enlightened to remain under it, when it has been stirred up by guardians incapable of all enlightenment." K 4:170.

85. Thus the subtitle of the second volume of Beales's biography of Joseph. It fits in principle, of course, the whole Enlightenment.

86. K 4:89.

87. "Der Bauern Gott, der Bürger Not, Des Adels Spott liegt auf dem Tod." Quoted in Bodi, *Tauwetter in Wien*, 396.

88. Pezzl, *Faustin*, chapter 43, "Die Philosophie auf dem Thron," especially 371ff.

89. *Briefe zu Beförderung der Humanität*, letter 10. H 7:55–70.

90. Beales, *Enlightenment and Reform*, 639ff.; Gagliardo, *Germany under the Old Regime*, chapter 21.

91. Quoted in Beales, *Enlightenment and Reform*, 178.

92. Gay, *The Enlightenment*, 1:373.

93. Cf. ibid., 2:447, 499–501.

CHAPTER 2. A WORLD OF OUR OWN

1. *Vorlesungen zur Einführung in die Psychoanalyse*, lecture 18. Freud, *Studienausgabe* 1:283.

2. *Critique of Pure Reason*. Introduction to the second edition of 1787, K 3:18.

3. Kant to Christian Garve, 7 August 1783, K 9:226.

4. *Critique of Pure Reason*, K 3:45, B 18f.

5. "Die Metaphysik von der Metaphysik." Kant to Markus Herz, 1781?, K 9:198.

6. AA 20:44.

7. "*Lasst uns unser Glück besorgen, in den Garten gehen und arbeiten!*" (emphasis in the original). *Träume eines Geistersehers*, K 2:390.

8. The translation seems to be Kant's own. Contemporary versions, e.g., *Kandide oder es ist doch die beste Welt*, published by Himburg in 1782, stay close to the original.

9. Kant to Johann Bering, 7 April 1786, K 9:295.

10. *Prolegomena*, K 4:10, perhaps taking further Hume's metaphor of an ambitious sea voyage in a "leaky weather-beaten vessel" in *A Treatise of Human Nature*, 263.

11. *Critique of Pure Reason*, first introduction, K 3:7n.

12. K 3:306ff., 312ff., 318ff.; B 454, 462, 473.

13. *Critique of Pure Reason*, introduction to the first edition, K 3:5.

14. See Kant to Christian Gottfried Schütz, 10 July 1797.

15. "The so-called religious disputes, spattered with blood." *Religion within the Limits of Mere Reason*, K 6:253.

16. Goethe to Herder, 4 September 1788, WA 4:9, 28.

17. Lbg 1:652.

18. *Decline and Fall*, book I, chapter xxi.

19. E.g., the seventeenth-century poet Daniel Czepko: "Before me was no time, none will be after me. / With me time has been born, with me will cease to be."

20. Kleist to Wilhelmine von Zenge, March 1801, in Kleist, *Sämtliche Werke*, 2:634.

21. "Die Frage, ob die Gegenstände außer uns objektive Realiktät haben . . . ist fast so törigt, als die: ob die blaue Farbe wirklich *blau* sei?," Lbg 1:892.

22. "Bloß ein Grenzbegriff, um die Anmaßung der Sinnlichkeit einzuschränken, und also nur von negativem Gebrauche." *Critique of Pure Reason*, K 3:221ff., B 311.

23. "Unser Zeitalter ist das Zeitalter der Kritik, der sich alles unterwerfen muß. *Religion*, durch ihre *Heiligkeit*, und *Gesetzgebung*, durch ihre *Majestät*, wollen sich gemeiniglich derselben entziehen. Aber alsdenn erregen sie gerechten Verdacht wider sich und können auf unverstellte Achtung nicht Anspruch machen, die die Vernunft nur demjenigen bewilligt, was ihre freie und öffentliche Prüfung hat aushalten können." K 3:7.

24. See the preface (1785) to Mendelssohn, *Morgenstunden*, 3. The statement slightly differs from what Mendelssohn wrote privately to Kant, that tackling the Critique was "a criterion of health," and that he was venturing to read it whenever he felt stronger. Mendelssohn to Kant, 10 April 1783, K 9:213.

25. "Einwirkung der neueren Philosophie," HA 13:27.

26. See Kant to Markus Herz, 7 June 1771 and 21 February 1772, K 9:97, 103. The formulation "Critique of Pure Reason" (*Critik der reinen Vernunft*) first occurs, though not yet as a proposed title, in an undated letter to Herz that Cassirer places between October 1773 and February 1774. K 9:116.

27. Lbg 1:693.

28. Ludwig, *Kant für Anfänger*, 5.

29. K 2:311.

30. For more on this see below, pp. 75, 98.

31. "Das Abenteuer der Vernunft," *Critique of Judgment*, §80, K 5:498n.

32. Wilbur, "Copernicus," *New and Collected Poems*, 70.

33. The lecture, "Vom leichteren und vom gründlichen Vortrag der Philosophie," still survived when Borowski wrote his contemporary account of Kant's life. Crucial though it is as evidence that Kant was aware of the presentational problem, it is rarely referred to by later biographers. See Vorlaender, *Kant: der Mann und das Werk*, 1:76. Goetschel refers to it in his useful study *Kant als Schriftsteller*, 43, but by omitting the second *von*, he allows the possible reading that Kant was presenting ease and thoroughness of presentation not disjunctively but as a compatible pair.

34. *Grundlegung*, K 4:266. As is often the case in his polemics, Kant mentions no names. He was corresponding cordially with, e.g., Garve, who was certainly a *Popularphilosoph*, as was, in some measure, Kant's friend Mendelssohn. Friedrich Nicolai, who attacked Kant's critical philosophy as damagingly obscure, would definitely be a candidate. On Nicolai see below, pp. 161ff.

35. AA 20:30.

36. "Kant wollte auf eine 'alle Welt' vor den Kopf stoßende Art beweisen, dass 'alle Welt' Recht habe: das war der heimliche Witz dieser Seele. Er schrieb gegen die Gelehrten zu Gunsten des Volks-Vorurteils, aber für Gelehrte und nicht für das Volk." *Die fröhliche Wissenschaft*, §193.

37. "So ist eine solche Critik nicht abgefaßt, um den Einfältigen, sondern den subtilsten Vernünftlern vorgetragen zu werden, welche sich keine Sache zu hoch zu sein meyneten. Da dann diese Critik eben beweisen soll, dass sie [= solche Sachen] ihnen und jedermann zur spekulativen Einsicht viel zu hoch sind, und sie in dem Wahn der letzteren zu verwirren (da es ihre eigene Schuld ist, darin zu beharren)." AA 18:628.

38. "Die erste Betäubung . . . wird sich verlieren." Kant to Christian Garve, 7 August 1783, K 9:225. The most recent biography suggests the condition is still with us; see Geier, *Kants Welt*, 168.

39. Kant to Moses Mendelssohn, 16 August 1783, K 9:232ff.

40. See *Über den Gebrauch teleologischer Prinzipien in der Philosophie*, K 4:514ff.

41. Kant to Garve, 7 August 1783, K 9:224. "Twelve years" is demonstrably an underestimate for the gestation of the project. (See the letter to Mendelssohn, n. 39.) It is not clear whether the period of actual writing included or followed the production of a first draft which Kant refers to at K 3:10.

42. Kant to Herz, undated, K 9:198.

43. "Gedanken ohne Inhalt sind leer, Anschauungen ohne Begriffe sind blind." K 3:80, B 75.

44. "Die leichte Taube, indem sie im freien Flug die Luft teilt, deren Widerstand sie fühlt, könnte die Vorstellung fassen, dass es ihr im luftleeren Raum noch viel besser gelingen werde." K 3:39.

45. This is from his early Latin dissertation, *De mundi sensibilis atque intelligibilis forma et principiis* (The Form and Principles of the Sensory and Intellectual World). TP 405.

46. The frontispiece to Samuel Grosser, *Pharus intellectus sive logica electiva* (1697), shows the ship of reason (Noonautica) steering between the rocks of error and ignorance to the harbor of the city of truth (Alethopolis). Reproduced in Schneiders, *Aufklärung und Vorurteilskritik*, 8.

47. Kant: "dem eigentlichen Sitze des Scheins, wo manche Nebelbank und manches bald wegschmelzendes Eis neue Länder lügt." K 3:212, B 294ff. Forster's original English: "the fallacious conformation of fog-banks, or that of islands half-hid in snowstorms"; mariners were "deceived by such appearances." *A Voyage round the World*, in Forster, AA, 1:72.

48. See Kant to Johann Schultz, 4 March 1784, K 9:249; and Vaihinger, "Die Kant-Medaille mit dem schiefen Turm zu Pisa," in *Kant-Studien*, 109–15.

49. "Freilich fand es sich, daß, ob wir zwar einen Turm im Sinne hatten, der bis an den Himmel reichen sollte, der Vorrat der Materialien doch nur zu einem Wohnhause zureichte." K 3:481, B 736.

50. *The Prelude*, 3:63.

51. Coleridge, *A Book I Value*, 44 (emphasis in the original).

52. See Landau, *Rezensionen der Kantschen Philosophie*.

53. Ludwig Heinrich Jacob to Kant, 4 May 1790, K 10:30.

54. *Critique of Pure Reason*, K 3:25, B XXXI. See further below, pp. 105, 175.

55. See chapter 10.

56. Leibniz declares "the knowledge of God" to be "the foundation and aim of all learning." If both, it is plainly a circular proposition. Leibniz to Bayle, 1687; quoted in Hettner, *Geschichte der deutschen Literatur im achtzehnten Jahrhundert*, 3:1, 119.

57. Quoted in Grigson, *Before the Romantics*, 81.

58. P. F. Strawson, in a review reprinted in Chadwick, *Immanuel Kant: Critical Assessments*, 1:242.

59. Adorno, *Kant's "Critique of Pure Reason,"* 59.

CHAPTER 3. HOPE IN HISTORY

1. Most notably Bossuet's *Histoire universelle* (1681).

2. Gibbon, *The History of the Decline and Fall of the Roman Empire*, book 1, chapter 3.

3. Spalding, *Betrachtung über die Bestimmung des Menschen*.

4. "Was der Mensch zu seiner Glückseligkeit zu wissen nötig hat, das weiß er gewiss ohne alle Offenbarung, als die, die er seinem Wesen nach besitzt." Lbg 1:671.

5. Eighth Proposition, K 4:161 (emphasis in original).

6. Saine, "Natural Science and the Ideology of Nature."

7. Ninth Proposition, K 4:161.

8. See the references to the labyrinth in the odes "An Gott" of 1748 and "An Bodmer" of 1750, as well as Canto 12 of the epic *Der Messias*, lines 1–12.

9. Fifth proposition, K 4:156.

10. "Hat mich außerordentlich befriedigt." Schiller to Körner, 29 August 1787.

11. 14 June 1789, K 9:424.

12. Cf. High, "Schiller, National Wars for Independence, and 'Merely Political' Revolutions," 219–40.

13. "Entkleidet sich großmütig seines fürstlichen Daseins, steigt zu einer freiwilligen Armut herunter und ist nichts mehr als ein Bürger der Welt." Sch 4:36.

14. "Auch erwarte man hier keine hervorragende, kolossalische Menschen." Ibid., 34.

15. They make a fine triple zeugma: "ein neuer jugendlicher Staat [war] mächtig durch Eintracht, seine Wasserflut und Verzweiflung." Ibid., 36.

16. "Dieses schöne Denkmal bürgerlicher Stärke" is calculated to arouse "in der Brust meines Lesers ein fröhliches Gefühl seiner selbst." Ibid., 33.

17. "Die Kraft also, womit es [das Volk] handelte, ist unter uns nicht verschwunden; der glückliche Erfolg, der sein Wagestück krönte, ist auch uns versagt, wenn die Zeitläufte wiederkehren und ähnliche Anlässe uns zu ähnlichen Taten rufen." Ibid., 1020, excised from its original place on 34.

18. "Die letzte vollendende Hand—der erleuchtete unternehmende Geist, der diesen großen politischen Augenblick haschte und die Geburt des Zufalls zum Plan der Weisheit erzöge." Ibid., 36.

19. "Die verzögerte Gegenwehr [ließ] dem Werke des Ohngefährs Zeit, zu einem Werke des Verstandes zu reifen." Ibid., 42.

20. "Der Mensch verarbeitet, glättet und bildet den rohen Stein, den die Zeiten herbeitragen; ihm gehört der Augenblick und der Punkt, aber die Weltgeschichte rollt der Zufall." Ibid., 45. The metaphor is already there in Posa's soliloquy before the audience scene in *Don Carlos*, act 3, scene 9, lines 2960ff: "Und was / Ist Zufall anders als der rohe Stein, / Der Leben annimmt in des Bildners Hand? / Den Zufall gibt die Vorsehung—zum Zwecke / Muss ihn der Mensch gestalten."

21. Sch 4:444, 481, 646; retrospect 714.

22. "Der große Zeitpunkt fand nur *mittelmäßige* Geister auf der Bühne, und unbenutzt blieb das [sic] entscheidende Moment, weil es den Mutigen an Macht, den Mächtigen an Einsicht Mut und Entschlossenheit fehlte." Sch 4:446. Similarly 4:381.

23. "Wäre es irgend erlaubt, in menschliche Dinge eine höhere Vorsicht zu flechten, so wäre es bei dieser Geschichte, so widersprechend erscheint sie der Vernunft und allen Erfahrungen." Sch 4:34.

24. "Diese unnatürliche Wendung der Dinge scheint an ein Wunder zu grenzen." Ibid., 37.

25. "So verschwindet das Übernatürliche dieser Begebenheit"; but then "des Fatums unsichtbare Hand." Ibid., 44. "Sonderbare Fügung des Himmels." Ibid., 51.

26. K 6:447.

27. See especially the close of the introduction to *Abfall der Niederlande*, Sch 4:46, where ancient wars are said to have been conducted humanely because they were not fought for religious causes.

28. "Gott der Allmächtige blies, / Und die Armada flog nach allen Winden." Sch 1:146.

29. Cf. *Abfall der Niederlande*, Sch 4:63: "Die ganze Weltgeschichte ist ein ewig wiederholter Kampf der Herrschsucht und Freiheit."

30. "Es steht uns frei, über die kühne Geburt des Zufalls zu erstaunen, oder einem höheren Verstand unsere Bewunderung zuzutragen." Sch 4:45.

31. Ibid., 764.

32. Ibid., 766.

33. Schiller to Körner, 9 February 1789, Sch 1:173.

34. This local sensation, and Schiller's experience of speaking before a packed hall, are graphically described in his letter to Körner of 28 May 1789.

35. "So manches wirksame Genie für das kommende Zeitalter." Sch 4:749.

36. Ibid., 766ff.

37. At least, that is what it must have meant to say. What it actually says, reprinted uncorrected in each of the nine volumes, is "the discipline that hesitates to forget its founding fathers" (dass diejenige Wissenschaft, die zögert, ihre Begründer zu vergessen, verloren ist). It plainly didn't hesitate to forget Schiller. Nor apparently did Schiller write any single work of history worthy of a place among the 246 titles by 228 authors summarized in Reinhardt, *Hauptwerke der Geschichtsschreibung*, a reference work international in scope but with an avowed leaning toward German examples, which again include Schiller's predecessors and contemporaries. Again, in the 450 pages of Muhlack, *Geschichtswissenschaft im Humanismus und in der Aufklärung*, which presents humanist and Enlightenment historiography as the prehistory of *Historismus*, Schiller is nowhere mentioned, not even in the chapter on universal history, a topic on which he made some striking remarks in what must be the most famous of all German inaugural lectures.

38. Thus Schiller barely appears in Meinecke, *Weltbürgertum und Nationalstaat*, despite being one of the three great historically visionary German *Weltbürger*. He is referred to in passing in the chapter on Humboldt and otherwise only as the author of the poem-fragment "Deutsche Größe." He is in good company: Kant, the key figure for the concept of cosmopolitanism, also barely appears. His relevant texts are not analyzed, and he is patronizingly dismissed for his "unhistorical dream" of eternal peace (Meinecke, *Weltbürgertum und Nationalstaat*, 70, 239). It is not clear how Meinecke's two-concept title can ever have been seriously meant. Ranke for his part is reported to have declared that Schiller had no natural aptitude for history (keinen Beruf zum Geschichtsschreiber— quoted in Schieder, "Schiller als Historiker," 32). Schiller as author of the *Geschichte des Dreißigjährigen Kriegs* gets no mention in Ranke's *Wallenstein*. Nor, naturally, does Schiller's mere dramatic masterpiece, the *Wallenstein* trilogy.

39. Though there have always been doubts about the claim to objectivity, Ranke's influence still secures him the leading place in Wehler, *Deutsche Historiker*, which includes the elite. For a concise but comprehensive critique of Ranke and his contemporary affiliations, see Croce, "Historicism Complete and Incomplete," 93ff.

40. "Man hat der Historie das Amt, die Vergangenheit zu richten, die Mitwelt zum Nutzen zukünftiger Jahre zu belehren, beigemessen: so hoher Aemter unterwindet sich gegenwärtiger Versuch nicht: er will bloß zeigen, wie es eigentlich gewesen." *Vorrede* to *Geschichte der romanischen und germanischen Völker von 1494 bis 1514* (1824), *Sämtliche Werke* 33:vii.

41. Schiller was clear about this appropriation of the past from his very beginnings as a historian. Cf. *Abfall der Niederlande*, Sch 4:29, 31, where he speaks of the shape that his own imagination gave his subject matter from the outset, and of the power that every good writer exerts over the way the reader will see things.

42. Two fragments, *Idee der Universalhistorie* and *Einleitung zu einer Vorlesung über Universalhistorie;* and the Inaugural, *Über die Verwandtschaft und den Unterschied der Historie und der Politik*, in Ranke, *Sämtliche Werke*. The latter was originally written in Latin and translated by another hand, so the precise German formulations are not Ranke's. The substance nevertheless remains unambiguous.

43. Ranke, *Sämtliche Werke*, 53/54:665ff., and *Idee der Universalhistorie*, 300ff.: "dass [der Kampf] sich nach Gottes Willen entscheiden wird."

44. Ranke, *Politisches Gespräch*, 61.

45. Ranke, *Sämtliche Werke*, 53/54:89ff.

46. "Wie könnte irgend etwas seyn ohne den göttlichen Grund seiner Existenz?" Ranke, *Idee der Univeralhistorie*, 295.

47. "Es ist nicht notwendig, dass wir das Inwohnen des Ewigen in dem Einzelnen lange beweisen; dies ist der religiöse Grund, auf welchem unser Bemühen beruht." Ibid.

48. "Indem wir uns den Ansprüchen einer gewissen beschränkten Theologie entziehen, bekennen wir doch, dass alles unser Bemühen aus einem höhern, aus einem religiösen Ursprung entquillt." Ibid.

49. "Blind chance," *Über die Verwandtschaft und den Unterschied der Historie und der Politik*, 283; prejudiced individuals, ibid., 287; "just and healthy," ibid., 281; "like the eighteenth-century philosophers with their universal theories, always questioning the present political arrangements," ibid., 291.

50. "Gang Gottes durch die Natur," and "der Finger Gottes [hat] alle Umwälzungen und Schattierungen auf der Erde umschrieben." *Ideen zur Philosophie der Geschichte der Menschheit*, H6:16, 36.

51. Hegel, *Vorlesungen über die Philosophie der Geschichte*, 1:28.

52. "Quod erat demonstrandum und nicht 'mitzubringen.'" Burckhardt, *Über das Studium der Geschichte*, 152.

53. Hegel, *Philosophie des Rechts*, 33.

54. On reason ruling the historical world, *Idee der Universalhistorie*, 305ff.; that the World Spirit is realized through the "cunning of reason," ibid., 306; that people wish to change the state only because they do not truly know it, *Über die Verwandtschaft und den Unterschied der Historie und der Politik*, 287. Ranke is gentler with critics of the status quo than is Hegel; his tone is more that of Mark Antony on the conspirators who murdered Caesar: "So are they all, all honourable men." Ibid., 280.

55. *Sonderweg* is the thesis, proposed or resisted in post-1945 German historiography, that all roads of German history led inevitably to the catastrophe of Nazism. For a concise account of the Prussian school, see the final chapter of Gooch, *Frederick the Great*.

56. Cf. the second of the *Unzeitgemäße Betrachtungen*, "Vom Nutzen und Nachteil des Historie für das Leben," §8, on Hegel's "nackte Bewunderung des Erfolges . . . Götzendienst des Tatsächlichen," N 1:263; and *Genealogie der Moral*, "Was bedeuten asketische Ideale?," §19, on the "kluge Indulgenz gegen die Stärke" typified by Ranke, "diesem klügsten aller 'Tatsächlichen,'" N 2:879. Not coincidentally, this was the moment when the concept of *Realpolitik* was coined by Rochau. See Gebhardt, *Handbuch der deutschen Geschichte*, 3:146.

57. *Vom Nutzen und Nachteil*, §9, 265f., and §10, N 1:276ff.

58. "Wenn die Philosophie ihr Grau in Grau malt, ist eine Gestalt des Lebens alt geworden, und mit Grau in Grau lässt sie sich nicht verjüngen. Die Eule der Minerva beginnt erst in der Dämmerung ihren Flug." Introduction to Hegel, *Philosophie des Rechts*, 7:37.

59. "Blinde Macht der Fakten." *Vom Nutzen und Nachteil*, §8, N 1:265.

60. "Monumentale Geschichte." *Vom Nutzen und Nachteil*, §2, N 1:219–25.

61. "Die Welt, als historischer Gegenstand, ist im Grunde nichts anders als der Konflikt der Naturkräfte untereinander selbst und mit der Freiheit des Menschen, und den Erfolg dieses Kampfs berichtet uns die Geschichte." "Über das Erhabene," Sch 5:803. One further wistful reference to a plan in history occurs in the draft for a poem on "German Greatness." In the wake of the harsh Peace of Campo Formio it asserts, against political events, the values of a culture which must one day make the latecomer Germany dominant in the world—"if, that is, the world has any plan, if human life has any meaning at all." Sch 1:474. The German self-assertion here is a surprising drift away from Enlightenment to nationalism; but at least Schiller never completed the poem, perhaps for self-critical reasons.

62. Ibid., 802.

63. "Ein unempfängliches Geschlecht"/ "eine verderbte Generation." Letter 5, Sch 5:580, and Schiller to the Duke of Schleswig-Holstein-Augustenburg, 13 July 1793.

64. Kant, *Conflict of the Faculties*, K 7:397ff., 400ff. Similarly, Wordsworth, in lines less well-known than his initial reaction to the Revolution ("Bliss was it in that dawn to be alive"), having, like Kant, confronted the atrocities of the Reign of Terror (*The Prelude* [1805], 10:237ff.), can write: "Yet not for this will sober reason frown / Upon that promise, nor the hope disown." "Descriptive Sketches," lines 648ff.

65. "Eine Aufgabe für mehr als *ein* Jahrhundert." Letter 7, Sch 5:590. See more fully chapter 9.

66. "An Karl Theodor von Dalberg, mit dem 'Wilhelm Tell.'" Sch 1:462.

67. "Die Vorsehung leitete die Entwicklung weiter" (H 4:19); but it is also "Werk des Schicksals" (H 4:65) and there is even a triple apposition of "chance, fate, divinity" (*Zufall, Schicksal, Gottheit*). H 4:58.

68. *Auch eine Philosophie der Geschichte zur Bildung der Menschheit.* The subtitle continues the gesture of world-weary irony: "One more contribution to many contributions of the century."

69. *Auch eine Philosophie*, H 4:23.

70. Ibid., 53ff.

71. Herder, *Journal meiner Reise im Jahr 1769*, H 4.

72. *Auch eine Philosophie*, H 4:74.

73. See chapter 5 on Forster's account of Cook's second circumnavigation, which Herder knew. *Briefe zu Beförderung*, letter 116, H 7:701.

74. Ibid., letter 114, H 7:672.

75. *Auch eine Philosophie*, H 4:83.

76. *Briefe zu Beförderung*, letter 27, H 7:148.

77. Ibid., letter 114, H 7:688.

78. Ibid., letter 115, H 7:687.

79. *Ideen zur Philosophie der Geschichte der Menschheit*, H 6:626.

80. Ibid., 668.

81. Ibid., H 6:634.

82. Ibid., H 6:655, 667ff.

83. *Auch eine Philosophie*, H 39.

84. *Briefe zu Beförderung*, letter 119, H 7:722ff.

85. *Ideen zur Philosophie der Geschichte der Menschheit*, H 4:187ff.

1. "Was kann eine gute stehende Bühne eigentlich wirken?" Sch 5:828.

2. Hessian subjects took part, in some numbers. Hessians and Prussians were earlier offered to fight against the Scottish clans in the 1745 uprising. True to Schiller's depiction (Lady Milford's diamonds), rulers used proceeds for luxuries, e.g., the celebrated *Dragonervasen*, oriental vases that August the Strong of Saxony was able to acquire by selling a regiment of dragoons.

3. See the chapter "Miller the Musician" in Auerbach, *Mimesis*.

4. "The Stage as a Moral Institution" (its final title), Sch 5:823.

5. Schiller to Dalberg, 7 June and 24 August 1784.

6. Schiller to Dalberg, 7 June 1784.

7. Schiller to his brother-in-law Reinwald, 27 March and 14 April 1783.

8. Schiller, *Briefe über Don Carlos*, letter 6, Sch 2:245.

9. German princes commonly referred to themselves—Karl Eugen of Württemberg often did—as "fathers of their people." Cf. Tocqueville, *L'ancien régime et la révolution*, 1:xii.

10. Milton, *Paradise Lost*, book 5, lines 394ff.

11. It echoes Frederick the Great's bitter comment on the reported progress of education in Silesia, based now on a Rousseauian belief in human goodness: "Ah, mon cher Sulzer, vous ne connoissez pas assez cette maudite race à laquelle nous appartenons." Quoted in Kant, *Anthropologie*, K 8:227.

12. Quoted in Parker, *Philip II*, 36.

13. *Über naïve und sentimentalische Dichtung*, Sch 5:776.

14. K IV:170.

15. The protagonist overthrows a tyrant, and will either rejoice in the city's freedom or take power himself. The uncertainty was Schiller's—he wrote three divergent endings.

16. Carl August to Wieland, 27 July 1772.

17. Wieland, *Agathon*, book 9, chapter 3. W 1:710, 717ff.

18. D'Alembert, "Essai sur la société des Gens de lettres et des Grands," in *Œuvres*, Paris 1822, 4:357ff.

19. W 7:59, 61.

20. Ibid., 156.

21. Tocqueville, *L'ancien régime et la révolution*, 3:247.

22. "Comme le principe du gouvernement despotique est la crainte, le but en est la tranquillité, mais ce n'est point une paix, c'est le silence de ces villes que l'ennemi est près d'occuper." *De l'esprit des lois*, book 5, chapter 14, in Montesquieu, *Oeuvres*, 1:96.

23. *Egmont*, act 4, "Albas Wohnung" scene, HA 4:430.

24. *Don Carlos*, act 3, scene 10, verses 3196ff.

25. Ibid., verse 3160.

26. *Egmont*, HA 4:429.

27. "Gedanken ohne Inhalt sind leer, Anschauungen ohne Begriffe sind blind." *Critique of Pure Reason*, K 3:80, B 75.

28. In act 1, scene 2, Arkas urges her to marry the king lest he carry out his threat

and reverse the social progress she has brought to Tauris. Agreeing would make her once again a sacrifice, this time to the cause of Enlightenment.

29. There are exact parallels with the finally benevolent Pascha in Mozart's *Abduction from the Seraglio*.

30. Orestes to Iphigenia: "Now I begin to see [Apollo's] purpose: he intended that I should find you here." But this Orestes is still going to steal the statue, and this Iphigenia has no scruples about going along with his plan. Euripides, *Alcestis and Other Plays*, 104. Racine's Iphigénie is more passive still in the face of male plans, even for her own sacrifice.

31. "What Is Enlightenment?," K 4:169, and *Anthropologie*, K 8:97ff., a lecturer's joke (to his wholly male audience) linking *mündig* with its seeming derivation from *Mund*.

32. Line 1716: "Rettet mich Und rettet euer Bild in meiner Seele." Lines 1917ff.: "Wenn Ihr wahrhaft seid wie ihr gepriesen werdet, / So zeigt's durch euern Beistand und verherrlicht / Durch mich die Wahrheit."

33. *Critique of Pure Reason*, K 3:396, B 596–98. For a fuller treatment, see below, p. 164.

34. Robertson, "Torture Is My Pleasure."

35. It is striking that in the last days before he was murdered by the Nazis, three of Dietrich Bonhoeffer's jailers helped smuggle out the letters that would become classic documents of the German resistance. See Schlingensiepen, *Dietrich Bonhoeffer*, 356ff.

36. "Der Dichter . . . sucht sich von den Zuständen beider kämpfenden Teile zu durchdringen, wo er denn, wenn Vermittlung unmöglich wird, sich entschließen muss, tragisch zu enden." *Campagne in Frankreich*, HA 10:361.

37. Lessing's foreword, Lg 2:748. In the text this is most explicit in the Templar's speech in act 2, scene 5: "Where and when has the pious crazed belief / Your god is better, and you must impose / This better god on everybody else, / Shown up in darkest form but here and now? / If *here* the scales do not fall from your eyes. . . ."

38. For the ethical implications, see below, p. 97.

39. Goethe, "Über das deutsche Theater," MA 11.2:164, quoted in Lg 2:754. Soberingly, contemporary reception as reported by Moses Mendelssohn (ibid., 2:751ff.) was cold: so far from having addressed the sophisticated intellectual culture the play's existence seemed to prove, Lessing found himself ostracized by former friends and acquaintances who had taken the criticism of Christianity personally. Incidentally, the play was banned in Vienna, and Lessing said he knew no place in Germany where it could yet be put on. Quoted in Herder, *Briefe zu Beförderung der Humanität*, H 7:647.

CHAPTER 5. COSMOPOLITAN QUANDARIES

1. A selection was published for the first time in the edition of the German text in Forster, *Reise um die Welt*.

2. They are printed at AA 4:447ff.

3. The phrase used by an assailant who had been on the voyage with them. See Georg's "Reply to Mr Wales's Remarks," AA 5:15, which shows him also fully at home in the mode of English eighteenth-century polemic, as does his pamphlet "A Letter to the Earl of Sandwich," AA 5:61ff.

4. AA 1:13ff.

5. AA 5:210.

6. *Cook als Entdecker*, AA 5:217.

7. AA 1:660.

8. Ibid., 572.

9. Ibid., 411.

10. Ibid., 269, 491.

11. Ibid., 227.

12. Ibid., 593ff.

13. Ibid., 308.

14. Ibid., 412.

15. Forster to Herder, 21 October 1787, Br 483. Given the density of quotations from letters in the later sections of this chapter, I add page references to the edition listed in the sources.

16. *Cook als Entdecker*, AA 5:249. The notorious Bligh of the *Bounty* served under Cook on his third voyage.

17. Ibid., 235ff.; AA 1:606.

18. AA 5:274.

19. Ibid., 243ff.

20. AA 1:137, 437.

21. On all this in full, see Hough, *Captain James Cook*.

22. The etymological point is made in Wuthenow's book of that title.

23. E.g., in New Zealand, in *Cook the Discoverer*, AA 5:214.

24. *Noch etwas über Menschenrassen*, F 1:33.

25. AA 5:178. For an imaginative reconstruction of the actions and attitudes of both parties, see Matthew Kneale's remarkable novel *English Passengers* (London: Penguin, 2000).

26. AA 5:292ff.; AA 1:483.

27. F 1:69.

28. F 1:67ff.; AA 1:456, 645.

29. AA 1:542.

30. Ibid., 351.

31. AA 8:358ff.; F 1:74ff.

32. AA 5:201.

33. Forster to Jacobi, 15 November 1789, Br 583.

34. F 1:82ff.

35. *Noch etwas über Menschenrassen*.

36. To Körner, 25 November 1789. Br 586.

37. *Anthropologie*, K 8, fn. 4.

38. Forster to Heyne, 30 August 1790, and to Jacobi, 19 November 1788, Br 527 and 619.

39. See above, p. 12.

40. See above, p. 12ff.

41. *Geschichte der Farbenlehre*, HA 14:91. See below, p. 125.

42. E.g., in his essay "Ein Blick in das Ganze der Natur," AA 8:358ff.

43. From a sonnet addressed to a dead friend, "Sennucio mio." Martin McLaughlin kindly located the source.

44. AA 1:178.

45. AA 1:35.

46. In "What Is Enlightenment?," K 4:170.

47. F 2:123ff., 163ff.

48. Ibid., 315.

49. Ibid., 315ff.

50. Ibid., 361, 389.

51. Ibid., 405.

52. "Richtigen Begriffen von unsern wesentlichen Bedürfnissen." Lbg 1:688.

53. The French text in Wuthenow, *Vernunft und Republik*, 89ff.

54. Br 701.

55. *Darstellung der Revolution in Mainz*, F 1:191.

56. HA 10:264.

57. To C. G.Voigt, 15 October 1792.

58. *Campagne in Frankreich*, HA 10, p. 235.

59. Forster to Huber, 25 October 1792, Br 770.

60. To Heyne, 12 July 1791, Br 667.

61. To Voss, 21 December 1792, Br 808.

62. To Heyne, 5 June 1792, Br 718.

63. To Heyne, 23 October 1792, Br 769.

64. To Heyne, 26 October 1792, Br 771.

65. To Heyne, 10 November 1792, Br 781.

66. To Huber, 24 October 1792, Br 766.

67. Goethe to Huber, 26 October 1792, Br 772.

68. *Darstellung der Revolution in Mainz*, F 1:156.

69. Forster to Huber, 5 December 1792, Br 803.

70. *Revolutionsschriften*, AA 10:1, 647.

71. Ibid., 1, 173.

72. Forster to Therese Forster, 31 December 1792, Br 814.

73. Forster to Therese Forster, 28 January 1793, Br 824.

74. Forster to Therese Forster, 2 January 1793, Br 818.

75. Forster to Therese Forster, 28 January and 4 February 1793, Br 828, 833.

76. Br 847.

77. Br 848.

78. Br 886.

79. Br 901.

80. Providence, e.g., Br 922, 925, 927; Fate, Br 959.

81. Br 939.

82. *Parisische Umrisse*, F 1:230ff.

83. *Über die Beziehung der Staatskunst auf das Glück der Menschheit*, F 1:148ff.

84. *Parisische Umrisse*, F 1:243.

85. Ibid., 233.

86. Ibid, 224.

87. Ibid., 217ff.

CHAPTER 6. THE EMPTY HEAVENS

1. "Luth'risch, Päpstisch und Calvinisch, diese Glauben alle drei / Sind verhanden; doch ist Zweifel, wo das Christentum dann sei." Haufe, *"Wir vergehn wie Rauch von starken Winden."*

2. Gagliardo, *Germany under the Old Regime*, 177.

3. For details of the intrigues against Wolff, see Georg Volkmar Hartmann, in Killy 2:1027ff. Praising the ethical Chinese was not even a novelty—Leibniz had said much the same. See Perkins, *Leibniz and China: A Commerce of Light.*

4. Quoted in Hettner, *Geschichte der deutschen Literatur im achtzehnten Jahrhundert*, 212.

5. See above, pp. 48ff.

6. Quoted respectively in Scholz, *Die Hauptschriften zum Pantheismusstreit*, 52, and Nicolai, *Goethe und Jacobi*, 312.

7. Cf. Weimar, "'Ihr Götter!'"

8. To Lavater, 28 October 1779.

9. In stanza 7 of the poem from the *West-Östlicher Divan*, "Vermächtnis altpersischen Glaubens": *"Schwerer Dienste tägliche Bewahrung, / Sonst bedarf es keiner Offenbarung."* HA 2:105 (emphasis in original). Similarly, Goethe to Eckermann, 25 February 1824, on the idea of immortality as something for idle aristocrats, especially ladies, or for those whom life has treated unkindly, and irrelevant to anyone who has practical things to strive for on earth.

10. Goethe to Lavater, 9 August 1782.

11. See the essay "Of Miracles," in Hume, *Essays Moral, Political and Literary*, 2:93ff.

12. To Gottlob Friedrich Ernst Schönborn, 1 June–4 July 1774.

13. Goethe to Jacobi, 5 May 1786. In an earlier letter to Jacobi (21 October 1785), Goethe had rejected the "unstable airy realm" of "belief sophists" who were unable to "shake the foundations of truth." That Spinoza's metaphysics provided a basis for science is an idea not peculiar to Goethe. See Hampshire, *Spinoza*, 47ff. Further to Goethe's science, see below, pp. 122ff.

14. Goethe to Jacobi, 9 June 1785.

15. Cf. the opening of Büchner's Zurich trial lecture of 1836, "On the Cranial Nerves," arguing that organisms are governed by a fundamental "law of beauty"; and the last page of Darwin's *Origin of Species*, a meditation on how "from so simple a beginning endless forms most beautiful and most wonderful have been, and are being, evolved."

16. Goethe to Lavater, 9 August 1782.

17. Goethe to Lavater, 4 October 1782.

18. Goethe to Auguste von Stolberg, 17 April 1823.

19. See Altmann, *Moses Mendelssohn*, 16ff. There were other pettifogging pressures, such as the requirement placed on Jews to buy unwanted sets of Berlin porcelain, that

point toward to the ever intensifying harassments that Jews still surviving in the cities were subjected to by the Nazis, as chronicled in Klemperer, *Tagebücher.*

20. See chapter 1 of Robertson, *The "Jewish Question" in German Literature;* and Schulte, *Die jüdische Aufklärung.*

21. Dohm, *Über die bürgerliche Verbesserung der Juden.* Dohm had worked through the issues with Mendelssohn.

22. Lg 8:13.

23. Goethe may have had this celebrated passage in mind when he wrote, in the notes to his collection of oriental poems the *West-Östlicher Divan,* that "the original value of every religion can only be judged from their effects after the elapse of centuries." HA 2:149.

24. Forster to Jacobi, 7 December 1784.

25. *Eine Duplik,* Lg 8:31. Again there is an echo of Montaigne: "Car nous sommes niais à quester la vérité; il appartient de la posséder à une plus grande puissance." *Essais* 3, viii, "De l'art de conférer." Montaigne, *Essais,* 1038.

26. Quoted in Herder, *Briefe zu Beförderung der Humanität,* H 7:641.

27. See "Natural History of Religion," in Hume, *Essays Moral, Political and Literary,* 2:337.

28. Gibbon, *History of the Decline and Fall of the Roman Empire,* book 1, chapter 21.

29. Kant, "Versuch über die Krankheiten des Kopfes," K 2:311.

30. Boie to Bürger, January 1778.

31. Lg 5:72. The motif of "seeing with one's own eyes" crops up in an early fragment of Lessing's in praise of the independent Herrnhut sect.

32. Quoted in Hazard, *La crise de la conscience européenne,* 183.

33. Arnold, *Unparteyische Kirchen- und Ketzergeschichte.* The book was a major influence on the young Goethe. Cf. *Dichtung und Wahrheit,* book 8, HA 9:350.

34. Lg 7:17. As was already clear to the twenty-year-old Lessing. See the letter of 30 May 1749 to his irate father.

35. Lg 7:494. The metaphor was duly mocked by the contemporary neologist theologian Johann Salomo Semler. See Schweitzer, *The Quest of the Historical Jesus,* 15. Schweitzer incidentally calls the *Fragments* "one of the greatest events in the history of criticism . . . written in the just consciousness of so absolute a superiority to contemporary opinion." Ibid. More drastically, the "death of God" has been dated from the *Fragments* controversy. Timm, *Gott und die Freiheit,* 1:22.

36. "Bibliolatrie." Lg 7:672. Similarly his riposte to a zealot who wanted to deny him "all claims to the name of a Christian." Lg 7:959.

37. "Die Religion Christi," §2. Lg 7:711ff.

38. "Aus den Papieren des Ungenannten: Gegensätze des Herausgebers." Lg 7:458.

39. *Die Erziehung des Menschengeschlechts* (1780). Lg 8:489ff.

40. Cf. Christie-Murray, *A History of Heresy,* 111.

41. See Nisbet, *Lessing,* 748.

42. In the fourth of the dialogues on Freemasonry, *Ernst und Falk* (1778). "*Wer wollte einem raschen Knaben, weil er dann und wann noch fällt, den Gängelwagen wieder einschwätzen?*" (emphasis in original). Lg 8:474.

43. Kant, *Critique of Pure Reason*, opening pages; Goethe to Herder, 4 September 1788; Lichtenberg, Lbg 1:652.

44. Gay, *The Enlightenment*, 1:151 (not coined apropos Lessing).

45. *Religion within the Bounds of Mere Reason*, K 6:252. Emphasis in original.

46. The first fifty-three sections were originally published in 1777 as a response to Reimarus. There is evidence for thinking that the remaining forty-seven were already written by then.

47. Gibbon, *History of the Decline and Fall of the Roman Empire*, book 1, chapter 2. Montesquieu uses the same argument in his *Politique des Romains dans la religion*.

48. "Selbstbesprechung," Sch 1:627.

49. Lbg 2:443.

50. Quoted in Hettner, *Geschichte der deutschen Literatur im achtzehnten Jahrhundert*, 212ff.

51. K 4:175.

52. MacCulloch, *History of Christianity*, 26.

53. K 4:175.

54. "Wie viel andächtig schwärmen leichter als / Gut handeln ist." *Nathan der Weise*, act 1, scene 2; Lg 2:218.

55. Lbg 1:947.

56. In the brief essay "Vom Gebet," K 4:525ff.

57. *Grundlegung*, K 4:265.

58. *Religion innerhalb*, K 6:253. Lucretius, *De rerum natura*, line 101. Incidentally, the reference is to Agamemnon's sacrificing of Iphigenia.

59. K 6:353.

60. K 6:257.

61. Which Kant knew. See the reference in the essay *Theory and Practice*, K 6:392. He also naturally knew about the controversial Reimarus *Fragments* (K 6:224n).

62. In the "Transcendental Dialectic," K 3:405–40, B 611–69.

63. Freud, *The Future of an Illusion*, in *Studienausgabe*, 9:166.

64. *Grundlegung*, K 4:302.

65. See below, p. 119.

66. K 3:396, B 597ff.

67. *Grundlegung*, K 4:279. Though Kant does earlier concede (*Der einzig mögliche Beweisgrund des Daseins Gottes*, K 2:170) that the unsustainable ontological proof of God's existence—postulating the thing than which nothing can be greater—can at least imbue people with "elevated feelings that are fruitful in noble activity," a parallel to Goethe's idea of the ennobling effects of hypothetical belief in "Das Göttliche."

68. *Grundlegung zur Metaphysik der Sitten*, K 4:287.

69. Ibid., 291, 295, 323.

70. Ibid., 317. There is a close parallel with Goethe's account of human freedom within nature's "iron laws" in "Das Göttliche."

71. K 5:168.

72. *Critique of Practical Reason*, §6, K 5:34ff.

73. *Grundlegung*, K 4:315.

74. *Grundlegung*, respectively K 4:246, 260, 250.

75. *Theory and Practice*, K 6:369.

76. *Tagebücher, 1775–1787*, WA 3:1, 24, 54, 74, 94. There are numerous other passages sometimes applying the term to Duke Carl August.

77. Biester to Kant, 29 June 1784, AA 11:516ff.

78. Kiesewetter to Kant, 14 June 1790, K 10:78.

79. Reprinted in Schwarz, *Der erste Kulturkampf*, 100.

80. Kiesewetter to Kant, 3 March 1790, K 10:7ff.

81. Arguments have been put forward for the Edict as in some respects enlightened, e.g., Clark, *Iron Kingdom*, 270–74. The balance is against them. The Edict did, it is true, confirm tolerance between sects, but that was no longer new. Its central point was *intolerance toward free opinion*; and censorship is never enlightened. True, there were allegations of slackness and simony in the church at the time, which needed reform but they are not what the Edict was aimed against. See Hinze, "Die Epochen des evangelischen Kirchenregiments in Preussen," in Büsch and Neugebauer, 3:1229.

82. Johann Christoph (von) Wöllner. Frederick the Great had refused to ennoble this "deceitful intriguer of a priest." Piltz, *Friedrich II: Wonach er sich zu richten hat*, 45.

83. K 7:316. For the full episode, see below, p. 150.

84. Thus in a letter to Goethe of 2 August 1799. Two epigrams in the satirical *Xenien*, whether by Goethe or Schiller is not clear (the *Xenien* were a joint work), satirize Kant's rigorism and the problem it raises: "Friends I am happy to help, but alas! it's just inclination. / So I'm often upset that I'm not moral at all." And the ironic answer: "There's nothing for it, you'll simply have to try and despise them / And with revulsion perform everything duty commands."

85. See the long footnote to the second edition of *Religion within the Bounds of Pure Reason*, K 6:161ff. For Schiller's relieved reaction to Kant's reaction, see his letter to Körner of 18 May 1794.

86. "das morsche Gebäude der Dummheit geflickt." Schiller to Körner, 28 February 1793.

87. Non-Germanists may know at least the eloquent stanza picked out by Schubert as the text of his song "Die Götter Griechenlands."

88. "*Einen* zu bereichern" (l:155). The closest parallel in English is a little-noticed sonnet of John Keats, "Written in Disgust of Vulgar Superstition," which includes the lines "Surely the mind of man is closely bound / In some black spell." But Keats believes Christianity is "dying like an outburnt lamp." His own elegiac devotion to Greece ("Ode on a Grecian Urn," "Ode to Psyche") needs no emphasizing.

89. This was to overlook the inspiration some science (Newton's especially) gave to poetry, as documented in Nicolson, *Newton Demands the Muse*.

90. Fambach, *Schiller und sein Kreis*, 54, 55, 59, 56.

91. Ibid., 68.

92. "Das Lob des einzigen Gottes, ein Gegenstück zu den Göttern Griechenlands," *Teutscher Merkur*, August 1789. (Schiller's poem had appeared there in March 1788.) In an endnote Wieland reserved the right to adjudicate between them in a later number of his journal, but he seems never to have done so.

93. For more detail see chapter 10.

94. Goethe to Lavater, 29 July 1782. What follows shows that Goethe has tired of Lavater's excesses.

95. *Nathan der Weise*, act 4, scene 7; Lg 2, 316. Compare such colloquialisms as *unchristliche Stunde* (uncomfortably early time to get up) and *unchristliches Wetter* (dreadful weather).

96. Goethe to Charlotte von Stein, 27 June 1785.

97. Ten volumes, 1783–93. The term *Seele*, though in German never so exclusively religious a term as the English "soul," bespeaks its Pietistic origins.

98. *Menschliches, Allzumenschliches*, I, §131, N 1:530.

99. Goethe to Eckermann, 6 June 1831.

100. The Austrian orientalist Joseph von Hammer-Purgstall published his translation of Hafiz in 1812.

101. HA 2:146.

102. Ibid., 130, 145.

103. Ibid., 143.

104. Ibid., 144.

105. "Vom Himmel steigend," *Book of Parables*, HA 2:102.

106. "Höheres und Höchstes," *Book of Paradise*, HA 2:116.

107. "Deine Liebe, dein Kuss," *Book of Paradise*, HA 2:114.

108. One poem does declare oral tradition—the alleged mode of transmission of the Koran—to be mere fantasy: "Glaubst du denn," *Book of Ill-Humour*, HA 2:48ff. A poem referring to Goethe's bête noire, the cross—"Süßes Kind, die Perlenreihen" (HA 2:122)—was left out on the pleading of Goethe's Catholic friend Sulpiz Boisserée.

109. "Wer sich selbst und andre kennt," HA 2:121. This, it is true, was unaccountably left in the Nachlass section.

110. "Närrisch, dass jeder," *Book of Aphorisms*, HA 2:56.

111. "Keinen Reimer wird man finden," *Book of Ill-Humour*, HA 2:43.

112. "Talismane," *Book of the Singer*, HA 2:10.

113. HA 2:127. The prepublication announcement of his new collection says, less plausibly, that he "does not reject the suspicion he is himself a Muslim." HA 2:268.

114. The phrase occurs twice in Spinoza's *Ethics*, part 4, Preface, and Proposition IV, Proof, but en passant as something presupposed, not a major new insight. Peter Hacker kindly located it. See *Ethics*, 142, 147.

CHAPTER 7. APPLES AND AFTER

1. Gay, *The Bridge of Criticism*, 9.

2. As late as 1735 a prominent defender of the church against science, the Prussian theologian Valentin Ernst Löscher, was still attacking the "extremely uncertain doctrines that the sun stands still and our globe revolves around it." Killy 1:20ff.

3. Wordsworth, *The Prelude* (1928 ed.), book 3, line 61.

4. Cf. Brooke, "The God of Isaac Newton," 169.

5. Newton, *Opticks*, 402.

6. See above, pp. 43, 104.

7. "Soizein ta phainomena." Plutarch, *Moralia, De facie in orbe lunae,* 932A. I owe the reference to Donald Russell.

8. Book 8, lines 81ff.

9. Kant, *Träume eines Geistersehers,* K 2:364ff.

10. Lbg 1:65.

11. "Die Sinne betrügen nicht, . . . weil sie gar nicht urteilen, weswegen der Irrtum immer nur dem Verstande zur Last fällt." *Anthropologie,* §11, K 8:31. The crucial distinction had already been made by Bacon in *The Advancement of Learning.*

12. Lbg 3:173; HA 14:81.

13. As was neatly pointed out by Ludwig Wittgenstein in a conversation with Elizabeth Anscombe reported in her *Introduction to Wittgenstein's "Tractatus,"* 151.

14. Kant, *Träume eines Geistersehers,* K 2:364ff. A later maxim of Goethe's, from the Nachlass, gets it right, exactly reproducing Kant's insight: "The senses do not deceive. The judgment deceives" (Die Sinne trügen nicht, das Urteil trügt). Another maxim from the same batch spells it out more fully, recommending a progressive skepticism that will arrive through ordered experience at a kind of conditional reliability. HA 12:406. The same view informs the very Kantian late poem "Vermächtnis," HA 1:370. For more on this, see p. 195.

15. Quoted in Andrade, *Sir Isaac Newton,* 72ff.

16. Lbg 1:130; 2, 83.

17. Lichtenberg to F. W. Wolff, 30 December 1784. An achromatic telescope was developed by Herschel.

18. Lichtenberg to Wolff, 6 January 1785, Lbg 4:603.

19. Lichtenberg to Samuel Sömmering, 26 December 1785, Lbg 4:657ff. This was an impression of the bust by Louis-François Roubiliac.

20. Lbg 2:693.

21. *Gedanken von der wahren Schätzung der lebendigen Kräfte.* K 1:5, 8, 15.

22. An epigram played on the title of this work. In estimating "live forces," had Kant not overestimated his own? Lg 1:47. Kant does appear to have overestimated his own grasp of current mathematical thinking. See Cassirer, *Kants Leben und Lehre,* 28.

23. "Der glücklichste Versuch, den der menschliche Verstand in der Erkenntnis der Natur noch getan hat." K 1:480.

24. "Besondere Klumpen." K 1:342. The earth is similarly called "the great lump we live on" (der große Klumpen, den wir bewohnen). K 1:442.

25. K 1:223.

26. K 1:225.

27. Plato, *Laws,* §889, in *Dialogues,* 4:457ff.

28. Foreword, K 2:71.

29. "Der sich selbst überlassenen Natur." K 1:223.

30. Heisenberg, "Die Einheit des naturwissenschaftlichen Weltbildes," in *Wandlungen in den Grundlagen der Naturwissenschaft,* 78.

31. "Gebt mir nur Materie, ich will euch eine Welt daraus bauen." There are slight variations at each occurrence, K 1:231, 232. Given that evolution by natural selection needs genetic materials from somewhere to work on, and given that the origins of the

Big Bang are still (as of April 2014) not fully understood, that seems to be the unchanged position of modern science.

32. *Critique of Judgment*, §75, K 5:476ff. Once again, the natural genesis of a "blade of grass" is his illustration (p. 479). The increasingly powerful idea of a self-ordering universe is also in Hume's *Dialogues Concerning Natural Religion* (1779), parts II and IV.

33. K 1:236. Cassirer, *Kants Leben und Lehre*, 72. Cassirer was writing in 1918, before the rehabilitation of the Kant-Laplace hypothesis.

34. K 1:223. Cf. above, p. 34. On Pierre Laplace, see Holmes, *The Age of Wonder*, 198.

35. K 1:316.

36. See Broadie, *The Scottish Enlightenment*, 212ff.

37. K 1:311.

38. "Finger Gottes," K 1:341; earlier, "Hand Gottes," K 1:264.

39. K 1:349ff. Spinoza had long ago made the same point about the "conveniences and inconveniences" of nature, which happened "promiscuously to the pious and impious." *Ethics*, book 1, Appendix, 31ff.

40. K 1:429.

41. K 1:430.

42. "Poème sur le désastre de Lisbonne," in Voltaire, *Mélanges*, 305.

43. K 1:468.

44. Goeze, *Zwo Predigten*.

45. "Der Mensch ist von sich selbst so eingenommen, dass er sich lediglich als das einzige Ziel der Anstalten Gottes ansiehet. . . . Wir sind ein Teil derselben und wollen das Ganze sein." K 1:472.

46. Mann, *Der Zauberberg*, in *Sämtliche Werke*, 5.1:726.

47. Voltaire begins with the rhetoric of suffering and protest but ends by humbly accepting the actions of providence; doubt is resolved by Revelation, leaving a vague hope that "un jour tout sera bien"—presumably in the afterlife. As Voltaire wrote to Madame de Fontaine on 17 March 1756, perhaps ironically, but accurately, he has argued "très chrétiennement." *Mélanges*, 1389.

48. HA 14:259.

49. MA 10:275.

50. Ibid., §§6–8.

51. Ibid., §28.

52. "Heilige Scheu," "die alte starre Konfession," ibid., §31.

53. "Vorurteil—ein Urteil vor der Untersuchung," "taschenspielerisch," "durch solches Hokuspokus betrügen," ibid., §§30, 45.

54. *Maximen und Reflexionen*, nr. 690, HA 12:463.

55. "Dass wirklich nunmehr das Ganze nicht mehr einer freiwirkenden Republik, sondern einem despotischen Hofe ähnlich wird." *Der Versuch als Vermittler von Objekt und Subjekt*, HA 13:16.

56. HA 13:537.

57. See Steinle, "'Das Nächste an das Nächste reihen.'"

58. The heading to §6 in the "didactic part" of the *Farbenlehre*, HA 13:494.

59. "Der größte und genaueste physikalische Apparat, den es geben kann." HA 12:458.

60. "Mikroskope und Fernröhre verwirren eigentlich den reinen Menschensinn." *Maxims and Reflexions (MuR)*, no. 469, HA 12:430.

61. See Kemp, *The Science of Art*, especially chapter 7. On Goethe and Runge, see 295ff.; on Goethe and Turner, see 303ff. Of Turner's "Goethe paintings," one (Kemp, plate X) has an express reference in the title: *Light and Color (Goethe's Theory)—The Morning after the Deluge*. See also Currie, *Goethe's Visual World*.

62. *MuR*, no. 450, HA 12:427.

63. *MuR*, no. 465, HA 12:429, unidentified quotation.

64. *MuR*, no. 461, ibid.

65. *MuR*, no. 631, HA 12:451.

66. "Am meisten freut mich ietzo das Pflanzenwesen, das mich verfolgt. . . . Es zwingt sich mir alles auf, ich sinne nicht mehr darüber, es kommt mir alles entgegen und das ungeheure Reich simplificirt sich mir in der Seele, daß ich bald die schwerste Aufgabe gleich weglesen kann. . . . Es ist ein Gewahrwerden der wesentlichen Form, mit der die Natur gleichsam nur immer spielt und spielend das manigfaltige Leben hervorbringt. Hätt ich Zeit in dem kurzen Lebensraum; so getraut ich mich es auf alle Reiche der Natur— auf ihr ganzes Reich—auszudehnen." Goethe to Charlotte von Stein, 10 July 1786.

67. *Italienische Reise*, 17 April 1787, HA 11:266.

68. Staiger, *Goethe*, 2:413.

69. "Das schönste Glück des denkenden Menschen ist, das Erforschliche erforscht zu haben und das Unerforschliche ruhig zu verehren." *MuR*, no. 718, HA 12:467.

70. "Baco, dem in der Breite der Erscheinung alles gleich war. . . . Ehe man durch Induktion . . . zur Vereinfachung und Abschluß gelangen kann, geht das Leben weg und die Kräfte verzehren sich." HA 14:91.

71. "Das Höchste wäre zu begreifen, daß alles Faktische schon Theorie ist. . . . Man suche nur nichts hinter den Phänomenen: sie selbst sind die Lehre." *MuR*, no. 488, HA 12:432.

72. "Was ist das Allgemeine? Der einzelne Fall. Was ist das Besondere? Millionen Fälle." *MuR*, no. 489, ibid., 433.

73. In the account of his first meeting with Schiller, at the meeting of a Jena scientific society in 1794. "Glückliches Ereignis," HA 10:540.

74. "Werdend betrachte sie nun," line 9 of "Die Metamorphose der Pflanzen," HA 1:199.

75. HA 13:583ff. Similarly, Fontenelle's *Entretiens sur la pluralité des mondes* of 1701 and Algarotti's *Newtonianismo per le dame* of 1736.

76. "Den Blick und die Freude." Goethe to Charlotte von Stein, 10 July 1786.

77. "Die Reiche der Welt und ihre Herrlichkeit," 12 April 1782. Cf. Matt. 4:8.

78. "Die gehässigen Knochen und das öde Steinreich." Quoted in HA 13:587.

79. "Zweck sein selbst ist jegliches Tier." From "Metamorphose der Tiere," line 12, HA 1:201.

80. "Es ist wie der Schlußstein des Menschen." Goethe to Herder, 27 March 1784.

81. "Bewegliche Ordnung." From "Metamorphose der Tiere," line 51, HA 1:203.

82. "Natürlich System, ein widersprechender Ausdruck. Die Natur hat kein System, sie hat, sie ist Leben und Folge aus einem unbekannten Zentrum, zu einer nicht erkennbaren Grenze." *Probleme*, HA 13:35.

83. "Die Metamorphose der Pflanzen," lines 67ff.

84. "Maifest," stanzas 2 and 3; HA 1:30.

85. Whether Goethe's quasi-poetic vision constitutes a distinct form of consciousness, itself difficult to define in nonmystical terms, is dubious. See Bortoft, *The Wholeness of Nature*.

86. "Die Natur nicht gesondert und vereinzelt vorzunehmen, sondern sie wirkend und lebendig, aus dem Ganzen in die Teile strebend darzustellen.""Glückliches Ereignis," HA 10:540.

87. See above, p. 110.

88. "Es ist der nackte, schneidende Verstand, der die Natur, die immer unfaßlich und in allen ihren Punkten ehrwürdig und ergründlich ist, schamlos ausgemessen haben will und mit einer Frechheit, die ich nicht begreife, seine Formeln, die oft nur leere Worte und immer nur enge Begriffe sind, zu ihrem Maßstabe macht. Er hat keine Einbildungskraft; und so fehlt ihm, nach meinem Urtheil das nothwendigste Vermögen zu seiner Wissenschaft—denn die Natur muß angeschaut und empfunden werden, in ihren einzelnsten Erscheinungen, wie in ihren höchsten Gesetzen." Schiller to Körner, 6 August 1797.

89. As suggested in Krätz, *Goethe und die Naturwissenschaften*, 118.

90. "Dadurch allein, dass wir die ganze Energie unsers Geistes in *einem* Brennpunkt versammeln und unser ganzes Wesen in eine einzige Kraft zusammenziehen, setzen wir dieser einzelnen Kraft gleichsam Flügel an und führen sie künstlicherweise weit über die Schranken hinaus, welche die Natur ihr gesetzt zu haben scheint." *Briefe über die ästhetische Erziehung des Menschen*, letter 6, Sch 5:587.

91. "Kann aber wohl der Mensch dazu bestimmt sein, über irgendeinem Zwecke sich selbst zu versäumen?" Ibid, 588.

92. "Earthquake . . . whose effects were so admirably investigated by . . . Kant." Humboldt, *Cosmos*, 1:206. "Speculated with admirable sagacity on . . . star formation." Ibid., 4:301.

93. Humboldt, *Kosmos*, 4, 6ff., 905.

94. Humboldt to Varnhagen von Ense, end of 1834.

95. Quoted in Holmes, *The Age of Wonder*, 198.

96. "Das Weihnachtsfest unserer neuen Zeit." Diary entry for 24 June 1831, WA 3:13, 99.

97. "Fing sich ein neuer Himmel und eine neue Erde an." In "Nicolaus Copernicus," Lbg 3:171, quoting Rev. 21:1.

98. "Die Naturwissenschaft handelt nicht mehr von der Welt, die sich uns unmittelbar darbietet, sondern von einem dunklen Hintergrund, den wir durch unsere Experimente ans Licht bringen." Heisenberg, "Die Goethesche und die Newtonsche Farbenlehre im Lichte der modernen Physik," in *Wandlungen in den Grundlagen der Naturwissenschaft*, 69.

99. Lbg 1:559. Gerlach Adolf von Münchhausen was in practice the founder and first curator of the university. Its first administrative head was the Swiss poet and scientist Albrecht von Haller.

100. Quoted in Promies, *Lichtenberg in Selbstzeugnissen und Bilddokumenten*, 57.

101. Ibid., 63.

102. Lbg 2:205. The Montgolfier brothers had invented and flown the aerostatic balloon.

103. "Ein großer Fehler . . . war, dass ich den Plan zum Gebäude zu groß anlegte." Lbg 2:401.

104. "Die Kunst alle Dinge recht tief unten anzufangen." Lbg 2:85.

105. Lbg 1:155.

106. Lbg 1:1256.

107. Lbg 2:615.

108. "Rich confusion," Lbg 2:333; "use everything," Lbg 2:195.

109. Cf. Schöne, *Aufklärung aus dem Geist der Experimentalphysik*.

110. Lbg 1:294.

111. Lbg 1:532.

112. There are statues of Lichtenberg in the central square in Göttingen and in front of the university library.

113. Lbg 3:270ff.

114. Knigge, *Über den Umgang mit Menschen*, 74.

115. His contributions, on physiognomics generally and on images of Brutus and Rameau, are reprinted in vol. 17 of Goethe, *Werke, Briefe und Gespräche*, 439–51.

116. *Dichtung und Wahrheit*, book 19, HA 10:162–65.

117. Lavater, *Physiognomische Fragmente*, 3:218ff.

118. Lbg 4:181.

119. For more on this novel and on the Pietistic background, see above, pp. 145ff.

120. "Fakta, und kein moralisches Geschwätz." M 1:811.

121. "Vorschlag zu einem Magazin einer Erfahrungs-Seelenkunde." Ibid., 795.

122. Hume, *A Treatise of Human Nature*, xix.

123. "Vorschlag," 793.

124. Lbg 1:447.

125. "Fragment von Schwänzen. Ein Beitrag zu den Physiognomischen Fragmenten." Lbg 3:533ff.

126. Lbg 1:899.

127. As suggested in Čapek, *The Gardener's Year*, 11.

CHAPTER 8. GOOD GUARDIANSHIP

1. Montaigne, "De l'institution des enfants," in *Essais*, 1:xxvi. Fénelon's *Télémaque* is likewise not a public program but one more "mirror for princes" in narrative form—Telemachus, son of Odysseus, is heir presumptive of Ithaca—and favored as such by Frederick the Great in his youth. Fénelon's explicit recommendations are, like Montaigne's, addressed to a noble lady, this time for the more guarded upbringing of a daughter: "Avis à une dame de qualité sur l'éducation de Mademoiselle sa fille," in *Oeuvres*. On the conception of children that lay behind educational methods, see Ariès, *Centuries of Childhood*.

2. Comenius, *The Great Didactic*, title page and 4ff. Comenius (Komensky) acknowledges several German predecessors, despite that country's "terribly oppressed state." Ibid., 8. They include Luther, who in 1525 apparently called for schools for both sexes and included peasants and artisans. Ibid., 76.

3. Ibid., 66–81.

4. Ibid., 100, 142.

5. Ibid., 89.

6. On Pestalozzi's program and its problems, including parental resistance, see his own account in Killy 2:1072ff.

7. Goethe, *Götz von Berlichingen*, act 1, "Jaxthausen. Götzens Burg," HA 4:88.

8. "Dass ich erkenne, was die Welt / Im Innersten zusammenhält, / Schau' alle Wirkenskraft und Samen, / Und tu' nicht mehr in Worten kramen." *Faust*, lines 382–85. Goethe's own education as a child of the *haute bourgeoisie* seems to have been a relaxed one with private tutors, including one who offered to teach him English in four weeks flat. They parted on good terms, the clients apparently satisfied. See *Dichtung und Wahrheit*, book 4, HA 9:123.

9. This "remarkable mortal" (Goethe to Lavater, 29 July 1782) deserves a brief excursus. Aged sixteen, as a grandson of "old Dessau" (*der alte Dessauer*) who had been a celebrated general in the Prussian army, he served at the start of the Seven Years' War but soon resigned and devoted the rest of his life to peaceful projects and the improvement of his subjects' lives. Frederick scorned him as "the princeling" (*le princillon*) and continued to recruit soldiers and demand subsidies from Anhalt-Dessau. Franz ensured tolerance in a municipality that had a substantial Jewish community (which included, in his childhood, Moses Mendelssohn). Besides education, he instituted public health, including treatment for vagrants passing through, gave the public free access to libraries, a theater and picture galleries. In collaboration with his architect Friedrich Wilhelm von Erdmannsdorf, he built handsome, but by the standards of the day modest, buildings. Together they laid out gardens inspired by stays in England and by Winckelmann's classicism. The Dessau-Wörlitz grounds, designated a Unesco World Heritage site in 2000, were in turn the inspiration for gardens in Potsdam, Bavaria, and Weimar (though Dessau's working model of Vesuvius, unveiled in 1794, remained unique). The great parklands were also partly cultivated for crops. In hard times Franz eased the burden of taxes and created work programs, especially after the floods of 1770–71. His dying words are said to have been, "Do they all have work and bread?" It comes incidentally as no surprise that there should have been a Princess of Anhalt-Dessau to whom the leading mathematician and physicist, Leonhard Euler, found it worth writing over two hundred letters on science and mathematics (Stedall, *The History of Mathematics*, 60). For a full account of Franz's duchy and its influence, see Hirsch, *Dessau-Wörlitz: Zierde und Inbegriff des 18. Jahrhunderts* (the subtitle is a comment of Wieland's).

10. This intriguing case of a still half-wild young man leading another is movingly explored in Goethe's poetic retrospect "Ilmenau" (1783).

11. For Klopstock as he worked on his decades-long project of the epic *Der Messias*; and with a three-year pension for the chronically ill Schiller, when the rumor of his death brought home to Danish admirers the urgency of his need.

12. Basedow, *Allgemeines christliches Gesangbuch für alle Kirchen und Sekten*. It is dedicated to sects that practice toleration and to all Christians who have doubts about divisive sectarian doctrines (*Unterscheidungslehren*). It is not clear which Christians, if any, ever used Basedow's hymnal.

13. Weisse, *Der Kinderfreund*, part 3, 132ff.

14. Basedow, *Für Cosmopoliten*.

15. Goethe's brother-in-law Schlosser; the Swiss thinker Isaak Iselin; the artist Chodowiecki; the dramatist Johann Elias Schlegel; the philosopher Moses Mendelssohn; the theologian Semler; the local historian Möser; Kant's publishers Kanter and Hartknoch, doubtless enlisted by him. Ibid., 56.

16. *Dessau 1776*, K 2:463ff. It was no doubt Kant's doing that his friend Robert Motherby, a Scottish businessman resident in Königsberg, sent his son George to the Philanthropin, as a natural follow-on from a relaxed Rousseauian upbringing. See Kant to Christian Heinrich Wolke, 28 March 1776, K 9:147ff.

17. "Insgesamt im ersten Zuschnitt verdorben, weil alles darin der Natur entgegenarbeitet"; "gewöhnliche Griffe . . . des sich auf seinem Miste verteidigenden alten Herkommens." *An das gemeine Wesen*, K 2:465–67.

18. Brechter, *Anmerkungen über das Basedowische Elementarwerk 1,1*, 12.

19. See Kant to William Crichton, 29 July 1778 (K 9:177), on the Philanthropin as destined to be "the mother of all good schools in the world," and to Wolke, 4 August 1778 (K 9:180), on how Kant was going about getting Crichton on board. This cool calculation throws light on Kant's tactics vis-à-vis Frederick the Great in "Was ist Aufklärung?" See chapter 1.

20. "Zwischen Lavater und Basedow," HA 1:90.

21. K 8:460. These were an obligation that Königsberg professors of philosophy took turns to fulfill—an institutional interest in educational principles that was rare in universities of the day. Published in 1798, Kant's set had clearly been given much earlier, probably from the mid-1770s, and in total four times. See the original editor's foreword, K 8:457, and Caygill, *A Kant Dictionary*, 20.

22. K 8:472.

23. K 8:465. There is one serious flaw in Kant's liberalism. For the male, sexually mature but too young in modern society to marry and father children, Kant says relations with women are to be preferred to the alleged damage of masturbation. It is not clear which women are to serve the young man's turn, and how this can be squared with the "decent respect for the other sex" that is to lead to the "prize of a happy marriage"—or, more fundamentally, with Kant's ethical requirement to use nobody as a mere means. K 8:506ff. He may have been sharing a period assumption formulated in Mandeville's *Fable of the Bees, or Private Vices, Public Benefits* (1724), of the "necessity of sacrificing one part of womankind to preserve the other."

24. Lbg 1:466. Of his own education, Frederick the Great said his father treated him "as a kind of human moldable clay" (*Knetmasse*). Quoted in Dollinger, *Friedrich II. von Preußen*, 13. Frederick's education could not have been more brutal.

25. These are Kant's arguments in the "announcement of his upcoming courses" for 1765–66, K 2:319ff.

26. Cassirer, *Kants Leben und Lehre*, K 11:17.

27. "Erstlich den *verständigen*, dann den *vernünftigen* Mann und endlich den *Gelehrten* bilden." Tellingly, the third stage is already a noun, a professional person, no longer simply a man plus a positive attribute. "Announcement," K 11:319.

28. "Er munterte auf, und zwang angenehm zum *Selbstdenken*; Despotismus war seinem Gemüt fremde." Number 79 of the *Briefe zu Beförderung der Humanität*,

H 7:424ff. Equally eloquent is the variant in letter 21 of the book's first draft, "Briefe, die Fortschritte der Humanität betreffend," H 7:794f.

29. Kant's two reviews are at K 4:177–200. Later still, when Herder attacked Kant's epistemology, he tried misleadingly to project back a critical view of Kant into those early years, when in fact he was wholeheartedly devoted to him. See Rudolf Haym, *Herder*, 1:45–65, especially 51.

30. *Welches sind die wirklichen Fortschritte*, K 8:265.

31. The term "enchanted world" echoes the title of Balthasar Bekker's *Betoverde Weereld* (Amsterdam, 1691–93), which caused "the biggest intellectual controversy of the early Enlightenment." See Israel, *Radical Enlightenment*, 382.

32. K 8:267.

33. Numerous major eighteenth-century figures were forced by necessity to be private tutors early on: Kant, Gottsched, Hamann, Herder, Mendelssohn, Wieland, Jung-Stilling, Fichte, Hölderlin, Schelling, Hegel, Lenz, Schleiermacher, Voss, Jean Paul, and Fröbel. On all aspects of the tutor, and much of value on education generally, see Fertig, *Der Hofmeister*. For a rare case of the ideal tutor, see Friedrich von der Trenck's account of his education, Killy 2:1013ff.

34. On Pietism and its effects in Prussia, see Clark, *Iron Kingdom*, 124–39; Gagliardo, *Germany under the Old Regime*, 181–87. On Pietism's quasi-establishment in Prussia as compared with its lesser role in Württemberg, and with the role of Puritanism in England, see Fulbrook, *Piety and Politics*, especially chapter 7.

35. Cf. Hinrichs, "Hallescher Pietismus als Reformbewegung," in Büsch and Neugebauer, *Moderne preußische Geschichte*, 3:1300.

36. Kant as recorded by Hippel, quoted in Cassirer, *Kants Leben und Lehre*. K 11:13.

37. Ruhnken to Kant, 10 March 1771, K 9:94. As a fellow academic, he was writing in Latin.

38. Cassirer, *Kants Leben und Lehre*, 14.

39. See above, p. 119.

40. See Reisiger, *Johann Gottfried Herder*, 14.

41. See the fragment *Journal meiner Reise im Jahr 1769*, in *Sturm und Drang Schriften*, 314–42. Exuberant as he is, Herder is also au fait with educational and sociological thought from Rousseau and Montesquieu to Basedow. The whole program is to be conducted "in the spirit of Kant." Ibid., 326.

42. The reference is presumably to the sentence "le silence de ces espaces infinis m'effraie" in Pascal's *Pensées*. For what looks like Kant's response, see below, p. 198.

43. Kant, *Anthropologie*, §4, K 8:17ff. Haller's "Incomplete ode on Eternity" of 1743–48 shows him overwhelmed by the dread implications of vastness, with nothing comforting to offset them. A note attached to the poem reads: "Lest anyone take offense at the phrases that speak of death as the end of being or of hope, let me say that all these formulations were meant to be objections that I would have answered, if I had been capable of bringing the ode to completion." Stenzel, *Epochen der deutschen Lyrik*, 173ff.

44. Cf. Aner, *Der Aufklärer Friedrich Nicolai*, 9ff. See Nicolai's account of the latter school's practicality—economics taught by visits to farms and factories, architecture by measuring the school building, mechanics through working models. Killy 2:1011ff.

45. M 1:95ff.

46. Lessing, *Nathan der Weise,* act 4, scene 7. Lg 2:315.

47. Cf. Schings, *Melancholie und Aufklärung,* 227-55.

48. "Erquickendes Licht," "er schmeckte zuerst die *Wonne des Denkens.*" M 1:215.

49. *Neues ABC-Buch, zugleich eine Anleitung zum Denken für Kinder,* M 3:381. This first exploration of the world through pictures and text ultimately shares the impulse behind the great illustrated *Encyclopédie* of Diderot and D'Alembert.

50. "Vorschlag zu einem Magazin einer Erfahrungs-Seelenkunde," M 1:403, 407.

51. M 1:411ff.

52. M 1:439.

53. Gay, *The Enlightenment,* 2:520ff.

54. Goethe to Charlotte von Stein, 11 November 1785. For Goethe's sympathies in this direction, see Freitag, *Goethes Alltagsentdeckungen.*

55. "Damit es an gelahrten Leuten in unsern Landen nicht Mangel gewinne"—the title of Dorfmüller and Konetzny's *Schulpforta* reader. The school's alumni included Klopstock, Fichte, and Nietzsche.

56. On the Karlsschule, see above, pp. 20ff.

57. An engraving of one such school by Chodowiecki is reproduced in Fertig, *Die Hofmeister,* 12. At the fair, the Kinderfreund family come across a book by Friedrich Eberhard von Rochow—also incidentally called *Der Kinderfreund*—designed for use in his *Landschule.* Daughter Luischen is reproved for pride ("What are peasants' children to me?" The tutor's answer: "They're more useful than children of the nobility"). Part 3, 127, 129.

58. Quoted above, p. 233, n. 11.

59. Piltz, *Friedrich II: wonach er sich zu richten hat,* p. 42.

60. E.g., under Ernst the Pious in Sachsen-Gotha.

61. Dollinger, *Friedrich II. von Preußen,* 85.

62. K 3:3.

63. "Also ist die Freiheit der Feder . . . das einzige Palladium der Volksrechte." K 6:388.

64. Zedlitz to Kant, 1 August 1778. K 9:179.

65. Abel, *Jacob Friedrich Abel: eine Quellenedition zum Philosophieunterricht.*

66. See Karl Friedrich von Klöden, in Killy 2:1048.

67. Löscher (see above, p. 241). Killy 1:20.

68. Kiesewetter to Kant, 15 November 1789, K 9:451.

69. Quoted by Kant at the start of his *Conflict of the Faculties,* K 7:316.

70. Biester to Kant, 17 December 1794, K 10:258.

71. The phrase is Peter Gay's, though not coined apropos Kant. Gay, *The Enlightenment,* 1:24.

72. *Der Streit der Fakultäten,* K 7:338.

73. Ibid., 332.

74. Ibid., 345.

75. Ibid., 337.

76. "Provideant consules, ne quid respublica detrimenti capeat." Ibid., 380.

77. Ibid., 402. This appears not to have happened under the new king, Frederick William III; but the king had a utilitarian view of study, favoring "useful arts and sciences"

over what he called "abstract knowledge for the enlightenment of the learned." See his
"Thoughts on the Art of Ruling," set down just before he came to the throne. Kotowski,
"Wilhelm von Humboldt und die Universitäten," in Büsch and Neugebauer, *Moderne
preußische Geschichte*, 3:1351.

78. "Dass die Letzten . . . die Ersten würden." K 7:346. Cf. Matt 20:16; Mark 10:31;
Luke 13:30.

79. This went further than the most liberal university of the day, Göttingen, which
had declared all faculties equal, was committed to freedom of thought, speech, and
publication ("the creeping, despotically treated academic will never produce anything of
value"), and, when headhunting for the new foundation, had expressly sought tolerant
and rational colleagues in theology (among them the Mosheim who is repeatedly praised
in Gibbon's footnotes). See Gerlach Adolf von Münchhausen, in Killy 2:1033ff. Not for
nothing did Kant dedicate *The Conflict of Faculties* to a Göttingen colleague. The university became a cradle for liberal-minded future servants of the state.

80. Johann Benjamin Erhard, "Über die Einrichtung und den Zweck der höheren Leh-
ranstalten," in Engel and Müller, *Gelegentliche Gedanken über Universitäten*, 19–29.

81. Schleiermacher, "Gelegentliche Gedanken über Universitäten," in ibid., 198.

82. Hardenberg and in particular Schuckmann, who persuaded the king that academic
freedom did not necessitate financial independence. Humboldt had suggested creating an
endowment from the income of feudal domains. Ibid., afterword and notes, 309, 327.

83. *Schools and Universities*, in Arnold, *The Complete Prose Works*, 4:207, 262.

84. Goethe did not invent the label, and there had been anticipations of the thing.
Wieland's *Geschichte des Agathon* (1761–67) is an obvious candidate, Moritz's *Anton
Reiser* (1785) another.

85. The manuscript, transcribed by Goethe's Swiss friend Barbara Schulthess, was
discovered in 1910. I quote from Maync's 1911 first edition.

86. Goethe to Jacobi, 3 March 1790.

87. *Wilhelm Meisters theatralische Sendung*, book 6, chapter 14, 414–16.

88. Ibid., book 1, chapter 15, 34.

89. "Was kann eine gute stehende Schaubühne eigentlich wirken?" Sch 5:828–30. See
above, p. 25.

90. The Hamburg project did, however, give rise to a major piece of literary criticism,
Lessing's *Hamburg Dramaturgy*.

91. HA 12:240ff.

92. The same topical warning can be seen in an epigram of Goethe's, often quoted
merely as evidence of Weimar liberal humanism. Germans should give up "national
hopes," and instead "shape" (*bilden*[!]) themselves more freely into human beings: "Zur
Nation euch zu bilden, ihr hoffet es, Deutsche, vergebens: / Bildet, ihr könnt es, dafür
freier zu Menschen euch aus."

93. See the *Annals* (*Tag- und Jahreshefte*), the section "To 1786", HA 10:432.

94. HA 7:446, 495. At moments (e.g., 7, 484, 55off.) this is stated a touch less apodic-
tically. A total denial of Wilhelm's talent would have made the novel's whole conception
implausible.

95. Lothario: "Wenn ein gebildeter Mensch . . . das Gemüt hat, Vormund von
vielen zu sein, sie leitet, dasjenige zur rechten Zeit zu tun, was sie alle doch gerne tun

möchten." HA 7:608. The "alle doch gerne" expresses a guardian's usual presumption that he is guiding his charges in the direction they themselves would want if they did but know it.

96. HA 7:504ff.

97. "Wenn so viele Menschen an dir teilnahmen, deinen Lebensweg kannten und wussten, was zu tun sei, warum führten sie dich nicht strenger? warum nicht ernster? Warum begünstigten sie deine Spiele, anstatt dich davon wegzuführen?" HA 7:495. Other passages (e.g., 7, 443, 537, 594) express the same willingness to let others decide, act, or speak for him. On one occasion Wilhelm does listen to the voices of his own "heart and good sense" and refuses a position offered him. HA 7, 568ff. Schiller, reading the novel appreciatively book by book as it was composed, welcomes precisely this act against the run of play as a mark of Wilhelm's completed education. Schiller to Goethe, 5 July 1796.

98. Goethe to Herder, May 1794. The force of the "Pseudo" is not clear.

99. Schiller to the Duke of Schleswig-Holstein-Augustenburg, 13 July 1793.

100. Sch 5:592.

101. Ibid., 580.

102. Ibid., 590.

103. HA 8:154–57.

104. HA 8:150,153.

105. Already with robust common sense by Goethe's first biographer; see Lewes, *The Life of Goethe*, 539–41.

CHAPTER 9. COMMUNICATION AND BEYOND

1. On this, see "The literary journals" in Blackall, *The Emergence of German as a Literary Language*, and more generally Martens, *Die Botschaft der Tugend*.

2. E.g., the question Frederick had raised of whether laws could be brief. Svarez's talk was published in the *Monatsschrift* 12 (1788): 99ff.

3. Mirabeau called the journal "ce noble antagoniste de la superstition et du fanatisme." *De la monarchie prussienne sous Frédéric le Grand* 5:87. The "flint" metaphor is quoted in Hinske's selection from the journal's first four years; introduction, xvi.

4. For the whole debate, see Hinske and Albrecht, *Was ist Aufklärung?*, 145–369; "a Protestant monthly," ibid., 354; Garve on papal infallibility, ibid., 186.

5. Cf. "Das Geheimnis des Kosmopolitenordens," W 3, especially 556.

6. Nicolai, "*Kritik ist überall, zumal in Deutschland, nötig,*" 428.

7. Ibid., 277.

8. *Grundlegung zur Metaphysik der Sitten*, §2. K 4:266ff.

9. For a fuller account, see Selwyn, *Everyday Life in the German Book Trade*, which discusses Nicolai's immense and largely unexplored correspondence.

10. In the *Briefe die neueste Literatur betreffend*, and in a published tripartite correspondence on the nature of tragedy.

11. Wieland to Tobias Gebler, 7 April 1775,

12. In Goethe's skit *Götter, Helden und Wieland* (1775), Hercules pours scorn on Wieland's "feeble" classicism. Wieland in return celebrated the young Goethe, newly

arrived in Weimar, as a positively magical phenomenon. See the poem "An Psychen," W 4:623ff.

13. See Lessing's praise of Wieland's *Agathon* as "the first and only novel for the thinking mind, of classical taste" in the teeth of widespread disapproval of the novel genre in general and the cold reception of Wieland's novel in particular. *Hamburgische Dramaturgie*, §69, Lg 4:555.

14. Schiller to Cotta, 19 May 1794.

15. "Ankündigung der Horen," Sch 5:870ff.

16. "What effect can a standing theater actually have?" Sch 5:828.

17. *Critique of Pure Reason*, B 596ff., K 3:396.

18. Schopenhauer, *Die Welt als Wille und Vorstellung*, 3:17; *Sämtliche Werke*, 3:499.

19. As suggested in Rorty, "Human Rights, Rationality and Sentimentality," 128, 133ff.

20. Gottfried August Bürger, "The Peasant to His Serene Tyrant" (Der Bauer an seinen Durchlauchtigen Tyrannen), *Gedichte*, 1:55.

21. "Brief eines reisenden Dänen," Sch 5:879.

22. *Critique of Judgment*, §2, K 5:273.

23. All the more because he recognizes that architecture never denies its practical purpose and hence has only "adherent beauty." Ibid., 299ff.

24. K 3:7.

25. *Critique of Judgment*, §§6 and 8. K 5:280, 283ff.

26. See below, p. 191.

27. In a letter to Körner of 25 January 1793, which became the first of the fragmentary *Kallias Letters* (*Kallias oder über die Schönheit*), Sch 5:394ff.

28. Baumgarten, *Reflections on Poetry* (originally published in 1750 as *Meditationes philosophicae de nonnullis ad poema pertinentibus*).

29. Winckelmann, *Geschichte der Kunst des Altertums*, 136.

30. Ibid., 348, 360, 310ff.

31. Butler, *The Tyranny of Greece over Germany*.

32. "Gedanken über die Nachahmung der griechischen Werke in der Malerei und Bildhauerkunst," in Winckelmann, *Kleine Schriften und Briefe*, 1:59-143.

33. Herder, "Shakespeare," in *Sturm und Drang: Kritische Schriften*, 565ff.

34. Lessing, *Laokoön* (1766), §16, Lg 6:28. The phrase "edle Einfalt und stille Größe" comes in the essay "On the Imitation of Greek Works," in Winckelmann, *Kleine Schriften und Briefe*, 1:81.

35. Herder, "Erstes Wäldchen," in *Kritische Wälder*, §16, H 2.

36. Herder, *Fragmente* (= *Über die neueste deutsche Literatur*), 1767, H 1: 161-598; Lessing, *Literaturbriefe* (= *Briefe die neueste Literaturbetreffend*), 1759-65, Lg 5:30-326; and *Hamburgische Dramaturgie*, 1769, Lg 4:229-708.

37. *Diary of the Italian Journey*, 19 October 1786, in Goethe, *The Flight to Italy*, 96.

38. See above, pp. 109-11.

39. Schiller to Körner, 25 May 1792.

40. Schiller to Goethe, 28 August 1794.

41. Mann, *Goethe und Tolstoi* (1925), in *Sämtliche Werke* 15/2:812. Mann was inci-

dentally excusing his failure to write "Geist und Kunst," a planned overview of German culture around 1910.

42. Cf. Wordsworth: "And long orations which in dreams I pleaded / Before unjust tribunals." *The Prelude*, X, 377ff.; and ibid., 193ff., where he imagines how he might have "[made] common cause / With some who perished, haply perished too."

43. They included Washington, Paine, Bentham, Wilberforce, Kosziusko, and Pestalozzi. Schiller's diploma did not arrive until 1798, by which time all the signatories had been guillotined.

44. Likewise Lichtenberg on what was needed: "It isn't possible to build a republic from the materials of a torn-down monarchy until every stone has first been carved afresh, and that takes time." Lbg 2:429.

45. *Kallias*, Sch 5:421.

46. *Über Anmut und Würde*, Sch 5:460.

47. Ibid., 463.

48. Forster to Christian Gottlob Heyne, 30 July 1789.

49. Forster to his wife Therese 8 April 1793. See above, p. 89.

50. Forster to his wife, 16 April 1793.

51. Forster to his wife, 4 June 1793.

52. In a speech to the National Convention on 18 Floréal Year 2 (7 May 1794).

53. 13 July 1793. "A corrupt generation" is also Goethe's phrase in the section "Das Zeitalter" of the narrative poem *Hermann und Dorothea*, HA 2:480. But the politically conservative Goethe's account there of the initial expectations is as generous as any.

54. Letter 15, Sch 5:614.

55. Letter 16, ibid., 620.

56. "Sich selbst versäumen." Letter 6, ibid., 588.

57. Letters 9 and 15, ibid., 595ff. and 617.

58. "Eine Aufgabe für mehr als *ein* Jahrhundert." Letter 7, ibid., 590.

59. Letter 16, ibid., 618.

60. Letter 21, ibid., 635.

61. Letter 9, ibid., 593.

62. Schiller to Goethe, 1 November 1795 and 25 June 1799.

63. "Die Künstler" (The Artists), lines 64ff and 393ff, Sch 1:175, 184.

64. Richter (Jean Paul), *Ideengewimmel*, p. 161.

CHAPTER 10. THE FULL EARTH

1. See the opening of the section "Transcendental Doctrine of Method," K 3:481; B 736.

2. K 3:405, 419; B 611, B 636.

3. Ibid., 413, B 624. Technically, "existence" cannot be a predicate (414, B 626). That is, to use the grammatical subject "God" already posits existence, to which the verb "exists" adds no new "synthetic" knowledge.

4. Ibid., 416ff., B 631.

5. "Null und nichtig." In the concluding subsection "Critique of All Theology That Proceeds from Speculative Principles of Reason." K 3:436ff., B 664.

6. Ibid., 429, B 652.

7. Ibid., 434, B 661.

8. "So dass sich unser Urteil vom Ganzen in ein sprachloses, aber desto beredteres Erstaunen auflösen muss." Ibid., 428, B 650. Already for Plato "wonder is the feeling of the philosopher, and philosophy begins in wonder." *Theaetetus*, 155d, in *The Dialogues*. I owe this reference to Christoph Sauer.

9. Schmidt, "Barthold Hinrich Brockes," 8.

10. The poem "Some Natural Forces, Laws and Characteristics," Killy 1:372. Wolff at about the same time was applying the fashionable microscope to a cherry. Killy 1:369ff.

11. "Beschäftigt euch, und lernt, aufmercksam, GOTT zu Ehren, / Empfinden, schmecken, sehn und hören"—from the poem "Skill in Reading the Book of Nature," Killy 1:372. All the other poems referred to can be found in Stenzel, *Epochen der deutschen Lyrik* 5.

12. As William James put it, the god of any coherent universe must be running "a wholesale, not a retail business." *Varieties of Religious Experience*, 472.

13. "Sich einem Höhern, Reinern, Unbekannten / Aus Dankbarkeit freiwillig hinzugeben. / Enträtselnd sich den ewig Ungenannten; / Wir heißen's: fromm sein." "Elegie," centerpiece of the *Trilogy of Passion*, lines 79ff., HA 1:384.

14. Diderot, *Oeuvres completes*, 1:138.

15. Boyle, *The Poetry of Desire*, 25.

16. For the progression from *Individualismus der Freiheit* to *Individualismus der Einzigkeit*, see Simmel, *Kant: sechzehn Vorlesungen*, 180.

17. *Annette*, published in Leipzig in 1767.

18. Goethe to Ernst Theodor Langer, 24 November 1768. The key phrase is "durch die Anhänglichkeit an die Welt zerflattert."

19. "Dwell in himself," Goethe to Gottlob Friedrich Ernst Schönborn, 1 June–4 July 1774; "free world" etc., "Auf dem See," final version, line 2; Goethe to Jacobi, 31 August 1774; Goethe to Auguste von Stolberg, 13 February 1775; Goethe to Carl August, 2 September 1786; Goethe to Herder, 27 December 1788.

20. "Ich sah die Welt mit liebevollen Blicken / Und Welt und ich, wir schwelgten im Entzücken." The opening lines of the poem "Einsamste Wildnis," one of a sequence published with a set of engravings from his drawings in 1821; FA 2:523, 1115, and illustrations.

21. Goethe to Lavater, 28 October 1779.

22. "Gehab' dich wohl," HA 1:106. Sent in a letter of 23 December 1775.

23. See Goethe, *Elegie von Marienbad*.

24. "Wandrers Nachtlied 2" ("Über allen Gipfeln"), HA 1:142.

25. Recent versions have made Goethe's quality more accessible. See Goethe, *Selected Poems* (trans. Luke); Goethe, *Selected Poetry* (trans. Whaley); and Goethe, *Goethe Poems* (ed. Reed).

26. "Alle gleichen wir uns, denn wir sind eines Geschlechtes; / Allen gleichen wir nicht, sagt einem jeden das Herz." FA 1:269.

27. HA 1:392, 403.

28. "Geb Gott dir Lieb zu deinem Pantoffel / Ehr jede krüpliche Kartoffel / Erkenne jedes Dings Gestalt / Sein Leid und Freud Ruh und Gewalt / Und fühle wie die ganze

Welt / Der hohe Himmel zusammenhält." The poem, "Hier schick' ich dir ein teures Pfand," was sent to his friend Johann Heinrich Merck in 1774 with a set of drawings and never published in his lifetime; FA 1:189.

29. *Faust*: "Dass ich erkenne, was die Welt / Im Innersten zusammenhält." *Faust*, part 1, lines 382ff. The poem to Merck: "Erkenne jedes Dings Gestalt / . . . Und fühle wie die ganze Welt / Der große Himmel zusammenhält." HA 1:92.

30. The original is conceptually and rhythmically the despair of translators: *Erdgeist*: "In Lebensfluten, im Tatensturm / Wall' ich auf und ab, / Wehe hin und her! / Geburt und Grab, / Ein ewiges Meer. / Ein wechselnd Weben, / Ein glühend Leben, / So schaff ich am sausenden Webstuhl der Zeit / Und wirke der Gottheit lebendiges Kleid." *Faust*, part 1, lines 501ff.

31. "Die verzehrende Kraft, die in dem All der Natur verborgen liegt; die nichts gebildet hat, das nicht seinen Nachbar, nicht sich selbst zerstörte. Und so taumle ich beängstigt. Himmel und Erde und ihre webenden Kräfte um mich her: ich sehe nichts als ein ewig verschlingendes, ewig wiederkäuendes Ungeheuer." HA 6:53.

32. "Goethe and the avoidance of tragedy" was a thesis of Heller, *The Disinherited Mind*. It rests largely on a late self-deprecating comment of Goethe's own. Heller's snappy formulation has become a cliché, but as these examples make plain, his essay is really a case of "Goethe and the avoidance of evidence." If Goethe's obiter dicta are to count, then so must the very different one that he was quite capable of writing another *Werther* that would make people's hair stand on end. To Zelter, 3 December 1812.

33. "Die schönen Künste von Sulzer," HA 12:17. The review was published in the *Frankfurter gelehrte Anzeigen*, the organ in the early 1770s of the contrarian younger generation.

34. "Handwerker trugen ihn. Kein Geistlicher hat ihn begleitet." HA 6:124. This late in the eighteenth century, churchyard burial like Werther's was becoming possible for suicides. Incidentally, Goethe did not write the last five words. He took them over from Kestner's report on the death of their mutual friend Karl Wilhelm Jerusalem. But montage can be as effective as primal creation. Notably, Goethe left out Kestner's "das Kreuz ward vorausgetragen" (the cross was carried before).

35. Strangely, the most elaborate recent treatment of Goethe's early poetry reads into this palpably exuberant poem a "crisis of vision," "trauma," and "a troubled condition." Wellbery, *The Specular Moment*, 37.

36. "Die Nacht schuf tausend Ungeheuer— / Doch tausendfacher war mein Mut; / Mein Geist war ein verzehrend Feuer, / Mein ganzes Herz zerfloss in Glut." For the two versions, see HA 1:27ff.

37. "Und doch, welch Glück! geliebt zu werden, / Und lieben, Götter, welch ein Glück!" HA 1:28.

38. "Krachts gleich bricht's doch nicht, / Bricht's gleich, bricht nicht mit dir." HA 1:131. Also FA 1:326 with the revised, more clearly didactic title "Mut" (Courage).

39. "Und vertrauet, scheiternd oder landend, / Seinen Göttern." HA 1:49.

40. Goethe to Charlotte von Stein, 6 September 1780.

41. Goethe to Herder, 12 May 1775.

42. "Wandrers Sturmlied" opens with the line "Wen du nicht verlässest, Genius." HA 1:33.

43. HA 1:48. The chutzpah is much reduced in a later revised version.

44. *Dichtung und Wahrheit*, books 7 and 8, HA 9:293 and 339ff.

45. Goethe to Jacobi, 11 January 1808.

46. "Alles gaben Götter, die unendlichen, / Ihren Lieblingen ganz, / Alle Freuden, die unendlichen, / Alle Schmerzen, die unendlichen, ganz." Enclosed in a letter to Auguste Gräfin zu Stolberg, 17 July 1777, HA 1:142. This, incidentally, is the poem he sang to himself as he emerged from his swim in the Ilm.

47. The lines "Vom Vater hab ich die Statur" end with the ironic comment that, if so much came from his parents and grandparents, not much of him can be original. HA 1:320. More seriously analytical is the companion piece ("Wenn Kindesblick begierig schaut," HA 1:310), which traces a child's acculturation in a world of fixed forms that leave little room for originality—very much the Enlightenment's problem of the pressures against daring to think for oneself.

48. "Eine Kindheitserinnerung aus *Dichtung und Wahrheit*" (1917); Freud, *Studienausgabe*, 10:266.

49. "Mir ist das All, ich bin mir selbst verloren, / Der ich noch erst der Götter Liebling war." HA 1:385.

50. "Zum Bleiben ich, zum Scheiden du erkoren, / Gingst du voraus—und hast nicht viel verloren." It is 1824, the fiftieth anniversary of his first appearance; an unjubilant jubilee, too near the quick of present disaster. I use John Whaley's version for both quotations.

51. Goethe to Pfenninger, 26 April 1774.

52. "Tüchtige Menschen . . . die Gemeinschaft der Heiligen, zu der wir uns bekennen." Goethe to Zelter, 18 June 1831.

53. "Dass die echten Menschen aller Zeiten einander voraus verkünden, aufeinander hinweisen, einander vorarbeiten." *History of the Theory of Colour*, quoting an aperçu of Kepler's, HA 14:100.

54. "Ich halte mich fest und fester an die Gottesverehrung des Atheisten." Goethe to Jacobi, 5 May 1786. On Spinoza's *Ethics* as the book closest to his conception of nature, see Goethe to Jacobi, 21 October 1785.

55. He also wrote it up at great length, and in (somewhat shaky) Italian, though it was first published only recently. Johann Caspar Goethe, *Reise nach Italien*.

56. Goethe, *The Flight to Italy*, 4. The diary, covering the first eight weeks up to Goethe's arrival in Rome, often has the ring of a personal letter. It was indeed sent in installments to Frau von Stein, who was thus the muse of a new phase that would lead to Goethe's break with her.

57. Diary, 29 October 1786.

58. Diary, 11 September 1786.

59. Diary, 27 September 1786.

60. "Wie wahr! wie *seiend!*" Diary, 9 October 1786.

61. Goethe to his Weimar friends, 1 November 1786.

62. Diary, 24 September 1786.

63. Goethe to Charlotte von Stein, 7 November 1786; Goethe to the Herders, 10 November 1786.

64. Goethe to Charlotte von Stein, 23 December 1786.

65. "Alles Willkürliche, Eingebildete, fällt zusammen, da ist die Notwendigkeit, da ist Gott." *Italienische Reise*, 6 September 1788, HA 11:395.

66. Diary, 16 September 1786.

67. "Sarkophagen und Urnen," HA 1:174.

68. Pater, *The Renaissance*, 217.

69. Diary, 19 October 1786. The passage was taken over unchanged into the later *Italienische Reise*, but this vehement sentence is notably omitted from the Auden-Mayer translation; see *Italian Journey*, 110.

70. Diary, 19 October 1786. This matches Vasari's view of the damage Christianity had done from the first to the profession and practice of the arts as they had come down from antiquity. See Vasari, *The Lives of the Artists*, 5.

71. Diary, 8 October 1786.

72. Diary, 27 September 1786.

73. Diary, 19 September 1786.

74. Goethe to Carl August, 17 November 1787.

75. Goethe to Charlotte von Stein, 24 November 1786. The followers of the Greek philosopher took a vow to first be silent for five years.

76. Goethe to Herder, 13 January 1787.

77. Goethe to the Herders, 2 December 1786.

78. Goethe to Philipp Seidel, 13 January 1787.

79. Elisabeth Goethe to her son, 17 November 1786. Katharina Elisabeth Goethe, *Briefe*, 1:157.

80. "Jeden anderen Meister erkennt man an dem, was er darstellt, / An dem, was er verschweigt, kennt man den Meister des Styls." FA 1:538.

81. Originally entitled "Erotica Romana." They were first published in Schiller's journal *Die Horen* as *Elegien*, later as *Elegien: Rom 1788*, and in editions since 1806 as *Römische Elegien*. Goethe omitted four other elegies. For a full account, with facing texts of the manuscript and first edition, see FA 1:392–441, 1083–1127. The elegy numbers are given in the text.

82. Goethe knew the *Basia* and addressed an admiring poem to (and in) "the Spirit of Johannes Secundus" ("Lieber, heiliger, großer Küsser," HA 1:140). He enclosed the text in a letter to Charlotte von Stein in 1776, at the start of a relationship that may not have been the kissing kind.

83. "The Definition of Love," in Marvell, *Selected Poetry*. For the school of Battista Marino, whose mode Marvell was following, despair was obligatory: "a noble heart thinks its excellence diminished if hope intrudes its flattering foot to reduce the ardent flames— base comfort of common minds, depart!" Thus a Marinist poem, "Amante che si pregia di non avere alcuna speranza," quoted in Marvell, *Selected Poetry*, xxviii.

84. "Reizendes Hindernis will die rasche Jugend: ich liebe / Mich des versicherten Guts lange bequem zu erfreun."

85. The Renaissance scholar Scaliger first called them the *triumviri amoris*.

86. "Und belehr' ich mich nicht, indem ich des lieblichen Busens / Formen spähe, die Hand leite die Hüften hinab? / Dann versteh ich den Marmor erst recht; ich denk und vergleiche, / Sehe mit fühlendem Aug, fühle mit sehender Hand." There are perhaps

echoes here of Herder's 1768 essay *Plastik*, which emphasized touch as the most fundamental of the senses.

87. Kommerell, *Gedanken über Gedichte*, 231. Cynthia gets a mention in the omitted Elegy XIVa.

88. "War das Antike doch neu, als jene Glücklichen lebten! / Lebe glücklich, und so
lebe die Vorzeit in dir!"

89. "Aber ihr Männer, ihr schüttet mit eurer Kraft und Begierde / Auch die Liebe
zugleich in den Umarmungen aus."

90. *Pace* Vaget, for whose notion that these two poems were "clearly meant to form
a frame" for the cycle (Goethe, *The Erotic Poems*, xxvii) there is no manuscript evidence
and massive counterevidence in the tenor of the entire cycle. Priapus is any case more
a grotesque guardian of gardens than a sex symbol. The suggestion that he, and not the
genius loci, is invoked in Elegy I (ibid., xxix) ignores the cycle's other essential balance,
between erotic experience and the all-determining city. Priapus gets such brief reference
as he needs at the end of Elegy XI.

91. "Freue dich also, Lebend'ger, der lieberwärmeten Stätte, / Ehe den fliehenden Fuß
schauerlich Lethe dir netzt."

92. Kommerell, *Gedanken über Gedichte*, 239. This variety of love is hinted at in
the opening lines of Elegy III, on arrows from Amor's bow: "einige ritzen, / Und vom
schleichenden Gift kranket auf Jahre das Herz" (some of them scratch you / And the
poison steals in, making the heart sick for years).

93. Charlotte von Stein to Charlotte Schiller, 27 July 1795.

94. "Uns ergötzen die Freuden des echten, nacketen Amors / Und des geschaukelten
Betts lieblicher knarrender Ton" (printed in critical editions as IIa).

95. "Aller Güter der Welt erstes und letztes."

96. Schiller to Goethe, 28 October 1794.

97. "Sage, wie lebst du? Ich lebe, und wären hundert und hundert / Jahre dem
Menschen gegönnt, wünscht' ich mir morgen wie heut."

98. Goethe to Herder, 11 September 1790.

99. Recognized in the *Venetian Epigrams* "Oft erklärtet ihr euch" and "Klein ist
unter den Fürsten," HA 1:178.

100. Cf. Wieland's letter of 18 February 1789 to his son-in-law, the Kantian philosopher Reinhold in Jena: "Goethe has for some time been studying Kant's [First] Critique,
and with great assiduity." Goethe's pencil markings in his copy are reproduced in Molnár,
Goethes Kant-Studien.

101. Goethe to Jacobi, 21 October 1785.

102. "So ruht der *Stil* auf den tiefsten Grundfesten der Erkenntnis, insofern uns erlaubt ist, es in sichtbaren und greiflichen Gestalten zu erkennen." "Einfache Nachmung,
Manier, Stil," HA 12:32.

103. An argument pressed in Boyle, *Revolution and Renunciation*.

104. "Wenn die gesunde Natur des Menschen als ein Ganzes wirkt, wenn er sich
in der Welt als in einem großen, schönen, würdigen, werten Ganzen fühlt, wenn das
harmonische Behagen ihm ein reines, freies Entzücken gewährt—dann würde das Weltall,
als an sein Ziel gelangt aufjauchzen und den Gipfel des eigenen Werdens und Wesens

bewundern. Denn wozu dient alle der Aufwand von Sonnen und Planeten und Mon-
den, von Sternen und Milchstraßen, von Kometen und Nebelflecken, von gewordenen
und werdenden Welten, wenn sich nicht zuletzt ein glücklicher Mensch seines Lebens
erfreut?" HA 12:98.

105. HA 2:135ff.

106. "Den Sinnen hast du dann zu trauen, / Kein Falsches lassen sie dich schauen, /
Wenn dein Verstand sich wach erhält."

107. "Genieße mäßig Füll' und Segen."

108. "Der Augenblick ist Ewigkeit."

109. "Das Zentrum findest du da drinnen . . . / Denn das selbständige Gewissen / Ist
Sonne deinem Sittentag." Ibid.; HA 1:370.

110. "Eins und Alles," HA 1:368.

111. Goethe draws on his own past work—*Werther* and *Torquato Tasso*—for support
in the present emergency. He then arranges the sequence of poems in the *Trilogy of Passion* to end with "Reconciliation," where genetically they ended with the dark address
"To Werther" and only a half-promise that expressing pain may ease it.

112. Left untitled by Goethe, later called "Schiller's Relics" or "In Contemplation of
Schiller's Skull."

113. "Dass in des Raumes Moderkält' und Enge / Ich frei und wärmefühlend mich
erquickte, / Als ob ein Lebensquell dem Tod entspränge." HA 1:366.

114. Act 5, scene 1, line 186.

115. Goethe calls the poem "Schillers Reliquien" in a letter to Zelter, 24 October
1827. In the poem "Memento mori! gibt's genug" (FA 2:690), he sets "vivere memento"
explicitly against the "reminders of mortality" tradition.

116. Goethe uses the form on only one other occasion, in the opening scene of
Faust II.

117. The translation is again Whaley's.

118. Strictly speaking, "Früh," with which the poem begins in the present, syntactically embraces all that follows, even the future sunset—a contradiction in the poem's
chronology. But it is an endearing flaw, showing how the poet was drawn on from immediate observation to profound reflection. As Robert Frost famously said, a poem begins
in beauty and ends in wisdom.

119. "Schwärmerisch-erschreckende Empfindungen," which Kant rejects along with
those of the Pietist cult figure Madame Bourignon as products of an introversion that can
only be cured by returning the individual to the "order of things accessible to the outer
senses" (*die Ordnung der Dinge, die den äußeren Sinnen vorliegen*). *Anthropologie,* §24,
K 8:48. Kant is alluding to Pascal's famous line "Le silence éternel de ces espaces infinis
m'effraie." *Pensées,* 392. The Pascalian sequence terror/divine refuge is precisely enacted
in Brockes's poem "Das Firmament"; Stenzel, *Epochen der deutschen Lyrik,* 85.

120. Lichtenberg sets against the intellectual achievements of the young Pascal the
religious apologist's belief that his sister's eye complaint could be cured by a relic. Lbg
1:348.

121. That the motion of the so-called fixed stars was imperceptible from earth was
due to their distance, some twenty thousand times that between earth and sun, and to

their orbiting time of one and a half million years, which produced just one degree of movement in four thousand years—in turn a measure of the depth of the universe.

122. K 5:174f.

123. "Denn edlen Seelen vorzufühlen / Ist wünschenswertester Beruf." The final lines of "Vermächtnis," HA 1:370. Whaley's version again.

124. "Wie der Mensch von innen heraus leben, der Künstler von innen heraus wirken müsse." "Noch ein Wort für junge Dichter," HA 12:360.

125. Arnold, "Heinrich Heine," in, *Lectures and Essays in Criticism*, in *Complete Prose Works*, 3:110. Regrettably, Arnold did not feel able to take on the whole Goethe in an essay—it would be "an alarming task." Arnold to his sister Fanny, December 1877, in *Letters of Matthew Arnold*, 2:165. Goethe's late self-assessment as an example to Germans, and Arnold's judgment—"really subversive," "radically detached"—may together offset the view that Goethe's "liberation from the status quo" was only "for the higher individual." Israel, *The Democratic Enlightenment*, 21ff., 698ff. Goethe was certainly no "revolutionary democrat" but in the long term has perhaps moved in a mysterious way.

CHAPTER 11. PEACE IN WHOSE TIME?

1. Hobbes, *Leviathan*, part 1, chapter 13, "Of the Natural Conditon of Mankind as Concerning Their Felicity and Misery," 143.

2. The text at K 1:473; the dating, ibid., 535ff.

3. Bräker, *Der arme Mann*, chapter xlix.

4. Quoted in Kugler, *Geschichte Friedrichs des Großen*, 146. This is the standard popular life memorably illustrated by Adolf Menzel, never out of print since the 1840s.

5. Ibid., vii. The several formulations of the "servant" notion are located in Meinecke, *Die Idee der Staatsräson*, 364n.

6. Gooch, *Frederick the Great*, 122.

7. See Giersberg, "Architecture, Urban Planning and Garden Design," in Streidt and Feierabend, *Prussia: Art and Architecture*, 158–223.

8. Ibid., vi.

9. Lbg 1:865.

10. Schieder, *Friedrich der Große: ein Königtum der Widersprüche*.

11. Frederick had made the case for "preventive war" in his *Antimachiavell*. More generally, once the routine extenuating arguments are allowed—"preventive war," "precautionary war," "operational aggression that is really strategic defense"—few wars lack a fig leaf.

12. The comprehensive statistic is from White, *Atrocitology*, 257. The Seven Years' War ranks fortieth. For comparison, the Thirty Years' War ranks seventeenth, with 17.5 million dead.

13. Streidt and Feierabend, *Prussia: Art and Architecture*, 72.

14. Seen in MS by Voltaire. Quoted in Berenhorst, *Betrachtungen über die Kriegskunst*, 227.

15. Quoted in Holmsten, *Friedrich II*, 115.

16. Quoted in Fraser, *Frederick the Great*, 384. As a former general, Fraser gives the most sympathetic (though by no means uncritical) view of Frederick as both king and soldier.

17. Berenhorst, *Betrachtungen über die Kriegskunst*, 109.

18. Winckelmann to Wilhelm Muzel-Stosch, November and December 1757.

19. Quoted in Hirsch, *Wörlitz-Dessau*, 69.

20. The grounds for the assumption are statistically questioned in Gittings, *The Glorious Art of Peace* and in an even wider-ranging historical argument by Pinker, *The Better Angels of Our Nature*.

21. Clausewitz, *Vom Kriege*, 641.

22. Johann Georg Schlosser, 1784, quoted in Dahnke, *Debatten und Kontroversen*, 1:88.

23. *Avant-propos* to the *Histoire de mon temps*, quoted in Meinecke, *Die Idee der Staatsräson*, 356. Meinecke attempts a systematic account of Frederick's thought but does not show the philosopher ever much denting the outlook of the politician.

24. Quoted in Schieder, *Friedrich der Große*, 133.

25. For casualties among officers from the noble families, see ibid., 65.

26. "The nobility, as the first estate of the realm, has by definition as its main function the defence of the state" (section 9, para. 1). The middle class was defined only negatively as whatever lay between the nobility and the peasantry. "A Gothic head on a modern body" was Tocqueville's description of the new code. *L'ancien régime et la révolution*, 345ff.

27. Steinberg, *Bismarck*, 290ff., 383. Only the less smart arms—artillery and engineer regiments—were officered by bourgeois. For the social atmospherics, see the late nineteenth-century novels of Theodor Fontane.

28. For a detailed account, see Henze-Dühring, *Friedrich der Große: Musiker und Monarch*.

29. Remarkably, though, the article "Prusse" in the *Encyclopédie* is full of extravagant praise for Frederick the writer: a year or two spent in Paris would make him one of the first poets of French literature, and only the lightest breath from a man of taste was needed to blow away a few grains of Prussian sand.

30. In an essay of 1780, in French of course: *De la littérature allemande; des défauts qu'on peut lui reprocher; quelles en sont les causes; et par quels moyens on peut les corriger.*

31. Reprinted in Elschenbroich, *Deutsche Dichtung im 18. Jahrhundert*, 186ff. Gellert also suggested that making peace would be a good basis for a native culture—this at the midpoint of the Seven Years' War.

32. The responses of a few minor writers are documented in Kästner, *Friedrich der Große und die deutsche Literatur*.

33. *Dichtung und Wahrheit*, book 7; HA 9:279ff. For Gleim, see, e.g., "Battle Song" and "Song after the [lost] Battle of Kolin," a morale raiser in post-Dunkirk mood, in *Epochen der deutschen Lyrik*, 5:279ff.; for Ramler, see likewise a "Battle Song," in *Epochen der deutschen Lyrik*, 6:113; but his finest poem is a threnody on peace written in the midst of the war in 1760, in *Epochen der deutschen Lyrik*, 5:24.

34. See Nisbet, *Lessing*, 446ff.

35. Schiller to Körner, 21 April 1789 and 28 November 1791.

36. "Die deutsche Muse," Sch 1:214.

37. "Zum ewigen Frieden," K 6:429.

38. "Presumable Origin of Human History," K 4:340.

39. K 6:427.

40. Wieland's essay *Über Krieg und Frieden*, written in 1794 in the midst of the Revolutionary Wars, cites from Cicero the ambiguous Latin oracle "Ajo te, Aeacidas, Romanos vincere posse" ("I tell you, Pyrrhus, that you can defeat the Romans"; or, syntactically just as plausible: ". . . that the Romans can defeat you.") Günther, *Die französische Revolution*, 582ff.

41. "Of the Original Contract," in Hume, *Essays Moral, Political, and Literary*, 2:457.

42. *Briefe zu Beförderung der Humanität*, 1:10, H 7:62.

43. For the Preliminary articles, see K 6:417–32; for the Definitive Articles, see ibid., 433–46.

44. See, e.g., Johann Benjamin Jachmann's letter to Kant dated Paris, 14 October 1790 (K 10:47ff.). Kant may also have known on-the-spot observations of another correspondent of his. See Reichardt, *Vertraute Briefe aus Paris, 1792*, especially 108ff., "Die Nationalversammlung."

45. *Don Carlos*, act 3, scene 10, verse 3160, Sch 2:124.

46. Quoted in Mann, "Schiller als Historiker."

47. K 6:455.

48. The most insidious instance of lip service to philosophy is the formulation *raison d'état* or *Staatsräson* itself. It misappropriates the concept of reason for what from the mid-nineteenth century on was more frankly termed *Realpolitik*.

49. Eulogius Schneider, "Hymnus an die Publicität," Killy 2:1197.

50. Frederick for his part only once briefly entertained the idea of "international" cooperation, for a European congress to eradicate the duel, which was costing aristocratic lives. Schieder, *Friedrich der Große*, 63.

51. In an otherwise humane-sounding letter of 11 December 1880 to a pacifist academic, Professor Bluntschli—a nice coincidence of names with the unmilitary soldier-hero of George Bernard Shaw's *Arms and the Man*. A professional soldier naturally welcomed war: Bismarck noted that Moltke looked ten years younger whenever war seemed imminent. Klein, *Der Kanzler*, 252.

52. "Denn nichts kann Schädlicheres und eines Philosophen Unwürdigeres gefunden werden, als die pöbelhafte Berufung auf vorgeblich widerstreitende Erfahrung, die doch gar nicht existieren würde, wenn jene Anstalten zu rechter Zeit nach den Ideen getroffen würden und an deren Statt nicht rohe Begriffe eben darum, weil sie aus Erfahrung geschöpft worden, alle gute Absicht vereitelt hätten." *Critique of Pure Reason*, K 3:258, B 373.

53. *Foundation of the Metaphysics of Morals*, K 4:264ff.

54. K 6:466.

55. The historic movements and measures toward peace and supranational control are surveyed in the later chapters of Gittings, *The Glorious Art of Peace*, and more fully in Mazower, *Governing the World*. Both pay ample tribute to Kant's essay.

56. In the essay of 1793 "On Theory and Practice," K 6:394.

57. White, *Atrocitology*, ranks the First World War second, with 15 million deaths, against the Second World War, in first place with 66 million. On the spurning of diplomacy by the warmongers of 1914, see Namier, "Men Who Floundered into the War." Most recently, Clark, *The Sleepwalkers*, tries to distribute historical responsibility more evenly. Kraus's monumental attack on the war mentality is the vast apocalyptic drama *Die letzten Tage der Menschheit* (The Last Days of Humanity) of 1926.

58. "Bis an die Sterne reichte einst ein Zwerg, / Sein irdisch Reich war nur ein Königsberg. / Doch über jedes Königs Burg und Wahn / Schritt eines Weltalls treuer Untertan." Kraus, "Zum ewigen Frieden." Kraus, *Gedichte*, 267.

59. Ibid., 339.

60. Most prominently Theodor Körner, the son of Schiller's oldest friend, killed in action in 1813.

61. The painting hangs in the Munich Neue Pinakothek.

62. As suggested by the small separate study for this figure, also in the Neue Pinakothek.

63. "Gestern noch auf hohen Rossen, / Heute durch die Brust geschossen." Hauff, "Reiters Morgengesang," in *Werke* 3.1:353.

64. K 7:398.

65. K 7:392ff.

66. K 7:396.

67. Dilthey, *Gesammelte Schriften*, 134, 248.

68. Stangneth, "Antisemitische und antijudaistische Motive bei Kant," especially 64–69, responding to Halberstam's drastically titled article "From Kant to Auschwitz."

69. "Das Wort entschlief, als jene Welt erwachte," from the poem "Man frage nicht . . . ," playing on the dual sense of *entschlafen* and the Nazi slogan "Deutschland erwache!" Kraus, *Gedichte*, 637.

70. "Dass aber Hitler nicht siegen wird u. nicht als verklärter Friedensfürst die von ihm geordnete Welt regieren wird, bleibt irrationale Überzeugung." 18 April 1941, Mann, *Tagebücher, 1940–1943*, 254ff.

71. "Die Demokratie, als säkularisiertes Christentum, ist nicht reif, von diesem falschen Sendling gestürzt zu werden." Ibid., 46.

72. "War ich sehr erschöpft gewesen, wurde aber nachher stärker, als ich mit Bermann auf die deutschen Dinge zu sprechen kam, sie im großen Stil betrachtete, die gegenwärtigen als eine neue Form der alten deutschen Kultur-Quatscherei charakterisierte und die verringerten Chancen für das Gelingen dieser Unternehmung ins Auge fasste. Eine verlorene Sache, auch wenn es sich wieder wie beim Kriege, von dem sie die klare Fortsetzung ist, um eine Reihe von Jahren handelt. Ein großes Ablenkungsmanöver, eine Riesen-Ungezogenheit gegen den Willen des Zeitgeistes, ein kindisches Hinter die Schule laufen." 2 May 1933, Mann, *Tagebücher, 1933–1934*, 68.

73. Thomas Mann Archive Zurich, manuscript Mp IX, 173, sheet 52.

74. *Ordine nuovo*, Number 1.

75. Not for nothing did André Malraux give the novel of 1938 that records his experiences as a pilot on the republican side in the Spanish civil war the title *L'espoir*. Spain was for contemporaries a crucial historical moment, most dramatically focused in W. H.

Auden's great poem "Spain." There, much in Schiller's spirit, the observer's mind is consciously poised at the decisive point between the whole human past and a still malleable future.

76. See, for encouragement, Garton Ash, *We the People*, on the 1989 Eastern bloc revolutions, and Gordimer, *Living in Hope and History*, published after the once barely imaginable end of apartheid in South Africa. Even allowing for the grim start to the twenty-first century, an Enlightenment history of human progress has some firm ground.

77. Julia Kristeva, in a lecture to the British Academy on 24 May 2010, http://www .britac.ac.uk/audio.cfm/assetfileid/9601. She duly adds, "As envisaged by Immanuel Kant."

A CONCLUSION? TOWARD ENLIGHTENMENT

1. This, surprisingly, from an outstanding and immensely well-informed historian. Judt, *Postwar*, 492.

2. Cf. Goethe, *Wilhelm Meister's Apprenticeship*, book 5, chapter 16, HA 7:347ff.

3. *Aufklärer*, as Kant knew, were thought by the state to be dangerous. K 8:402. Especially after the French Revolution, Lichtenberg noted, any rational demand would be regarded as a seed of unrest. Lbg 2:426.

4. On attempts to reach down to that constituency, see Knudsen, "On Enlightenment for the Common Man."

5. For a balanced view of the Enlightenment's origins, tradition, achievements, and the continuing obstacles to its realization, see Louden, *The World We Want*.

6. Or historically would have looked like. For an amusing but deeply serious counterfactual sketch of European history without the Enlightenment (and a factual sketch of how the Islamic world has got on without an Enlightenment of its own) see Pagden, *The Enlightenment*, 345ff.

7. "Die Aufklärung hat die Geisterwelt umgestaltet, ohne dass ein Mensch auf einen Paragraphen wäre vereidigt gewesen." Burckhardt, *Über das Studium der Geschichte*, 274.

BIBLIOGRAPHY

EDITIONS AND REFERENCE CODES

Forster, Georg. *Briefe*. Edited by Gerhard Steiner. Frankfurt am Main, 1970.

———. *Sämtliche Schriften, Tagebücher und Briefe*. Edited by Gerhard Steiner et al. Berlin, 1958. [AA]

———. *Werke*. Bibliothek deutscher Klassiker. Edited by Gerhard Steiner. Berlin, 1968. [F]

Goethe, Johann Wolfgang. *Briefe*. Edited by Karl Robert Mandelkow. Hamburg, 1962.

———. *Sämtliche Werke*. Frankfurter Ausgabe. Edited by Karl Eibl et al. Frankfurt am Main, 1987. [FA]

———. *Sämtliche Werke*. Münchener Ausgabe. Edited by Karl Richter et al. Munich, 1986. [MA]

———. *Sämtliche Werke*. Weimarer Ausgabe. Edited by Erich Schmidt et al. Weimar, 1887. [WA]

———. *Werke*. Hamburger Ausgabe. Edited by Erich Trunz et al. Munich, 1981. [HA]

———. *Werke, Briefe und Gespräche*. Gedenkausgabe. Edited by Ernst Beutler. Zurich, 1948.

Herder, Johann Gottfried. *Werke*. Edited by Hans Dietrich Irmscher et al. Frankfurt am Main, 1988. [H]

Kant, Immanuel. *Kants Werke*. Edited by Ernst Cassirer et al. Berlin, 1912. [K]

———. *Kant's Gesammelte Schriften*. Akademie Ausgabe. Published by the Königliche Preußische Akademie der Wissenschaften. Berlin, 1900. (For Kant's *Critique of Pure Reason*, I also give the standard "B" reference to the pagination of the 1787 second edition.) [AA]

———. *Theoretical Philosophy, 1755–1770*. Translated and edited by David Walford and Ralf Meerbote. Cambridge and New York, 1992. [TP]

Lessing, Gotthold Ephraim. *Werke*. Edited by Herbert G. Göpfert et al. Munich, 1970. [Lg]

Lichtenberg, Georg Christoph. *Schriften und Briefe*. Edited by Wolfgang Promies. Munich, 1967. [Lbg]

Marx, Karl. *Frühschriften*. Edited by Siegfried Landshut. Stuttgart, 1964.

Moritz, Karl Philipp. *Werke*. Edited by Horst Günther. Frankfurt am Main, 1981. [M]

Nietzsche, Friedrich. *Werke*. Edited by Karl Schlechta. Munich, 1960. [N]
Schiller, Friedrich. *Sämtliche Werke*. Edited by Herbert G.Göpfert et al. Munich, 1958.
    [Sch]
———. *Schillers Sämtliche Werke*. Edited by Karl Goedeke. Stuttgart, 1893.
Wieland, Christoph Martin. *Werke*. Edited by Fritz Martini et al. Munich, 1964. [W]

ANTHOLOGIES OF PRIMARY TEXTS

Bahr, Eberhard. *Was ist Aufklärung? Thesen und Definitionen*. Stuttgart, 1986.
Dahnke, Hans-Dietrich. *Debatten und Kontroversen*. Berlin, 1989.
Dorfmüller, Petra, and Rudolf Konetzny. *"Damit es an gelahrten Leuten in unsern
    Landen nicht Mangel gewinne": Schulpforta; 450 Jahre Schulgeschichte; Ein Lese-
    buch*. Leipzig, 1993.
Elschenbroich, Adalbert. *Deutsche Dichtung im 18. Jahrhundert*. Munich, 1960.
Engel, Johann Jacob, and Ernst Müller. *Gelegentliche Gedanken über Universitäten*.
    Leipzig, 1990.
Grigson, Geoffrey. *Before the Romantics: An Anthology of the Enlightenment*. Edin-
    burgh, 1984.
Günther, Horst. *Die französische Revolution*. Bibliothek der Geschichte 12. Frankfurt am
    Main, 1985.
Haufe, Eberhard, ed. *"Wir vergehn wie Rauch von starken Winden": Deutsche Gedichte
    des 17. Jahrhunderts*. Berlin, 1985.
Hinske, Norbert, and Michael Albrecht. *Was ist Aufklärung? Beiträge aus der Berlini-
    schen Monatsschrift*. Darmstadt, 1977.
Killy, Walther. *18. Jahrhundert: die deutsche Literatur; Texte und Zeugnisse IV*. Munich,
    1983. [Killy]
Kopper, Joachim, and Rudolf Malter. *Immanuel Kant zu ehren*. Frankfurt am Main, 1974.
Loewenthal, Erich, ed. *Sturm und Drang: Kritische Schriften*. 3rd ed. Heidelberg, 1972.
Pickerodt, Gerhart, ed. *Epochen der deutschen Lyrik*. Vol. 6, *1770–1800*. Munich, 1970.
Stenzel, Jürgen, ed. *Epochen der deutschen Lyrik*. Vol. 5, *1700–1770*. Munich, 1969.

OTHER PRIMARY SOURCES

Abel, Jacob Friedrich von. *Jacob Friedrich Abel: eine Quellenedition zum Philosophieun-
    terricht an der Stuttgarter Karlsschule (1773–1782)*. Edited by Wolfgang Riedel.
    Würzburg, 1995.
Arnold, Gottfried. *Unparteiische Kirchen- und Ketzergeschichte*. Leipzig, 1699–1700.
Arnold, Matthew. *The Complete Prose Works of Matthew Arnold*. Edited by R. H. Super.
    Ann Arbor, 1962.
———. *Letters of Matthew Arnold*. London, 1901.
Bacon, Francis. *The Advancement of Learning*. Oxford, 1906.
Basedow, Johann Bernhard. *Allgemeines christliches Gesangbuch für alle Kirchen und
    Sekten*. Riga, 1781.
———. *Das Elementarwerk*. Bremen, 1772.
———. *Für Cosmopoliten: etwas zu lesen, zu denken, und zu thun; in Ansehung eines*

in Anhalt-Dessau errichteten Philanthropins oder Seminars von ganz neuer Art, die schon alt seyn sollte. Leipzig, 1775.

Baumgarten, Alexander Gottlieb. *Reflections on Poetry: Meditationes philosophicae de nonnullis ad poema pertinentibus*. Berkeley and Los Angeles, 1954.

Berenhorst, Georg Heinrich von. *Betrachtungen über die Kriegskunst*. Berlin, 1798.

Bräker, Ulrich. *Der arme Mann im Tockenburg*. Zurich, 1789.

Brechter, Johann Jakob. *Anmerkungen über das Basedowische Elementarwerk* Zurich, 1772.

Burckhardt, Jakob. *Über das Studium der Geschichte*. Edited by Peter Ganz. Munich, 1982.

Bürger, Gottfried August. *Gedichte*. Edited by Ernst Consentius. Leipzig, n.d.

Čapek, Karel. *The Gardener's Year*. London, 1932.

Clausewitz, Carl von. *Vom Kriege*. 10th ed. Berlin, 1915.

Comenius, John Amos. *The Great Didactic of John Amos Comenius*. Translated by M. W. Keatinge. London, 1910.

D'Alembert, Jean le Rond. *Œuvres*. Paris, 1822.

Diderot, Denis. *Oeuvres complètes*. Edited by Jules As_zat. Paris, 1875.

Dilthey, Wilhelm. *Gesammelte Schriften*. Vol. 3. Leipzig, 1927.

Döblin, Alfred. *Berlin Alexanderplatz*. Freiburg, 1967.

Dohm, Christian Konrad Wilhelm von. *Über die bürgerliche Verbesserung der Juden*. Berlin, 1781.

Euripides. *Alcestis, and Other Plays*. Translated by Philip Vellacott. Harmondsworth, 1953.

Fambach, Oscar, ed. *Schiller und sein Kreis*. Vol. 2 of *Ein Jahrhundert deutscher Literaturkritik, 1750–1850*. Berlin, 1957.

Fénelon, François de Salignac de LaMothe. *Oeuvres*. Edited by Jacques Le Brun. Paris, 1997.

Forster, Georg. *Reise um die Welt: illustriert von eigener Hand*. Frankfurt am Main, 2007.

Freud, Sigmund. *Studienausgabe*. Edited by Alexander Mitscherlich, Angela Richards, and James Strachey. Frankfurt am Main, 1970.

Gibbon, Edward. *The History of the Decline and Fall of the Roman Empire*. Edited by David Womersley. Harmondsworth, 1994.

Goethe, Johann Caspar. *Reise nach Italien im Jahre 1740/Viaggio in Italia*. Translated and edited by Albert Meier. Munich, 1986.

Goethe, Johann Wolfgang von. *Elegie von Marienbad: Urschrift*. Edited by Jürgen Behrens and Christoph Michel. Frankfurt am Main, 1991.

———. *The Erotic Poems*. Edited by Hans Rudolf Vaget. Oxford, 1988.

———. *The Flight to Italy: Diary and Selected Letters*. Translated by T. J. Reed. Oxford, 1999.

———. *Goethe Poems: A New Collection Published to Celebrate the 250th Anniversary of the Birth of Johann Wolfgang Goethe and the 600th of the Birth of Johann Gutenberg*. Edited by T. J. Reed. Newtown, 2000.

———. *Italian Journey*. Harmondsworth, 1970.

———. *Selected Poems*. Translated by John Whaley. London, 1998.

————. *Selected Poetry*. Translated and edited by David Luke. London, 1990.

————. *Wilhelm Meisters theatralische Sendung*. Edited by Harry Maync. Stuttgart, 1911.

Goethe, Katharina Elisabeth. *Briefe der Frau Rath Goethe*. Edited by Albert Köster. Leipzig, 1911.

Goeze, Johann Melchior. *Zwo Predigten, welche durch das fürchterliche und so weit verbreitete Gericht Gottes im Erdbeben, veranlasset worden*. Hamburg, 1756.

Hauff, Wilhelm. *Werke*. Edited by Felix Bobertag. Leipzig, n.d.

Hegel, Georg Wilhelm Friedrich. *Philosophie des Rechts*. Vol. 7 of *Werke*, edited by Hermann Glockner. Stuttgart, 1932.

————. *Vorlesungen über die Philosophie der Weltgeschichte*. Edited by Johannes Hoffmeister. Hamburg, 1955.

Hobbes, Thomas. *Leviathan*. Edited by John Plamenatz. London, 1967.

Humboldt, Alexander von. *Cosmos: A Sketch of a Physical Description of the Universe*. London, 1849.

————. *Kosmos: Entwurf einer physischen Weltbeschreibung*. Edited by Ottmar Ette and Oliver Lubrich. Frankfurt am Main, 2004.

Hume, David. *Dialogues Concerning Natural Religion*. New York, 1948.

————. *Essays Moral, Political, and Literary*. Edited by T. H. Green and T. H. Grose. London, 1882.

————. *A Treatise of Human Nature*. Edited by L. A. Selby-Bigge. Oxford, 1973.

Kleist, Heinrich von. *Sämtliche Werke und Briefe*. Edited by Helmut Sembdner. Munich, 1961.

Klemperer, Viktor. *Tagebücher, 1933–45*. Berlin, 1998.

Knigge, Adolf Freiherr von. *Über den Umgang mit Menschen*. Hannover, 1788.

Lawrence, D. H. *Phoenix*. London, 1961.

Lavater, Johann Caspar. *Physiognomische Fragmente zur Beförderung der Menschenkenntnis und Menschenliebe*. Leipzig, 1968.

Locke, John. *Thoughts Concerning Education*. London, 1693.

Mann, Thomas. *Sämtliche Werke*. Frankfurt am Main, 2002.

————. *Tagebücher, 1933–1934*. Edited by Peter de Mendelssohn. Frankfurt am Main, 1977.

————. *Tagebücher, 1940–1943*. Edited by Peter de Mendelssohn. Frankfurt am Main, 1982.

Marvell, Andrew. *Selected Poetry*. Edited by Frank Kermode. New York, 1967.

Mendelssohn, Moses. *Morgenstunden*. Vol. 3, Pt. 2 of *Gesammelte Schriften*, edited by Leo Strauss. Stuttgart–Bad Cannstatt, 1974.

Mill, John Stuart. *On Liberty*. Oxford, 1962.

Montaigne, Michel Eyquem de. *Essais*. Paris, 1953.

Montesquieu, Charles de Secondat de. *Oeuvres*. Paris, 1839.

Newton, Isaac. *Opticks; Or, A Treatise of the Reflections, Refractions, Inflections & Colours of Light; Based on the 4th Ed., London, 1730*. New York, 1952.

Nicolai, Friedrich. *"Kritik ist überall, zumal in Deutschland, nötig": Satiren und Schriften zur Literatur; Mit 20 zeitgenössischen Abbildungen*. Edited by Wolfgang Albrecht and Ralph F. H. Böttcher. Munich, 1987.

Pascal, Blaise. *Pensées.* Edited by Louis Lafuma. Paris, 1952.

Pezzl, Johann. *Faustin: oder Das philosophische Jahrhundert.* Hildesheim, 1982.

Piltz, Georg, ed. *Friedrich II: wonach er sich zu richten hat; Urteile und Verfügungen.* Berlin, 1995.

Plato. *The Dialogues.* Edited by Benjamin Jowett. Oxford, 1953.

Plutarch. *Moralia.* Edited by W. R. Paton. Leipzig, 1925.

Ranke, Leopold von. "Einleitung zu einer Vorlesung über Universalhistorie." *Historische Zeitschrift* 178 (1954).

———. "Idee der Universalhistorie." *Historische Zeitschrift* 178 (1954).

———. *Politisches Gespräch.* Edited by Theodor Schieder. Göttingen, 1955.

———. *Sämtliche Werke.* Leipzig, 1867–90.

———. *Über die Verwandtschaft und den Unterschied der Historie und der Politik.* Vol. 24 of *Sämtliche Werke.*

Reichardt, Johann Friedrich. *Vertraute Briefe aus Paris, 1792.* Edited by Rolf Weber. Berlin, 1980.

Reinhold, Carl Leonhard. *Briefe über die Kantsche Philosophie.* Jena, 1788.

Reisiger, Hans. *Johann Gottfried Herder: sein Leben in Selbstzeugnissen, Briefen und Berichten.* Darmstadt, 1970.

Richter, Jean Paul. *Ideengewimmel: Texte aus dem Nachlass.* Edited by Joachim Wirtz and Kurt Wölfel. Munich, 2000.

Schiller, Friedrich. *On the Aesthetic Education of Man: In a Series of Letters.* Edited by Elizabeth M. Wilkinson and L. A. Willoughby. Oxford, 1968.

Schopenhauer, Arthur. *Sämtliche Werke.* Edited by Arthur Hübscher. Wiesbaden, 1960.

Spalding, Johann Joachim. *Betrachtung über die Bestimmung des Menschen.* 3rd ed. Berlin, 1749.

Spinoza, Benedictus de. *Ethics, and, On the Correction of the Understanding.* London, 1963.

Staël, Germaine de. *De l'Allemagne.* London, 1813.

Thomasius, Christian. *Vom Laster der Zauberei: über die Hexenprozesse.* Edited by Rolf Lieberwirth. Weimar, 1967.

Tocqueville, Alexis de. *L'ancien régime et la révolution.* Paris, 1967.

Vasari, Giorgio. *The Lives of the Artists.* Edited by Julia Conaway Bondanella and Peter E. Bondanella. Oxford, 1991.

Voltaire. *Mélanges.* Edited by Emmanuel Berl and Jacques van den Heuvel. Paris, 1965.

Weisse, Christian, ed. *Der Kinderfreund: ein Wochenblatt.* Leipzig, 1776.

Wieland, Christoph Martin. *Der goldene Spiegel.* In *Werke,* vol. 7, edited by Karl Philipp Reemtsma. Hamburg, 1990.

———. *Politische Schriften, insbesondere zur französischen Revolution.* Edited by Jan Philipp Reemtsma. Nördlingen, 1988.

Wilbur, Richard. *New and Collected Poems.* London, 1989.

Winckelmann, Johann Joachim. *Geschichte der Kunst des Altertums.* Munich, n.d.

———. *Kleine Schriften und Briefe.* Edited by Hermann Uhde-Bernays. Leipzig, 1925.

Wordsworth, William. *The Prelude.* 1805 text. Oxford, 1969.

———. *The Prelude.* Parallel texts. Edited by A. de Selincourt. Oxford, 1928.

SECONDARY SOURCES

Adams, David and Galin Tihanov, eds. *Enlightenment Cosmopolitanism*. Oxford, 2011.

Adorno, Theodor. *Kant's "Critique of Pure Reason."* Translated by Rodney Livingstone. Oxford, 2001.

Altmann, Alexander. *Moses Mendelssohn: A Biographical Study*. London, 1973.

Andrade, E. N. da C. *Sir Isaac Newton*. London, 1961.

Aner, Karl. *Der Aufklärer Friedrich Nicolai*. Giessen, 1912.

Anscombe, Elisabeth. *Introduction to Wittgenstein's "Tractatus."* London, 1963.

Ariès, Philippe. *Centuries of Childhood: A Social History of Family Life*. London, 1962.

Auerbach, Erich. *Mimesis*. Bern, 1946.

Beales, Derek. *Enlightenment and Reform in Eighteenth-Century Europe*. London, 2005.

———. *Joseph II*. Cambridge, 1987–2009.

Beck, Ulrich. *Der eigene Gott: von der Friedensfähigkeit und dem Gewaltpotential der Religionen*. Frankfurt am Main, 2008.

Behrens, Catherine B. *Society, Government and the Enlightenment: The Experiences of 18th-Century France and Prussia*. London, 1985.

Beiser, Frederick. *The Fate of Reason*. London, 1987.

Blackall, Eric A. *The Emergence of German as a Literary Language, 1700–1775*. Cambridge, 1959.

Blanning, T. C. W. *The Culture of Power and the Power of Culture: Old Regime Europe, 1660–1789*. Oxford, 2002.

Bodi, Leslie. *Tauwetter in Wien: zur Prosa der österreichischen Aufklärung, 1781–1795*. Frankfurt am Main, 1977.

Bortoft, Henri. *The Wholeness of Nature: Goethe's Way toward a Science of Conscious Participation in Nature*. Hudson, NY, 1996.

Boyle, Nicholas. *The Poetry of Desire, 1749–1790*. Vol. 1 of *Goethe: The Poet and the Age*. Oxford, 1991.

———. *Revolution and Renunciation, 1790–1805*. Vol. 2 of *Goethe: The Poet and the Age*. Oxford, 2000.

Broadie, Alexander. *The Scottish Enlightenment: The Historical Age of the Historical Nation*. Edinburgh, 2007.

Brooke, John. "The God of Isaac Newton." In *Let Newton Be! A New Perspective on His Life and Work*, edited by John Fauvel, Raymond Flood, Michael Shortland, and Robin Wilson. Oxford, 1988.

Browning, Robert M. *German Poetry in the Age of the Enlightenment*. University Park, PA, 1978.

Bubner, R. *Geschichtsprozesse und Handlungsnorm*. Frankfurt am Main, 1984.

Buchwald, Reinhold. *Schiller*. Wiesbaden, 1954.

Burschell, Friedrich. *Schiller*. Reinbek bei Hamburg, 1968.

Büsch, Otto, and Wolfgang Neugebauer. *Moderne preußische Geschichte*. Berlin, 1981.

Butler, Eliza M. *The Tyranny of Greece over Germany*. Cambridge, 1935.

Cassirer, Ernst. *Kants Leben und Lehre*. Vol. 11 of K. Berlin, 1921.

Caygill, Howard. *A Kant Dictionary*. Oxford, 1995.

Chadwick, Ruth, ed. *Immanuel Kant: Critical Assessments*. London, 1992.

Christie-Murray, David. *A History of Heresy*. Oxford, 1991.

Clark, Christopher. *Iron Kingdom: The Rise and Downfall of Prussia*. Harmondsworth, 2007.

———. *The Sleepwalkers: How Europe Went to War in 1914*. London, 2012.

Coleridge, Samuel Taylor. *A Book I Value: Selected Marginalia*. Edited by H. J. Jackson. Princeton, 2003.

Conrad, Hermann. "Das Allgemeine Landrecht von 1794." In Büsch and Neugebauer, *Moderne preußische Geschichte*.

Croce, Benedetto. "Historicism Complete and Incomplete." In *History as the Story of Liberty*. London, 1941.

Currie, Pamela. *Goethe's Visual World*. Leeds, 2013.

Demandt, Alexander. *Metaphern für Geschichte: Sprachbilder u. Gleichnisse im historisch-politischen Denken*. Munich, 1978.

Dollinger, Hans. *Friedrich II. von Preußen: sein Bild im Wandel der Zeiten*. Munich, 1986.

Duffy, Christopher. *The Army of Frederick the Great*. London, 1974.

Engfer, Hans-Jürgen. "Die Philosophie der Aufklärung und Friedrich II." In Ziechmann, *Panorama der Friderizianischen Zeit*.

Fertig, Ludwig. *Die Hofmeister: ein Beitrag zur Geschichte des Lehrerstandes und der bürgerlichen Intelligenz*. Stuttgart, 1979.

Fraser, David. *Frederick the Great*. London, 2000.

Freitag, Egon. *Goethes Alltagsentdeckungen: "das Volk interessiert mich unendlich."* Leipzig, 1994.

Fulbrook, Mary. *Piety and Politics: Religion and the Rise of Absolutism in England, Württemberg, and Prussia*. Cambridge, 1983.

Gagliardo, John G. *Germany under the Old Regime, 1600–1790*. London, 1991.

Garton Ash, Timothy. *We the People: The Revolution of '89 Witnessed in Warsaw, Budapest, Berlin and Prague*. Cambridge, 1990.

Gay, Peter. *The Bridge of Criticism: Dialogues among Lucian, Erasmus, and Voltaire on the Enlightenment; on History and Hope, Imagination and Reason, Constraint and Freedom, and on Its Meaning for Our Time*. New York, 1970.

———. *The Enlightenment: An Interpretation*. London, 1966–69. [Gay]

Gebhardt, Bruno. *Handbuch der deutschen Geschichte*. Stuttgart, 1970.

Geier, Manfred. *Kants Welt: eine Biographie*. Reinbek bei Hamburg, 2003.

Gittings, John. *The Glorious Art of Peace: From "The Iliad" to Iraq*. Oxford, 2012.

Goetschel, Willi. *Kant als Schriftsteller*. Vienna, 1990.

Gooch, G. P. *Frederick the Great: The Ruler, the Writer, the Man*. London, 1947.

———. *Germany and the French Revolution*. London, 1920.

Gordimer, Nadine. *Living in Hope and History*. Harmondsworth, 1999.

Grass, Günter. *Der Traum der Vernunft: vom Elend der Aufklärung; eine Veranstaltungsreihe der Akademie der Künste, Berlin*. Darmstadt, 1985.

Grimminger, Rolf, ed. *Deutsche Aufklärung bis zur französischen Revolution*. Hansers Sozialgeschichte der deutschen Literatur 3. Munich, 1980.

Gronke, Horst. *Antisemitismus bei Kant und anderen Denkern der Aufklärung: prä-*

mierte Schriften des wissenschaftlichen Preissausschreibens "Antisemitische und
    antijudaistische Motive bei Denkern der Aufklärung." Würzburg, 2001.

Habermas, Jürgen. Strukturwandlung der Öffentlichkeit. Darmstadt, 1962.

Halberstam, Joshua. "From Kant to Auschwitz." Social Theory and Practice 14 (1988).

Hampshire, Stuart. Spinoza. Harmondsworth, 1962.

Haym, Rudolf. Herder. Berlin, 1958.

Hazard, Paul. La crise de la conscience européenne, 1680–1715. Paris, 1961.

Heisenberg, Werner. Wandlungen in den Grundlagen der Naturwissenschaft. Leipzig,
    1945.

Heller, Erich. The Disinherited Mind: Essays in Modern German Literature and Thought.
    Cambridge, 1959.

Henze-Dühring, Sabine. Friedrich der Große: Musiker und Monarch. Munich, 2012.

Hettner, Hermann. Geschichte der deutschen Literatur im achtzehnten Jahrhundert. 6th
    ed. Braunschweig, 1913.

High, Jeffrey L. "Schiller, National Wars for Independence, and 'Merely Political' Revo-
    lutions." In Schiller: National Poet—Poet of Nations, edited by Nicholas Martin.
    Amsterdam, 2006.

Hinske, Norbert. "Kants Theorie von der Unmöglichkeit des totalen Irrtums." In Kant
    als Herausforderung an die Gegenwart. Freiburg, 1980.

Hinze, Otto. "Die Epochen des evangelischen Kirchenregiments in Preussen." In Büsch
    and Neugebauer, Moderne preußische Geschichte.

Hirsch, Erhard. Dessau-Wörlitz: Zierde und Inbegriff des XVIII. Jahrhunderts. Munich,
    1985.

Holmes, Richard. The Age of Wonder: How the Romantic Generation Discovered the
    Beauty and Terror of Science. London, 2009.

Holmsten, Georg. Friedrich II. in Selbstzeugnissen und Bilddokumenten. Reinbek bei
    Hamburg, 1969.

Horkheimer, Max. The Eclipse of Reason. New York, 1944.

———. "Kants Philosophie und die Aufklärung." In Gesammelte Schriften. Vol. 7. Frank-
    furt, 1985.

Horkheimer, Max, and Theodor W. Adorno. Dialektik der Aufklärung. New York, 1944.

Hough, Richard. Captain James Cook. London, 1994.

Hubatsch, Walther, ed. Absolutismus. Darmstadt, 1973.

Israel, Jonathan I. Democratic Enlightenment: Philosophy, Revolution, and Human
    Rights 1750–1790. Oxford, 2011.

———. Enlightenment Contested: Philosophy, Modernity, and the Emancipation of Man,
    1670–1752. Oxford, 2006.

———. Radical Enlightenment: Philosophy and the Making of Modernity, 1650–1750.
    Oxford, 2001.

James, William. The Varieties of Religious Experience: A Study in Human Nature. Lon-
    don, 1960.

Judt, Tony. Postwar: A History of Europe since 1945. New York, 2005.

Kästner, Erich. Friedrich der Große und die deutsche Literatur: die Erwiderungen auf
    seine Schrift "De la littérature allemande." Stuttgart, 1972.

Kemp, Martin. *The Science of Art: Optical Themes in Western Art from Brunelleschi to Seurat.* New Haven, 1990.

Klein, Tim. *Der Kanzler: Bismarck; Briefe, Reden, Anekdoten.* Munich, 1915.

Knudsen, Jonathan. "On Enlightenment for the Common Man." In *What Is Enlightenment? Eighteenth-Century Answers and Twentieth-Century Questions,* edited by James Schmidt. Berkeley and Los Angeles, 1996.

Kommerell, Max. *Gedanken über Gedichte.* Frankfurt am Main, 1943.

Košenina, Alexander. *Literarische Anthropologie: die Neuentdeckung des Menschen.* Berlin, 2008.

Kotowski, Georg. "Wilhelm von Humboldt und die Universitäten." In Büsch and Neugebauer, *Moderne preußische Geschichte.*

Krätz, Otto. *Goethe und die Naturwissenschaften.* Munich, 1992.

Krieger, Leonard. *The German Idea of Freedom: History of a Political Tradition.* Chicago, 1972.

Kugler, Franz. *Geschichte Friedrichs des Großen: gezeichnet von Adolf Menzel.* Leipzig, 1926.

Landau, Albert, ed. *Rezensionen der Kantschen Philosophie.* Bebra, 1991.

Langen, August. *Der Wortschatz des deutschen Pietismus.* Tübingen, 1968.

Lee, Meredith. *Displacing Authority: Goethe's Poetic Reception of Klopstock.* Heidelberg, 1999.

Lewes, George Henry. *The Life of Goethe.* London, 1875.

Louden, Robert B. *The World We Want: How and Why the Ideals of the Enlightenment Still Elude Us.* Oxford, 2007.

Ludwig, Ralf. *Kant für Anfänger.* Munich, 1998.

MacCulloch, Diarmid. *History of Christianity.* Harmondsworth, 2010.

Manger, Klaus. *Klassizismus und Aufklärung: das Beispiel des späten Wieland.* Frankfurt am Main, 1991.

Mann, Golo. "Schiller als Historiker." *Schiller Jahrbuch* 4 (1960).

Martens, Wolfgang. *Die Botschaft der Tugend: die Aufklärung im Spiegel der deutschen moralischen Wochenschriften.* Stuttgart, 1968.

Mazower, Mark. *Governing the World: The History of an Idea.* London, 2012.

Meinecke, Friedrich. *Weltbürgertum und Nationalstaat.* Edited by Hans Herzfeld. Vol. 5 of *Werke.* Munich, 1962.

Minor, Jakob. *Schiller.* Berlin, 1890.

Mirabeau, Victor Riquette, Marquis de. *De la monarchie prussienne sous Frédéric le Grand.* London, 1788.

Möller, Horst. *Vernunft und Kritik.* Frankfurt am Main, 1986.

Molnár, Gésa von. *Goethes Kant-Studien.* Weimar, 1994.

Mommsen, Katharina. *Goethe und der Alte Fritz.* Leipzig, 2012.

Muhlack, Ulrich. *Geschichtswissenschaft im Humanismus und in der Aufklärung: die Vorgeschichte des Historismus.* Munich, 1991.

Namier, L. B. "Men Who Floundered into the War." In *Vanished Supremacies: Essays on European History, 1812–1918.* Harmondsworth, 1958.

Neiman, Susan. *Moral Clarity: A Guide for Grown-up Idealists.* Princeton, 2009.

————. *The Unity of Reason: Rereading Kant*. New York, 1994.

Nicolai, Heinz. *Goethe und Jacobi: Studien zu ihrer Freundschaft*. Stuttgart, 1965.

Nicolson, Marjorie Hope. *Newton Demands the Muse: Newton's "Opticks" and the Eighteenth Century Poets*. Princeton, 1946.

Nilges, Yvonne. *Schiller und das Recht*. Göttingen, 2012.

Nisbet, H. B. *Lessing: eine Biographie*. Munich, 2008.

O'Neill, Onora. *Constructions of Reason: Explorations of Kant's Practical Philosophy*. Cambridge, 1989.

Outram, Dorinda. *The Enlightenment*. Cambridge, 1995.

Pagden, Anthony R. *The Enlightenment: And Why It Still Matters*. Oxford, 2013.

Parker, Geoffrey. *Philip II*. London, 1979.

Pater, Walter. *The Renaissance: Studies in Art and Poetry*. London, 1877.

Perkins, Franklin. *Leibniz: A Guide for the Perplexed*. London, 2007.

————. *Leibniz and China: A Commerce of Light*. Cambridge, 2004.

Pinker, Steven. *The Better Angels of Our Nature: The Decline of Violence in History and Its Causes*. London, 2011.

Porter, Roy. *Enlightenment: Britain and the Creation of the Modern World*. Harmondsworth, 2000.

Promies, Wolfgang. *Georg Christoph Lichtenberg in Selbstzeugnissen und Bilddokumenten*. Reinbek bei Hamburg, 1964.

Pütz, Peter. *Erforschung der deutschen Aufklärung*. Königstein, 1980.

Reinhardt, Volker, ed. *Hauptwerke der Geschichtsschreibung*. Stuttgart, 1997.

Reki, B., et al. *Kant lebt*. Paderborn, 2006.

Robertson, Ritchie. *The "Jewish Question" in German Literature, 1749–1939: Emancipation and Its Discontents*. Oxford, 1999.

————. "Torture Is My Pleasure." *Times Literary Supplement*, 2 May 2014.

Rorty, Richard. "Human Rights, Rationality and Sentimentality." In *Oxford Amnesty Lectures on Human Rights*. New York, 1993.

Saine, Thomas P. *Georg Forster*. New York, 1972.

————. "Natural Science and the Ideology of Nature." *Lessing-Jahrbuch* 8 (1976).

Schieder, Theodor. *Friedrich der Große: ein Königtum der Widersprüche*. Frankfurt am Main, 1983.

————. "Schiller als Historiker." *Historische Zeitschrift* 190 (1960).

Schings, Hans-Jürgen. *Die Brüder des Marquis Posa: Schiller und der Geheimbund der Illuminaten*. Tübingen, 1996.

————. *Melancholie und Aufklärung: Melancholiker und ihre Kritiker in Erfahrungsseelenkunde und Literatur des 18. Jahrhundert*. Stuttgart, 1977.

Schlingensiepen, Ferdinand. *Dietrich Bonhoeffer, 1906–1945: eine Biographie*. Munich, 2010.

Schmidt, Arno. "Barthold Hinrich Brockes, oder nichts ist mir zu klein." In *Nachrichten von Büchern und Menschen*. Frankfurt am Main, 1971.

Schmidt, James, ed. *What Is Enlightenment? Eighteenth-Century Answers and Twentieth-Century Questions*. Berkeley and Los Angeles, 1996.

Schneiders, Werner. *Aufklärung und Vorurteilskritik: Studien zur Geschichte der Vorurteilstheorie*. Stuttgart–Bad Cannstatt, 1983.

———. *Lexikon der Aufklärung: Deutschland und Europa.* Munich, 1995.

———. *Die wahre Aufklärung: zum Selbstverständnis der deutschen Aufklärung.* Freiburg, 1974.

Scholz, Heinrich, ed. *Die Hauptschriften zum Pantheismusstreit zwischen Jacobi und Mendelssohn.* Berlin, 1916.

Schöne, Albrecht. *Aufklärung aus dem Geist der Experimentalphysik: Lichtenbergs Konjunktive.* Munich, 1982.

Schulte, Christoph. *Die jüdische Aufklärung: Philosophie, Religion, Geschichte.* Munich, 2002.

Schulz, Gerhard. *Philosophers and Kings: Variations on an Old Theme.* Canberra, 1991.

Schulz, Ursula, and Günter Schulz. *Die Berlinische Monatsschrift (1783–1796): eine Bibliographie.* Bremen, 1968.

Schwarz, Paul. *Der erste Kulturkampf.* Berlin, 1925.

Schweitzer, Albert. *The Quest of the Historical Jesus: A Critical Study of Its Progress from Reimarus to Wrede.* Baltimore, 1998.

Seifert, Siegfried. *Die Zeit schlägt ein neues Buch in der Geschichte auf: zum französischen Revolutionskalender und zu seiner Aufnahme in Deutschland.* Weimar, 1989.

Selwyn, Pamela Eve. *Everyday Life in the German Book Trade: Friedrich Nicolai as Bookseller and Publisher in the Age of Enlightenment, 1750–1810.* University Park, PA, 2000.

Sengle, Friedrich. *Wieland.* Stuttgart, 1949.

Sheehan, James J. *German History, 1770–1866.* Oxford, 1989.

Simmel, Georg. *Kant: sechzehn Vorlesungen.* Leipzig, 1904.

Staiger, Emil. *Goethe.* Zürich, 1963.

Stangneth, Bettina. "Antisemitische und antijudaistische Motive bei Immanuel Kant." In Gronke, *Antisemitismus.*

Stedall, Jacqueline A. *The History of Mathematics.* Oxford, 2012.

Steinberg, Jonathan. *Bismarck: A Life.* Oxford, 2011.

Steinle, Friedrich. "'Das Nächste an das Nächste reihen': Goethe, Newton und das Experiment." *Philosophia Naturalis* 39, no. 1 (2002).

Storz, Gerhard. *Karl Eugen: der Fürst und das "alte gute Recht."* Stuttgart, 1981.

Strawson, P. F. Review in Chadwick, *Immanuel Kant: Critical Assessments.*

Streidt, Gert, and Peter Feierabend. *Prussia: Art and Architecture.* Cologne, 1999.

Timm, Hermann. *Gott und die Freiheit: Studien zur Religionsphilosophie der Goethezeit.* Frankfurt am Main, 1974.

Vaihinger, Hans. "Die Kant-Medaille mit dem schiefen Turm zu Pisa." *Kant-Studien* 2 (1898).

Venturi, Franco. *Utopia and Reform in the Enlightenment.* Cambridge, 1970.

Vorlaender, Karl. *Kant: der Mann und das Werk.* Leipzig, 1925.

Ward, Albert. *Book Production, Fiction and the German Reading Public, 1740–1800.* Oxford, 1974.

Warda, Arthur, and Johann Friedrich Gensichen. *Immanuel Kants Bücher.* Berlin, 1922.

Watson, Peter. *The German Genius: Europe's Third Renaissance, the Second Scientific Revolution and the Twentieth Century.* London, 2010.

Wehler, Hans-Ulrich, ed. *Deutsche Historiker*. Göttingen, 1971–82.

Weigelt, Horst. *Johann Kaspar Lavater: Leben, Werk und Wirkung*. Göttingen, 1991.

Weigl, Engelhard. *Schauplätze der deutschen Aufklärung: ein Städterundgang*. Reinbek bei Hamburg, 1997.

Weimar, Klaus. "Ihr Götter!" In *Goethes und Schillers Literaturpolitik*, edited by Wilfried Barner. Stuttgart, 1984.

Weimar, Klaus, ed. *Goethes Gedichte, 1769–1775*. Paderborn, 1982.

Wellbery, David E. *The Specular Moment: Goethe's Early Lyric and the Beginnings of Romanticism*. Stanford, 1996.

White, Matthew. *Atrocitology: Humanity's 100 Deadliest Achievements*. Edinburgh, 2012.

Wundt, Max. *Die deutsche Schulphilosophie im Zeitalter der Aufklärung*. Tübingen, 1945.

Wuthenow, Ralf Rainer. *Die erfahrene Welt: Europäische Reiseliteratur im Zeitalter der Aufklärung*. Frankfurt am Main, 1980.

———. *Vernunft und Republik*. Bad Homburg, 1970.

Ziechmann, Jürgen, ed. *Panorama der friderizianischen Zeit*. Bremen, 1985.

INDEX

Printed in Great Britain
by Amazon

38108333R00177